From the Depths of Despair
to the Promise of Presence

Siphrut
Literature and Theology of the Hebrew Scriptures

Editorial Board

From the Depths of Despair to the Promise of Presence

A Rhetorical Reading of the Book of Joel

Joel Barker

Winona Lake, Indiana
EISENBRAUNS
2014

Library of Congress Cataloging-in-Publication Data

Barker, Joel, 1979–
    From the depths of despair to the promise of presence : a rhetorical
    reading of the book of Joel / Joel Barker.
            pages cm.—(Siphrut : literature and theology of the Hebrew
    Scriptures ; 11)
        Includes bibliographical references and index.
        ISBN 978-1-57506-287-7 (hardback : alk. paper)
        1. Bible. Joel—Criticism, interpretation, etc.   I. Title.
        BS1575.52.B37   2014
        224′.7066—dc23

                                                            2013042211

Contents

Preface

This book represents a slightly revised version of my Ph.D. dissertation, which was submitted to McMaster Divinity College in April 2011. I am grateful to Professors Stephen B. Chapman, Tremper Longman III, and Nathan MacDonald for accepting this monograph for publication in the Siphrut series. Thanks are also due to Jim Eisenbraun, Beverly McCoy, and the rest of the Eisenbrauns team for contributing their publishing and editing expertise, which has certainly enriched my work.

I owe a great debt of thanks to Dr. Mark Boda, my doctoral supervisor, for his guidance and friendship throughout my time at McMaster Divinity College. He offered a wonderful combination of scholarly acumen and personal concern that was invaluable in bringing my studies to completion. His probing critiques and thoughtful suggestions greatly improved this project. The contribution of Dr. Paul Evans, my second reader, is also noteworthy because he stepped in to shepherd this project through a critical phase. I am also thankful for my external examiner, Dr. Robert Chisholm, who contributed his vast breadth of knowledge and offered many suggestions that enhanced the final product.

My parents, Dr. David and Mrs. Lorraine Barker were indispensable throughout the time of my research. They provided many words of encouragement in times of struggle and celebrated with me as this project came to completion. My mother's willingness to provide "granny day care" was essential throughout the course of my research. Special thanks are also due to Philpott Memorial Church for its provision of a stipend for students involved in theological studies. I also want to thank McMaster Divinity College and Dr. Stanley Porter, its president, for providing a stimulating intellectual environment as well as an opportunity to begin my teaching career in conjunction with my studies.

Finally, this project would have been impossible without the faithful support of my wife, Karen. Her unflagging devotion and encouragement were essential in giving me the strength to pursue my studies to the end. This project is dedicated to her as well as our children, Abigail, Hannah, and Isaac, each of whom was born near a significant milestone of this research.

Note to the Reader

One notable omission in this book is the recent monograph by Elie Assis entitled *The Book of Joel: A Prophet between Calamity and Hope* (LHB/OTS 581; New York: Bloomsbury, 2013). Unfortunately, it came out after my work was in the final publication process. Readers who are interested in my reflections on Assis's contribution, including his novel proposal for Joel's date and setting, are encouraged to read my review for the *The Journal of Hebrew Scriptures* (www.jhsonline.org; forthcoming).

Abbreviations

General

LXX   Septuagint
MT   Masoretic Text
Syr   Syriac version of the Bible
Tg. J.   *Targum of Jonathan*

Reference Works

AB	Anchor Bible Commentary
ABD	*Anchor Bible Dictionary*
AJSL	*American Journal of Semitic Languages and Literatures*
ANETS	Ancient Near Eastern Texts and Studies
AOAT	Alter Orient und Altes Testament
BASOR	*Bulletin of the American Schools of Oriental Research*
BBR	*Bulletin for Biblical Research*
BEATAJ	Beiträge zur Erforschung des Alten Testaments und des Antiken Judentums
BHS	K. Elliger and W. Rudolph, editors. *Biblia Hebraica Stuttgartensia*. Stuttgart: Deutsche Bibelgesellschaft, 1984
Bib	*Biblica*
BibInt	*Biblical Interpretation*
BIS	Biblical Interpretation Series
BJS	Brown Judaic Studies
BSac	*Bibliotheca Sacra*
BZ	*Biblische Zeitschrift*
BZAW	Beiheft zur Zeitschrift für die alttestamentliche Wissenschaft
CBQ	*Catholic Bible Quarterly*
CBR	*Currents in Biblical Research*
CSCD	Cambridge Studies in Christian Doctrine
CTM	*Concordia Theological Monthly*
DTIB	*Dictionary for Theological Interpretation of the Bible*
ETR	*Etudes theologique et religieuse*
ESIEC	Emory Studies in Early Christianity
ExpTim	*Expository Times*
FTL	Forum Theologicae Linguisticae
GKC	E. Kautzsch. *Gesenius' Hebrew Grammar*. 2nd English ed. Translated by A. Cowley. Oxford: Clarendon, 1910
HBT	*Horizons in Biblical Theology*
HDR	Harvard Dissertations in Religion

HSM	Harvard Semitic Monographs
HUCA	*Hebrew Union College Annual*
IEJ	*Israel Exploration Journal*
Int	*Interpretation*
ITC	International Theological Commentary
JANES(CU)	*Journal of the Ancient Near Eastern Society (of Columbia University)*
JBL	*Journal of Biblical Literature*
JETS	*Journal of the Evangelical Theological Society*
JHS	*Journal of Hebrew Scriptures*
JNES	*Journal of Near Eastern Studies*
JNSL	*Journal of Northwest Semitic Languages*
JSNTSup	Journal for the Study of the New Testament Supplement Series
JSOT	*Journal for the Study of the Old Testament*
JSOTSup	Journal for the Study of the Old Testament Supplement Series
JSPSup	Journal for the Study of the Pseudepigrapha Supplement Series
JSS	*Journal of Semitic Studies*
KAT	Kommentar zum Alten Testamentum
LHB/OTS	Library of Hebrew Bible / Old Testament Studies
MBPS	Mellen Biblical Press Series
NAC	New American Commentary
NBS	Numen Book Series
NCBC	New Century Bible Commentaries
NICOT	New International Commentary on the Old Testament
NSBT	New Studies in Biblical Theology
OBT	Overtures to Biblical Theology
OTG	Old Testament Guides
OTL	Old Testament Library
OtSt	Oudtestamentische Studiën
PTL	*A Journal for Descriptive Poetics and Theory of Literature*
RB	*Revue Biblique*
ResQ	*Restoration Quarterly*
RSR	*Revue des sciences religieuses*
SBLAB	Society of Biblical Literature Academia Biblica
SBLDS	Society of Biblical Literature Dissertation Series
SBLHB/OT	Society of Biblical Literature Hebrew Bible / Old Testament
SBLEJL	Society of Biblical Literature: Early Judaism and Its Literature
SBLMS	Society of Biblical Literature Monograph Series
SBLSP	Society of Biblical Literature Seminar Papers
SBLSS	Society of Biblical Literature Symposium Series
SEÅ	*Svensk Exegetisk Årsbok*
SHS	Scripture and Hermeneutics Series
SOTBT	Studies in Old Testament Biblical Theology
TDOT	*Theological Dictionary of the Old Testament*
TJT	*Taiwan Journal of Theology*
TOTC	Tyndale Old Testament Commentaries

UBT	Understanding Biblical Themes
UUÅ	Uppsala Universitets Årsskrift
VT	*Vetus Testamentum*
VTSup	Supplements to Vetus Testamentum
WBC	Word Biblical Commentary
WEC	Wycliffe Exegetical Commentary
WTJ	*Westminster Theological Journal*
WUNT	Wissenschaftliche Untersuchungen zum Neuen Testament
ZAW	*Zeitschrift für die alttestamentliche Wissenschaft*
YABRL	Yale Anchor Bible Reference Library

Introduction

The book of Joel provides many interpretive opportunities worthy of detailed exploration. This book combines impressive imagery, literary artistry, and persuasive potential in a powerful prophetic proclamation. It begins with a vivid depiction of a locust plague and drought, followed by the terror-inducing threat of Yʜᴡʜ marching against Zion at the head of an invading army. This prompts a prophetic call to return that eventually leads to total restoration that is guaranteed by the presence of Yʜᴡʜ in Zion. Joel details how Yʜᴡʜ reverses both spiritual and material threats and concludes by announcing Yʜᴡʜ's intention to judge the nations and bless those who dwell in Jerusalem. This book also creatively employs the day-of-Yʜᴡʜ motif to announce both threat and restoration for the Judahite community throughout the book. Joel has an impact on our understanding of the broader canon of the Old Testament that belies its size since it recalls and adds new layers of meaning to other biblical texts with which it interacts.[1]

In this book, I propose to explore afresh the layers of imagery and meaning in this prophetic proclamation. I approach Joel through the prism of rhetorical criticism, a discipline that delves deeply into the heart of the text and considers its persuasive intent and effect. This approach provides a valuable window into the language of prophecy and its struggle to present the reality of Yʜᴡʜ through the limitation of human speech and thought.[2] A rhetorical-critical approach is also appropriate for a book of this length, since it allows the interpreter to enter the world of the text and thoroughly examine a discrete literary unit. It also prompts the interpreter to consider the effects of the book's literary artistry and to explore the ways in which it persuades an audience to adopt its point of view and respond appropriately.[3]

---

1. J. Crenshaw, *Joel* (AB 24c; New York: Doubleday, 1995) 27–28. Crenshaw lists 22 occurrences where there are close connections between Joel and other books or quotations by Joel of other books in the rest of the Prophets, Torah, and Psalms. I interact with a number of these allusions in my discussions of rhetorical strategy. See also R. Mason, *Zephaniah, Habbakuk, Joel* (OTG; Sheffield: Sheffield Academic Press, 1994) 117–20; R. Coggins, *Joel* (NCBC; Sheffield: Sheffield Academic Press, 2000) 21–23; J. Strazicich, *Joel's Use of Scripture and the Scripture's Use of Joel: Appropriation and Resignification in Second Temple Judaism and Early Christianity* (BIS 82; Leiden: Brill, 2007) 59–254.

2. D. B. Sandy, *Plowshares and Pruning Hooks: Rethinking the Language of Biblical Prophecy and Apocalyptic* (Downers Grove, IL: InterVarsity, 2002) 32. Sandy articulately casts prophetic language between the poles of something exhilarating to describe and something impossible to describe fully.

3. On the nature of the "audience(s)" that this study considers, see the discussion of rhetorical effectiveness in the following chapter.

1

Survey of Research

The book of Joel continues to engender significant scholarly attention due to a variety of issues that defy expeditious resolution. Its wealth of interpretive challenges prompted Merx to label Joel as a problem child of Old Testament exegesis in 1879.[4] Consequently, it is worth situating the book by highlighting some of the major *crux interpreti* that continue to call for careful analysis. I locate the study that follows within the broader field of research on the book of Joel. Following this discussion, I also establish a foundation for using rhetorical-critical methodology in my study of Joel. I survey the development of this field of inquiry and trace its growth to the specific model that guides this study.

The Date of Joel

Any survey of scholarship on Joel will note the interminable discussions about when the book was composed. The debate continues unabated since Joel itself provides little concrete evidence that would point to a resolution. Most notably, unlike many other prophetic books, Joel contains no information in its superscription that would at least provide a point of reference around which to orient the discussion. In its absence, commentators look at a myriad of other features, including Joel's vocabulary, syntax, literary expression, and relationship to extrabiblical data to try to locate the composition of this book temporally.[5] The difficulties that arise from the numerous attempts are apparent in the fact that the range of proposed dates stretches from the ninth to the second centuries B.C.E.

The earliest suggested date of composition is during the reign of Joash. One reason put forward for this proposal is the position of the book between Hosea and Amos in the Masoretic tradition, since they are two prophetic books that locate themselves in the monarchic era. A second suggestion is that the presence of Jehoiada's regency could explain the lack of reference to a king in Joel (2 Kings 11–12).[6] This line of argumentation no longer carries significant sway since it relies heavily on Joel's location in the order of the Minor Prophets, which is not a firm foundation on which to make chronological judgments.[7] Consequently, theories of Joel's

---

4. A. Merx, *Der Prophetie des Joel und Ihrer Ausleger von den ältesten Zeiten bis zu den Reformatoren: Eine exegetisch-kritische und hermeneutisch-dogmengeschichtliche Studie* (Halle: Waisenhaus, 1879) iii. "Denn der Joel ist gradezu ein Schmerzenskind der alttestamentlichen Exegese."

5. Crenshaw, *Joel*, 23.

6. See especially K. Credner, *Der Prophet Joel: Übersetz und eklärt* (Halle: Waisenhauses, 1831) 40.

7. D. Hubbard, *Joel and Amos* (TOTC 25; Downers Grove, IL: InterVarsity, 2009) 24. Allen correctly notes that the different location assigned to Joel in the LXX version of the Minor Prophets is problematic for using canonical order as a strategy to establish chronology (L. Allen, *The Books of Joel, Obadiah, Jonah, and Micah* [NICOT; Grand Rapids: Eerdmans, 1976] 21). See also the following discussion in this chapter concerning the relationship between Joel and the rest of the Minor Prophets, or "The Book of the Twelve."

early composition have not gained significant traction in contemporary scholarship.

Arguments for a later preexilic time of composition are attributed primarily to Kapelrud, who asserts that the time of composition was just prior to the fall of Jerusalem.[8] He looks at references to other nations made in the book and suggests that the mention of the Philistines in Joel 4:4–8 reflects similar references in Zeph 1:14–18 and Jer 47:4 (Jer 47:4 also includes Tyre and Sidon). Based on a supposedly more secure date for these passages to which Joel alludes, Kapelrud claims that Joel is situated prior to the exile.[9] He notes Joel's failure to mention a king and suggests that this reflects the prophet's intent to include all people within the text's intended audience, further suggesting that Joel's summons tend to group people according to age, rather than social rank (Joel 1:2; 2:16).[10] Stuart follows a similar path, suggesting a late preexilic date, which is connected to his understanding of the locusts in Joel 1:1–2:11 as symbols of an invading Babylonian horde.[11] For Stuart, the crisis that drives Joel is the ominous threat of Babylonian invasion and the destruction of the Judahite kingdom.

Despite Kapelrud's and Stuart's contributions, the weight of recent scholarship falls on dating Joel to a time after the fall of Jerusalem and during the Second Temple period, although this still encompasses a significant range of dates. Evidence adduced to support this period includes the lack of mention of a major enemy (i.e., Assyria or Babylon), the absence of a royal figure, and the commands for the community to gather under priestly leadership, which is thought to suggest a period of theocratic leadership.[12] Numerous commentators follow some variation of this line of argument, although most acknowledge that they cannot make this claim with a significant degree of certainty.[13]

---

8. A. Kapelrud, *Joel Studies* (UUÅ 4; Uppsala: Lundequist, 1948) 191.

9. Ibid., 152–53. Kapelrud also considers the reference to Greeks in Joel 4:4–8, appealing to extrabiblical evidence to suggest points of contact between Mesopotamia and Greece that would have preceded the Babylonian captivity.

10. Ibid., 191. He claims that the absence of a king "is not really decisive" in determining Joel's date of composition.

11. D. Stuart, *Hosea–Jonah* (WBC 31; Waco, TX: Word, 1987) 225–26. The question of whether or not the locusts are intended to be literal or symbolic will be discussed in detail in the text analysis of Joel 1:1–14 and 2:1–11. For now, what is important is Stuart's reliance on a symbolic interpretation of the locust imagery in order to support his understanding of Joel's date of composition.

12. W. Prinsloo, *The Theology of the Book of Joel* (BZAW 163; Berlin: de Gruyter, 195) 6.

13. See G. Ogden and R. Deutsch, *Joel and Malachi: Promise of Hope—A Call to Obedience* (ITC; Grand Rapids: Eerdmans, 1987) 14; H. Wolff, *Joel and Amos* (Hermeneia; Philadelphia: Fortress, 1977) 6; Allen, *Joel*, 24–25; Crenshaw, *Joel*, 24–25; Hubbard, *Joel*, 27. Representative of these assessments is Allen, who states that "[t]his survey of the main chronological views and supporting arguments must leave the reader without a single clear impression." The most recent entry into the conversation comes from Ganzel, who proposes that Joel functions as a prophetic bridge between Ezekiel and Haggai. Essentially, Joel transitions between Ezekiel, who foresees a restoration authored by God alone, and

Ahlström also considers the possibility that the rebuilt temple contained improper syncretistic elements against which Joel spoke, which are revealed by the prophet's sevenfold use of the phrase יְהוָה אֱלֹהֵיכֶם 'YHWH your God' (Joel 1:14; 2:13, 14, 23, 26, 27; 4:17).[14] This would mean that Joel employs this suffix to separate YHWH from the other deities that may have crept into the community's worship practices. This concern, along with evidence drawn from lexical analysis, suggests to Ahlström a date between 515 and 505 B.C.E.[15] Taking a slightly different approach, some scholars leverage the image of a city wall in Joel 2:1–11 to try to attribute Joel to the time of Nehemiah (ca. 445 B.C.E.) and the completion of Jerusalem's wall.[16] This line of interpretation depends on the assumption that the image of an invader breaching the city walls is most appropriate in a context in which Jerusalem had functioning city walls.

Alongside these interpretations of Joel's imagery and language, some commentators rely more explicitly on extrabiblical data to support theories of Joel's composition during the Second Temple period. Myers extrapolates a time of composition from references to Greeks, Sabeans, and their involvement in slave trading in Joel 4:4–8.[17] He uses this passage to ground a detailed examination of the political and social situation of the ancient world that focuses on the mostly likely points of contact between these nations and Judah. He suggests that the right conditions for these events to occur converged around 520 B.C.E., at a time when "the devastated Judan [sic] territory was more or less at the mercy of the neighboring states who

---

Haggai, who calls the community to work in order to restore God's favor. Joel interweaves themes of both divine sovereignty and appropriate human response. See T. Ganzel, "The Shattered Dream. The Prophecies of Joel: A Bridge between Ezekiel and Haggai," *JHS* 11 (2011), http://www.jhsonline.org/Articles/article_153.pdf.

14. G. Ahlström, *Joel and the Temple Cult of Jerusalem* (VTSup 21; Leiden: Brill, 1971) 27–28. The idea is that the title "YHWH your God" implies that there were other deities whom the community may have been worshiping alongside YHWH. Ahlström then suggests that this mild correction found in Joel develops into Malachi's full rebuke of improper priestly practices (Mal 1:11; 2:11, 13).

15. Ibid., 1–22, 129. Ahlström begins his monograph with a collection of word studies including יְעַבְּטוּן, מִנְחָה וָנֶסֶךְ, and הַשֶּׁלַח. The intention of these studies is to argue that these words do not necessarily indicate a late time of origin for the book of Joel. Instead, Ahlström's understanding of an early postexilic date remains a viable option.

16. Strazicich, *Joel's Use of Scripture*, 55. See Joel 2:7 and the description of the invading horde running over the top of the wall, which fails to keep them at bay.

17. J. Myers, "Some Considerations Bearing on the Date of Joel," *ZAW* 74 (1962) 177–95. Myers's strongest arguments consist of his detailed research on various signs of Greek and Sabean presence in Palestine at the time of composition that he prefers, alongside research into the development of slave-trading in both cultures. He also reflects on Joel 2:9 and its mention of invaders running over a wall, and he tries to demonstrate that this does not necessitate a date of composition during the time of Nehemiah, since parts of the wall were likely to have remained standing even after the Babylonian assault (cf. 2 Kgs 25:10; 2 Chr 36:19; Jer 52:14). This argument, however, is not persuasive since the image of a divinely authorized army breaching city walls does not need to have any particular correlation to the state of actual city walls at that time.

had moved into the vacuum created by the captivity and subsequent decline of the Neo-Babylonian Empire."[18]

Stephenson similarly approaches the question of Joel's date of composition through extrabiblical material. He uses astronomical data to establish
that solar eclipses occurred in 357 and 366 B.C.E. He argues that they would
have been the points of reference for Joel's use of imagery concerning the
darkening of heavenly bodies.[19] Treves pushes the date of Joel into the
Ptolemaic era, suggesting that the book's concern with Egypt in Joel 4:19
reflects a time when Egypt's influence was in ascendance.[20] Finally, the lat-
est date proposed for Joel's composition is during the second century B.C.E.
Duhm is the primary proponent of this theory, and he roots it in his understanding of the dual nature of the book's composition, according to which
Joel 2:17–4:21 and the references to the day of Yhwh in Joel 1:1–2:17 should
be attributed to a Maccabean preacher who attempted to recontextualize
prophetic literature to serve his concerns regarding the day of Yhwh.[21]

This survey demonstrates that none of the lines of argumentation articulated above has succeeded in providing the final word in this debate. It is
quite possible to award differing degrees of significance to internal criteria
such as the lack of mention of a royal figure, the mention of a temple, or the
mention of outside nations. Further, references of this sort are difficult to
restrict to specific times and places, as seen by the fact that the absence of a
royal figure in Joel is advanced as evidence for both the Josianic era and the
time after the Babylonian capture of Jerusalem.[22] Additionally, attempts to
date the book that proceed according to these arguments assume that the
text directly reflects the circumstances of its immediate sociopolitical sur-
roundings. It is improbable, for example, that every mention of convulsion
or darkening of the heavenly bodies in prophetic literature has an actual
astronomical event behind it (cf. Jer 13:16; Amos 4:13, 5:8). The same holds
true for the reference to the city wall in Joel 2:7–9 and perhaps even the
idea of a functioning Temple that undergirds the imagery of Joel 1:1–2:17.[23]

---

18. Ibid., 190.

19. F. Stephenson, "The Date of the Book of Joel," *VT* 19 (1969) 229.

20. M. Treves, "The Date of Joel," *VT* 9 (1959) 154.

21. B. Duhm, *Israels Propheten* (Tübingen: Mohr, 1922) 398. Duhm's theory and its
significance will be discussed further in the following section on the debate over the unity
of Joel's composition. See also S. Cook, *Prophecy and Apocalypticism: The Postexilic Social
Setting* (Minneapolis: Fortress, 1995) 168.

22. Allen, *Joel*, 19.

23. Linville offers an intriguing perspective when he argues that scholars are too quick
to assign extratextual reality to the images and metaphors contained within Joel. He
concludes that the only Joel to whom later interpreters have access is the Joel revealed in
the text of the prophetic book, which may or may not resonate with actual political and
social settings in ancient Judah. Linville may tilt the balance too far in removing nearly
every trace of historicity from the text, but his work offers a useful corrective to scholarly
attempts to find a one-to-one correspondence between prophetic imagery and real world
scenarios (J. Linville, "Bugs through the Looking Glass: The Infestation of Meaning in
Joel," in *Reflection and Refraction: Studies in Biblical Historiography in Honour of A. Graeme*

In summary, all of these different discussions regarding the date of Joel have not yielded consensus, nor is there much probability of future agreement. Consequently, further studies of Joel will either rehash the above-mentioned issues before settling on a particular, contested date of composition, or they will adopt a different approach entirely and leave aside such questions for the sake of reading the book of Joel as a received text. Prinsloo offers the best synopsis of the situation, claiming that since, "it is virtually impossible to date it exactly on the basis of its contents," the exegete must, "use the text of Joel itself to the utmost to try and discover its actual message and intention."[24] As a result, while the date of Joel is one of its enduring issues and merits review, this study is unlikely to shed any new light on it. Instead, it will use the preceding survey to ground a rhetorical approach that focuses on the persuasive strategies that the text employs, without explicitly linking it to a specific time of composition.

The Unity of Joel

Closely related to the question of the date of Joel's provenance is the question of its compositional unity. A cursory reading of the book quickly reveals a dramatic shift in its tenor between Joel 1–2 and 3–4. Joel 1–2 is largely oriented around the image of a locust plague that causes tremendous devastation and destruction. Against this backdrop, the text interweaves images of the day of Yhwh, military invasion, and a call for divine mercy that finally culminates in a systematic reversal of the preceding crises. Joel 3–4, on the other hand, departs from the locust plague and instead focuses on the outpouring of the divine Spirit, Yhwh's authority to judge all nations, and a promise of future blessing for Judah and Jerusalem that is rooted in Yhwh's presence in Zion.

The origin of the discussion concerning the authorship of Joel goes back to Vernes, who proposed in 1872 that Joel 1–2 refers to a day of Yhwh that preceded the prophetic declaration, while Joel 3–4 looks ahead to a day of Yhwh to come. For Vernes, these different orientations indicate that there are different authors for the two "halves" of the book. Vernes declares, "[I]l est résulté pour nous la convinction très-nette que nous avons affaire ici à deux œuvres fort différentes . . . qui ne sauraient appartenir à un même auteur."[25] Vernes specifically draws attention to the lack of mention of locusts, drought, or agricultural crises in Joel 3–4 to suggest that these chapters must have a different provenance.[26] He posits that the two parts of Joel were united later because they both make use of the day of Yhwh,

---

Auld [ed. R. Rezetko, T. Lim, and W. Aucker; Cambridge: Cambridge University Press, 2006] 283–98).

24. Prinsloo, *Theology*, 92.

25. M. Vernes, *Le peuple d'Israel et ses espérances relative à son avenir depuis les origines jusqu' à l'epoque persane Ve siècle avant J. C.* (Paris: Sandos & Fischbacher, 1872) 47.

26. Ibid., 49.

even though they treat it quite differently.[27] This proposal provides the foundation for further research into the text's compositional unity, while adding a new layer to the already unresolved question of the book's date of composition. Conceivably, the interpreter would need to locate temporally the composition of the two halves, which may have been separated by a period of centuries.

Following Vernes, the most influential theory of Joel's disunity comes from Duhm. He differs from Vernes in that he locates the key point of disjunction between Joel 2:17 and 2:18, while also asserting that Joel 1:15; 2:1b–2a, and 11b arose from the hand that composed the latter half of the book.[28] This would also seem to be a logical point of division, since Joel 1:1–2:17 deals with the challenges and threats to the Judahite community's existence, while Joel 2:18–4:21 offers resolution of and restoration from both physical and spiritual threats through Yhwh's intervention. Duhm essentially reduces the message of the "original" prophet to a call toward lament in the wake of a locust invasion and its ensuing agricultural disasters. Consequently, material that looks beyond the immediate horizon of the locusts must belong to a later layer of composition. Duhm attributes the day-of-Yhwh material and the rest of Joel 3–4 to a synagogue preacher in the Maccabean era who was attempting to transform Joel's discussion of the locust plague into a harbinger of a coming eschatological event.[29]

The assertion that passages referring to the day of Yhwh must have a late provenance is somewhat surprising given the broad range of references to the day of Yhwh in the Old Testament. Prophets as early as Amos employ the day of Yhwh in a way that suggests it was a reasonably well-known concept from which prophets could draw (cf. Amos 5:18–20).[30] Consequently, it does not seem necessary to attribute the day-of-Yhwh references in Joel 1:1–2:17 to later redactional activity. Furthermore, efforts to separate the discussion of the day of Yhwh from the description of the locust plague require a radical bifurcation between history and events in the natural

---

27. Ibid., "Du reste, la deuxième partie de Joël nous a semblé trahir une imitation assez directe des deux premières chapitres." Vernes then suggests that the author of Joel 3–4 composed it with the knowledge of what was contained in Joel 1–2.

28. Significantly, the verses in Joel 1:1–2:17 that Duhm attributes to the creator of the latter half are the references to the day of Yhwh. Duhm asserts that the reference to the day of Yhwh in Joel 1:15 does not fit the context of the book, and the phrase's appearance in Joel 2:11 does not fit the metrical scheme of the verse; B. Duhm, "Anmerkungen zu den zwölf Propheten," *ZAW* 31 (1911) 184–88.

29. Ibid., 187. He finds evidence for the Maccabean era in the mention of Greeks in Joel 4:4–8.

30. I will delve into the day of Yhwh in greater detail in the discussion about the rhetorical strategies of the passages that use the day of Yhwh. See especially the discussion of the rhetorical strategy of Joel 1:15 since it also explores the origins and range of the day-of-Yhwh motif.

world.[31] This does not properly capture Joel's perspective because, as Simkins rightly notes, "Joel has fused together the human and natural dimensions, the historical and cosmological dimensions into one complex day of Yahweh which involves all creation."[32] In this view, the locust plague is certainly capable of being a harbinger of Yʜᴡʜ's action in the affairs of Judah and the nations. The devastation that the text portrays creates an appropriate milieu for the prophet to announce the day of Yʜᴡʜ.

Plöger offers a slightly different perspective by proposing a complex compositional history for the book of Joel. He follows Duhm in positing that Joel reflects a historical message related to a locust infestation that a later eschatological outlook enlarges and embellishes.[33] He considers Joel 1:4–10 to be the kernel of the original message, to which the day-of-Yʜᴡʜ references in Joel 2:1b, 2, and 11 added a later theological reflection.[34] The remainder of Joel 1–2, with its calls to cry out to Yʜᴡʜ, shifts the focus of the text away from the inbreaking of the day of Yʜᴡʜ and toward remedies mediated by the cult.[35] Plöger then asserts that the provenance of Joel 3–4 rests with an eschatological group of outsiders opposed to the theocratic programme of Joel 1–2. This group "retained their respect for the old prophetic word," which "provoked definite reactions, namely to hold fast to the eschatological meaning of certain parts of the prophetic message."[36] In other words, Joel 3–4 reflects an attempt to resignify the prophetic message of Joel 1–2 and to use it to paint a picture of eschatological hope when Yʜᴡʜ chose to intervene in power.[37]

Plöger's theory of dispossessed outsider groups adding an eschatological tinge to a prophetic message has its critics. In particular, Cook disputes the sociological basis of Plöger's theory, suggesting that it is not only out-

31. R. Simkins, *Yahweh's Activity in History and Nature in the Book of Joel* (ANETS 10; Lewiston, NY: Edwin Mellen, 1991) 81. For Simkins's cogent argument on the false dichotomy between the historical and natural realms of the biblical world, see especially pp. 43–76. Instead, he argues for a fusion of these realms in the creative activity of Yʜᴡʜ, which guides both the cosmos and events in human history.

32. Ibid., 277.

33. O. Plöger, *Theocracy and Eschatology* (trans. S. Rudman; Richmond: John Knox, 1968) 97–106. Blenkinsopp essentially follows the same line of reasoning, claiming that Joel 3–4 reflects a later, eschatologically driven interpretation of an actual locust plague in Joel 1–2 (J. Blenkinsopp, *A History of Prophecy in Israel: Revised and Enlarged* [Louisville: Westminster John Knox, 1996] 224).

34. Plöger, *Theocracy and Eschatology*, 98.

35. Ibid., 100.

36. Ibid.

37. Plöger is also unique in that he posits that this group added Joel 4 prior to the addition of Joel 3. In his reading, Joel 4 opens the door for Israel's eschatological rescue, while Joel 3 restricts it to those who believe in this eschatological hope (ibid., 103–4). This reading requires finding dissonance between the assertion in Joel 3:1 that Yʜᴡʜ will pour out the divine Spirit on "all flesh" and the statement that everyone "who calls on the name of Yʜᴡʜ" will be saved in Joel 3:5. See Cook, *Prophecy and Apocalypticism*, 169.

sider or oppressed groups who adopt eschatological rhetoric.[38] Instead, he notes Joel's concern to draw the audience together by summoning different subgroups in the first call to assemble in Joel 1:1–14 and commanding everyone from the oldest to the youngest to gather at the temple in Joel 2:15–17. Cook also points out the lack of animus toward the cult and its figures, since they are the ones who guide the community in crying out to Yhwh.[39] Further, the declaration in Joel 3:1 that Yhwh will pour out the divine Spirit on כָּל־בָּשָׂר 'all flesh' suggests that the book is trying to maintain unity within its audience.[40] All of this successfully argues against the need to posit a disenchanted group that sought to reinterpret a prophetic message to suit its particular concerns.

Theories of Joel's multilayered history of composition continue in contemporary interpretation. Barton takes Vernes and Duhm as the points of departure for his own analysis and focuses on the seemingly disjointed nature of Joel 3–4, which he sets in contrast to Joel 1–2 which "gives every impression of being well-ordered."[41] For Barton, Joel 1–2 consists of two parallel cycles of oracles reflecting on a current dire situation and calling for the audience to cry out to Yhwh (Joel 1:2–20; 2:1–17). This cycle concludes with a declaration that Yhwh heeds such cries and acts salvifically (Joel 2:18–27).[42] Joel 3–4, however, appears to reflect a different world with prophetic oracles that reflect on Yhwh's judgment of the nations and the future for Judah and Jerusalem.[43] Consequently, Barton divides Joel 3–4 into individual pericopes that he examines independently of one another.

In contrast to suggestions for a fragmented compositional history, there are also many defenders of Joel's essential literary unity. Dennefeld responds to Vernes's distinction between the two days of Yhwh, suggesting instead that the locusts in Joel 1–2 serve as forerunners of a coming day of Yhwh, which is introduced in Joel 1:15; 2:1, and 11 and described in detail in Joel 3–4.[44] He notes that the proposed victims of the day of Yhwh differ between Joel 1–2 (Judah) and Joel 3–4 (the nations), but this is not necessarily contradictory, since the prophetic narrative provides an opportunity for Judah to return to Yhwh and escape in Joel 2:12–14.[45] He

---

38. Ibid., 56–83. This chapter contains an impressive cross-cultural examination of eschatologically oriented groups who exist in central positions in their societies.

39. Ibid., 207.

40. I will return to the range intended by the phrase כָּל־בָּשָׂר in my rhetorical analysis of Joel 3:1–5, but I will state here that, at a minimum, the phrase encompasses the entire Judahite community.

41. J. Barton, *Joel and Obadiah: A Commentary* (OTL; Louisville: Westminster John Knox, 2001) 13.

42. Ibid., 13.

43. Ibid., 27–28.

44. L. Dennefeld, "Les problèmes du livre de Joel" *RSR* 4 (1924) 555–75.

45. Ibid., 562.

further demonstrates congruence throughout the book in stylistic matters, including allusion to other texts, which permits him to conclude that, "La prétendue contradiction entre la première et la seconde partie, en particulier entre quelques versets et le reste de la première partie, n'éxiste pas."[46] Dennefeld's thorough, detailed work provides a solid scholarly foundation for defending Joel's compositional unity.

Scholars following in Dennefeld's wake have contributed to making the compositional unity of Joel the majority view.[47] Kapelrud derives the unity of the book from its resonances with cultic laments followed by divine responses from Yhwh.[48] Kapelrud further takes issue with Duhm's insistence that the day-of-Yhwh references in Joel 1:1–2:17 must be later insertions. Kapelrud asserts that the day-of-Yhwh references are appropriate to their contexts as the prophet attempts to take the occurrence of a locust plague and use it as a harbinger of the forthcoming day.[49] He appeals to the long history of the day-of-Yhwh tradition to suggest that it would be appropriate for the prophet to refer to it, convincingly arguing that the day of Yhwh does not need to be a later eschatological interpolation. This work deftly traces the movements within the book, from the description of devastation and warning of further disaster to divine promises of restoration that effectively reverse the threats articulated in previous pericopes.[50]

Another approach to defending the literary unity of Joel comes from Wolff. Similar to Duhm, Wolff notes the abrupt transition between Joel 2:17 and 2:18 but argues that the same author is at work in both halves.[51] Instead, he constructs a symmetrical structure for the book in which the same issues recur in both parts. These include: (1) the lament about agricultural scarcity in Joel 1:4–20 that Joel 2:21–27 reverses; (2) the announcement of imminent eschatological catastrophe for Jerusalem in Joel 2:1–11 that turns to an announcement of security and salvation in Joel 4:1–3 and 9–17; and (3) the call to return to Yhwh in Joel 2:12–17, which Yhwh seems to answer in the affirmative in the pouring out of the divine Spirit

---

46. Ibid., 575.

47. See the brief discussion in R. Coggins, "Joel," *CBR* 2 (2003) 93–94.

48. Kapelrud, *Joel Studies*, 9. Ahlström appropriately nuances the identification of Joel as a lament by stating that it bears resemblances to the style of a lament and perhaps reflects a situation in which a lament should be offered up to Yhwh in hopes of redress; Ahlström, *Joel*, 130–31. The connection between Joel and lament reappears in Ogden's, which portrays the four oracles in Joel 4 (4:1–3, 4–8, 9–17, 18–21) as prophetic responses indicating that earlier pleas to Yhwh will lead to Judah's restoration and salvation from foreign enemies (G. Ogden, "Joel 4 and Prophetic Responses to National Laments," *JSOT* 26 [1983] 97–106).

49. Kapelrud, *Joel Studies*, 178. Kapelrud claims that "[t]his is the core of Joel's message, and it is incomprehensible that critics could delete it."

50. Ibid., 178–79.

51. Wolff, *Joel and Amos*, 7.

in Joel 3:1–5.[52] Consequently, since Joel 1:1–2:17 mirrors the concerns of Joel 2:18–4:21, it is appropriate to consider the book an integrated literary composition.

This breakdown of Joel's structure is not without its difficulties, specifically, its insistence that Joel 2:1–11 references a different kind of crisis from Joel 1:1–20.[53] However, Wolff's identification of crises in Joel 1:1–2:17 that YHWH addresses and redresses in Joel 2:18–4:21 is helpful for demonstrating the integrated nature of the subject material in this book. This work provides the foundation on which other scholars propose similar understandings of Joel's structure.[54]

Prinsloo adopts a different approach in arguing for the unity of Joel's composition by denying that there is a radical bifurcation between the two proposed halves of the book. Instead, he puts forward a theory that each passage in the book refers to preceding passages through lexical and thematic repetitions. Consequently, the governing structure of the book is that of a *Steigerung* 'heightening', which builds towards the book's climax.[55] This is especially notable in his discussions of the passages where other interpreters find the greatest disjunction. In Joel 2:18–27, Prinsloo identifies a connection through the word חֶרְפָּה 'reproach' between the plea of the people that YHWH not put them into this state in Joel 2:17 (וְאַל־תִּתֵּן נַחֲלָתְךָ לְחֶרְפָּה) and YHWH's declaration in Joel 2:19 that it will not occur (וְלֹא־אֶתֵּן

---

52. Ibid., 7. Notably, Joel 2:18–20, 4:4–8 and 4:18–21 are absent from this symmetrical scheme, because Wolff considers them to be redactional additions. Prinsloo aptly notes that Joel 2:19 and 4:18–21 also point powerfully to the end of the lack of sustenance, and therefore, their excision from Wolff's structure is troubling (W. Prinsloo, "The Unity of the Book of Joel," *ZAW* 104 [1992] 73).

53. See the discussion of rhetorical strategy in Joel 2:1–11 for additional critique of Wolff's understanding of this passage. Essentially, I argue that the text is reusing the imagery of the locust invasion to set up YHWH's turn against Jerusalem, rather than pointing toward an eschatological event.

54. See Ahlström, *Joel*, 135. Ahlström refers to the "correlative" nature of Joel's structure, in which the second part of the book reverses every facet of the negative fate prophesied for Judah and Jerusalem in the first part. Additionally, Allen modifies Wolff's theory so that Joel 4:4–8 also has a parallel to a previous section of the book, Joel 2:21–23 (Allen, *Joel*, 28). Garrett goes to great lengths in constructing a symmetrical understanding of the book, proposing that Joel contains a "double-hinge" structure in which two overlapping chiasms have their hinge points in 2:17/18 and 2:27/3:1. The first chiasm covers Joel 1:1–2:27, while the second stretches from 2:20 to 4:21. The first consists of two elements of punishment (A. 1:1–20; B. 2:1–11), two elements of forgiveness (A′. 2:20; B′. 2:21–27), and a middle point of repentance plus a transition to YHWH's response (C. 2:12–17 plus 2:18–19). The second chiasm consists of "outer" passages of judgment (A. 2:20; A′. 4:1–21) and "inner" passages of grace (B. 2:21–27; B′. 3:1–5; D. Garrett, "The Structure of Joel," *JETS* 28 [1985] 289–97). Garrett stretches the boundaries of what should be considered a chiasm farther than is likely with the lopsided nature of certain elements in his structural proposal. See M. Boda, "Chiasmus in Ubiquity: Symmetrical Mirages in Nehemiah 9," *JSOT* 71 (1996) 56–57.

55. See Prinsloo, "Unity," 66–81.

אֶתְכֶם עוֹד חֶרְפָּה בַּגּוֹיִם).[56] Similarly, in Joel 3:1–5 he draws attention to the introductory phrase וְהָיָה אַחֲרֵי־כֵן 'And it will be after this', which he views as an interpretation of the *waw*-consecutive phrases that commence in Joel 2:18.[57] After the material restoration of Joel 2:18–27, spiritual restoration follows in Joel 3:1–5. While I do not follow Prinsloo's structural divisions precisely, the way in which he identifies points of continuity that stretch across significant points of apparent disjunction is helpful in tracing the flow of Joel's prophetic message.

Moving beyond the various proposals for Joel's structure, we must realize that the use and reuse of similar lexemes, images, and themes throughout the book are key features upon which numerous commentators rely. The day of Yнwн is a key *Leitmotiv* that occurs throughout the book and requires reflection as the nature of this day develops.[58] Further, Joel 2:27 and 4:17 both use the same statement of knowing that Yнwн is God based on divine actions on Judah's behalf. Other images that span this prophetic book include the גּוֹיִם 'nations' who invade and destroy the land. The idea of an invading nation first appears in Joel 1:6 as a metaphor for locusts. It then recurs in Joel 4:12, where Yнwн summons the nations to a place of judgment. Joel 2:11 describes the strength of Yнwн's army and the terrifying nature of the day of Yнwн when Yнwн speaks and leads an assault against Zion. The image of Yнwн's voice recurs in Joel 4:16, this time promising sanctuary for those who dwell in Zion, since Yнwн is in their midst.[59] Similarly, images of agricultural fertility and its lack permeate the entire book (Joel 1:5, 11; 2:22; 4:13, 18).[60] Overall, the lexical correspondences that span the length of Joel provide evidence of its unity.

In summary, the weight of the arguments concerning Joel's composition seems to fall on the side of scholars who consider it a unified work. Coggins may be correct to claim that the unity of the book is unlikely to return to the forefront of Joel studies, but it has undoubtedly been one of the most significant issues in the history of research.[61] The following analysis will speak to the issue by working through the rhetorical structure and strategies that Joel employs. By identifying the strategies through which Joel communicates a persuasive message, I intend to buttress the arguments that Joel is a unified composition.

---

56. Ibid., 78.

57. Ibid., 79.

58. Strazicich, *Joel's Use of Scripture*, 47. Identifying the day of Yнwн as a signal of literary unity presumes that mentions of this day in Joel 1–2 are not later redactional insertions.

59. Wolff, *Joel and Amos*, 8.

60. Ahlström, *Joel*, 133. I examine the rhetorical effects of this reuse of imagery in detailed studies of the appropriate passages. Thompson also provides a thorough list of lexical and thematic repetitions throughout the book and argues that these are a signal of the book's literary unity; J. Thompson, "The Use of Repetition in the Prophecy of Joel," in *On Culture and Religion* (ed. M. Black and W. Smalley; The Hague: Mouton, 1974) 108.

61. Coggins, "Joel," 94.

Joel and the Book of the Twelve

A more recent development in the discussion of Joel is its relationship to the burgeoning field of studies on the *Book of the Twelve*. This term refers to the twelve Minor Prophets, a corpus that has been transmitted on a single scroll and was considered a single literary collection. [62] In recent years, scholars have taken an interest in this collection as a literary corpus and examined evidence of intentional shaping in the collection. This is a development from previous scholarly projects that tended to focus on stripping away extraneous material to get to the "authentic" prophetic kernel of each book. [63] Exploring the Book of the Twelve as a collection may have the potential to open up new avenues of interpretation through consideration of the way that the books within the corpus interact. [64] The existence of the Book of the Twelve and the competing theories of its composition are not at the heart of my study, but the debate surrounding the composition of the Book of the Twelve does raise certain issues that affect the way in which one approaches the rhetoric of Joel. Specifically, the debate surrounding the Book of the Twelve casts doubt on the method of interpreting an individual book in the corpus as its own discrete literary unit. In the following survey, I engage the literature surrounding the Book of the Twelve and provide a foundation for the reading strategy that I adopt in this book.

The most significant theory about the composition of the Book of the Twelve that relates to this study is Nogalski's work on an apparent *Stichwort* 'catchword' phenomenon that links the various books within the corpus. He locates keywords at the end of each prophetic book in the corpus that seem to recur at the beginning of the subsequent book. [65] These

---

62. For additional details on the Book of the Twelve as a corpus, see J. Nogalski, *Literary Precursors to the Book of the Twelve* (BZAW 217; Berlin: de Gruyter, 1993) 2–3; B. Jones, *The Formation of the Book of the Twelve: A Study in Text and Canon* (SBLDS 149; Atlanta: Scholars Press, 1995) 1–13; R. Fuller, "The Form and Formation of the Book of the Twelve: The Evidence of the Judean Desert," in *Forming Prophetic Literature: Essays on Isaiah and the Twelve in Honour of John D. W. Watts* (ed. J. Watts and P. House; JSOTSup 235; Sheffield: Sheffield Academic Press, 1996) 86–101; P. Redditt, "The Production and Reading of the Book of the Twelve," in *Reading and Hearing the Book of the Twelve* (ed. J. Nogalski and M. Sweeney; SBLSymS 15; Atlanta: Scholars Press, 2000) 11–33; D. Schneider, *The Unity of the Book of the Twelve* (Ph.D. diss., Yale University, 1979) 235–41. Redditt notes that the idea of the Minor Prophets as a single volume stretches back to 200 B.C.E. and Jesus Ben Sira, who mentions The Twelve alongside Isaiah, Jeremiah, and Ezekiel (Sir 49:10; Redditt, "Production and Reading," 14).

63. Coggins refers to the preponderance of this project by declaring, "We have all come to be disciples of, shall we say, Bernard Duhm, and the tradition that he exemplifies" (R. Coggins, "The Minor Prophets: One Book or Twelve," in *Crossing the Boundaries: Essays in Biblical Interpretation in Honour of Michael D. Goulder* [ed. S. Porter, P. Joyce, and D. Orton; Leiden: Brill, 1994] 58).

64. Ibid., 65–68. Coggins organizes the trajectory of the Book of the Twelve around the themes of Israel in relation to foreign powers and the attitude toward cultic worship.

65. See the collection of catchwords that he gathers, in Nogalski, *Literary Precursors*, 21–58.

key words provide the reading logic for the broader corpus, helping the reader to keep the former book in mind when transitioning into the next book in the corpus. Applying this approach to Joel, Nogalski compares Hos 14:5–10 with Joel 1:1–12, noting shared vocabulary that includes the words יֹשְׁבֵי 'inhabitants', דָּגָן 'grain', יַיִן 'wine', and גֶּפֶן 'vine'.[66] On the other end, the catchwords connecting Joel 4:1–21 and Amos 1:1–2:16 include the shared declaration of Yhwh's roar (Joel 4:16; Amos 1:2), names of foreign nations against whom Yhwh moves (Tyre, Philistia, Edom), and Zion and Jerusalem.[67] As I discuss in a later chapter, the way in which Nogalski uses these catchwords to integrate the contexts of prophetic books within The Twelve has significant ramifications for the way the interpreter approaches an issue such as the prophetic call to return to Yhwh in Joel 2:12–17.[68]

Beyond the proposed existence of catchwords, Nogalski summarizes other lines of inquiry that have led to a consensus concerning the Book of the Twelve as a redactional literary composition. These include most significantly the priority of the Masoretic sequence of books over other possibilities.[69] Establishing the priority of the Masoretic sequence is significant since Nogalski's catchword connections only work if the prophetic books are arranged in this way. The Masoretic sequence is compared with that of the Septuagint, which lists the first six books in a variant order, and one Qumran manuscript that seems to have Jonah in the final position

---

66. Ibid., 21–23.

67. Ibid., 24–27. There is some variation in these catchwords since Joel 4:4 employs a generic "regions of Philistia," while Amos 1:7–8 mentions specific cities including Gaza, Ashdod, Ashkelon, and Ekron, before using the blanket term "remnant of the Philistines" as a summary statement.

68. Other theories about the composition of the Book of the Twelve differ in the number of redactional layers that can be found within the corpus. Schart posits several additional redactional layers, including one that combined Hosea–Amos, followed by a four-book collection that included Micah and Zephaniah. The four-book layer presented a theological message that transgressions were perceived as being directed against Yhwh and that Israel's problems were a result of falling away from Israel's core identity as established in the exodus. The following layer added Nahum and Habakkuk, followed by a layer consisting of Haggai and Zech 1–8. This led to the addition of Joel, Obadiah, and Zech 9–14, which was oriented around passages about the day of Yhwh. Finally, the satirical narrative of Jonah and the book of Malachi completed the corpus; A. Schart, "Reconstructing the Redaction History of the Twelve Prophets: Problems and Models," in *Reading and Hearing the Book of the Twelve* (ed. J. Nogalski and M. Sweeney; SBLSymS 15; Atlanta: Scholars Press, 2000) 42–46; A. Schart, *Entstehung des Zwölfprophetenbuchs* (BZAW 260; Berlin: de Gruyter, 1997) 304–6.

69. E. Ben Zvi and J. Nogalski, *Two Sides of a Coin: Juxtaposing Views on Interpreting the Book of the Twelve / the Twelve Prophetic Books* (Analecta Gorgiana 201; Piscataway, NJ: Gorgias, 2009) 12. The third line of inquiry that Nogalski notes is the proposed existence and transmission of two literary units within the broader Book of the Twelve: (1) Hosea-Amos-Micah-Zephaniah; (2) Haggai-Zech 1–8.

of the Book of the Twelve.[70] Joel's location in these different sequences is significant because it shifts from second to fourth position (following Micah) in the LXX tradition. This shift is attributed to the intention of the LXX editors to preserve older prophetic writings at the beginning of the collection.[71]

The priority of the Masoretic order in the Book of the Twelve is not an entirely closed question. Jones makes the opposite case, suggesting that Joel and Obadiah were crafted specially to bridge the gap between the judgments against Israel in Hosea-Amos-Micah and the announcements of judgment against foreign nations in Nahum and Habakkuk.[72] In this understanding, the LXX sequence has temporal priority. Although his conclusion does not appear to have been widely adopted, Jones's work indicates that there is credence to the dissenting view. It is not in the purview of this book to resolve the issue of canonical priority, but this issue does raise interesting questions concerning the role of Joel in the proposed Book of the Twelve. Nogalski may be correct in asserting that arguments for the priority of the LXX sequence have not succeeded in swaying the consensus, but the presence of varying sequences should at least lend some caution to approaches to unifying the Book of the Twelve that depend on all of the books remaining in their Masoretic location.[73]

Interestingly, scholars further supplement the work on proposed redactional layers with synchronic and literary studies of the Book of the Twelve. Joel plays a significant role in many of these studies. For example, Sweeney proposes that Joel in its present location in the Masoretic Text balances out Hosea in presenting the program of the Book of the Twelve. Whereas Hosea is concerned with the dissolution of the relationship between Yhwh and Israel, Joel shifts the concern to the fate of unnamed nations who threaten God's people.[74] Rendtorff traces the use of the day of Yhwh throughout the collection, proposing that it is a dominating theme that helps unify the

---

70. The LXX order of the Minor Prophets is Hosea, Amos, Micah, Joel, Obadiah, Jonah, Nahum, Habakkuk, Zephaniah, Haggai, Zechariah, and Malachi. The scroll 4QXII[a] may preserve an order in which Jonah follows Malachi. See Fuller, "Form and Formation," 95–97; Jones, *Formation*, 223.

71. Schneider, *Unity*, 223–26. Schneider differentiates the LXX order from the Masoretic order by claiming that the former is determined by chronology while the latter is determined by context. See also Nogalski, *Literary Precursors*, 2–3.

72. Jones, *Formation*, 239–41.

73. Ben Zvi and Nogalski, *Two Sides of a Coin*, 13.

74. M. Sweeney, "Sequence and Interpretation in the Book of the Twelve," in *Reading and Hearing the Book of the Twelve* (ed. J. Nogalski and M. Sweeney; SBLSymS 15; Atlanta: Scholars Press, 2000) 59. Sweeney also contrasts Joel's position in the Masoretic order with the sequence of the Septuagint. In the Septuagint, the first three books focus heavily on the fate of Israel before Joel interjects and shifts the scene toward Judah and Jerusalem (M. Sweeney, "The Place and Function of Joel in the Book of the Twelve," in *SBL 1999: Seminar Papers* [SBLSP 38; Atlanta: Society of Biblical Literature, 1999] 592).

Book of the Twelve.[75] Again, Joel plays a vital role, presenting the day of
YHWH as something for YHWH's people to fear (cf. Amos 5:18–20; Zeph 1:4–7,
14–16), as well as a potential signal of divine restoration through judgment
on foreign nations (cf. Obad 15–21; Zeph 2:1–9).

Nogalski goes even further and proposes that Joel is the "literary anchor" of a synchronic reading of the collection since Joel's introduction
mirrors the conclusion of Hosea by calling the audience to repentance,
while Joel's final chapter mirrors the beginning of Amos by threatening
judgment against foreign nations.[76] Further, the language of agricultural
fertility in Joel 1–2, especially the triad of "grain, wine, and oil," in Joel
1:10; 2:19; 2:24, occurs in other locations in the Twelve, suggesting its significance in drawing the corpus together (cf. Hos 2:23–25; Amos 4:9; Hag
1:10–11; 2:9).[77] Nogalski proposes that Joel transcends the chronological
context, explaining why events in later books within the sequence of the
Twelve happened as they did and grounding hope of restoration in the call
to return to YHWH.[78] This synchronic examination of Joel runs counter to
typical diachronic approaches in that it reverses the lines of literary dependence and is also noticeably dependent on the sequence of the Masoretic
text to provide meaning for this reading.

The idea of a Book of the Twelve and theories related to its composition and coherence have not gone unchallenged. One stream of criticism
claims that Nogalski's use of catchwords adopts too narrow of a focus in
concentrating on the beginnings and endings of prophetic books in relationship with the books that surround them. Coggins, for example, points
out several stark examples of thematic and linguistic connections between
Joel and other prophetic books that do not immediately precede or follow
it. These include Joel 1:15 and Isa 13:6 and Joel 4:10 with Isa 2:4 which are
clearly in conversation with each other.[79] Similarly, Isa 24:7 shares signifi-

---

75. R. Rendtorff, "How to Read the Book of the Twelve as a Theological Unity," in
Reading and Hearing the Book of the Twelve (ed. J. Nogalski and M. Sweeney; SBLSymS 15;
Atlanta: Scholars Press, 2000) 75–87.

76. J. Nogalski, "Joel as 'Literary Anchor' for the Book of the Twelve," in *Reading and
Hearing the Book of the Twelve* (ed. J. Nogalski and M. Sweeney; SBLSymS 15; Atlanta: Scholars Press, 2000) 92. See the discussion on rhetorical strategy in Joel 2:12–17, where I consider whether Nogalski is correct to import guilt from Hosea into Joel.

77. Ibid., 102–4.

78. Ibid., 107. Nogalski provides an extended list of examples that includes Nahum's
affirming that YHWH punishes the guilty (Nah 1:3) while comparing Assyria and Babylon
to locusts (Nah 3:15–17). Further, Zephaniah draws on day-of-YHWH sayings first found in
Joel to threaten disobedient Judah.

79. R. Coggins, "Interbiblical Quotations in Joel," in *After the Exile: Essays in Honour of
Rex Mason* (ed. J. Barton and D. Reimer; Macon, GA: Mercer University Press, 1996) 77–78.
Mason also notes the "almost identical verbal parallels," before detailing how the two
passages differ in their targets; Mason, *Zephaniah*, 117. Isaiah 13:6 describes the Divine
Warrior's activity in defeating Babylon, while Joel 1:15 points to the devastation that the
locusts wreak over the Judean countryside.

cant vocabulary relating to lamentation about agricultural produce with Joel 1:10, 12, which opens up the question of why the proposed sequential linkages between the books of this corpus should be elevated to a privileged position.

Another critique leveled against the catchword phenomenon concerns the criteria for identifying words of this sort. Specifically, the proposed catchwords linking Hosea and Joel are called into question. Ben Zvi incisively notes that words like יֹשְׁבֵי 'inhabitants', דָּגָן 'grain', יַיִן 'wine', and גֶּפֶן 'vine' are relatively common and that it would almost require a reader to be anticipating a connection in order for these catchwords to be noticed and cataloged.[80] As mentioned above, words describing agricultural bounty or its lack are found throughout the Book of the Twelve. The focus on catchwords also requires diminishing the significance of the unique conclusion of Hos 14:10 and the introductory phrase in Joel 1:1, which both admirably serve the purpose of marking the boundaries of discrete literary units. Consequently, one can question whether the readers of Joel must import the conclusion of Hosea into their understanding of the situation underlying the prophetic text of Joel.

Another line of criticism of Nogalski's work challenges the viability of the idea of the Book of the Twelve more broadly. Petersen questions how one could examine twelve prophetic texts as a single literary composition and suggests instead that the Book of the Twelve is a thematic anthology oriented around the idea of the day of YHWH.[81] This permits the interpreter to examine thematic overlaps among the individual books without importing complex theories of composition and redaction into the discussion. Ben Zvi goes even further than Petersen and disputes the usefulness of employing the title *Book of the Twelve*. His orientation is toward ancient readers of the prophetic texts, whom he argues would not instinctively read across the superscriptions, incipits, and other signals that mark the

---

80. Ben Zvi and Nogalski, *Two Sides of a Coin*, 87–89. Coggins follows Ben Zvi and asserts that the commonality of the supposed catchwords significantly diminishes their probative value; Coggins, "Joel," 90. Jones offers a similar critique of the catchword connection between Micah and Nahum, noting that many of the words occur over 100 times in the Old Testament. The word list includes "anger," "sea," "mountain," "rivers," and "hand." Again, Jones calls into question the value of developing redactional linkages between books based on common words; Jones, *Formation*, 38.

81. D. Petersen, "A Book of the Twelve?" in *Reading and Hearing the Book of the Twelve* (ed. J. Nogalski and M. Sweeney; SBLSymS 15; Atlanta: Scholars Press, 2000) 9–10. Petersen grounds the idea of thematic coherence as the underlying feature of the Book of the Twelve with a similar understanding of the "Major" Prophets. He suggests that the focal theme for Isaiah is Zion, for Jeremiah it is the rhetoric of lament, and for Ezekiel it is the glory of God. Landy adroitly points out that one potential weakness of viewing the day of YHWH as the primary unifying theme of the Book of the Twelve is that there is no explicit reference to it in Hosea and Zechariah, the two largest books of the collection; F. Landy, "Three Sides of a Coin: In Conversation with Ben Zvi and Nogalski, *Two Sides of a Coin*," *JHS* 10 (2010), http://www.jhsonline.org/Articles/article_139.pdf, §19.

introduction of individual prophetic books.[82] He claims that ancient readers used the material to interact imaginatively with the personas of the
prophets, who are symbolically brought to life within their respective
books.[83] Consequently, the Minor Prophets speak with 12 different voices,
all of whom have unique contributions to make. Ben Zvi compares these
reading communities with contemporary synchronic approaches to the
text and claims that these communities were unlikely to work through proposed layers of redaction and editing in order to try to understand the prophetic books as a single collection.[84] Ben Zvi specifically notes that there is
no superscription or incipit denoting a collection called the "Book of the
Twelve." Instead, the superscriptions and incipits are limited to individual
books and thus seem to indicate that they ought to be read as discrete literary units.[85]

Ben Zvi also goes to great length to establish the idea of a prophetic book
as a self-contained literary unit, offering the following definition:

> a self-contained written text that was produced within ancient Israel, and
> characterized by a clear beginning and conclusion, by a substantial level
> of textual coherence and of textually inscribed distinctiveness vis-à-vis
> other books, and that, accordingly, leads its intended and primary readers
> (and re-readers) to approach it in a manner that takes into account this
> distinctiveness.[86]

This definition highlights the features of individual books within the
broader corpus of the proposed Book of the Twelve, noting specifically how

---

82. Ben Zvi and Nogalski, *Two Sides of a Coin*, 58. Sweeney also captures this sentiment
nicely when he declares, "No other superscription appears until the following book. . . .
The superscription marks the book of Joel as a discrete unit within the Book of the Twelve"
(Sweeney, "Place and Function," 576).

83. Ben Zvi and Nogalski, *Two Sides of a Coin*, 80–83.

84. Ibid., 58–60. Ben Zvi asserts that the individual texts do not contain explicit statements identifying the different redactional layers and that the readers would be willing
to accept that implied authors of prophetic books could use different styles and literary
forms within a single body of literature. Consequently, the supposed redactional seams are
less apparent than one might think. This line of argumentation bears some resemblance
to Barton's "trick of the disappearing redactor," where the more one shows that a redactor seamlessly integrates bodies of text, the less one has need of that redactor to interpret
the text (J. Barton, *Reading the Old Testament: Method in Biblical Study* [2nd ed.; Louisville:
Westminster John Knox, 1996] 159). In a literarily focused reading of the text, however,
the supposed disappearance of a redactor is not especially troubling since the ability to
read the text as a discrete unit is the primary concern.

85. Nogalski rightly notes that the Pentateuch does not have an overall title, yet few
would dispute the interconnected nature of these books. Ben Zvi appropriately counters
with an appeal to the nature of prophetic literature, suggesting that titles and incipits
place the books of the Minor Prophets on the same literary level as Isaiah, Jeremiah, and
Ezekiel. See Ben Zvi and Nogalski, *Two Sides of a Coin*, 16, 73–75.

86. E. Ben Zvi, "The Prophetic Book: A Key Form of Prophetic Literature," in *The
Changing Face of Form Criticism for the Twenty-First Century* (ed. M. Sweeney and E. Ben Zvi;
Grand Rapids: Eerdmans, 2003) 279–80.

each book has introductory and concluding signals and how each book establishes a unique literary and rhetorical situation into which it speaks. These concluding signals include what Ben Zvi terms "unique expressions" that delimit each book as well as a signal the book's particular choice of expression in comparison with other books in the collection (cf. Hos 14:10; Joel 4:21; Amos 9:15; Obad 21; Mic 7:20; Zech 14:21).[87] For example, Ben Zvi takes issue with Nogalski's assertion that Hosea ends and Joel begins with a call to repentance (Hos 14:1–8; Joel 1:1–2:17). Instead, Hosea actually concludes in Hos 14:10 with a unique statement, calling on its readers to reflect wisely on what has been said, while Joel commences with a superscription that associates the book with a prophetic figure who is different from Hosea.[88] Ben Zvi thus highlights points of distinction within individual prophetic books and argues that the readers would be likely to pay attention to their individualized settings.[89] This concern for the uniqueness of each prophetic book within the collection should guide further study.

A helpful view on this issue comes from Landy, who addresses the debate over the nature of the Book of the Twelve, looking specifically to the contrasting views of Nogalski and Ben Zvi. Landy uses Nogalski and Ben Zvi's coauthored book, *Two Sides of a Coin: Juxtaposing Views on Interpreting the Book of the Twelve / the Twelve Prophetic Books*, as the point of departure and offers several valuable insights. Landy approaches the debate from a literary perspective that resonates closely with the concerns of this book. Landy's first notable contribution concerns his analysis of the features of coherence and contrast within the Book of the Twelve. He suggests that it is difficult to find poetic unity across the Book of the Twelve since readers must overcome the disjunctive effects of superscriptions as well as the "powerful internal coherence" of each respective book.[90] Landy also takes issue with theories of thematic coherence across different prophetic books, claiming that it is difficult to conceive of a biblical book that is *not* concerned with "the fertility of the land, the fate of God's people, and the theodicy problem."[91] Consequently, the threshold of what an interpreter ought to consider as a shared prophetic theme probably needs to be raised.

Further, Landy notes the tension between theories of redactional layering and poetic imagination. Essentially, if one is concerned with identifying the nature and agenda of each proposed layer of redactional shaping, it is possible to sublimate the artistic interplay of nuanced arguments and disjunctive elements. While denying neither poetic creativity nor

---

87. Ben Zvi and Nogalski, *Two Sides of a Coin*, 78.
88. Ibid., 87.
89. Ben Zvi, "Prophetic Book," 287.
90. Landy, "Three Sides of a Coin," §17.
91. Ibid., §19. See also Nogalski's claim that the concerns of the Book of the Twelve closely mirror those of Isaiah; J. Nogalski, *Redactional Processes in the Book of the Twelve* (BZAW 217; Berlin: de Gruyter, 1993) 280.

redactional activity, Landy locates himself toward the poetic end of the spectrum, raising the apt question how the work of redactors "came to be universally accepted, and how they concealed themselves so thoroughly (and yet, according to redaction critics so transparently) in the text."[92] While redactional work on the Minor Prophets continues apace, the injunction to experience the uniqueness and the fragmented nature of the 12 prophetic books provides a much needed counterbalance.

In summary, while there appears to be sufficient thematic coherence and linguistic overlap for continued research into the Minor Prophets as a redactionally shaped collection called the Book of the Twelve, it is an equally appropriate reading strategy to consider the individual books within the collection and to examine their composition and specific nuances of meaning. Effectively, one's perspective on the unity and interrelationship of the individual books of the Minor Prophets is in large part shaped by the reading strategy that one adopts.[93] The foundation that Ben Zvi and Landy establish provides the opportunity to examine Joel as a literary whole in its own right. This does not deny the existence of redactional processes within Joel and the broader corpus of the Minor Prophets, nor does it preclude examination of citations, allusions, and reinterpretations of other biblical texts. This approach, however, roots the interpretive process in Joel as a creative, poetic, and rhetorically powerful literary unit.

Reading Joel

In recent years, several important studies dealing with literary and reader-oriented perspectives on prophetic literature have emerged that include Joel in the conversation. These studies are relevant to this project since they concern the effects of reading the text as a literary whole. Conrad borrows terminology from Umberto Eco's semiotic theory and proposes that prophetic books encode information that a Model Reader should have the capacity to comprehend.[94] For prophetic books, Conrad suggests that their openings and superscriptions provide the key coded information that unlocks the way in which the reader ought to approach them.[95] He divides

---

92. Landy, "Three Sides of a Coin," §20.

93. Ben Zvi and Nogalski, *Two Sides of a Coin*, 64. Note Ben Zvi's assertion that, if one begins from the hypothesis that the Book of the Twelve is a redactional unit, one is likely to discover "structures, macrostructures, general themes and other markers of textual coherence."

94. Eco's summation of the task states that "the author has to assume that the ensemble of codes he relies upon is the same as that shared by his possible reader. The author thus has to foresee a model of the possible reader (hereafter Model Reader) supposedly able to deal interpretively with the expressions in the same way as the author deals generatively with them" (U. Eco, *The Role of the Reader* [Bloomington: Indiana University Press, 1979] 7).

95. E. Conrad, "Forming the Twelve and Forming Canon," in *Thematic Threads in the Book of the Twelve* (ed. P. Redditt and A. Schart; BZAW 325; Berlin: de Gruyter, 2003) 96.

prophetic books into three forms, based on the opening words of Isaiah (חָזוֹן 'vision'), Jeremiah (דִּבְרֵי 'words of'), and Ezekiel (וַיְהִי 'and it was'). He suggests that characteristics of prophetic books that follow the Isaianic code include diminishing the character of the prophet and inaugurating a period of waiting for the promised restoration to come.[96] In contrast, prophetic books that follow the Jeremianic pattern are about words from the outside being brought into cultic reality, while prophetic books in the Ezekielian pattern are more narrative in scope, fitting in with the introductory וַיְהִי 'and it was'.[97]

Conrad's attempt to apply Eco's literary theory encounters serious difficulties in its consideration of Joel's role within the broader scheme of prophetic literature. Conrad classifies Joel as a חָזוֹן 'vision' in the manner of Isaiah, even though the word חָזוֹן never appears in Joel. He defends this classification on the grounds that, like Isa 1:2, Joel 1:2 commences the prophetic discourse with a call to hear.[98] This is especially problematic considering the actual opening of Joel, דְּבַר־יְהוָה אֲשֶׁר הָיָה אֶל־יוֹאֵל 'The word of YHWH that was to Joel'. This opening more closely resembles those that Conrad attributes to Jeremiah and Amos (Jer 1:1, דִּבְרֵי יִרְמְיָהוּ; Amos 1:1, דִּבְרֵי עָמוֹס). The parallel is not exact since Joel's opening attributes the prophetic "word" to YHWH, mediated through the prophet Joel. Jeremiah 1:2, however, closely resembles Joel since it also indicates that Jeremiah is receiving the word of YHWH (אֲשֶׁר הָיָה דְבַר־יְהוָה אֵלָיו 'which was the word of YHWH to him'). Given the similarities to Jeremiah, if Conrad's argument is that Model Readers will be able to decode correctly the nature of prophetic books based on their opening lexical choices, Joel's code is very confusing. The Model Reader needs to ignore the initial verse, which supposedly provides the key to the code, and instead look down at the next verse.

Other studies that focus on the reading of Joel employ the literary-critical discipline of intertextuality.[99] Prophetic literature would seem to

---

96. E. Conrad, *Reading the Latter Prophets: Towards a New Canonical Criticism* (JSOTSup 376; London: T. & T. Clark, 2003) 242.

97. Ibid., 159, 180.

98. Conrad, *Forming the Twelve*, 100–101; cf. also Mic 1:1–2.

99. Intertextuality is distinguished here from what Strazicich describes as "source and influence" studies, which approach interrelated texts with the primary objective of determining what texts were used in constructing the text being examined; Strazicich, *Joel's Use of Scripture*, 6–7. Bergler is probably the most accomplished exemplar of the "source and influence" approach in Joel studies. See S. Bergler, *Joel als Schriftinterpret* (Frankfurt am Main: Peter Lang, 1988). He argues that the prophet combined poems about drought and enemy invasion with allusions and themes from other biblical sources to proclaim a new message (p. 28). Joel's primary function is that of a *Schriftinterpret* ('interpreter of Scripture') who appropriates previous biblical texts and reapplies them in a new context. Bergler suggests that Joel's purpose in reincorporating sacred texts was to indicate that divine promises had not failed and were still in the process of coming to fruition, claiming that "Keines der Worte der Alten is dahingefallen" (p. 29). This perspective is linked to a sociotemporal location of Joel in a time when prophetic declarations were waning while linking one's

offer fertile ground for this approach since it often seems to be in conversation with other texts.[100] The unpublished dissertation of Kathryn Kit-King Leung adopts this approach and focuses specifically on how intertextuality helps to explain Joel's use of the day-of-YHWH motif. She works from a definition of intertextuality as a reader-oriented approach that seeks to find relationships between the studied text and others that may have chronologically preceded or followed it.[101] Notably, Leung attempts to rein in some of the perceived excesses of intertextuality by claiming that intertextuality discovered by the reader needs to cohere with the intertextuality intended by the author, while maintaining a temporal perspective in which "prior texts" contribute to the meaning of the passages being studied.[102] Leung further reflects on the challenges of bringing synchronic and diachronic sensibilities to intertextual studies, noting that it is difficult completely to sever ties to diachronic approaches when one wants to speak of one text as reading an antecedent text.[103]

The majority of Leung's work considers Joel's use of covenant, theophany, and holy war motifs in the broader picture of the text's development of the day of YHWH. Leung detects lexical and structural resonances with other passages, which suggest that Joel invoked these ancient traditions in order to construct the meaning of the prophetic message.[104] Consideration of lexical references is shared by most commentaries on Joel, which often point out the number of apparent allusions and references to other texts.[105] This leads to lengthy consideration of the structure and form of the texts to which Joel refers since Leung attempts to construct fully the meaning of

---

material with established prophecies appeared to provide a means of authentication. Key to Bergler's approach is the identification of Joel's allusion to the Egyptian plagues, especially those involving blood, darkness, and locusts. While Joel does not explicitly cite these passages, Bergler argues that they resonate in the background, informing the prophetic portrayal of the present situation. For example, Bergler finds a parallel between the description in Exod 10:14 of the innumerable locusts and the fourfold synonyms for locusts used in Joel 1:4, which also suggests a vast quantity (pp. 272–76). Bergler's identification of scriptural parallels is debatable in certain instances, but his detailed examination of Joel's use of scriptural traditions establishes a useful point of departure for further research.

100. Speaking of the strategies that biblical prophets employ, Jemielity eloquently writes that "they allude, they repeat, they use and invert established patterns, they invoke the authority of earlier prophets—in short, they constantly employ the language of the past to strengthen their present position (T. Jemielity, *Satire and the Hebrew Prophets* [Louisville: Westminster John Knox, 1992] 171–72).

101. K. Leung, *An Intertextual Study of the Motif-Complex* Yom Yahweh *in the Book of Joel* (Ph.D. diss., Fuller Theological Seminary, 1997) 16. Leung derives this definition from O. Miller, "Intertextual Identity," in *Identity of the Literary Text* (ed. M. Valdés and O. Miller; Toronto: University of Toronto Press, 1985) 30.

102. Leung, *Intertextual*, 17.

103. Ibid., 39.

104. Ibid., 270.

105. For example, see the lists in Coggins, *Joel*, 21; Crenshaw, *Joel*, 27–28.

those texts before discussing their appropriation in Joel.[106] Overall, Leung offers a useful examination of the applicability of intertextuality to biblical texts and Joel's multiple references to other biblical passages. Her work, however, leaves room to go beyond establishing the presence of allusions and references to other texts, offering the opportunity to examine the intended effects of these references.

The final approach to reading Joel comes from John Strazicich, whose monograph considers the book of Joel with detailed reference to its proposed intertextual linkages. He considers the book of Joel to be a skillful theological response to twin crises of locust infestation and drought. The key to Joel's response is located in its use of other scriptural traditions, which Strazicich articulates using the categories of appropriation and resignification.[107] Essentially, Joel displays signals that it is appropriating other texts and placing them into a different context that intends to bring new meaning to the fore.[108] Uniquely, this monograph attempts to address both the question of the texts that inform the composition of Joel as well as the use of Joel in New Testament contexts. Strazicich derives his approach to intertextuality largely from Bakhtin and Kristeva, and he defines *intertextuality* as "the heuristic enterprise of discerning the appropriation and resignification of antecedent texts."[109] He notes that Bakhtin and Kristeva both try to maintain a role for an author, stressing the transposition of meaning

---

106. See the lengthy discussion of Exod 32–34 in conversation with the reuse of Exod 34:6–7 in Joel 2:12–14 in Leung, "Intertextual," 106–18. In this particular case, her identification of a chiastic structural parallel between Exod 32–34 and Joel 1–2 is rather questionable. She argues that both texts move from breach of covenant to restoration of covenant with features of punishment, restoration, divine appearance, and affirmation of divine character appearing within these boundaries. Her approach, however, involves omitting a number of verses in Exodus that she deems to be irrelevant to the discussion, which casts doubt on the validity of finding a chiastic structure. There is clearly some level of relationship between the two passages, which I explore in more detail in another chapter, but here I can state that Leung's identification of structural patterning is questionable.

107. Strazicich, *Joel's Use of Scripture*, 1–2. He defines *appropriation* as "the acquisition of an antecedent text or tradition" and *resignification* as "the transformation of an antecedent text or tradition." Strazicich distinguishes his work from Bergler's by means of these definitions; whereas Bergler argues that Joel is a Scripture interpreter, Strazicich maintains that Joel's approach is to resignify Scripture by placing it in a different literary context. This may lead to a new understanding of the referenced passage, but it does not necessarily reflect intentional interpretation.

108. Probably the most famous example of this process is the reversal of Isa 2:4 and Mic 4:3 in Joel 4:10.

109. Strazicich, *Joel's Use of Scripture*, 14. For more on the theory of *intertextuality* that Strazicich appropriates, see especially M. Bakhtin, *The Dialogic Imagination* (Austin: University of Texas Press, 1981); J. Kristeva, *Sēmeiōtikē: Recherche pour une semanalyse* (Paris: Seuil, 1969). For a helpful summary of employing intertextual concepts in biblical studies, see P. Tull, "Rhetorical Criticism and Intertextuality," in *To Each Its Own Meaning: An Introduction to Biblical Criticisms and Their Application—Revised and Expanded* (ed. S. Haynes and S. McKenzie; Louisville: Westminster John Knox, 1999) 164–82.

that the antecedent texts undergo when brought into conversation with the text being studied.[110]

Strazicich's work is also notable for the density of allusions and intertextual references that he attributes to Joel. He goes beyond what other scholars have previously attributed, and there are relatively few verses in which he does not detect the presence of an intertextual linkage. His criteria for determining intertextuality include the use of antecedent sources to which readers would have access, signs of deliberate use of these texts, and evidence of readers assigning levels of meaning to both texts in a way that corresponds with the author's intended meaning.[111] Contributing to the wide range of texts that he brings into conversation with Joel is his adoption of a Kristevan perspective, borrowing her assertion that all texts are a mosaic of citations and reflect the interplay and transformation of previous texts.[112]

Strazicich's examination of Joel is invaluable for the detail it provides about Joel's potential relationship with other scriptural traditions. The dual concepts of appropriation and resignification appropriately describe Joel's use of scriptural traditions, which my analysis of specific passages in later chapters will reveal. His approach also resonates with Ben Zvi's understanding of reading models, which suggests that the intended audience reading Joel had access to "a large world of knowledge that they use to decode the meaning of the text."[113] I part company with Strazicich when I place a greater emphasis on the flow of rhetorical argumentation within Joel. Strazicich's analysis is painstakingly thorough but leaves room for an approach that seeks to consider Joel's use of scriptural traditions alongside the text's other rhetorical strategies.

---

110. Strazicich, *Joel's Use of Scripture*, 11–13. Strazicich provides a summary of intertextual approaches to the problem of authorship and authorial intent that includes the theories that attempt to eliminate the author from conversation, placing the identification of intertextual linkages solely on the reader. He pulls back, suggesting that intertextuality in biblical studies must take into account how the writer intended the text to be understood.

111. Ibid., 27. Strazicich relies on literary theorist Z. Ben-Porat for a working definition of *allusion*, which she describes as "a device for the simultaneous activation of two texts." A marker in the base text activates the context of the alluded text. Markers could include words, phrases, or images that invoke another text (Z. Ben-Porat, "The Poetics of Literary Allusion," *PTL* 1 [1976] 107–8). This is an often-cited definition of allusion that has also found its way into other biblical studies (see M. Jauhiainen, *The Use of Zechariah in Revelation* [WUNT 2/199; Tubingen: Mohr Siebeck, 2005] 129).

112. Strazicich, *Joel's Use of Scripture*, 60; cf. Kristeva, *Recherche pour une semanalyse*, 146.

113. Ben Zvi and Nogalski, *Two Sides of a Coin*, 91. Ben Zvi puts forward this model to argue against Schart, who seems to argue for sequential limits on the texts that can inform a reading of Joel; cf. A. Schart, "The First Section of the Book of the Twelve Prophets: Hosea-Joel-Amos," *Int* 61 (2007) 142.

Summary

The preceding survey presents some of the issues that influence this study. The continuing lack of consensus regarding Joel's date of composition is significant since it opens the door for a synchronically oriented approach. The research into Joel's unity is important to this book since I attempt to trace and explore the persuasive strategies throughout the book of Joel, examining how the entire book builds its arguments. Joel's relationship to current research into the Book of the Twelve reveals the usefulness of considering larger textual units, but it also reminds us that it is valuable to read the constituent prophetic books in their own right. I explore Joel's allusions to other texts, but I do not depend on reading Joel within the framework of the Book of the Twelve. My survey of literary approaches reveals some intriguing interpretive perspectives, especially as they relate to Joel's potential intertextual links to a broad scope of scriptural traditions. I also move beyond the identification of intertextual connections to considering their rhetorical purpose in the text. Overall, I will demonstrate the vibrancy and broad range of scholarly discussion on Joel, while orienting the study that follows in the context of these issues.

Methodological Survey

In light of the issues discussed above, I propose to examine the text through the prism of rhetorical criticism. This seems highly appropriate given the concerns over Joel's compositional unity as well as the discussion about the way one ought to read individual books within the broader collection of the Book of the Twelve. This method also permits us to consider Joel's connection to other texts and the effects of reading Joel as a literary unit. The nature of rhetorical criticism requires a close reading of the text in order to discern how its form, structure, and use of imagery point toward its persuasive intent. Consequently, a relatively short book such as Joel provides fruitful ground for a rhetorical-critical examination, since the interpreter can examine a well-defined literary unit in significant detail. Further, prophetic literature is especially receptive to rhetorical analysis, since one can argue convincingly that it represents a rhetorical tour de force in which the prophets attempted to persuade their audience that what was happening to them came about as the result of divine necessity.[114] The following

---

114. J. Barton, "History and Rhetoric in the Prophets," in *The Bible as Rhetoric: Studies in Biblical Persuasion and Credibility* (ed. M. Warner; Warwick Studies in Philosophy and Literature; London: Routledge, 1990) 52–53. Barton considers the genius of prophetic literature to be its ability to take a variety of events and successfully portray them as following the outworking of a divinely guided plan. See also Fox, who states, "[B]y any definition prophecy is rhetoric. The prophets were concerned with persuasion and they are indeed persuasive" (M. Fox, "The Rhetoric of Ezekiel's Vision of the Valley of the Bones," *HUCA* 51 [1980] 4).

is a brief survey of the origins and development of this methodological approach in the study of the Old Testament. It will provide a foundation for discussing the specific rhetorical-critical model that I employ and adapt for my work on Joel.

The inauguration of a rhetorical approach to the biblical text is attributed to James Muilenburg's presidential address to the Society of Biblical Literature in 1968.[115] In the address entitled "Form Criticism and Beyond," Muilenburg encouraged biblical scholars to consider approaching the text in a fashion that appreciates its literary character and uniqueness.[116] He called for scholars to pay attention to the various literary devices and structural strategies that give the text its artistic qualities and claimed that "rhetorical criticism" would be an appropriate name for this approach.[117] He intended for this approach to move beyond identifying the text's generic elements, which had tended to be the interest of form criticism, toward appreciating each text's individual compositional strategies and literary character.[118] While he acknowledged the continued importance of form criticism, he viewed this move toward rhetorical criticism as the next step in better appreciating the uniqueness of individual biblical texts. This discipline draws interpreters into a close reading of the text, calling on them to scrutinize the broad range of literary devices that constitute the artistry of the text.[119]

Following this seminal article, the discipline of rhetorical criticism began to make its mark in the broader field of biblical studies. Muilenburg's call essentially conferred legitimacy on literary approaches to the biblical

---

115. J. Muilenburg, "Form Criticism and Beyond," *JBL* 88 (1969) 1–18.

116. Hauser correctly places this approach as a call to adopt a different program from form and source criticism, where the focus is reconstructing literary units for the purpose of reconstructing a picture of life in ancient Israel. Rhetorical criticism instead focuses on the artistry of a particular passage and the ways it would affect its intended audience (D. Watson and A. Hauser, *Rhetorical Criticism of the Bible: A Comprehensive Bibliography with Notes on History and Method* [BIS 4; Leiden: Brill, 1994] 9.

117. Muilenburg, "Form Criticism and Beyond," 8. "What I am interested in, above all, is in understanding the nature of Hebrew literary composition, in exhibiting the structural patterns that are employed for the fashioning of a literary unit, whether in poetry or in prose, and in discerning the many and various devices by which the predications are formulated and ordered into a unified whole."

118. Ibid., 5. For example, he looks at Deut 32 and Mic 6:1–8 as examples of lawsuit oracles, but suggests that their stylistic differences outweigh a generic resemble. Consequently the individual features of each text are worthy of close analysis. Tull captures the tension between the disciplines, noting that form critics risk ignoring the unique features of texts within the broader categories of form, while rhetorical critics risk focusing their attention too narrowly and missing the role of other texts in shaping readers' comprehension (P. Tull, "Rhetorical Criticism and Beyond in Second Isaiah," in *The Changing Face of Form Criticism for the Twenty-First Century* [ed. M. Sweeney and E. Ben Zvi; Grand Rapids: Eerdmans, 2003] 327–28).

119. Muilenburg, "Form Criticism," 12–13.

text, which is a field that continues to grow exponentially.[120] One potential source of confusion in tracing the development of rhetorical criticism as a scholarly discipline is the terminology. On one hand, following most closely in the manner of Muilenburg, rhetorical criticism has engaged in what Trible calls the "art of composition," which focuses on the literary and stylistic features of a given text.[121] The monographs of scholars such as Bar-Efrat, Berlin, Alter, and Sternberg on Old Testament narrative and poetry reflect arguably the fullest articulation of this sort of approach.[122] This approach continues to have an impact on biblical studies through scholars such as Fitzgerald, who explicitly adopts Muilenburg's approach in order to find markers of literary cohesion in Isa 56–66.[123]

The other trajectory of rhetoric in biblical studies is rhetorical criticism as the "art of persuasion."[124] This type of analysis has its roots in the classical works of figures such as Aristotle, who defined rhetoric as a counterpart of logic. According to this definition, rhetoric is more than verbal embellishment; it reflects specific techniques of argumentation and intends to analyze texts in terms of their persuasive capacity.[125] In the last century, the study of the persuasive nature of communication returned to prominence with the development of the New Rhetoric associated with Perelman and Olbrechts-Tyteca.[126] Their work focuses on studying the methods of proof used to secure adherence to different concepts or ideas. It focuses on the arguments that claim to be either credible or plausible, since their truth could not be calculated with mathematical certainty.[127]

Throughout their lengthy monograph, they discuss many different ways of arguing that may serve to strengthen adherence to a given proposition.

---

120. Tull, "Rhetorical Criticism and Intertextuality," 160.

121. P. Trible, *Rhetorical Criticism: Context, Method, and the Book of Jonah* (Minneapolis: Fortress, 1994) 48. Trible provides a useful list of studies that seem to fit most appropriately into the two aforementioned categories.

122. S. Bar-Efrat, *Narrative Art in the Bible* (New York: T. & T. Clark, 2004); R. Alter, *The Art of Biblical Poetry* (New York: Basic Books, 1985); R. Alter, *The Art of Biblical Narrative* (New York: Basic Books, 1981); A. Berlin, *The Dynamics of Biblical Parallelism* (Bloomington: Indiana University Press, 1985); idem, *The Interpretation of Biblical Narrative* (Sheffield: Almond, 1983); M. Sternberg, *The Poetics of Biblical Narrative: Ideological Literature and the Drama of Reading* (Bloomington: Indiana University Press, 1985). Interestingly, in their 1994 bibliography on rhetorical criticism, Watson and Hauser highlight the above-mentioned studies as key examples of rhetorical criticism in the Old Testament (Watson and Hauser, *Rhetorical Criticism*, 15–18).

123. C. Fitzgerald, *A Rhetorical Analysis of Isaiah 56–66* (Ph.D. diss., Dallas Theological Seminary, 2003) 26–34.

124. Trible, *Rhetorical Criticism*, 41.

125. Ibid., 6.

126. C. Perelman and L. Olbrechts-Tyteca, *The New Rhetoric* (Notre Dame, IN: University of Notre Dame Press, 1969); C. Perelman, *The New Rhetoric and the Humanities: Essays on Rhetoric and Its Applications* (Dordrecht: Reidel, 1979).

127. Perelman and Olbrechts-Tyteca, *New Rhetoric*, 1.

Perelman defines the task of argumentation, claiming that "the purpose of the discourse in general is to bring the audience to the conclusion offered by the orator, starting from premises that they already accept."[128] Consequently, the study of biblical rhetoric as the "art of persuasion" seeks to explore and understand the strategies through which the text intends to secure the adherence of its audience.

One of the most significant conclusions of the New Rhetoric is its claim that rhetoric characterizes all of human discourse. Consequently, by elucidating the theories and techniques of argumentation, Perelman and Olbrechts-Tyteca demonstrate how rhetoric can make reasonable choices available to the listeners/readers of a given communication through drawing attention to the strategies through which that communication intends to persuade.[129] This understanding prepares the ground for the authors to bring the techniques of argumentation into the world of biblical literature and use these techniques to describe how the Old and New Testaments attempt to persuade their audience of the validity of their message.

This focus on the "art of persuasion" is what now drives rhetorical-critical approaches to the Old Testament. This development represents a conscious attempt to move beyond the boundaries of Muilenburg's "art of composition." It makes use of rhetorical theories of persuasion from Aristotle to contemporary theorists such as Perelman and Olbrechts-Tyteca.[130] A sharp distinction between the two branches of rhetorical study is developing, with scholars asserting that the "rhetoric in the Bible must not be limited to the exploration of commonplaces and the hunting down of rhetorical devices so that they can be displayed in articles, complete with Latin name tag, like exhibitions in a Victorian museum."[131] In this view,

---

128. Perelman, *New Rhetoric and the Humanities*, 18.

129. Trible, *Rhetorical Criticism*, 56.

130. For example, see T. Renz, *The Rhetorical Function of the Book of Ezekiel* (VTSup 76; Leiden: Brill, 1999); R. Duke, *The Persuasive Appeal of the Chronicler: A Rhetorical Analysis* (JSOTSup 88; Sheffield: Almond, 1990); R. Duke, "The Ethical Appeal of the Chronicler," in *Rhetoric, Ethic, and Moral Persuasion in Biblical Discourse: Essays from the 2002 Heidelberg Conference* (ed. T. Olbricht and A. Eriksson; ESIEC; New York: T. & T. Clark, 2005) 33–51; R. Clifford, *Fair Spoken and Persuading: An Interpretation of Second Isaiah* (New York: Paulist Press, 1984); D. Patrick, *The Rhetoric of Revelation in the Hebrew Bible* (OBT; Minneapolis: Fortress, 1999); D. Patrick and A. Scult, *Rhetoric and Biblical Interpretation* (JSOTSup 82; Sheffield: Almond, 1990); D. Patrick and A. Scult, "Rhetoric and Ideology," in *The Rhetorical Interpretation of Scripture: Essays from the 1996 Malibu Conference* (ed. S. Porter and D. Stamps; JSNTSup 180; Sheffield: Sheffield Academic Press, 1999) 63–83; Fox, "Rhetoric of Ezekiel's Vision," 1–15; G. Oeste, *Legitimacy, Illegitimacy and the Right to Rule: Windows on Abimelech's Rise and Demise in Judges* (LHB/OTS 546; New York: T. & T. Clark, 2011); C. Shaw, *The Speeches of Micah: A Rhetorical-Historical Approach* (JSOTSup 145; Sheffield: JSOT Press, 1993); K. Möller, *Prophet in Debate: The Rhetoric of Persuasion in the Book of Amos* (JSOTSup 372; London: Sheffield Academic Press, 2003).

131. P. Phillips, "Rhetoric," in *Words and the Word: Explorations in Biblical Interpretation and Literary Theory* (ed. D. Firth and J. Grant; Nottingham: Apollos, 2008) 259.

the practice of rhetorical criticism should move beyond the "art of compo-sition" and focus its energies on the "art of persuasion."

In a well-known article that focuses on the development of rhetorical criticism in the New Testament, Wuellner provocatively states a preference for rhetoric as the "art of persuasion" by stating that this would liberate bib-lical rhetorical criticism from the "Babylonian captivity of rhetoric reduced to stylistics."[132] Although this statement is harsh, it does call attention to the value of focusing on biblical texts as acts of persuasive communica-tion. Wuellner then describes this persuasive branch of rhetorical studies as "rhetoric revaluated" or "rhetoric reinvented."[133] Wuellner's article helps to shape the development of the rhetorical-critical field and focuses attention on the seemingly neglected study of the means and manner of persuasion in biblical texts.

The call to focus on rhetorical criticism as the "art of persuasion" is evident in Old Testament studies by Hauser, who states that the role of the rhetorical critic is both to analyze the literary features of the text and to articulate the impact of the given unit on its audience.[134] The second step is to determine what separates this trajectory of rhetorical criticism from purely literary studies.[135] Gitay adds to the chorus by emphasizing the value of rhetorical-critical work on the "art of persuasion" and describing it as a method that will enable the critic systematically to study the strategy and techniques of biblical discourse in order to understand its communica-tive efficacy better.[136] Gitay uses this approach to study Isaiah, which he examines through a rhetorical method that seeks to discover the comple-mentary roles of the author, the text, and the audience in determining a text's persuasive power.[137]

---

132. W. Wuellner, "Where Is Rhetorical Criticism Taking Us?" *CBQ* 49 (1987) 457.

133. Ibid., 453. See also Amador, who surveys the development of rhetorical criticism in the wake of Wuellner's appeal. Amador asserts that rhetorical critics have not fully fol-lowed Wuellner's call and ought to devote more time to studying the rhetoric *of* the text rather than the rhetoric *within* the text itself (J. Amador, "Where Could Rhetorical Criti-cism [Still] Take Us?" *Currents in Research: Biblical Studies* 7 [1999] 195–222).

134. Watson and Hauser, *Rhetorical Criticism*, 14.

135. D. Howard, "Rhetorical Criticism in Old Testament Studies," *BBR* 4 (1994) 103. Howard is another helpful voice in Old Testament studies who echoes Wuellner's con-cerns, proposing that Old Testament rhetorical critics reclaim persuasion as the principal focus of their work. He asserts that this is the correct approach, noting that all religious writing can be said to make rhetorical claims since it intends to change behavior and convince its readers. Consequently, the strategies and efficacy of textual persuasion are an important element of truly rhetorical studies.

136. Y. Gitay, "Rhetorical Criticism," in *To Each Its Own Meaning: An Introduction to Biblical Criticisms and Their Application* (ed. S. R. Haynes and S. L. McKenzie; Louisville: Westminster John Knox, 1993) 135–52. Gitay summarizes this point of view pithily by stating, "That 'how' (style, form) is as important as 'what' (message, content)," in under-standing the persuasive power of biblical texts; Gitay, "Rhetorical Criticism," 139.

137. Idem, *Prophecy and Persuasion: A Study of Isaiah 40–48* (FTL 14; Bonn: Linguistica Biblica, 1981) 35–45. This approach raises the question of the degree of certainty with

The preceding discussion notes numerous calls for rhetorical criticism to focus on rhetoric as the "art of persuasion." The exact way that one ought to engage in this task remains an open question. One frequently discussed approach roots itself in the work of Kennedy, who engages in detailed rhetorical analysis of New Testament passages. His most salient work on the subject is entitled *New Testament Interpretation through Rhetorical Criticism.* Kennedy proposes that an effective program for rhetorical analysis first delimits the rhetorical unit under discussion by seeking to find elements that indicate its beginning, middle, and end.[138] The next stage is to determine the rhetorical situation of the address, which Kennedy considers to be roughly equivalent to the Sitz im Leben of form criticism.[139] This is then followed by an attempt to determine the rhetorical problem with which the originator of the communication (or "rhetor") wishes to interact. Kennedy includes at this point problems such as lack of willingness on the part of the audience to hear the message and the potential for the message to be so far from what the audience expects that they will not entertain the possibility of listening.[140]

The fourth step is to consider the arrangement of material in the text, or its rhetorical strategy. At this point, the interpreter searches for the subdivisions of the rhetorical piece and attempts to determine what literary devices it employs to add to its persuasive force.[141] The final step is to consider the rhetorical effectiveness of the piece and to consider the impact it may have had on the speaker or audience. Kennedy asserts that rhetorical composition is a creative act that requires its interpreters to interact with it on deeper levels than simple mechanistic analysis of its parts.[142] He stresses the need to pay attention to the whole rhetorical composition and to be willing to look beyond it to an awareness of the human condition in order to see how it might reveal religious or philosophical truth.[143]

At the beginning of an extensive study on the rhetoric of Amos 1–4, Möller suggests that Kennedy's five steps for rhetorical interpretation discussed above can serve as a useful methodology for studying prophetic

---

which one can successfully identify the text's author and original audience in particular. I will address this issue at some length in the forthcoming discussion of the specific model of rhetorical criticism that I employ.

138. G. Kennedy, *New Testament Interpretation through Rhetorical Criticism* (Chapel Hill: University of North Carolina Press, 1984) 33.

139. Ibid., 34.

140. Ibid., 36.

141. Ibid., 37. The concern with the wider meaning that is being emphasized in a collection of literary or poetic devices is what keeps the discussion of rhetorical strategy in the realm of the "art of persuasion." Wendland suggests that elements of literary artistry build dynamic tension that reinforces the appeal of the text's persuasive intent (E. Wendland, "The Discourse Analysis of Hebrew Poetry: A Procedural Outline," in *Discourse Perspectives on Hebrew Poetry in the Scriptures* [ed. E. Wendland; UBS Monograph Series 7; New York: United Bible Society, 1994] 16).

142. Kennedy, *New Testament Interpretation*, 38.

143. Ibid.

texts.[144] He believes that it is a well-articulated model that gives the interpreter something concrete to bring into conversation with particular texts in the Old Testament. While Wuellner rightly cautions that rhetorical criticism is a dynamic process that will defy perfect systemization because of the tremendous creativity in form and approach of biblical literature, it is helpful to have a basic methodological framework from which to begin.[145] Möller adapts these five steps slightly to fit better into his understanding of Old Testament prophetic rhetoric. The principal distinction that he makes is to combine Kennedy's second and third steps of rhetorical situation and rhetorical problem into one. Möller then adds in the consideration of rhetorical genre as a separate step in his methodology. Kennedy categorizes the texts that he studies according to rhetorical genre but does not argue for these classifications as part of his methodology.[146]

After beginning with Kennedy's broad outline about how we ought to do rhetorical criticism in the New Testament, and taking into account necessary adaptations for studying prophetic texts of the Old Testament, we still must consider how to orient ourselves before engaging in a rhetorical-critical reading of biblical texts. First, there are difficulties in understanding how rhetorical criticism interacts with other disciplines. It is difficult to pin down the best manner in which to frame the relationship between rhetorical criticism and synchronic and diachronic understandings of the text. Literary approaches, with which rhetorical criticism is frequently associated due to the influence of Muilenburg, tend to be more concerned with synchronic readings, with scholars arguing that the text is a worthwhile subject of analysis in its final form. Kessler, for example, emphasizes the synchronic nature of the rhetorical approach, proposing that rhetorical criticism ought to be understood as "the leading candidate for synchronic criticism."[147] He makes this explicit in the methodology he presents, which contains nine separate elements. Two of these ("authorship," "setting") set up a general diachronic background for the study, but the remaining seven elements are synchronic in focus and are given much greater significance in his articulation of his approach.[148]

---

144. Möller, *Prophet*, 37.

145. Wuellner, "Rhetorical Criticism?" 463.

146. Möller, *Prophet*, 40. The discussion of the specific model that I employ in my analysis of Joel below delves into the usefulness of Möller's categories.

147. M. Kessler, "A Methodological Setting for Rhetorical Criticism," in *Art and Meaning: Rhetoric in Biblical Literature* (ed. D. Clines, D. Gunn, and A. Hauser; JSOTSup 19; Sheffield: JSOT Press, 1982) 14. Howard challenges Kessler's proposal, suggesting that rhetorical criticism should adopt a narrower focus on the elements of persuasion instead of attempting to serve as a generic category for studies rooted in the world of the text (Howard, "Rhetorical Criticism," 103).

148. Kessler, "Methodological Setting," 9. His seven "synchronic" elements that correspond with the two "diachronic" elements are: whole piece, medium, *Gattung*, stance, form, structure, style, metastyle, and ratio.

Many rhetorical critics, however, would not wish for their work to deal
only with the text as a literary artefact. Kennedy notably proposes that
rhetorical criticism can fill the void between diachronic and synchronic
approaches such as form and literary criticisms by considering the text "as
we have it" and ways that this text would have been received by an audience of "near contemporaries."[149] Renz constructs rhetorical analyses in
accordance with an understanding of redactional layering within the text,
thus basing his reading on previous diachronic results.[150] Consequently,
what he articulates is a rhetorical reading of redactional layers, which is
a worthwhile project if he can correctly delineate the text's growth and
development. Boadt adopts a similar approach, claiming that divorcing a
text from its historical and social context makes it harder to determine its
persuasive power.[151]

In an attempt to speak to the synchronic/diachronic balance, Möller
pushes beyond Renz and Boadt and argues that rhetorical-critical studies
can challenge the results of diachronic criticisms when they discover literary seamlessness within a text. These may render theories of complex redaction and secondary additions unnecessary.[152] Rhetorical criticism, then,
is a bridge between synchronic and diachronic approaches, but it need not
rely solely on the results of previous diachronic analysis. It can offer results that affect both the synchronic and diachronic understandings of the
text. This is a welcome development in rhetorical criticism because it places
this approach on par with diachronic approaches that developed earlier.
Essentially, both streams of interpretation can interact and offer mutual
corrections.

The debate over the priority of synchronic or diachronic approaches or
rhetorical criticism also moves the discussion into the world in front of
the text, taking into consideration the role of the interpreter in determining meaning. For example, Patrick argues that the final form of the text is
the most appropriate subject of analysis, regardless of a text's redactional
history.[153] He focuses on prophetic texts as rhetorical communications that
speak persuasively not only to original "hearing" audiences but also to later
"reading" audiences.[154] This allows interpreters to determine the perspective that they will bring to the rhetorical study of a text. Interpreters can

---

149. Kennedy, *New Testament Interpretation*, 3–4.

150. Renz, *Rhetorical Function*, 5–8.

151. L. Boadt, "The Poetry of Prophetic Persuasion: Preserving the Prophet's Persona,"
CBQ 59 (1997) 1–22. Note in particular Boadt's examination of Isa 5:1–7 and Ezek 15,
where he describes the poetic features of both passages, while then trying to place them
in a historical location.

152. Möller, *Prophet*, 5–10. In this way, Möller tries to show that Barton's "trick of the
disappearing redactor" is also wedded to the assumption that these redactors must exist
(Barton, *Reading*, 57).

153. Patrick, *Rhetoric of Revelation*, 126.

154. Ibid., 157–58.

position themselves positively toward the text as effective communication in Patrick's manner, or they can use their position in front of the text to criticize its methods and messages. This is most notable in the fusion of rhetorical and ideological criticisms.[155]

These wide-ranging concerns indicate that one of rhetorical criticism's strengths is its potential to examine the three primary foci of interpretation, which are the author ("the world behind the text"), the discourse ("the world of the text"), and the reader ("the world in front of the text").[156] Although not all rhetorical-critical studies attempt to cover the full scope of this wide range, the history of rhetorical-critical interpretation does suggest ways of approaching all three levels of interpretation. A rhetorical-critical study must establish its orientation toward these levels of interpretation when a scholar approaches a particular text.

Summary

The discipline of rhetorical criticism continues to branch out significantly from the vision articulated in Muilenburg's inaugural address. The examination of the literary nature of the biblical text and the unique qualities that lend it esthetic power and appeal are welcome additions. Beyond esthetics, however, rhetorical criticism as the "art of persuasion" offers the most potential for present and future studies of the text. This is most evident in the numerous scholarly appeals for interpreters to focus on this project. The wide range of issues that it encompasses allows it significant scope for interpreting the text. Rhetorical criticism frequently tries to bridge the diachronic/synchronic dichotomy, wishing to abandon neither referentiality and social context in presenting the text's persuasive power nor the understanding of a text's rhetorical strategies to previously determined redactional levels. Further, rhetorical criticism makes forays into the world of the interpreter, considering how various preconceptions shape the interpreter's understanding of a text's persuasive power. It is a vibrant discipline, worthy of further exploration.

In this book, I enter into the milieu of rhetorical criticism and employ it to examine the persuasive power of the prophetic book of Joel. Joel's litany of literary strategies and fascinating imagery makes it a worthy text to examine. The issues surrounding its compositional unity also make it a valuable field of inquiry for determining the flow of argumentation. I plan

---

155. See, for example, W. Wuellner, "Reconceiving a Rhetoric of Religion: A Rhetoric of Power and the Power of the Sublime," in *Rhetorics and Hermeneutics: Wilhelm Wuellner and His Influence* (ed. J. Hester and J. Amador; ESIEC; New York: Continuum, 2004) 23–77; Bible and Culture Collective, "Rhetorical Criticism," in *The Postmodern Bible* (ed. E. Catelli et al.; New Haven: Yale University Press, 1995) 149–86; E. Schüssler Fiorenza, "Challenging the Rhetorical Half-Turn: Feminist and Rhetorical Biblical Criticism," in *Scripture and Theology: Essays from the 1994 Pretoria Conference* (ed. S. Porter and T. Olbricht; JSNTSup 121; Sheffield: Sheffield Academic Press, 1996) 28–53.

156. K. Möller, "Rhetorical Criticism," *DTIB* 689.

to articulate Joel's persuasive artistry as I engage in a detailed reading of the text. In my survey of the rhetorical-critical field, I lay the groundwork for deciding the specific model of rhetorical criticism to use in this book. In so doing, I engage with issues related to diachronic and synchronic approaches to the text and offer insight on choosing an appropriate location for the interpreter. In this way, I will be able to offer a useful reading of Joel and its persuasive appeal.

Purpose and Organization

The preceding discussions of the history of research and the development of rhetorical criticism provide the basis for this study. In this monograph, I build on that foundation to show that Joel is a unified work of prophetic literature that moves from scenes of devastation to promises of restoration by evoking divine and human responses in order to persuade the audience of the necessity of calling and relying on Yhwh in all circumstances. Essentially, this book demonstrates that Joel is a coherent, self-contained literary work that speaks persuasively to the situation that it creates.

I plan to reflecting further on my chosen method of interpretation in order to provide a detailed reading of the text. Following this introductory chapter, the first chapter contains a thorough consideration of the rhetorical-critical model that I employ. I derives this model from Kennedy and Möller and then examine each of the proposed steps and modify the structure to suit the task of reading Joel rhetorically. I also consider issues of synchrony and diachrony in reading a prophetic book that does not provide any overt indication of the time and place of its composition. I offer a few suggestions for improving weaknesses in the rhetorical-critical model developed by Kennedy and Möller, focusing on the rhetorical situation and the rhetorical effectiveness of prophetic discourse.

The following chapters consist of a rhetorical analysis of the entire book of Joel based on the modified model of Kennedy and Möller. I apply the same steps to the various textual units of the book. The second chapter contains a rhetorical analysis of Joel 1:1–14, considering issues such as the intended referent of the locust imagery, the relationship that Joel constructs between the prophetic message and the cult, and the way in which Joel constructs its implied audience through various calls to lament. I examine the persuasive force of this sort of imagery, considering how it could potentially affect its implied audience to respond.

The third chapter looks at Joel 1:15–20 and considers the text's use of drought imagery to reinforce the exigence of the locust plague. It also reflects on the rhetorical strategy of introducing the day of Yhwh with all of its ramifications, setting the stage for further references to the day of Yhwh in various contexts throughout the book. This chapter also explores the text's strategy of merging the prophet with the implied audience as it transitions from calls to lament to offering lament cries directly to YHWH.

The fourth chapter examines the rhetorical power of Joel 2:1–11. This chapter examines the strategies by which Joel reaches its nadir, heightening the picture of devastation and destruction in the previous chapter. This chapter considers the rhetorical effect of portraying YHWH as the one leading an assault on Zion in the wake of calls to appeal to YHWH in Joel 1:1–14 and 1:15–20. This chapter also examines how the prophet uses this revelation to coax the proper response from the text's implied audience.

The fifth chapter examines Joel 2:12–17 and engages in an extended study of the means by which the text turns this prophecy away from despair and begins to offer hope of divine restitution. It examines the prophetic call to "turn" that hopefully leads to a divine turning in response. This chapter peruses the relationship among Joel 2:12–17, Exod 34:6–7, and Jonah 3:9 and 4:2 as passages that reflect deeply on the character of YHWH and YHWH's relationship with Israel. It reflects on how the response to the prophetic command to "return to me" could motivate a divine response that brings restoration out of devastation.

The sixth chapter considers Joel 2:18–27 and shows how the text systemically and effectively begins the process of "liquidating the lack" that was described in Joel 1:1–14, 1:15–20, and 2:1–11.[157] It examines the means by which the text portrays the character and actions of YHWH as one who provides restoration after desperate circumstances and how this portrayal calls the community to trust in YHWH. It also continues to explore the idea of a conceptual gap between Joel 2:17 and 2:18 and engages interpreters by asking them to participate in constructing the text's meaning.

The seventh chapter looks at Joel 3:1–5 and explores its portrayal of a powerful outpouring of the divine Spirit that impacts the entire community. It also details the change in image-world from one in which locusts dominate to one that reflects cosmological phenomena as a response to YHWH's interventions. This chapter reveals the points of contact between Joel 3:1–5 and its surrounding material as constituting the persuasive strategy of the book, along with its portrayal of restoration, which is also tightly linked to the images of devastation found earlier in the text.

The eighth chapter examines Joel 4:1–21 and considers the persuasive potential of pairing the removal of external threats with the guarantees of material and spiritual renewal in Joel 2:18–27 and 3:1–5. It further considers the persuasive power of a rhetorical strategy in which the text permits genuine agency to YHWH alone in the context of discussing foreign

---

157. This phrase is borrowed from F. Deist, "Parallels and Reinterpretation in the Book of Joel: A Theology of Yom Yahweh?" in *Text and Context: Old Testament and Semitic Studies for F. C. Fensham* (ed. W. Claasen; JSOTSup 48; Sheffield: Sheffield Academic Press, 1988) 64.

nations, whom YHWH inevitably defeats. This chapter looks at Joel's use of the nations, both in general and specifically named as a rhetorical foil that establishes reasons to trust YHWH's promises of restoration.

I conclude by reflecting on the preceding analysis, tracing the interplay of persuasive strategies that bind the book of Joel into a coherent, rhetorically powerful work that moves the people in its audience from despair to restoration by persuading them to call on YHWH in the midst of desperate circumstances. The conclusion also reflects on the usefulness of the Kennedy and Möller model of rhetorical criticism and considers the effect of the changes proposed in my chapter on methodology. I also offer suggestions for continued study, pointing toward future refinement of this model for analysis of other texts.

Chapter 1

The Process of Persuasion:
A Rhetorical-Critical Model
for Studying Prophetic Literature

Introduction

Following the previous survey of the development of rhetorical-critical methods in the introduction, this chapter provides a more detailed examination of the methodological foundation of this book. I consider the contours of the model developed by Kennedy and modified by Möller. I critique various aspects before detailing the adaptations necessary to bring this model to the study of Joel. I focus on the strengths and weaknesses of the model, while offering suggestions about how it can be improved to handle better the challenges that are inherent in studying prophetic texts.

Model

The model of rhetorical criticism that this study follows began as an attempt to function in both the diachronic and synchronic realms of interpretation. Black supports the broad utility of Kennedy's version of the model for biblical studies, claiming that it represents the most comprehensive understanding of the field of rhetoric.[1] Möller defends the application of Kennedy's model to the Old Testament against charges of anachronism by arguing from the universal nature of persuasiveness in texts.[2] He claims that any discourse, whether written or oral, ancient or modern, is capable of being investigated and assessed by this method, providing that the critic is aware of the specific qualities of the given discourse.[3] Essentially, he argues that the categories of Kennedy's model reflect a universal approach to rhetoric in biblical studies, even though it originates in a New Testament context. Möller's own adaptation of Kennedy's model for studying

---

1. C. Black, "Rhetorical Criticism and Biblical Interpretation," *ExpTim* 100 (1989) 256–57.

2. Shaw has also used the model of Kennedy to examine Micah, but he does not adhere to the five steps of Kennedy's model as rigorously as Möller. For his particular rhetorical-critical approach, see C. Shaw, *The Speeches of Micah: A Rhetorical-Historical Approach* (JSOTSup 145; Sheffield: JSOT Press, 1993) 22–23.

3. K. Möller, "Rhetorical Criticism," *DTIB* 690. This defense is similar to the previously mentioned argument employed by Duke to justify his use of Aristotelian categories in his study of Chronicles (R. Duke, *The Persuasive Appeal of the Chronicler: A Rhetorical Analysis* [JSOTSup 88; Sheffield: Almond, 1990] 39).

the? book of Amos usefully articulates some of its persuasive features and merits further exploration here.

Rhetorical Unit

As currently constructed, the model presented above consists of five stages, beginning with the task of determining the *rhetorical units* of a given text. In this phase, the interpreter divides the text in question into various subunits for study. These subunits should contain attempts to persuade or to effect some sort of change in the audience.[4] Delineating a text's rhetorical units requires searching for various signals of aperture and closure that demarcate the discourse's prophetic oracles.[5] Within these subunits, the interpreter can identify the various strategies by which the text attempts to make its persuasive impact. This leads to an examination of the interrelationship of the various subunits with an eye toward articulating their function in building the argument of the larger rhetorical unit of the book.[6] In Möller's application of the model, the largest unit that he considers is the individual prophetic book, although he leaves room for future extension of his investigation to consider the role of an individual prophetic book within larger complexes, such as the Book of the Twelve or the Old Testament canon.[7] Möller is not specific in describing how this could be accomplished, however, which is unsurprising given the number of divergent paths that this move would create. Consequently, bringing the discussion up to the level of the individual prophetic book is probably the optimal use of this model.[8]

---

4. J. Hester, "Re-discovering and Re-inventing Rhetoric," *Scriptura* 50 (1994) 7. Hester states that, for a unit of text to be rhetorical, it must contain an argument that intends to affect its audience. This concern for argumentation is how Hester distinguishes a rhetorical unit from a literary unit. Further, Wuellner defines a rhetorical unit as an "argumentative unit affecting the reader's reasoning or the reader's imagination" (W. Wuellner, "Where Is Rhetorical Criticism Taking Us?" *CBQ* 49 [1987] 455).

5. For one proposal of ways to determine these signals, see E. Wendland, *The Discourse Analysis of Hebrew Prophetic Literature* (MBPS 40; Lewiston, NY: Edwin Mellen, 1995) 24–70. Since Wendland uses Joel as a test case for his criteria, I will interact with his work in some detail as the discussion progresses. For a synopsis of his conclusions concerning the organization of Joel's rhetorical units, see E. Wendland, *Prophetic Rhetoric: Case Studies in Text Analysis and Translation* (Longwood, FL: Xulon, 2009) 19–20.

6. See the list that Wuellner provides that begins with parables and metaphors and increases unit levels until it reaches the entire biblical canon; Wuellner, "Rhetorical Criticism?" 455.

7. K. Möller, *A Prophet in Debate: The Rhetoric of Persuasion in the Book of Amos* (JSOTSup 372; London: Sheffield Academic Press, 2003) 37. A preliminary consideration of the issue suggests that this is probably intended to be a synchronic move in which one considers how the persuasive appeal of a book such as Amos or Joel affects the broader message of the Book of the Twelve.

8. See also the discussion in the introduction above about the usefulness of reading prophetic books as unique literary compositions.

Rhetorical Situation

The second step of our rhetorical model is to determine the *rhetorical situation* of the discourse in question. Kennedy provides a basic formulation of this concept when he claims that it is roughly analogous to the Sitz im Leben of form criticism.[9] In other words, the purpose of determining a text's rhetorical situation is to try to look behind the text and examine the society, circumstances, and historical era that produced it. For Kennedy, examining the rhetorical situation is a diachronic step that grounds the text in a particular time and space that the interpreter can use as a backdrop to explain why and how the rhetor composed the text. The distinction between rhetorical situation and Sitz im Leben is that the rhetorical critic's primary objective is to consider the text's premises as an appeal or argument.[10] This still leaves the rhetorical situation rooted in the "world behind the text," but considering the text's argumentative premises begins to move the rhetorical situation away from simply establishing the text's historical and social background toward deliberating about its persuasive appeal in this context.

Kennedy derives his understanding of rhetorical situation from the influential work of communications theorist Lloyd Bitzer, which is rooted in a diachronic approach. Bitzer's three criteria for establishing rhetorical situations are: (1) exigences, which are problems and defects requiring solutions; (2) an audience capable of being persuaded to act on the exigence; and (3) sets of constraints that influence the rhetor and the audience.[11] For Bitzer, determining the rhetorical situation requires an analysis of these three factors and the way they interrelate. Each of these factors merits further comment.

First, the idea of exigence is essential for rhetorical communication. If there are no problems in the present situation, no theoretical questions needing answers, no objects or ideas awaiting discovery, then there is no need for rhetorical tasks such as persuasion, advocacy, or mediation.[12] Thus, Bitzer ties the rhetorical situation to a problem in a specific time and space that a rhetor believes requires addressing. In other words, to have a rhetorical situation, one must first have a problem, or exigence that a rhetorical discourse can address. Correctly identifying this exigence permits

---

9. G. Kennedy, *New Testament Interpretation through Rhetorical Criticism* (Chapel Hill: University of North Carolina Press, 1984) 34.

10. Wuellner, "Rhetorical Criticism?" 456.

11. L. Bitzer, "Functional Communication: A Situational Perspective," in *Rhetoric in Transition: Studies in the Nature and Uses of Rhetoric* (ed. E. White; University Park: Pennsylvania State University Press, 1980) 23. Although these criteria provide the framework for rhetorical communication, Bitzer attempts to leave space for the creativity of the rhetor by asserting that the situation does not predetermine the discourse.

12. Ibid., 25–26.

the rhetor to craft his or her arguments appropriately in order to persuade the intended audiences.

Second, Bitzer considers the rhetor's relationship with the audience, focusing on the exigence's factual conditions and the interest that it generates in the audience. Bitzer proposes four scenarios in which these criteria can interact: (1) the rhetor and the audience can have the same understanding of the factual conditions and interest in the topic; (2) the rhetor and audience may agree on the factual conditions but disagree on the level of interest; (3) the rhetor and audience can have the same level of interest but disagree on the factual conditions; and (4) the rhetor and audience may disagree on *both* the level of interest and the factual conditions.[13] These different scenarios require different approaches based on the relationship of interest and agreement between the speaker and the potential audience. In situations where the rhetor and the audience disagree on either the existence or the nature of an exigence, it is practically impossible to persuade the audience to respond.[14] Essentially, the situation becomes rhetorical when the audience and speaker acknowledge a common exigence that a given discourse could modify.[15] This opens up an additional role for the rhetor: he or she can attempt to guide the audience toward recognizing the exigence before proposing a fitting response.[16]

The different degrees of relationship between rhetor and audience help to demonstrate the subjective nature of determining an exigence. Binton takes Bitzer to task for promoting a highly "objective" look at exigence, because Bitzer considers an exigence to be a genuine defect in the world that a rhetorical act can modify.[17] This largely denies the creative role of

---

13. Ibid., 29–30.

14. M. Garrett and X. Xiao, "The Rhetorical Situation Revisited," *Rhetorical Society Quarterly* 23 (1993) 38.

15. J. Hester, "Speaker, Audience and Situations: A Modified Interactional Model," *Neotestamentica* 32 (1998) 78–79. Hester uses this definition to distinguish a "rhetorical situation" from a historical situation, which comprises factual components that an investigator can identify and study. The perception of an exigence and the sharing of common interests are what bind the speaker and audience together, allowing for rhetorical communication to occur.

16. One important factor to note in the discussion of audience is that Bitzer has in mind the audience that hears/reads the discourse in its original context; his formulation of rhetorical situation does not take into account later reading audiences who may still be moved by its persuasive appeal even if the original exigence is no longer operational. This merits consideration when one studies the biblical text since the text derives much of its significance from its ability to speak persuasively to audiences in situations far removed from its original exigence. In my discussion of *rhetorical effectiveness* below, I consider a more nuanced view of audiences that are called to respond to a text's persuasive appeal.

17. A. Binton, "Situation in the Theory of Rhetoric," *Philosophy and Rhetoric* 14 (1981) 242–43. Binton considers a few "odd consequences" of a thoroughly objective understanding of exigence, suggesting that this means that only a rhetor with a correct grasp of the facts of the situation is engaging in rhetoric. Since it is not possible for rhetors to know every conceivable fact about a given situation, clearly there is some room for

the rhetor in establishing the situation for the audience since it is patently untrue that everyone will perceive a given situation as flawed or have similar ideas about how to remedy the supposed deficiency. Vatz echoes this critique, arguing instead that "meaning is not discovered in situations, but *created* [italics his] by rhetors."[18] This leads to a higher level of responsibility for rhetors since the situation(s) that they strive to create have the potential to influence the thoughts, beliefs, and actions of their audiences.

In the case of prophetic rhetoric, it often appears that a prophet has a much higher degree of interest in the topic, and he often claims that Yhwh is sending a message that the audience should heed. A significant part of the prophet's task is to persuade the audience that it should take his analysis of the situation seriously.[19] Prophetic literature strives to bring the horizon of divine discourse into the reality of daily existence and to communicate this wider perspective to the audience. This gives a rather significant role to the prophetic rhetor, who must persuade an audience that the situation he addresses is worthy of deliberation, reflection, and action.[20] Prophetic literature often derives its exigence from the gap between the audience's understanding and the divinely mediated message that the prophet presents.

Third, the final factor in Bitzer's definition of rhetorical situation is the constraints that surround a rhetorical situation. For Bitzer these include: the degree of interest in the topic that the speaker and audience possess, the capacity for modification of the situation, the risk incurred in responding, the obligation and expectation of a response, the familiarity with a topic, and the immediacy of the situation.[21] All of these factors determine the nature of the rhetoric necessary for the rhetor to persuade the audience

rhetorical communication based on beliefs and perceptions. Binton is probably engaging in *reductio ad absurdum* here since Bitzer does permit a distinction between the "factual component" and the "interest component" of a rhetorical situation. The basic critique of overly relying on objective criteria, however, is a useful caution in this discussion; cf. Bitzer, "Functional," 28.

18. R. Vatz, "The Myth of the Rhetorical Situation," *Philosophy and Rhetoric* 6 (1973) 157. This is a thoroughly subjective understanding of situation that contrasts with Bitzer's concern for objectivity. Vatz permits the rhetor to shape the reality of the situation that he or she intends to address.

19. D. B. Sandy, *Plowshares and Pruning Hooks: Rethinking the Language of Biblical Prophecy and Apocalyptic* (Downers Grove, IL: InterVarsity, 2002) 73. Sandy recognizes this disparity of interest when he claims that part of the prophet's task is metaphorically to turn up the volume to communicate with an audience that is presented as deliberately deaf.

20. See C. Perelman and L. Olbrechts-Tyteca, *The New Rhetoric: A Treatise on Argumentation* (Notre Dame, IN: University of Notre Dame Press, 1969) 21. The authors claim that "the speaker should depart from his premises only when he knows that they are adequately accepted; if they are not, the speaker's first concern should be to reinforce them with all the means at his disposal." In other words, the creation of a shared interest in a given exigence is one of the first requirements of successful rhetorical communication.

21. Bitzer, "Functional," 31–33.

to respond appropriately. For example, if the solution that the rhetor proposes is beyond the capacity of the intended audience, then it is unlikely that the rhetor will succeed in swaying the audience in a given direction.[22] Similarly, the level of authority that an audience grants to the rhetor will influence the rhetor's persuasive potential. Consigny correctly uses this understanding of constraints to show that Vatz overstates the freedom of rhetors in constructing situations. There are still particularities related to persons, actions, and agencies that surround the proposed rhetorical communication that will guide the shape of a fitting response.[23] Rhetors may help in establishing the rhetorical situation, but they do not begin with a blank slate; the consideration of constraints reveals the limitations of the situation that they can construct.

The discussion of Bitzer's categories for rhetorical situations highlights some of the factors in play when we consider the rhetorical situations of Old Testament prophetic texts. The most significant challenge to using the concept of *rhetorical situation* as articulated by Bitzer and his interlocutors for studying the biblical text is his reliance on identifying the "world behind the text" or conflating the rhetorical situation with an objectively identifiable historical situation.[24] Bitzer's illustrations of rhetorical situations derive from either recent history or politics, which means that there are other significant resources available to use in constructing the exigence that gave rise to the rhetorical situation. Although no later description can encompass all facets of a given situation perfectly, the critic can argue with some degree of certainty that he or she has captured its essential elements. Similarly, the critic can make reasonable assumptions about the nature of the audience (and may even have information about the composition and response of the original audience) and the constraints that faced the rhetor because there is sufficient secondary evidence available.

Following Kennedy, biblical scholars who use the concept of *rhetorical situation* typically attempt to accomplish a similar goal, in spite of the difficulty of surmounting the temporal and geographical gap between the world that produced the text and the world of the interpreter. Kennedy's approach to the idea of rhetorical situation highlights the dynamic nature of the speaker's construction of text, the rhetorical problem, and the au-

---

22. Ibid., 33.

23. S. Consigny, "Rhetoric and Its Situations," *Philosophy and Rhetoric* 7 (1974) 175–85. Consigny deftly moves between the poles of situational particularities and rhetorical creativity, noting that the job of the rhetor includes both articulating specific problems out of indeterminate rhetorical situations and being receptive and engaged in the given situation so that the problems that the rhetor addresses remain relevant. He finds a middle ground between Bitzer's assertion that the rhetorical situation governs the rhetor's choices and Vatz's understanding of the rhetor's freedom to create a variety of exigences out of a given situation.

24. Although Hester and Wuellner try to keep distance between historical and rhetorical situations, this proves to be difficult to achieve in practice.

dience but maintains a heavy emphasis on reconstructing "real" history and finding a historical author.[25] The interpreter thus focuses on the text as an argument or an appeal from within the historical and social context that the interpreter determines.[26] The chronological distance and paucity of supporting evidence, however, mean that it is difficult to establish the "world behind the text" with certainty. At the very least, it is precarious to use this idea of rhetorical situation for texts in which theories about the date of composition may span centuries.[27]

In prophetic studies of the Old Testament, Shaw and Möller work most closely with the concept of rhetorical situation, and it is helpful to review their approaches.[28] Their adaptations of the concept help to reveal some of the challenges of employing rhetorical situation in the sense that Kennedy, following Bitzer, proposes for biblical studies. In reviewing their approach, I will also point out some of the challenges that future studies will encounter in using this concept. I will conclude with a proposal for a way to move forward.

In his work on Micah, Shaw acknowledges that "we have no account of the situation which has given rise to each discourse."[29] Essentially, he admits that the text is not explicit about when the prophet spoke, what the nature of his audience was, or what the occasion was that prompted the discourse. Further, there is not enough available evidence from outside the book of Micah to engage in a comprehensive reconstruction of its situation. Consequently, Shaw searches for the rhetorical situation by reflecting on clues within the discourse itself. Essentially, he argues that the elements of the prophetic speeches reveal the underlying exigences.[30] Shaw divides the

---

25. D. Stamps, "Rethinking Rhetorical Situation: The Entextualization of the Situation in New Testament Epistles," in *Rhetoric and the New Testament: Essays from the 1992 Heidelberg Conference* (ed. S. Porter and T. Olbricht; JSNTSup 90. Sheffield: Sheffield Academic Press, 1993) 195–96. See also Kennedy's statement that "[t]he ultimate goal of rhetorical analysis, briefly put, is the discovery of the author's intent and of how that is transmitted through a text to an audience" (Kennedy, *New Testament Interpretation*, 12). Kennedy's "goal" is predicated on the assumption that it is possible to recover the original author and the historical-cultural situation about which he was writing.

26. Wuellner, "Rhetorical Criticism?" 456.

27. Determining the date of composition is especially difficult with regard to Joel, for which interpreters put forward theories that locate the book anywhere from the ninth to the second centuries B.C.E.

28. Gitay also uses the idea of rhetorical situation when studying Deutero-Isaiah, but his approach essentially mirrors that of Kennedy. He devotes one short chapter to the rhetorical situation of Isa 40–48 in which he takes a diachronic stance and describes the purported political, social, and spiritual situation that prompted Deutero-Isaiah's discourse (Y. Gitay, *Prophecy and Persuasion: A Study of Isaiah 40–48* [FTL 14; Bonn: Linguistica Biblica, 1981] 50–60).

29. Shaw, *Speeches*, 25.

30. Ibid., 25. This approach to rhetorical situation is based on the assumption that "the close connection between the rhetorical situation and the discourse makes it inevitable that the major elements of the rhetorical situation are reflected in the discourse itself."

book of Micah into his understanding of its composite rhetorical units and attempts to determine a plausible rhetorical situation for each discourse. Shaw acknowledges that this is a somewhat subjective undertaking, requiring him to "attempt to judge when the speaker is setting forth the facts of the case and when he is exaggerating and using hyperbole."[31] Given the range of rhetorical strategies found in prophetic speech, this judgment process is fraught with peril.

In his analysis, Shaw divides the elements that make up rhetorical situations into "objective" and "subjective factors." He derives both sets of factors primarily from the text of Micah itself, a fact that leads to questions concerning the objectivity of his "objective factors." For example, in Mic 2:1–13, Shaw asserts as an objective factor that one social group in Israel is oppressing others. Reading between the lines of various descriptions, he eventually narrows this down to say that the "oppressors" in this situation are a powerful, well-defined group whose crimes include violently dispossessing and harassing a group that has "turned away from war."[32] Arriving at this conclusion requires significant exegetical work and many interpretive decisions. In Mic 2:8, Shaw acknowledges that he reads against the majority opinion in claiming that the reference to "stripping off the cloak of the poor" is not a reference to debt slavery.[33] Given the extent of the argument and discussion surrounding this and other issues, I find it difficult to grant the label "objective factor" to this element of the rhetorical situation that Shaw identifies.

While not quarreling with Shaw's exegetical prowess, I highlight in this survey some of the difficulties in relying on the text itself as the primary witness for constructing a "world-behind-the-text" rhetorical situation. The interpreter's judgments about what constitutes "stating the case" and "hyperbole" are necessarily visible throughout the process, which makes the terminology "objective factor" somewhat misleading. The prevalence of interpretive judgments renders it difficult to say that Shaw has managed to peer into the world behind the text well enough to describe it accurately. Shaw's concept of the text's rhetorical situation may fall victim to the danger of which Linville warns when he comments, "[T]here is a certain circularity to the process: the historical reality of the book's composition is derived from the text and the text is then interpreted in view of those conclusions."[34] Shaw may have established the situation that the text of

---

31. Ibid., 27.

32. Ibid., 84.

33. Ibid., 80. Shaw cites Willis as an example of what he understands to be the majority opinion (J. Willis, "Micah 2:6–8 and the 'People of God' in Micah," *BZ* 14 [1970] 82).

34. J. Linville, "Bugs through the Looking Glass: The Infestation of Meaning in Joel," in *Reflection and Refraction: Studies in Biblical Historiography in Honour of A. Graeme Auld* (ed. R. Rezetko, T. Lim, and W. Aucker; Cambridge: Cambridge University Press, 2006) 286. Linville makes this claim in his discussion of scholars who assume that the events described in Joel reflect an identifiable historical scenario. Instead, he examines Joel us-

Micah claims to address, but it requires a leap to claim that this accurately reflects an identifiable historical context.

Möller takes the discussion of rhetorical situation in a slightly different direction. He states that Shaw's approach will not work for Amos since he does not think that the book preserves "original" prophetic speeches.[35] Consequently, he does not try to trace the rhetorical situation of given passages. Instead, he examines the rhetorical situation on the level of the whole book. This is still predominantly a "world-behind-the-text" approach with the emphasis shifted from the original speaker and original audience to the book's "compilers" and the way that they frame the book for a later (but still historically locatable) audience.[36] This requires him to engage in a discussion of the book's date of composition and redactional history so that he can find a *terminus ad quem* for the book's compilation. He also considers geographical location as part of the book's rhetorical situation. Since he is not investigating the rhetorical situation behind its original utterances, he is not wedded to Samaria or the context of the Northern Kingdom. Instead, he prefers to view Amos against the backdrop of the Judahite tradents who preserved it after the Assyrian conquest of Israel.[37]

Essentially, Möller locates the rhetorical situation of Amos in the world of the Southern Kingdom of Judah during the period between the Assyrian conquest of Israel and the Babylonian conquest of Judah. The exigence that occasioned the book's compilation is the opportunity to use the fulfilled messages of doom to Israel found in Amos as warnings in the Judahite context; if the Judahites did not listen to this preserved prophetic word, they would suffer the same fate as Israel.[38] Möller argues that, in this situation, the travails and ultimate failure of Amos to convince Israel to reform would be particularly poignant since the Judahite audience could find evidence of the veracity of his claims in the ruins of their northern neighbor. Möller bases this conclusion on the results of his research into the probable date of compilation, arguing that reading it as a product of this time minimizes interpretive difficulties.

While this approach nuances the presentation of rhetorical situation by moving away from the explicit referents of the text to its transmission

---

ing solely the text's word-world and argues that this is the only "Joel ben Pethuel" with whom contemporary interpreters can interact. See below for further consideration of this particular understanding of rhetorical situation.

35. Möller, *Prophet*, 105. Instead, he considers Amos to be an edited collection of prophetic oracles and visions but does not necessarily subscribe to complex theories of redactional development and growth.

36. Ibid., 106.

37. Ibid., 119.

38. Ibid. For a different perspective on the intended hearing audience, see D. Patrick, *The Rhetoric of Revelation in the Hebrew Bible* (OBT; Minneapolis: Fortress, 1999) 158. He argues that "[t]he book is designed for an audience that does recognize the legitimacy of the Davidic scion, but which is not being ruled by a Davidide."

history, it remains grounded in the diachronic world behind the text.[39] Möller's construction of the rhetorical situation in Amos depends on his geographical-temporal theory of Amos's compilation and promulgation. In fact, establishing the validity of his theory about Amos's composition is one of his stated objectives since he is using this rhetorical-critical methodology to challenge the findings of redaction critics who propose a complex theory of composition for the book of Amos.[40] Möller has put forward a likely scenario that adequately handles the majority of the text's rhetoric and imagery, but his proposal remains hypothetical and subject to challenge from those with different theories regarding the text's transmission history.

Analyzing the book of Joel exacerbates the difficulties noted in Shaw's and Möller's conceptions of the rhetorical situation. Micah and Amos at least have a prophetic superscription that includes the names of the reigning kings during the period of their prophetic ministry. This offers at least one potential location in space and time in which to anchor the rhetorical situation. While Möller nuances the discussion by declaring that he is not looking for the rhetorical situation behind the original utterances, he at least has one explicit chronological marker from which to begin his work. Joel has no such date formulas and, as mentioned previously, suggestions for its date of origin vary tremendously. This absence of date formulas and historical references makes it difficult to determine the backdrop against which to read the book. Conceivably, one could argue for one of the proposed dates of the book's compilation and try to reconstruct a historically based rhetorical situation from that foundation.[41] Similarly, one could follow Möller and try to establish the situation of a later audience that preserved Joel's prophecy. Attempts of this sort, however, are unlikely to

---

39. One can also find indications in the text that suggest a shift to a Judahite readership, notably in the equation of Zion with Samaria in Amos 6:1 and in the promised Davidic restoration of Amos 9:11–12. The consistent focus on the Northern Kingdom and its iniquities, however, suggests that one should identify an Israelite rhetorical situation at the heart of this book.

40. Möller challenges Barton's critique of rhetorical criticism as a discipline that goes to great lengths to preserve the text's compositional unity, despite the weight of evidence from historical-critical disciplines. Barton claims that, "when rhetorical criticism comes in at the door, critical probing into the text's unity or disunity tends to go out the window, the demonstration of its unity being taken as an absolute imperative" (J. Barton, *Reading the Old Testament: Method in Biblical Study* [2nd ed.; Louisville: Westminster John Knox, 1996] 201). Möller responds, "The underlying assumption of Barton's criticism is that the 'traditional' historical-critical findings are correct after all, and that the text in question is *not* a unity. This, however, is precisely the disputed issue" (Möller, *Prophet*, 8). For a more extended look at Barton's critique of rhetorical criticism, see Barton, *Reading*, 201–5.

41. This also has ramifications for the interpreter's understanding of the text's composition. Those who argue that Joel 3–4 stems from another time and place than Joel 1–2 would develop a completely different understanding of the text's rhetorical situation than those who argue for it as a unified work.

withstand the weight of criticism since one can easily dispute any proposed date of composition or compilation. Criticism in this vein would render it difficult to discuss the persuasive character of the text in any proposed rhetorical situation.

The difficulty of constructing a viable "world-behind-the-text" understanding of the rhetorical situation for Joel leads us to consider whether it is possible to modify this concept so that it can work with a text such as Joel, which effectively camouflages its historical situation. Joel seems to have a "dehistoricized" nature because it lacks references that could anchor it in time and space, such as regnal formulas, or even a statement of the specific cause of the current catastrophe.[42] Essentially, Joel's cultic and mythic themes are general enough to be applicable to many different times of crisis, which leads to the conjecture that Joel as a whole is a liturgical text that could be cited during services of national lament.[43] Consequently, in looking at a text like Joel that obscures its original situation, we are justified in trying to understand the text's rhetorical situation in a manner that depends less on establishing a hypothetical "world behind the text."[44]

An alternative proposal to determining a text's rhetorical situation is to nuance the concept by using it synchronically. This involves viewing rhetorical situation as a phenomenon that occurs on the level of the "world of the text" and examining the situation or exigences that the text appears to create and to which it responds. This sort of approach may offer a way past the frustration of trying to lock Joel into a specific historical context. It highlights the timelessness of Joel's literary quality and potentially permits its persuasive power to have influence beyond the time and place of its original utterance.[45] Working out of the New Testament, Thurén argues that a synchronic approach to rhetorical situation is helpful, especially in cases where historical knowledge is lacking. Thurén also makes the thought-provoking point that, even if the interpreter can objectively determine the situation of the addressees, there is no guarantee that the text's author understood their situation in the same way.[46] These considerations open the door for a reformulation of the rhetorical situation.

It is important to acknowledge here that moving toward a synchronic approach to rhetorical situation undeniably cuts against Bitzer's original

---

42. Wendland, *Prophetic Rhetoric*, 21.

43. R. Mason, *Zephaniah, Habbakuk, Joel* (OTG; Sheffield: Sheffield Academic Press, 1994) 122; R. Dillard, "Joel," in *The Minor Prophets: An Exegetical and Expository Commentary* (ed. T. McComiskey; Grand Rapids: Baker, 1992) 243.

44. See W. Prinsloo, *The Theology of the Book of Joel* (BZAW 163; Berlin: de Gruyter, 1985) 92. Prinsloo comments on the wide range of proposed dates of composition for Joel before admitting that the historical context probably cannot be reconstructed and asserts instead that "the book has to be expounded within its intrinsic literary context."

45. Dillard, "Joel," 244.

46. L. Thurén, *The Rhetorical Strategy of 1 Peter with a Special Regard to Ambiguous Expressions* (Turku: Åbo Akademi Press, 1990) 71.

concept. In his article, he distinguishes between "real" and "fictive" situations, arguing that the situation created in a work such as a narrative or drama is not rhetorical since it is not historical in nature.[47] Bitzer, however, does acknowledge the existence of persistent or recurring rhetorical situations that no single rhetorical communication can resolve. These situations evoke texts that "exist as rhetorical responses *for us* [italics his] precisely because they speak to situations which persist—which are in some measure universal."[48] It is not too much of a stretch to assert that a text such as the Bible could be included in this body of "truly *rhetorical* [italics his] literature."[49] While Bitzer's concern is demonstrably with historically locatable situations, his acknowledgment of persisting situations and literature that seeks to respond to these situations may help to open the door to considering rhetorical situation in a different light.

This "world-of-the-text" or synchronic approach to rhetorical situation is similar to Shaw's approach to Micah in which he seeks to determine the rhetorical situation of the text primarily from the text itself, but it differs since it deliberately remains at the textual level and does not presume to capture the world behind the text. Focusing on the "world of the text" would help to eliminate Shaw's possible overreach in claiming that the situations that the book of Micah constructs are reliable reflections of an actual historical situation in ancient Israel. Instead, he could articulate the situation that the text of Micah creates in constructing its prophetic addresses. Wuellner pushes toward this approach in a study of Luke 12:1–13:9 in which he attempts to separate the rhetorical situation from a historical situation. He describes a "narrative story world" created by the author and its influence on readers, both past and present.[50] This entextualized world

---

47. L. Bitzer, "The Rhetorical Situation," in *Rhetoric: A Tradition in Transition* (ed. W. Fisher; Lansing, MI: Michigan State University Press, 1974) 257. Bitzer does acknowledge, however, that a drama or a narrative can be a response to a real-life rhetorical situation.

48. Ibid., 259. His examples include: the Gettysburg Address, Burke's Speech to the Electors of Bristol, and *Socrates' Apology*.

49. Ibid.

50. W. Wuellner, "Rhetorical Genre of Jesus' Sermon in Luke 12.1–13.9," in *Persuasive Artistry: Studies in New Testament Rhetoric in Honour of George A. Kennedy* (ed. D. Watson; JSNTSup 50; Sheffield: Sheffield Academic Press, 1991) 99–100. Gitay tries to find a middle ground between synchrony and diachrony in his discussion of the rhetorical presentation of Jeremiah. He claims that he is not interested in whether the prophet presented in Jer 1 reflects a historical figure or reflects a later textual presentation. He is concerned, however, with whether this presentation of Jeremiah would persuade an actual historical audience as well as later readers (Y. Gitay, "A Rhetorical Presentation of the Prophet Jeremiah," in *Prophecy and Prophets: The Diversity of Contemporary Issues in Scholarship* [ed. Y. Gitay; Atlanta: Scholars Press, 1997] 42). Notably, Gitay allows for a textual creation of the prophet but tries to maintain an extratextual understanding of the audience, which is a rather difficult line to walk.

is what gives rise to the persuasive capacity of the text in regard to its hearers and readers.[51]

Stamps helpfully defines a synchronic approach to rhetorical situation as "the situation embedded in the text and created by the text which contributes to the rhetorical effect of the text."[52] For this to be effective, the rhetor must construct the situation in a way that elicits correspondence with some if not the majority of the audience. The persuasiveness of the argument is linked tightly to the literary presentation of the situation; if there is correspondence, then the text may be capable of eliciting a fitting response from its audience.[53] The textual presentation of the situation becomes the basis for the argument of the whole communication and its individual rhetorical units. In positing its own rhetorical situation, the text conditions the speaker and the audience to accept a new reality in which the discourse operates.[54] This new reality should provoke the audience to response.

The role of the rhetor is to affect individuals in the audience through discourse and to persuade them to rectify the exigence by reacting in the way that the rhetor proposes.[55] The rhetor thus shapes the rhetorical situation through the discourse and constructs the exigence that requires a rhetorical response. The textuality of the rhetorical situation in this construction means that the speaker and the audience are literary constructions who only meet in the "world of the text." In meeting on this level, however, they have the capacity to construct a persuasive text that continues to draw in reading and hearing audiences whom the text can influence.

Consideration of the rhetorical situation is a dynamic process in this synchronic configuration since the argument of the discourse evolves throughout the text. Hauser's concept of the life cycle of rhetorical situations is applicable to this approach. Essentially, rhetors affect the life cycle of rhetorical situations, either by actively trying to move the audience to a desired opinion or action, or by reactively adapting their discourse as the situation shifts.[56] The rhetorical situation does not remain stagnant throughout a discourse. It changes as the argument of a discourse unfolds

---

51. Wuellner, "Jesus' Sermon," 100. Wuellner emphasizes the essential nature of the present tense of the verb "give rise" as opposed to the past "gave rise." In doing so, he highlights the fact that, in this construction of the rhetorical situation, the emphasis is on the textual world that exists in a perpetual present.

52. Stamps, "Rethinking," 199.

53. Ibid., 200.

54. Ibid., 210. See the discussion of rhetorical effectiveness for discussion about how one ought to use the concept of audience in a synchronic reading of the rhetorical situation.

55. D. Patrick and A. Scult, *Rhetoric and Biblical Interpretation* (JSOTSup 82; Sheffield: Almond, 1990) 34.

56. G. Hauser, *Introduction to Rhetorical Theory* (2nd ed.; Long Grove, IL: Waveland, 2002) 60.

according to the nature of the response.[57] In other words, a discourse, whether rejected or accepted, has an impact on those who hear it, and this receptivity has an influence on the nature of the situation that the text constructs.[58]

In studies of biblical texts, several interpreters have noted how rhetorical situations can develop over the course of a text. Thurén develops the life cycle of a rhetorical situation in his work on 1 Peter and notes that "an argumentative text is seldom so static that the rhetorical situation would remain the same throughout the text."[59] This claim receives further support from Hester, who considers the interplay between situation and audience in the construction of epistolary literature. Hester notes that, in an epistle, the author must anticipate the effect of the communication on the audience and consider how this effect might shift the situation.[60] This potential for development in a situation guides the construction of additional parts of the text. In a prophetic book such as Joel, one sees a similar dynamic. The prophet moves from describing a situation and calling for a response to describing its aftermath. Consequently, it might be helpful for us to look at different passages as progressive stages in the life cycle of the rhetorical situation and consider how the text responds to different developments in the rhetorical situation while leading towards final resolution.

In summary, the use of rhetorical situation on the level of the "world of the text" is indisputably problematic for most interpreters of the Bible. The interpreter cannot claim that the exigence or deficiency that is critical to Bitzer's understanding is an actual defect in the real world that the discourse intends to address. This use of rhetorical situation is more in line with arguments about the role of the rhetor in constructing the situation.[61]

---

57. Perelman and Olbrechts-Tyteca, *New Rhetoric*, 491. Perelman and Olbrechts-Tyteca speak of the "argumentative situation" rather than "rhetorical situation," but the terms are roughly parallel if rhetorical situation is understood synchronically. Perelman and Olbrechts-Tyteca's understanding of the argumentative situation encompasses the rhetor's persuasive intent and the challenges that s/he will face in gaining adherence. The argumentative situation is dynamic, shifting to accommodate the audience's responses to the discourse's progress. Perelman and Olbrechts-Tyteca also use the idea of argumentative situation to discuss the ordering of arguments in a persuasive discourse, demonstrating that a rhetor's choice of organization has an impact on the effectiveness of the discourse (Perelman and Olbrechts-Tyteca, *New Rhetoric*, 96, 460–61, 490–91).

58. Consigny, "Rhetoric," 181. The discussion of the dynamism of the rhetorical situation is similar to Consigny's condition of receptivity for the rhetor, permitting the rhetor to engage the different stages of the situation as they arise, not predetermining the problems and challenges that they will create.

59. Thurén, *Rhetorical*, 70.

60. J. Hester, "Kennedy and the Reading of Paul: The Energy of Communication," in *Words Well Spoken: George Kennedy's Rhetoric of the New Testament* (ed. C. Black and D. Watson; Waco, TX: Baylor University Press, 2008) 146. Hester attempts to put this proposal into practice in a reading of Galatians. See Hester, "Kennedy," 149–53.

61. See Vatz, "Myth,"160. Vatz asserts that rhetoric is "a *cause* not an *effect* [italics his] of meaning. It is antecedent, not subsequent to a situation's impact."

Similarly, it is possible to conceive of the audience in a broader sense than those who first heard the discourse. It also opens the door to the criticism that this broader understanding of rhetorical situation neglects the context necessary to understand a text's construction. In the case of Joel, whose historical exigence and date of composition are beyond our grasp, however, approaching the situation of the text from the textual perspective it presents is an appropriate way to proceed. Ultimately, the entextualized understanding of rhetorical situation that Stamps and Wuellner propose is the best way forward when establishing the "world behind the text" is almost impossible.

Rhetorical Genre

The third step in the model we are examining is to consider the *rhetorical genre* of the text. Reaching back to Aristotle, rhetorical critics typically distinguish a triad of genres differentiated by the responses demanded by the audience.[62] *Judicial rhetoric* asks hearers to judge past events, while *deliberative rhetoric* invites the audience to consider what would be beneficial for its future. Third, *epideictic rhetoric* aims at reinforcing certain values or beliefs shared by both audience and speaker, with a view toward harmonizing these values with the audience's circumstances.[63] Kennedy explicitly relies on these categories because he distinguishes his examples based on identifying their rhetorical genre.[64] He places a high priority on determining the appropriate rhetorical genre since each genre uses its own particular style of argumentation to shape its persuasive intent.[65] The genre of the text provides the framework for Kennedy's interpretation of the text.

Möller mentions these basic rhetorical categories but nuances the way in which they are applied to the biblical text. Specifically, Möller is less interested in dividing a text's rhetorical units into constitutive rhetorical genres than in discerning how these genres advance the text's persuasive strategies.[66] This is in keeping with developments in the field of genre criticism that push toward a functional interpretation in exploring the range of communication that is possible within the constraints of a genre. Brown defines genre as "a socially defined constellation of typified formal and thematic features in a group of literary works, which authors use in individualized ways to accomplish specific communicative purposes."[67]

---

62. Black, "Rhetorical Criticism," 254; Kennedy, *New Testament Interpretation*, 36–37.

63. Perelman and Olbrechts-Tyteca, *New Rhetoric*, 52–53.

64. "Deliberative" texts include The Sermon on the Mount and The Sermon on the Plain; an "epideictic" example is John 15–17; and a "judicial" example is 2 Corinthians.

65. Kennedy, *New Testament Interpretation*, 36. Kennedy's concern for rhetorical genre is strongest in his discussion of Galatians, which he categorizes as deliberative rhetoric: Paul seeks to persuade the Galatians to respond appropriately to the gospel.

66. Möller, *Prophet*, 40.

67. J. Brown, "Genre Criticism," in *Words and the Word: Explorations in Biblical Interpretation and Literary Theory* (ed. D. Firth and J. Grant; Nottingham: Apollos, 2008) 122.

This definition nicely captures the idea that there should be common features that bind a collection of texts together as a genre category while leaving sufficient space for individual creativity and adaptation within the confines of this category. [68]

Möller adds a new layer to the conversation when he distinguishes between the rhetorical genre of specific passages and the rhetorical genre of the prophetic book. [69] He describes most of Amos's oracles as judicial rhetoric, condemning Israel for its past misdeeds. He argues, however, that the overall strategy of the book is actually deliberative, attempting to bring about a change of attitudes and actions in the text's situational audience through these words of condemnation. [70] Möller's conception of a text's rhetorical genre as part of the rhetorical strategy is tied tightly to his construction of Amos's rhetorical situation. The book of Amos is deliberative rhetoric if it addresses a Judahite audience prior to the Babylonian captivity, when return and redress were still possible.

Borrowing terminology from speech-act theory—the deliberative slant that Möller brings to the rhetorical genre of Amos emphasizes the *perlocutionary* intent of the text to provoke response, rather than its *illocutionary* act of activating judgment. [71] In other words, Möller demonstrates that focusing on the rhetorical genre of the individual units in a prophetic book can be misleading after taking into consideration the book's broader persuasive strategy. In the case of Amos, identifying the condemnatory nature of the individual units could cause the interpreter to miss what Möller believes is a call to response and return in an identifiable rhetorical situation.

Moving from the genre of individual units to the genre of the broader discourse opens up a potential pitfall in this step of the methodology since it may be too easy to categorize all prophetic books as deliberative attempts to modify future behavior or belief. This concern for the text's continuing impact is an integral part of reading a text as authoritative Scripture. If

---

68. Similarly, Hester considers rhetorical genre to be a response to a text's audience and exigences. It is a functional part of the text's communicative strategy. See Hester, "Speaker," 84.

69. Brown, "Genre Criticism," 137–40. Brown discusses the ability of literary genres to "contain" shorter literary forms within their bounds, mentioning specifically the propensity of the Gospels to contain parables, proverbs, and prayers within the boundaries of an overarching narrative.

70. Möller, *Prophet*, 40. For more on the proposed prophetic ability to use oracles pronouncing judgment as attempts to modify current behavior, see K. Möller, "Words of (In-)evitable Certitude? Reflections on the Interpretation of Prophetic Oracles of Judgement," in *After Pentecost: Language and Biblical Interpretation* (ed. C. Bartholomew, C. Greene, and K. Möller; SHS 2; Grand Rapids: Zondervan, 2001) 352–86; T. Eagleton, "J. L. Austin and the Book of Jonah," in *The Book and the Text* (ed. R. Schwartz; Oxford and Cambridge, MA: Blackwell, 1990) 231–36; and W. Houston, "What Did the Prophets Think They Were Doing? Speech Acts and Prophetic Discourse in the Old Testament," *BibInt* 1 (1993) 167–88.

71. Möller, *Prophet*, 40.

one's philosophical or theological predispositions require reading the text as active in all contexts, this view will have an impact on one's consideration of a text's genre.[72]

Amador proposes the possibility of "hybrid genres" in the biblical text as one solution for moving past this particular trap. Amador argues that, for example, 1 Corinthians should be understood as deliberative-forensic with the ultimate aim of educating its audience.[73] This identification permits him to break free of the constraints of genre categories when passages in the text do not match the expectations of one specific category. A slightly different approach is to connect rhetorical genre to the exigences of a rhetorical situation. If one identifies multiple exigences for a rhetorical situation, it may be difficult to determine one controlling rhetorical genre. Further, a complex text tends to have a "dynamic rhetorical situation" that shifts throughout the discourse, again rendering it difficult to establish an overarching genre category.[74] Consequently, identifying the rhetorical genre of a larger work may prove difficult and perhaps not as helpful in determining its persuasive force as has been thought.

After discussing the limitations of genre categories in determining the persuasive appeal of a text, we should note that Möller differs greatly from Kennedy in the significance he attaches to the rhetorical genres identified in given texts. Möller essentially abandons the category of rhetorical genre in his discussion of Amos.[75] He devotes lengthy chapters to determining the text's macrostructure, rhetorical situation, and strategy before delving into exegetical analysis in the latter half of his monograph. Rhetorical genre does not reappear in the discussion of the different rhetorical units, suggesting that, for Möller, establishing a unit's rhetorical genre does not necessarily help to determine its persuasive strategy.

In the case of Joel, it is unclear whether determining the rhetorical genre of given units of the discourse will improve our understanding of the text's persuasive strategies and effects. Broadly speaking, it appears that the text employs deliberative rhetoric in the rhetorical units where there is a heavy concentration of imperatives to the implied audience to react or respond

---

72. Garrett and Xiao's work on the concept of discourse tradition elucidates this point. A discourse tradition encompasses the presuppositions and beliefs that rhetors bring to their communication; Garrett and Xiao, "Rhetorical," 34–38. Identifying a prophetic book as a prophetic book casts it into a certain discourse tradition that provides both the source and the limits of the communicative strategies. The freedom to construct the discourse is limited by the fundamental values and presuppositions of prophetic texts.

73. J. Amador, "Where Could Rhetorical Criticism (Still) Take Us?" *Currents in Research: Biblical Studies* 7 (1999) 198. For the educational role of epideictic rhetoric, see Perelman and Olbrechts-Tyteca, *New Rhetoric*, 51–54.

74. Hester, "Speaker," 86.

75. Similarly, "rhetorical genre" is completely absent from Shaw's discussion of Micah. Shaw pares the method of Kennedy down to "rhetorical unit," "rhetorical situation," and "rhetorical strategy." Also missing is a discussion of the text's "rhetorical effectiveness."

in a given manner (see Joel 1:1–14; 2:12–17), epideictic rhetoric in passages describing the character of Yʜᴡʜ (see Joel 2:1–11; 2:18–27), and potentially judicial rhetoric in passages condemning foreign nations (see Joel 4:1–21). Even within these units, however, one cannot make hard and fast distinctions, since the text may contain features of multiple genres in a given passage.[76] Consequently, I intend to follow Möller and, although I mention features that suggest a generic orientation for each rhetorical unit, I subordinate this sort of discussion to the rhetorical strategies that the text employs to make its persuasive appeal.

Rhetorical Strategy

The fourth step of this method of rhetorical criticism is to look at the *rhetorical strategy* employed in a particular text. It is at this stage of the analysis that the concerns of rhetorical criticism as the "art of composition" and as the "art of persuasion" are most closely intertwined. Essentially, rhetorical analysis must delve into stylistic concerns in order to draw out the tropes and figures that the rhetor employs to affect the audience.[77] The rhetorical critic here examines the way the text is structured as well as what type of imagery and metaphor is used to give it persuasive power. The goal is to determine how the particular choices of language and imagery organize the argument through different stylistic techniques. This involves identifying literary devices such as chiasmus, inclusio, metaphor, and rhetorical questions.[78] In rhetorical criticism as the art of persuasion, however, the interpreter does not simply articulate these devices as literary ornamentation but, rather, seeks to demonstrate how they relate to the process of convincing the hearers/readers to adhere to the argument in question.

Prophetic texts are particularly amenable to analysis of their persuasive intent. In a discussion of word order choices, van der Merwe and Wendland note that prophets and preachers typically try to modify the behavior of their audience; their poetic constructions rarely convey information for its own sake.[79] The information embedded in the stylistic flourishes contains data that ought to motivate an audience to give heed to the prophetic speech directed to them.

---

76. For example, Joel 2:12–17 calls for the audience to respond in a certain way in order to avert the calamity described in the previous rhetorical unit, which means that we would probably classify it as deliberative rhetoric. However, the primary reason that the text gives for calling for this response revolves around its description of Yʜᴡʜ, which aims to reinforce the audience's belief in his gracious and compassionate nature. Hester aptly states that "it is important to understand that the selection of genre is itself an inventional choice and has to be set into the context of the interaction between and among speaker, audience and situations" (Hester, "Speaker," 91–92).

77. Gitay, *Prophecy and Persuasion*, 40–41.

78. Möller, *Prophet*, 41.

79. C. van der Merwe and E. Wendland, "Marked Word Order in the Book of Joel," *JNSL* 36 (2010) 114–15.

The analysis of different approaches to persuasion also fits into this category. It may activate the classical distinctions of *ethos, pathos,* and *logos,* which correspond roughly to the character of the rhetor, the frame of mind that the text evokes, and the details of the text itself.[80] Employing these concepts allows the critic to explore the full range of persuasive approaches, from the rational and cognitive dimensions to those driven by emotion and imagination.[81] In particular, it is interesting to notice the relative absence of rhetorical *ethos* in Joel. The text hides the character of the prophet, offering no call or commissioning narrative for the prophet to establish his *bona fides.* The relative anonymity of the prophet in Joel makes some sense, given the status of a prophet as Yhwh's messenger; prophets' will and character are subjugated ultimately by their status as one who claims to speak for Yhwh.[82] In contrast to *ethos,* both *logos* and *pathos* are visible throughout Joel. The prophet claims to have a grasp of the situation and proposes seemingly fitting responses to it (*logos*), while conjuring up startling images of both desolation and blessing that will result if the audience either rejects or heeds his call (*pathos*). Thus, these categories are useful in providing insight into the different strategies that a text can use to construct its persuasive appeal.

Möller also extends his consideration of rhetorical strategy beyond examining the internal structure and devices of each rhetorical unit. He states that the critic's task is to examine the way the various rhetorical units work together to achieve a unified purpose or their failure to accomplish this.[83] The relationship between the rhetorical units is important to consider in the case of Joel, given the debate over the text's essential unity. If there is a discernible strategy or purpose that binds together all of the rhetorical units, then finding it may help to move the debate forward. Thus, the analysis of rhetorical strategy needs to be able to step outside the techniques employed within particular rhetorical units in order to examine how the text uses this material to create the broader rhetorical strategy that informs the persuasive appeal of the entire discourse.

Rhetorical Effectiveness

The fifth and final stage of our model is the *rhetorical effectiveness* of a particular text. Its purpose is to determine whether the unit in question could function as effective persuasion within the situation to which it is being applied. Kennedy uses rhetorical effectiveness to look back and examine the strength of the rhetorical strategies that the text employs and how well they fit the rhetorical situation. In this step, interpreters broaden their

---

80. Möller, *Prophet,* 41.
81. Wuellner, "Rhetorical Criticism?" 461.
82. J. Darsey, *The Prophetic Tradition and Radical Rhetoric in America* (New York: New York University Press, 1997) 28.
83. Möller, *Prophet,* 42.

perspective and reflect on the overall effect of the rhetorical unit. This step essentially permits Kennedy to summarize the previous discussion briefly and to expand its implications beyond the narrow boundaries of the text in question. For example, in his reflection on the Sermon on the Mount, Kennedy claims that his analysis reveals that it has unity of thought, that Jesus maintains a connection with the audience, and that the employed rhetorical devices are not ornamental but functional in creating audience contact and intensity.[84] Kennedy notes Matthew's claim that the audience was astounded at Jesus' speech and then asserts that "it has continued to startle and challenge readers for two thousand years."[85] Consequently, Kennedy views it as an example of "effective" rhetoric, emphasizing its continued ability to astound and confront readers, despite the passing of millennia.

Despite Kennedy's example, rhetorical effectiveness remains a nebulous concept. On a diachronic level, it is hard to gauge effectiveness because we rarely have a record of the response of the audience that heard the message.[86] Even in cases where the text does provide an account of the audience's response, including Kennedy's example of the Sermon on the Mount (Matt 7:28–29), one could understand it as both an account of the text's effectiveness on a particular audience and an additional rhetorical strategy to convince a later reading audience that Jesus' words ought to affect them similarly.

In an attempt to move rhetorical effectiveness beyond a search for records of audience response, Möller proposes considering whether or not the utterance is a fitting response to the exigence underlying the communication. He cannot state for certain whether the rhetorical work successfully modifies the exigence, since this depends on factors external to the text; instead, he proposes considering whether it has the potential to modify it on the basis of its internal logic and persuasive thrust.[87] This criterion is vague and potentially self-fulfilling, since an interpreter is likely to conclude that the text to which he or she has devoted a great deal of time and energy is capable of modifying whatever circumstances created its rhetorical situation.

Möller's own attempt to apply the "fitting response" criterion requires further reflection and development, since he devotes only the final two pages of his study to considering the potential effectiveness of Amos's rhet-

---

84. Kennedy, *New Testament Interpretation*, 63. Interestingly, Kennedy has a much more negative judgment of Luke's parallel "Sermon on the Plain." He concludes his analysis by claiming that Luke 6 is an ineffective speech and that any rhetorical impact it may have is due in large part to the *ethos* of Jesus, its speaker (p. 67).

85. Ibid., 63.

86. M. Fox, "Rhetoric of Ezekiel's Vision of the Valley of the Bones," *HUCA* 51 (1980) 4. In addition to the lack of information concerning audience response to a prophetic message, Fox also points out that prophets often tended to portray their audiences in a very negative light, presumably to try to spur them to hear their message.

87. Möller, *Prophet*, 42–43.

oric. He concludes that, although it obviously did not successfully modify the exigence of Judah's improper behavior, its depiction of Israel's behavior and ultimate fate certainly had the potential to do so.[88] In other words, the fault for Amos's ineffectiveness lies with the audience rather than with the rhetor or the message. One wonders how a text can be construed as "effective" if it fails to fulfill its primary rhetorical function—that is, to persuade its audience to modify its behavior or to adopt the text's point of view. Ultimately, the paucity of Möller's analysis indicates that, if this model of rhetorical criticism is to keep rhetorical effectiveness as a category, scholars must consider the concept more thoroughly.

The need to develop a more nuanced approach to rhetorical effectiveness cuts to the core of rhetorical criticism as a discipline. One of the repeated refrains of rhetorical critics is that the discipline too frequently remains content with describing a text's rhetoric, without moving to consider its actual persuasive impact. Wuellner laments the "ghetto" of biblical stylistics that he claims imprisons critics in a functionless, context-less approach to the biblical text.[89] Similarly, Hester appeals for rhetorical studies to move beyond analysis to actual criticism, or from descriptions of a text's arguments to consideration of its persuasive power.[90] In Kennedy's and Möller's approaches, rhetorical effectiveness could provide the potential for the interpreter to move from describing the text's rhetorical arguments to examining its persuasive potential and effect. The risk of the rhetorical approach's remaining primarily in the realm of stylistics is evident in critiques of Muilenburg, whom some consider to have essentially divorced the text from its rhetorical environment in his consideration of the text's rhetorical form and figures.[91] Consequently, the category of rhetorical effectiveness could offer the interpreter a significant opportunity to enhance the scope of the analysis.

In order to develop the analysis of rhetorical effectiveness, we may find it helpful to consider the notion of the audience whom the discourse seeks to affect in more detail. I mention above that "audience" is one of the three criteria Bitzer uses to determine a discourse's rhetorical situation but that Bitzer focuses almost exclusively on those who actually heard a particular

---

88. Ibid., 295–96. He allows for the potential that Amos's message may have persuaded some of those who heard it but admits the highly conjectural nature of this proposal. He suggests that the preserved oracles of Amos may have worked in concert with an Isaianic condemnation of Judahite elites. Again, however, even if this were the case, the oracles of Amos still failed to persuade its audience to reform and avoid divine judgment.

89. Wuellner, "Rhetorical Criticism?" 462.

90. Hester, "Kennedy," 154. His proposal is to examine ancient and modern theories of rhetoric in order to ground rhetorical strategies in the frameworks that help to explain their persuasive power.

91. P. Tull, "Rhetorical Criticism and Beyond in Second Isaiah," in *The Changing Face of Form Criticism for the Twenty-First Century* (ed. M. A. Sweeney and E. Ben Zvi; Grand Rapids: Eerdmans, 2003) 330.

discourse or whom a particular text addressed. Audience, in the discussion of rhetorical situation is significant since it guides rhetors in the rhetorical strategies and approaches they ought to adopt. The concept of *audience*, however, is also vital in considering a text's rhetorical effectiveness since this category requires that a text achieve its effects on someone or some group.[92]

Möller indicates that he does not want the effectiveness of prophetic rhetoric to rest solely on the actual response of an historical audience. Instead, his proposal to examine its capacity for modifying an exigence expands the boundaries of the audience that can judge a prophetic text's persuasive force. If Möller claims that Amos is "effective" rhetoric, despite the fact that its original audience did not heed its message, it is necessary to appeal to another audience who found it persuasive.

Prophetic literature as a broad category may even lend itself to a consideration of its effect on a wider audience. Alter helpfully notes that since biblical prophecy employs poetic language it can elevate its utterances to another level of significance; thus, what the text says in response to a given situation can be aligned with an archetypal horizon.[93] In this perspective, a prophetic message seemingly located in a given space and time can continue to speak and invite people from very different times and places to locate themselves within the text and allow it to have an impact on them.[94]

Considering rhetorical effectiveness beyond an immediate historical audience involves determining diverse levels of audiences that operate within the various orientations toward the text. A rhetor may craft a text to speak in a certain time and setting, but this particular situation does not encompass the full extent of the text's persuasive capability; there are other audiences whom the text may persuade. An introductory step in locating these audiences is found in an article by rhetoricians Hunsaker and Smith. They attempt to bring clarity to the categorization process by differentiating among a "situational audience" who perceives a given issue or exigence, a "rhetorical audience" who may act on the rhetor's appeals, and an "ac-

---

92. Y. Gitay, "Rhetorical Criticism and the Prophetic Discourse," in *Persuasive Artistry: Studies in New Testament Rhetoric in Honour of George A. Kennedy* (ed. D. Watson; JSNTSup 50; Sheffield: Sheffield Academic Press, 199) 124. Gitay locates rhetorical study in the relationship between the text and its audience. He has in mind the original hearing audience of a prophetic speech, which may prove difficult to isolate in other instances.

93. R. Alter, *The Art of Biblical Narrative* (New York: Basic Books, 1981) 146. Alter uses the example of prophetic condemnation of exploitation of the poor and oppressed as an example of a theme that can resonate with an audience beyond the audience to which it was originally addressed.

94. Fox argues similarly and points to an example such as the Gettysburg Address to indicate that the rhetorical force of a given discourse may far exceed its impact on its original audience (Fox, "Rhetoric of Ezekiel's Vision," 4).

tual audience" whom the rhetor chooses to address.[95] In other words, the immediate audience who first hears the discourse is only a small part of those whom the rhetor seeks to persuade. Hunsaker and Smith's use of the term "situational audience" is rooted firmly in the diachronic realm. They define the situational audience as a *"witness* [italics theirs] to the rhetorical situation: knowledge of the rhetorical exigence is direct."[96] Essentially, the situational audience is composed of individuals who share a common interest in a particular exigence, even if they were not in the actual audience of the discourse.

Perelman and Olbrechts-Tyteca's concept of the "universal audience" may also help us more thoroughly to consider rhetorical effectiveness. They describe the "universal audience" as the compilation of those capable of judging the truth-claims of an argument.[97] This universal audience exists primarily as an imaginative construct that the rhetor ought to keep in mind when putting together an argument. Arguments persuasive to the universal audience must be "of compelling character . . . self-evident, and possess an absolute and timeless validity, independent of local or historical contingencies."[98] The primary purpose of the universal audience is to serve as a check on the rhetors in constructing their arguments for particular audiences.[99] In other words, the rhetor ought not to employ any argument that could sway an audience if the argument were objectionable or repugnant to a broader, universal audience. Scult characterizes the relationship between audiences as one in which a particular, concrete audience keeps the concept of the universal audience from becoming an abstract irrelevancy, while the universal audience prevents the rhetor from succumbing to the temptation to go to any length to persuade a particular audience.[100] The universal audience, therefore, exists in the "world of the text" as the complex of readers or hearers upon whom the text may have persuasive appeal.

While they acknowledge that the *universal audience* can never be defined perfectly, Patrick and Scult adeptly argue that this concept can be used to articulate the rhetorical power of the biblical text. They claim that, by examining the text's arguments from the perspectives of both the

---

95. D. Hunsaker and C. Smith, "The Nature of Issues: A Constructive Approach to Situational Rhetoric," *Western Speech Communication* 41 (1976) 148–52.

96. Ibid., 148.

97. Perelman and Olbrechts-Tyteca, *New Rhetoric*, 31.

98. Ibid., 32.

99. Ibid., 31.

100. A. Scult, "Perelman's Universal Audience: One Perspective," in *The New Rhetoric of Chaim Perelman: Statement and Response* (ed. R. Dearin; New York: University Press of America, 1989) 159. Scult's example is a rhetor who may employ arguments designed to sway a racist audience. The test of the "universal audience" ought to persuade this rhetor that arguments of this sort are unlikely to stand close scrutiny.

historical audience whom it affected and the universal audience whom its truth-claims hope to persuade, the critic is in a better position to analyze the text's rhetorical power.[101] This approach allows the interpreter to explore the transactions between text and reader that shape the text's persuasive appeal on both historical and epistemological levels.[102] Patrick and Scult view the universal audience as an effective check of the rhetor's capacity to manipulate specific audiences, since the truth-claims that the text makes must withstand scrutiny from the universal audience.[103] Thus, the concept of universal audience may provide a way to speak of a text's rhetorical effectiveness beyond the time and place of its original composition.

Kennedy provides a view similar to Patrick and Scult in the final stage of his methodology by claiming that this stage permits the interpreter not only to bring the analyzed text into clearer focus but also to look beyond to its awareness of the human condition and perhaps even to religious or philosophical truth.[104] This move may be especially relevant to a book such as Joel, for which we have little evidence of its particular audience or its response to the text's rhetorical power. The book of Joel is constructed as a prophetic message from Yhwh to a particular audience at a particular time responding to a particular exigence that is difficult to locate in history. Consequently, it is difficult to talk about the rhetorical effectiveness of this text for its original audience. This text, however, continues to exist and have an impact on additional reading audiences. In this way, it may be possible to consider the text's rhetorical effectiveness as it seeks to communicate across time and space to this more universal audience.

---

101. D. Patrick and A. Scult, "Rhetoric and Ideology: A Debate within Biblical Scholarship over the Import of Persuasion," in *The Rhetorical Interpretation of Scripture: Essays from the 1996 Malibu Conference* (ed. S. Porter and D. Stamps; JSNTSup 180; Sheffield: Sheffield Academic Press, 1999) 79.

102. Ibid., 79. See also A. Scult, "The Relationship between Rhetoric and Hermeneutics Reconsidered," *Central States Speech Journal* 34 (1983) 226. Scult argues that one of the effects of reading a "sacred" rhetorical text is that its original rhetorical situation remains dormant so that the text's effects on the present can come to the forefront. Scult probably states the case too strongly since much of biblical interpretation revolves around determining the "original" situation of the text, but he is on the right track when he notes how the interpreter must move toward finding commonalities between the "original" situation and the interpreter's own situation in order properly to unleash the rhetorical power of the text.

103. Patrick and Scult make the fascinating move of considering God to be part of the biblical text's universal audience. In making this move, they argue that a primary purpose of the biblical text is to bear faithful witness to the deity who called forth this discourse. They argue that considering God to be part of the universal audience should mean that "the narrators and prophets did not consciously manipulate information and emotions to win their audience. They could not be 'base rhetors' in the presence of this conception of the universal audience" (Patrick and Scult, "Rhetoric and Ideology," 80).

104. Kennedy, *New Testament*, 38.

Perelman and Olbrechts-Tyteca's concept of the universal audience has parallels to the idea of the "implied reader" or "implied audience" found in narrative criticism. Both are text-immanent moves that hold that a discourse gives clues about who would be its ideal readers or audience.[105] The implied audience is bound to the text and functions as a communicative instance that guides the rhetor in the process of shaping his or her discourse.[106] If one can outline the parameters of this audience from the directives found in the text, perhaps one can also pass judgment on how a given discourse intends to affect it.[107] A preliminary consideration of the nature of an implied audience for Joel would take into account the strategies that the text uses to appeal for response. Specifically, the text employs imperatives directed at specific groups that may begin the process of constructing an implied audience (cf. Joel 1:2, 5–14; 2:1, 15–17; 4:4–8). In this book, I examine the construction of implied audiences and the persuasive appeal of the text's rhetoric to these audiences in my discussion of individual passages.

Patrick and Scult also employ the idea of an implied audience in their call for a "hermeneutics of affirmation" when reading biblical texts. This orientation toward the text permits it to have a persuasive impact on interpreters who read it many centuries after its original composition by allowing them to situate themselves among those to whom the text speaks and whom it intends to persuade.[108] They argue that "the interpreter should assume that the text seeks to persuade an intellectually, emotionally and morally competent audience, and judge as best one can whether it succeeds in doing so."[109] This orientation connects the interpreter to an appropriate understanding of the text's implied audience, which should help the interpreter experience the persuasive appeal of the text. This echoes the presentation of the literary nature of a text's situation to its implied audience since the implied audience must consent to the text's presentation of the

---

105. M. Powell, *What Is Narrative Criticism?* (Minneapolis: Fortress, 1990) 20. See also the discussion of Conrad's use of the "Model Reader," in the previous chapter.

106. A. van Wieringen, *The Implied Reader in Isaiah 6–12* (BIS 34; Leiden: Brill, 1998) 25.

107. Powell differentiates between rhetorical-critical approaches and narrative criticism by claiming that the "real" audience is of less concern in narrative criticism. It is only the implied audience or reader who needs to be determined. He later claims, however, that he does not want to divorce the study of the Bible from "referentiality," arguing that historical and narrative approaches need to be laid side by side (Powell, *Narrative Criticism*, 15, 98).

108. Patrick and Scult, "Rhetoric and Ideology ," 66. See also Iser, who views the ability of the reader to enter the world of the text as an essential element in what allows literature to transcend its time and place in history (W. Iser, "Indeterminacy and the Reader's Response in Prose Fiction," in *Aspects of Narrative: Selected Papers from the English Institute* [ed. J. Miller; New York: Columbia University Press, 1971] 44).

109. Patrick and Scult, "Rhetoric and Ideology," 65 n. 4.

situation in order for the text to be persuasive.[110] When an audience accepts a text's presentation of the situation, it can experience the persuasive potential of that text.

Patrick and Scult derive their approach from the understanding of all interpreters as "situated" with preexisting conditions and commitments that they bring to the text. They are responding to readings that employ a "hermeneutic of suspicion" and seek to read against the grain of what appears to be the text's meaning. For example, the Bible and Culture Collective criticizes Kennedy's model of rhetorical criticism by claiming that it could be employed in an anticritical agenda, in which demonstrating the rhetorical strategies of the text passes too easily into assuming the success of those strategies, thereby arriving at the "truth" of the text and closing off further discussion or critique.[111] The potential silencing of dissenting voices is worth considering when discussing biblical rhetoric, since it is "a rhetoric with immense power in that it assumes that that world view is the only viable one for humanity to accept."[112] In other words, there is a significant collection of interpreters who worry that claiming that a biblical text succeeds in persuading its audiences (whether situational, implied, or universal) could equal stifling additional debate over the meaning or ethical import of the given text.

This concern has some legitimacy, since it reminds interpreters of the rhetorical nature of all discourse. Tull artfully encapsulates the nature of critical inquiry by claiming that "the very practice we are analyzing, we are also ourselves exercising, since any stance that an interpreter takes concerning the text is by nature a rhetorical stance."[113] One can assert, however, that it is also a valid approach to read the text as the "best text" it can be, allowing the potential validity of its truth claims to shape and guide the interpretation.[114] This approach does not necessarily seek to subsume all other orientations toward the text. It does demand, however, the same

---

110. Stamps, "Rethinking," 200.

111. Bible and Culture Collective, "Rhetorical Criticism," in *The Postmodern Bible* (ed. E. Castelli et al.; New Haven, CT: Yale University Press, 1995) 182.

112. Phillips, "Rhetoric," 259.

113. P. Tull, "Rhetorical Criticism and Intertextuality," in *To Each Its Own Meaning: An Introduction to Biblical Criticisms and Their Application—Revised and Expanded* (ed. S. Haynes and S. McKenzie; Louisville: Westminster John Knox, 1999) 163.

114. The call to read the text as the "best text" creates a fascinating duel of definitions. Patrick and Scult use the concept of "best text" to call the interpreter to measure the different meanings that a text has had against the interpreter's judgment about what the text, in its fullest, most consistent, and most natural sense could communicate (Patrick and Scult, *Rhetoric*, 21). In practice, this usually leads them to affirm the text's religious authority and significance as they encounter the text as Scripture. In contrast, the Bible and Culture Collective claim that the "best text" is one that resists pressures to "reify and commodify" exegesis (Bible and Culture Collective, "Rhetorical Criticism," 183–85). In other words, the "best text" should criticize overarching systems of interpretation. This makes them highly suspicious of any approach that seems to support a "conservative" interpretive tradition.

freedom of being explored as is given to "suspicious" readings of the text. Patrick and Scult suggest that this approach offers the advantage of promoting "a view of human existence in which the knowing subject is open to being taught by others. The interpreter can only *receive* [italics theirs] truth from a text if he or she is willing to entertain the possibility of its being true."[115] This perspective demonstrates that a rhetorical-critical approach can incorporate the stance of interpreters who position themselves as readers willing to be swayed by its persuasiveness.

In light of the preceding discussion, I explore rhetorical effectiveness in this book by means of two interrelated frameworks. First, I consider the signs and signals in the text that suggest a rhetorical effect on the text's implied audience and see how the text guides the implied audience through the course of the book. Second, I consider rhetorical effectiveness by using the idea of the universal audience who experiences this text beyond its original time and place. This approach opens up the scope of rhetorical effectiveness so that one may consider the continuing persuasive impact of a text.[116]

Conclusion

Rhetorical criticism as the "art of persuasion" is a valuable approach to studying prophetic literature. Prophetic literature functions as intermediation between the divine and earthly realms, with the prophetic figures themselves operating as agents who intend to persuade their earthly audience of the importance of the divine message.[117] Consequently, studies of prophetic literature that seek to draw forth its various means of persuasion are helpful in deepening our understanding of this corpus. Contemporary interpreters such as Gitay, Shaw, Möller, and Patrick offer examples of persuasive studies of prophetic rhetoric, but there remains much of this corpus that is available for rhetorical study.

---

115. Patrick and Scult, "Rhetoric and Ideology," 77.

116. E. Black, *Rhetorical Criticism: A Study in Method* (New York: Macmillan, 1965) 74–75. Black comes close to this understanding of rhetorical effectiveness when he argues for opening up the category to consider audiences other than the immediate hearing audience. He proposes numerous possibilities for further examination, suggesting that the critic can "assess all the differences that a rhetorical discourse has made in the world, or will make, and how the differences are made and why." While he adopts a diachronic approach for discussing multiple audiences for considering effectiveness, his imaginative illustration of the concept provides the chance to push it even further in this study.

117. J. Barton, "History and Rhetoric in the Prophets," in *The Bible as Rhetoric: Studies in Biblical Persuasion and Credibility* (ed. M. Warner; Warwick Studies in Philosophy and Literature; London: Routledge, 1990) 64. Barton makes the claim that one of the signs of the persuasive power of prophetic rhetoric is that these texts became normative in scriptural history and tradition. The general acceptance of the prophets' portrayal of Israel and Judah's sin and the necessity for divine punishment reflects the rhetorical skill of the prophets.

Given the history and development of rhetorical-critical studies in the prophets, the book of Joel provides an appealing test case for demonstrating the usefulness of rhetorical analyses in the prophets and for a modified version of Kennedy's and Möller's models. This potential is visible when Joel shifts image-worlds from one apparently rooted in natural catastrophes such as locust infestations and drought toward eschatological judgment oracles. The rhetorical effects of this progression are well worth considering. Furthermore, the development of the text's imagery helps to establish its structural divisions. Within these textual units, one can explore the various rhetorical strategies and literary devices at work that create its persuasive impact. One can also show interplay between the rhetorical genres that inform the structure of different oracles as the prophet moves from exhortation of his audience to promises of comfort and blessing and challenges addressed to other nations.

Joel's lack of historical specificity creates an intriguing challenge for working with the concepts of rhetorical situation and rhetorical effectiveness because it is so difficult to determine the audience to whom it was originally addressed or what impact it could have had. This virtually demands expanding these concepts so that rhetorical situation and rhetorical effect can be used to discuss the persuasive impact of the text beyond a presumed historical location. Instead, the interpreter can focus on the text's potential to speak to an implied audience who is constructed of individuals capable and willing to be persuaded by the argument of the discourse. I intend to discover and articulate the means of persuasion employed in the book of Joel and to place them in the context of rhetorical situations that the discourse constructs, while also considering their continuing persuasive impact.

To summarize, the intention of this book is to demonstrate that Joel is a unified work of prophetic literature that moves from scenes of devastation to promises of restoration through its persuasive evocation of divine and human responses in order to articulate the necessity of calling and relying upon YHWH in all circumstances. To achieve this goal, I employ a rhetorical-critical method consisting of four elements. First, I determine the text's rhetorical units. This step involves determining the signals of aperture and closure that demarcate these units. Second, I investigate the rhetorical situation of the text. Because it is almost impossible to look behind the text of Joel and locate it in time and space, I consider rhetorical situation as it is constructed in the "world of the text." Third, I examine the rhetorical strategies employed within the various rhetorical units that evoke divine and human responses. The discussion of rhetorical genre, which for Kennedy is its own discrete step, will be subordinated to its role in the development of the text's rhetorical strategies. Discussing rhetorical strategy will also involve considering the literary devices, themes, and imagery that the text invokes in order to persuade its audience. Although the bulk of the discussion focuses on the individual rhetorical units, I also consider how they build the persuasive thrust of the entire book. Finally, I examine the rhetorical effectiveness of the text.[118] This will involve considering the persuasive impact of the text's rhetorical strategies in its entextualized rhetorical situation on the implied audience whom the text constructs, as well as its influence on the universal audience for whom the text maintains its persuasive power.

118. The discussion of rhetorical effectiveness demonstrates the interrelated nature of the various stages of this rhetorical-critical model. The interpreter's consideration of the rhetorical unit's effectiveness is tightly tied to the way s/he constructs the rhetorical situation and its implied audience. It is also reliant on the way s/he assesses the text's potential impact on a universal audience who can be persuaded of its truth and rhetorical power. It also permits an assessment of the construction and arrangement of the argument that considers the effect of the various persuasive strategies that the text employs. If the interpreter can consider these elements, then the category of rhetorical effectiveness is a vital summary step in rhetorical analysis. The interpreter engages in the process by assessing the impact of the constituent parts as they work together to create the broader message of the whole discourse.

Chapter 2

Announcing the Crisis: Rhetorical Analysis of Joel 1:1–14

Introduction

We commence the rhetorical study of the book of Joel by exploring the persuasive strategies used in Joel 1:1–14 and the effect of these strategies on the audience. This will provide the foundation for examination of the book as a whole. This chapter locates the initial rhetorical situation against the backdrop of the text's use of locust imagery and agricultural devastation. It examines the way that the text uses a series of imperatives to construct its implied audience and motivate it to respond to the situation that it describes. Joel 1:1–14 deftly gathers the whole community into its implied audience by addressing it both as a whole and in its individual components, calling each part of the implied audience to respond. The appeals to the members of the implied audience culminate when the prophet directs the whole community to gather under priestly leadership and cry out to YHWH. Joel 1:1–14 effectively takes a natural disaster of a locust plague and uses it to direct the implied audience to respond by maintaining its commitment to YHWH, even amidst crisis.

Rhetorical Unit

The first stage of the rhetorical-critical model used in this book is to determine the boundaries of the rhetorical units within the text. At this stage, the goal is to divide the book into discrete passages in order to see both how they communicate their message and how they fit into the broader shape of the entire book.[1] As mentioned in the discussion of theories concerning Joel's compositional unity, Joel 2:18 is frequently viewed as a major break in the book since it begins the process of reversing the pictures of devastation and destruction articulated in previous verses.[2] Another recognizable disjunction occurs in Joel 3:1[Eng. 2:28],[3] where the image-world shifts

---

1. For a summary of all of these different structural proposals, see J. Crenshaw, *Joel* (AB 24c; New York: Doubleday, 1995) 29–34.

2. See L. Allen, *The Books of Joel, Obadiah, Jonah, and Micah* (NICOT; Grand Rapids: Eerdmans, 1976) 39–42; H. W. Wolff, *Joel and Amos* (Hermeneia; Philadelphia: Fortress, 1977) 7; G. Ahlström, *Joel and the Temple Cult of Jerusalem* (VTSup 21; Leiden: Brill, 1971) 130–32; E. Wendland, *Prophetic Rhetoric: Case Studies in Text Analysis and Translation* (Longwood, FL: Xulon, 2009) 20.

3. Joel 3:1–5 and 4:1–21 in the Hebrew text are equivalent to Joel 2:28–32 and 3:1–21 in English Bibles. Hereafter, I will use the Hebrew versification without making reference to the English.

from locusts, armies, agricultural devastation, and restoration to broader eschatological visions of the outpouring of Yʜᴡʜ's Spirit and a day of judgment against the nations.[4] Essentially, Joel 3–4 appears to shift the focus of the day of Yʜᴡʜ from a day in which Judah's existence is threatened to a day of restoration and salvation from its external enemies. The majority of interpreters base their analysis on one of these two points of division.[5]

Beyond the question of the book's principal hinge, there are several different proposals for determining the subunits of the book. Joel 1:1 is clearly its own distinct unit since it is the superscription for the whole book. Superscriptions stand as structurally independent from the body of the book, and they introduce and identify the material that follows.[6] Joel's superscription differs from many other prophetic books since it only reveals that what follows is the communication of Yʜᴡʜ. The superscription gives no other details that would help in the process of placing the book in the context of its original utterance, such as the location of the utterance, or regnal formulas to provide a historical context.

My intention in this book is to keep these structural proposals in mind, while beginning on a smaller scale and building toward a picture of the discourse as a whole, rather than offering any firm conclusions at this juncture.[7] Consequently, the place to begin is with a consideration of the text's first principal rhetorical unit after the superscription. The most viable place to demarcate the end of the first rhetorical unit that follows the superscription is Joel 1:14. Joel 1:1–14 reflects a call to communal complaint or lament about the locust plague described in this section.[8] The prophet uses imagery of locust attacks and agricultural devastation in order to set up his appeal to his implied audience to lament and cry out to Yʜᴡʜ. Joel

---

4. Nogalski states that dividing Joel 1–2 from Joel 3–4 is to divide it by content, while dividing Joel 1:1–2:17 from 2:18–4:21 is to divide in terms of form (J. Nogalski, *Redactional Processes in the Book of the Twelve* [BZAW 218; Berlin: de Gruyter, 1993] 2). Simkins provides a recent example of an interpreter who places the primary "hinge" between Joel 2:27 and 3:1 (R. Simkins, *Yahweh's Activity in History and Nature in the Book of Joel* [ANETS 10; Lewiston, NY: Edwin Mellen, 1991] 99, 201).

5. Prinsloo is an exception, arguing for an incremental building of the argument, with each unit related to its predecessor through shared vocabulary and phraseology (W. Prinsloo, *The Theology of the Book of Joel* [BZAW 163; Berlin: de Gruyter, 1982] 122–27).

6. M. Sweeney, *The Twelve Prophets: Vol. 1* (Berit Olam; Collegeville, MN: Liturgical Press, 2000) 152. See also Stuart, who refers to this verse as the simple title of Joel, limiting our knowledge of him to his patronymic and his identification as a prophet (D. Stuart, *Hosea–Jonah* [WBC 31; Waco, TX: Word, 1987] 237).

7. Coggins comments on the divergent proposals about structure, likening them to a form of reader-response criticism; they are welcome if they help a reader better interpret the text but should not necessarily be granted any objective status (R. Coggins, *Joel* [NCBC; Sheffield: Sheffield Academic Press, 2000] 18). Consequently, I do not claim that the divisions employed in this book are the only way to divide the text, but I do assert that they reflect the progression of the text as a persuasive argument.

8. Sweeney, *Twelve*, 154; Stuart, *Hosea–Jonah*, 239. See also Wendland, *Prophetic Rhetoric*, 20.

1:15–20 moves from a call to communal gathering of lament to offering up prayers of lamentation, which sets it apart from the material found in Joel 1:1–14.[9]

Joel 1:14 also provides two signals that it concludes this first rhetorical unit. First, it forms an inclusio with Joel 1:2 by directing its calls to assemble toward the זְקֵנִים 'elders' and the יֹשְׁבֵי הָאָרֶץ 'dwellers of the land'. Joel 1:2 begins the prophetic speech by addressing these groups before moving into appeals to specific subgroups within the broader community. By returning to the זְקֵנִים and the יֹשְׁבֵי הָאָרֶץ in Joel 1:14, the text signals the completion of its series of appeals to gather the audience. Second, the final imperative of Joel 1:14, וְזַעֲקוּ אֶל־יְהוָה 'cry out to YHWH', succinctly encapsulates all of the previous imperatives and marks the emotive peak of this first rhetorical unit.[10] All of the preceding calls to cry out culminate in the command to the people in the audience to focus their attention on YHWH.

Rhetorical Situation

As mentioned in the previous chapter, I propose to use the category of rhetorical situation in a different way from the majority of rhetorical-critical studies. Inability to determine the situation of the "world behind the text" of Joel with any degree of certainty drives the interpreter toward an understanding of the rhetorical situation of this prophetic book from criteria internal to the text. Although this approach may not prove satisfactory for placing the book in a specific historical situation, it can at least locate the passage in the situation that its words describe and reveal the concerns that the rhetor intends to address. From this understanding of the rhetorical situation of Joel 1:1–14, it will be possible to commence considering how the prophet's rhetorical strategy would affect the situation that the text describes.[11] The situation will develop throughout the text, but we can derive an understanding of the text's initial rhetorical situation from Joel 1:1–14.

Locust Infestation

First, the situation of this passage is closely linked to the metaphor of locusts in Joel 1:4–7, which is repeated in Joel 2:25. Scholars propose two possible image-worlds that inform the portrayal of the locusts in Joel 1:1–14.

---

9. Prinsloo, *Theology*, 28.

10. C. van der Merwe and E. Wendland, "Marked Word Order in the Book of Joel," *JNSL* 36 (2010) 120.

11. Stuart, *Hosea–Jonah*, 226. Stuart argues that the general message of the text and its impact remain strong despite the difficulty in locating it historically. This indicates that it may be possible to put forward some proposals about the sort of situation that might be most affected by the message that follows. Dillard suggests that the ambiguity of Joel's historical situation would actually favor its reuse in the face of ensuing calamities (R. Dillard, "Joel," 4 in *The Minor Prophets: An Exegetical and Expository Commentary* [ed. T. McComiskey; Grand Rapids: Baker, 1992] 243).

They view the locusts as either: (1) a metaphor for a foreign invader; or (2) a depiction of an actual locust infestation.[12] Adiñach, Stuart, and Ogden are among those who assert that the locusts are best understood as symbols for a foreign invader. Adiñach suggests that the use of locusts as an image for human armies was frequent in ancient Near Eastern literature and that the language and imagery that Joel attributes to locusts resembles other biblical descriptions of military activities (cf. Judg 6:3–5; 7:12; Jer 46:23; Nah 3:15–16).[13] Stuart argues that the hyperbolic language that Joel employs raises the relatively familiar occurrence of a locust plague to purely figurative heights.[14] Stuart proposes that Joel has in mind the Babylonian army since the death and destruction that it caused during its invasion of Judah was much greater than any conceivable invasion of locusts.[15] Ogden also asserts that the locusts of Joel 1:1–14 are representative of a foreign enemy. He argues that the book of Joel has its origins in a lament setting and that laments typically reflect military/political crises.[16] The text also explicitly refers to nations and peoples in Joel 1:5–6 and 2:2, which in Ogden's mind points to human invaders represented by locust imagery.

There are two difficulties with the theory that the locust images in Joel 1:1–14 create a rhetorical situation that was rooted in a foreign invasion. First, Stuart's insistence that the locust plague can only be a symbol since the effects of a locust invasion could not have caused devastation on a scale of such magnitude does not give proper credence to the potential of prophetic hyperbole. On the contrary—one can argue that the prophet seized on the idea of a natural disaster and used it to move the people's perspective from the natural to the supernatural as the text makes the transition from a description of the locusts to the coming day of Yʜᴡʜ.[17]

Second, the language that Joel employs to describe the activity of the locusts in this passage well suits a report of a literal locust infestation. Joel 1:7 describes the activity of the locusts in destroying two of Israel's most important agricultural resources: vines and fig trees. The picture of the locusts stripping off the bark so the bare branches become bleached (הִלְבִּינוּ שָׂרִיגֶיהָ) in that verse appears to be an accurate description of what happened in

---

12. P. Andiñach, "The Locusts in the Message of Joel," *VT* 42 (1992) 433–44. Andiñach details the opposing position before arguing for the theory of the foreign invader. I will revisit the identity of the invading force in my discussion of Joel 2:1–11, which appears to blend locust imagery with more overtly militaristic images.

13. Ibid., 433–44.

14. Stuart, *Hosea–Jonah*, 242.

15. Ibid., 240. He does not attempt to distinguish between the invasions of 597 B.C.E. and 586 B.C.E. Presumably, either would be traumatic enough to trigger the images of devastation that Joel employs.

16. G. Ogden and R. Deutsch, *Joel and Malachi: A Promise of Hope—A Call to Obedience* (ITC; Grand Rapids: Eerdmans, 1987) 11.

17. R. Simkins, "God, History, and the Natural World in the Book of Joel," *CBQ* 55 (1993) 437.

a locust infestation.[18] While one could argue that Joel includes this description simply to make the metaphor more striking, the specificity of the
prophet's description is potentially a sign that the locusts in Joel 1:4–7 are
more than symbolic of a foreign invader.[19] The text's approach is to construct an image-world that describes a known phenomenon and use it as a
precursor to move toward more explicitly theological concerns.

Overall, it is more likely that the prophet pictures an actual locust infestation that creates a striking backdrop for the prophetic message that he
hoped to communicate. The locusts begin to threaten the text's implied
audience and drive the text toward the prophetic call for response.[20] In
this text-immanent construal of the rhetorical situation, it is not necessary
to engage in the incredibly difficult search of trying to locate an actual
historical locust invasion. Instead, the focus is on the text's use of this
image-world to create the backdrop against which the text puts forward
its rhetorical strategies.[21] The locust backdrop of Joel 1 essentially permits
the prophet to portray the saving power of Yhwh in later oracles; thus the
detail with which the prophet paints the gravity of this locust invasion is
particularly striking.[22]

The Cult

Another significant element of the rhetorical situation in Joel 1:1–14
concerns the relationship that the text constructs between the prophet and
the cult in Jerusalem. It is clear that this is an important theme in Joel, especially in this rhetorical unit. Joel 1:1–14 contains repeated references to

---

18. Simkins, *Yahweh's Activity*, 130. Simkins cites a description of a 1915 locust infestation in Jerusalem that describes their activity in similar terms.

19. Interestingly, Boda identifies a possible parallel in Jer 14:1–15:4, where he sees that
a liturgy concerning a siege by foreign invaders has been incorporated into a liturgy regarding a drought (M. Boda, "From Complaint to Contrition: Peering through the Liturgical Window of Jer 14,1–15:4," *ZAW* 113 [2001] 196). This potential parallel may add some
support to the view that Joel is employing locust and drought imagery in conjunction
with the threat of a foreign invasion. The situations differ, however, in that Jer 14:17–21
clearly shifts the context from drought to siege with its description of individuals slain by
the sword in the countryside, while people who remain in the city experience disease and
hunger (Jer 14:18). Joel 1:6a does describe "a nation" invading Yhwh's land, but the calamity is first ascribed to locusts (Joel 1:4), and the ravages of the invader clearly resemble
locusts (Joel 1:6b–7). Consequently, it is more likely that Joel intends for the images of
locusts to be sufficiently frightening in their own right; it is not necessary to look for a
foreign invader lurking behind this imagery.

20. J. Linville, "Bugs through the Looking Glass: The Infestation of Meaning in Joel,"
in *Reflection and Refraction: Studies in Biblical Historiography in Honour of A. Graeme Auld* (ed.
R. Rezetko, T. Lim, and W. Aucker; Cambridge: Cambridge University Press, 2006) 296.

21. F. Deist, "Parallels and Reinterpretation in the Book of Joel: A Theology of Yom
Yahweh?" in *Text and Context: Old Testament and Semitic Studies for F. C. Fensham*. (ed.
W. Claasen; JSOTSup 48; Sheffield: Sheffield Academic Press, 1988) 63–79. Deist offers
further arguments for understanding the locusts as literary in nature.

22. Prinsloo, *Theology*, 127.

temple offerings and priests (Joel 1:9, 13) and calls for lament and sacred fasting (Joel 1:13–14). The nature of this relationship, however, is a matter of debate. Many, following the lead of Kapelrud, claim that the text portrays Joel as a cultic prophet, closely associating him with the temple in Jerusalem.[23] The text's assertion that YHWH will protect and restore Jerusalem in Joel 3–4 and the repeated calls in this passage for the people to engage in lament led by the priests indicate that the text portrays the prophet as standing in some degree of solidarity with the cultic leadership.[24] One can nuance the presentation of Joel as a cultic prophet somewhat by arguing that, while the social standing of the prophet cannot be located, the text provides "access to the terminology and characteristic concerns of the Jerusalem cult."[25]

In contrast, some argue instead that, while Joel is concerned with cultic matters, the text portrays the prophet as standing outside it and possibly even representing a group that was relegated to the periphery of society, partly as a result of his critiques. Wolff claims that the text's call to "return to YHWH" is reflective of a cult consumed by "pious self-sufficiency" that refused to understand that the day of YHWH would fall on Jerusalem itself.[26] Ahlström suggests that Joel saw the cult in Jerusalem as impure, even letting elements of idolatry taint the proper worship rituals.[27] The remedy for this situation is "a true cult that gives a true *tsĕdāqāh*."[28] Ahlström and Kapelrud appeal frequently to Canaanite fertility cult imagery to describe

---

23. A. Kapelrud, *Joel Studies* (UUÅ 4; Uppsala: Lundequist, 1948) 177. A unique interpretation of Joel's cultic connection comes from Conrad, who suggests that the text is referring to Bethel in Joel 1:14–16, since YHWH does not respond positively. Conrad posits a parallel to YHWH's refusal to intercede in the time of Amos. Conrad draws a distinction between 'the house of our God' (בֵּית אֱלֹהֵינוּ) in Joel 1:16 and the explicit references to Zion in Joel 2:15–16; E. Conrad, *Reading the Latter Prophets: Towards a New Canon Criticism* (JSOTSup 376; London: T. & T. Clark, 2003) 202. This interpretation, while creative, is extremely unlikely. There are many examples where בֵּית אֱלֹהֵינוּ refers to the Jerusalem temple, meaning that in this verse the phrase is probably not making an oblique reference to another sanctuary (Ezra 8:17, 25, 30, 33; Neh 10:33–40; Ps 135:2). Further, in the progression of the prophetic narrative, the temple in Jerusalem seems to be a better fit. YHWH's silence in Joel 1 sets up the divinely sanctioned assault on Zion in Joel 2:1–11 before the text presents the possibility of salvation in Joel 2:12–17.

24. Sweeney, *Twelve*, 151. Sweeney goes even further and suggests that Joel may have been a prophetic temple singer. This claim, however, stretches the available evidence of the text to a degree that it cannot sustain.

25. R. Coggins, "An Alternative Prophetic Tradition?" in *Israel's Prophetic Tradition: Essays in Honour of Peter Ackroyd* (ed. A. Phillips, R. Coggins, and M. Knibb; Cambridge: Cambridge University Press, 1982) 89–92.

26. Wolff, *Joel and Amos*, 13.

27. Ahlström, *Joel*, 25–26. His strongest evidence comes from the command in Joel 2:12 for the community to 'return to me' (שֻׁבוּ עָדַי). The suffixed prepositional phrase עָדַי suggests to Ahlström that there is the potential for idolatrous worship since the prophetic call highlights that the audience must return to YHWH.

28. Ibid., 61.

the worship practices found in this book. For example, Kapelrud puts forward the argument that the call to weeping in Joel 1:5 resonates with liturgical weeping for the slain deity Baal.[29] This seems speculative, however, given the gravity of the situation that the prophet presents. Calls to lament in the house of YHWH in the wake of an economic and agricultural disaster may well reflect a response congruent with appropriate worship of YHWH.

A different approach is to suggest that Joel's orientation toward the cult changes throughout the text. Redditt suggests that the book of Joel came together over a lengthy period of history and that those who added to it took an increasingly negative view of the cult. In the present passage, the prophet begins to decry the cessation of sacrifice in Joel 1:9, 13. A later redactional addition then eventually circumvents the cult by democratizing the Spirit of YHWH in Joel 3:1–5.[30] Allen, however, offers a trenchant critique of Redditt's theory, noting that the lapse of sacrifices would be inevitable in the wake of the agricultural disaster and that the text does not appear to affix any more blame on the priesthood than it does on the farmers or vine-growers, who are also unable to do their jobs.[31] This renders suspect Redditt's judgment concerning the relationship with the cult in Joel 3:1–5. In addition, if a rhetorical reading of Joel can demonstrate that the text makes sense as a unified composition, then Redditt's understanding of Joel's growth becomes even less likely to be useful in explaining the rhetorical situation of the relationship between the prophet and the priests found in this text.

In response to the arguments suggesting Joel's disapproval of the cult, it is helpful to take a closer look at the value that the text places on cultic ritual in Joel 1:1–14. The text effectively casts the message of Joel into a priestly world view, where rituals and rhythms are understood as part of the proper response to the difficult situation that is presently afflicting the implied audience.[32] In response to the devastating locust infestation and the subsequent agricultural failures, the text calls the people to enter the cultic world and lament and fast in the house of YHWH. This is part of the

---

29. Kapelrud, *Joel Studies*, 21.

30. P. Redditt, "The Book of Joel and Peripheral Prophecy," *CBQ* 48 (1986) 226.

31. L. Allen, "Some Prophetic Antecedents of Apocalyptic Eschatology and Their Hermeneutical Value," *Ex Auditu* 6 (1990) 21. Allen rightly asserts that the text does not shape the crisis in such a way that points to priestly culpability. Instead, the text dwells on the gravity of the situation in order to stress that only YHWH can provide the remedy. Prinsloo also challenges Redditt's use of an anthropological model that relies on the categories of peripheral and central prophecy, suggesting that this extratextual reality does not capture the context of Joel (W. Prinsloo, "The Unity of the Book of Joel," *ZAW* 104 [1992] 68–69). See also S. Cook, *Prophecy and Apocalypticism: The Postexilic Social Setting* (Minneapolis: Fortress, 1995) 207.

32. J. Linville, "The Day of Yahweh and the Mourning of the Priests in Joel," in *The Priests in the Prophets: The Portrayal of Priests, Prophets and Other Religious Specialists in the Latter Prophets* (ed. L. Grabbe and A. Bellis; JSOTSup 108; London: T. & T. Clark, 2008) 106.

natural response to tragedy: people seek solace in the familiar and expected in order to try to gain perspective on what is happening.[33] In this case, the text's repeated commands for the community to engage in ritual lament in the house of Yʜᴡʜ demonstrate that it portrays the cult as a place of reorientation and response.

The locust plague and subsequent agricultural ruin create a powerful scenario of doom and destruction. The insistence in Joel 1:1–14 on returning to the temple and its rituals suggests a way of appropriately understanding this threat in the context of the relationship with Yʜᴡʜ.[34] The locutionary commands to seek Yʜᴡʜ at his house directed to both priests and community also have the illocutionary purpose of reminding the community of the central role that the temple and the worship of Yʜᴡʜ play in the community's own identity.[35] The passage details considerable consternation about the cessation of the worship rituals of the community and calls for the people to cry out to Yʜᴡʜ from the house of Yʜᴡʜ (Joel 1:14). Essentially, the text's presentation of its rhetorical situation draws in the world of the cult and portrays it as a means through which the implied audience can respond to the exigence of the locust infestation.

The Implied Audience

Another significant element in the rhetorical situation that the text constructs is related to its implied audience. Joel 1:1–14 goes into significant detail to assemble the various facets of the implied audience for this particular prophetic oracle. This process begins in Joel 1:2 when the text employs the merismus of "elders" and "dwellers of the land." As mentioned above, this merismus is also found in Joel 1:14, signaling the conclusion of this rhetorical unit. It creates the contours of the implied audience, drawing in the entire community from its leaders to its regular citizens. Following the broad description of the implied audience in Joel 1:2, several verses in Joel 1:1–14 highlight certain subsections of the audience. Notably, many of the groups that the text identifies have intimate ties to the land.[36] The

---

33. Ibid., 103. Linville draws on the theory of normalizing response of ritual to tragedy put forward by Bell (C. Bell, *Ritual Theory, Ritual Practice* [Oxford: Oxford University Press, 1992] 108–9). This articulates a plausible understanding of the reason that the text would call for a cultic response, even if the standard practices of the cult were nonfunctional.

34. Cook, *Prophecy and Apocalypticism*, 171.

35. K. Möller, "Words of (In-)evitable Certitude? Reflections on the Interpretation of Prophetic Oracles of Judgement," in *After Pentecost: Language and Biblical Interpretation* (ed. C. Bartholomew, C. Greene, and K. Möller; SHS 2; Grand Rapids: Zondervan, 2001) 365–66. Möller attempts to make sense of the potential gap between the specific words and the meaning of prophetic communication by distinguishing between locutionary, illocutionary, and perlocutionary acts. A *locutionary* act concerns the exact nature of the words spoken, while *illocution* concerns the intended purpose of the words, and *perlocution* concerns the effects of the words.

36. Interestingly, the text uses a slightly different approach to construct its implied audience in Joel 2:1–11 with its description of an all-encompassing assault against Jerusalem.

first groups that the text identifies are the שִׁכּוֹרִים 'drunkards' and שֹׁתֵי יָיִן 'wine drinkers' in Joel 1:5, who depend on agricultural produce to find the escape that they seek. Joel 1:11 then addresses the אִכָּרִים 'farmers' and כֹּרְמִים 'vinedressers', whom the locust plague directly affects because the locusts are devouring their produce.[37] The text also links the other subsections of the community to the land and its bounty in several places within Joel 1:2–14. Joel 1:13 calls the priests to lament because the lack of agricultural produce threatens the sacrificial system, while the text further fleshes out the generic call to wail in Joel 1:8 with a list of devastated crops in 1:10.

The text's attempt to catalog a cross-section of its implied audience helps to develop the exigence of the rhetorical situation. While the text draws in the broadest possible audience with the merismus found in Joel 1:2, the process of identifying smaller entities within this audience adds immediacy to the crisis that it describes. By focusing on groups whom the locust plague directly affects, the text expresses the severity of the rhetorical situation and the necessity for appropriate response. The exigences of the locust plague have specific effects on the implied audience that create the milieu for the rhetorical strategies that the text employs to move this implied audience.

Summary

While the lack of historical data precludes placing Joel 1:1–14 in a specific, historically locatable rhetorical situation, the clues derived from the text itself suggest that the rhetorical situation that the text creates is one that seeks to provide an appropriate response to the exigence of a terrible locust plague and subsequent agricultural hardships. Further, the situation presupposes a functioning and genuine cult, since the prophet directs the addressees to go to the priests and the house of YHWH to respond to this situation. Although the cult faces serious challenges as a result of the locust plague, it is nevertheless the place to which the prophet directs the community in order to address the disaster appropriately. The close relationship of the prophet's implied audience to the land also drives the rhetorical situation of Joel 1:1–14. This rhetorical unit details the effects of the locust infestation throughout the society: it deprives many of sustenance and livelihood while threatening the sacrificial system. Ultimately, this scene of devastation creates a rhetorical situation in which the only course of action is to cry out to YHWH.

The agrarian focus of Joel 1 gives way to a picture of "fortress Jerusalem" succumbing to an attack.

37. J. Thompson, "Joel's Locusts in the Light of Near Eastern Parallels," *JNES* 14 (1955) 53–54. Thompson notes examples of Egyptian artists who depicted locusts devouring grapevines and wheat, while also finding an Assyrian parallel in locusts that were devouring the produce of a fruit tree. Consequently, the text is probably drawing from the realm of likely victims when it calls on these specific agricultural workers to cry out.

Rhetorical Strategy

After articulating the text's rhetorical units and describing the entextualized rhetorical situation against which the text can be read, we now turn to the rhetorical strategies that govern these units. This is the third and most detailed step of the method used in this study. At this stage, rhetorical criticism as the art of persuasion most closely resembles Muilenburg's art of composition. The interpreter now looks for the structural clues and literary devices that the text uses to communicate the intended message effectively. My method differs from Muilenburg's program, however, in that the rhetorical situation and genre play a greater role in describing the passage's communicative intent. The goal is to move beyond simply articulating the esthetic appeal of the passage. In this section, I seek to capture the way in which the passage's construction reveals its persuasive force. This ability to describe the text's persuasive appeal is what moves this approach from rhetorical analysis to rhetorical criticism.[38] Consequently, this study of the text's rhetorical strategies needs to keep its persuasive potential at the centre of the analysis.

Joel 1:1: Prophetic Superscription

Joel 1:1–14 begins with a prophetic superscription that roots the discourse that follows in the tradition of Yhwh's prophets. A prophetic superscription can be defined as "a title, sometimes expanded, over a book, a portion of a book, or a poem."[39] Such superscriptions are not standardized throughout prophetic literature, and different books provide varying degrees of information concerning the nature of the communication, the speaker, and the time and place of the prophetic utterance.[40] Joel 1:1 only provides the reader with the name of the prophet, his patronymic, and the claim that what follows is the word of Yhwh.[41] Five other prophetic books in the broader collection of the Book of the Twelve (Obadiah, Jonah, Nahum, Habakkuk, and Malachi) echo Joel in not providing a regnal formula

---

38. J. Hester, "Kennedy and the Reading of Paul: The Energy of Communication," in *Words Well Spoken: George Kennedy's Rhetoric of the New Testament* (ed. C. Black and D. Watson; Waco, TX: Baylor University Press, 2008) 154.

39. J. Watts, "Superscriptions and Incipits in the Book of the Twelve," in *Reading and Hearing the Book of the Twelve* (ed. J. Nogalski and M. Sweeney; SBLSymS 15; Atlanta: Society of Biblical Literature, 2000) 111.

40. For a detailed analysis of varying forms of prophetic superscriptions and their development, see G. Tucker, "Prophetic Superscriptions and the Growth of a Canon," in *Canon and Authority* (ed. B. Long and G. Coats; Philadelphia: Fortress, 1977) 56–70.

41. Joel 1:1 identifies the prophet as "Joel, the son of Pethuel." Pethuel is a name otherwise unattested in the Old Testament. The LXX identifies the name of Joel's father as Bethuel, a name that occurs notably in Gen 22:22–23; 24:15, 24, 47, and 50. That Bethuel is the father of Rebekah and the nephew of Abraham. Although it is impossible to say for certain, it seems most likely that the LXX tradition took a previously unknown name and brought it into line with a name that did occur elsewhere in the Old Testament.

that would help to define the provenance of the prophecy. These books stand in contrast to the remainder of the Twelve (Hosea, Amos, Micah, Zephaniah, Haggai, and Zechariah), which employ regnal year formulas to locate their messages spatially and temporally.

The rhetorical function of the superscription in Joel 1:1 is to establish a sense of prophetic commissioning, articulating that the prophet has received words from the divine that he is supposed to communicate.[42] This verse stands distinct from the remainder of the prophetic communication by introducing the nature of material to follow and the name of the prophet to whom the work is ascribed.[43] The phrase דְּבַר־יְהֹוָה אֲשֶׁר הָיָה 'The word of YHWH came to', which is common to the openings of Joel, Hosea, Micah, and Zephaniah, provides the primary identity of the following message as communication given by YHWH.[44] Of the group just mentioned, Joel alone contains no ensuing regnal formula.[45] The rhetorical effect of the uniqueness of the superscription could be that, by means of its sparseness, it intensifies the identity of the book as divine communication from YHWH since this particular superscription subordinates both the intermediary figure of the prophet and any concern over the time and place of its composition to the declaration that this book is "the word of YHWH."

The strategy of subordinating the person of the prophet is in keeping with the prophetic tradition, which emphasizes the surrender of the prophet's will to YHWH (Isa 49:5; Jer 1:5; Amos 3:8), although the silence of Joel 1:1 about the prophet's time of ministry goes even further in this regard. This silence may strengthen the timelessness of the message since no particular time period can conclusively be attached to it. Although the text employs all manner of strategies to persuade its audience, the heart of its authority rests in its identity as the word of YHWH. On this basis, the prophetic text can attempt to persuade its audience to respond. Essentially, the superscription in Joel 1:1 establishes the prophet as the agent of the divine communication.

---

42. Crenshaw, *Joel*, 79.

43. Sweeney, *Twelve*, 152.

44. Tucker notes that classifying speech as "the word of YHWH" is reserved for prophetic revelation but argues that this idea has a different sense when used as part of a superscription. In this case, it encompasses the whole of the prophetic word that was committed to writing. See Tucker, "Prophetic Superscriptions," 63–64.

45. Watts, "Superscriptions and Incipits," 121. Watts's concern in investigating prophetic superscriptions and incipits is to try to argue how they show redactional shaping in the Book of the Twelve. Essentially, he argues that where superscriptions and incipits overlap, there is evidence of redactional activity in attempting to connect the various corpora of the Book of the Twelve. This may prove to be a fruitful field of inquiry, but for the purposes of this project it is more important to focus on the rhetorical effect of commencing prophetic communication through the specific superscription of Joel 1:1.

Joel 1:2–4: The Crisis Revealed

The text's prophetic discourse commences following the superscription of Joel 1:1. First, Joel 1:2–3 introduces the content of the oracle that is to come in 1:2–14. The text begins with two parallel imperative commands: שִׁמְעוּ־זֹאת הַזְּקֵנִים 'Hear this, O elders', and וְהַאֲזִינוּ כֹּל יוֹשְׁבֵי הָאָרֶץ 'give ear, all dwellers of the land'. The prophet's use of dual commands for the audience to pay heed to the forthcoming message is a common rhetorical technique that introduces multiple literary forms, including wisdom instruction (Prov 4:1; 7:24), diplomatic discourse (2 Kgs 18:28–29), and prophetic oracles (Hos 4:1; Amos 3:1; Mic 6:1; Isa 1:10; Ezek 6:3).[46]

The text's use of imperatives in this verse also lays the foundation for the style of persuasion that Joel 1:1–14 employs. Imperatives dominate this rhetorical unit, a fact that suggests that the text is drawing from a deliberative rhetorical genre to guide its audience toward a certain course of action in response to the rhetorical situation (Joel 1:2, 3, 5, 8, 11, 13, 14).[47] The deliberative orientation of this passage creates the context through which the text intends to address the situation. By issuing a series of commands rooted in the prophet's knowledge of the situation, the text seeks to persuade the implied audience that it offers the proper response to the devastating locust plague.

The two terms denoting the scope of the implied audience form a merismus that summons the entire nation, since these terms bring together the leaders of the people at the local village or town level with all of the people themselves.[48] In other parts of the Old Testament, elders appeared on the

---

46. Sweeney, *Twelve*, 155. Wolff highlights the connection to wisdom literature, referring to the commands in Joel 1:2 as the ancient "call to receive instruction" (*Lehreröffnungsruf*). However, the wide-ranging variety of literary contexts that employ this type of construction suggest that one cannot locate its provenance within the wisdom tradition. See Wolff, *Joel*, 20; and Crenshaw, *Joel*, 84.

47. See Griffin's analysis of the proportionally high use of "verbal instruction" in Joel. He notes that this seems to identify the activity of the book as potential rather than realized activity, but the progression of the book indicates that the implied audience could have responded appropriately to these instructions (W. Griffin, *The God of the Prophets: An Analysis of Divine Action* [JSOTSup 249; Sheffield: Sheffield Academic Press, 1997] 140).

48. Sweeney, *Twelve*, 155. Some argue that the text employs "elders" in a nontechnical sense, meaning only elderly people who would have the ability to recall the past and acknowledge the uniqueness of the situation that is now unfolding around them (Crenshaw, *Joel*, 86; D. Garrett, *Hosea, Joel* [NAC 19A; Nashville: Broadman & Holman, 1997] 313). However, taking "elders" in the sense of the people's leaders makes more sense, given the following appeal to the "dwellers of the land." In this way, the text calls both the leaders and the remainder of the people to hear the prophetic word. For more on the role of elders as local authorities who performed judicial, representative, and cultic functions, see T. Willis, *The Elders of the City: A Study of the Elder-Laws in Deuteronomy* (SBLMS 55; Atlanta: Society of Biblical Literature, 2001) 307–8. J. Conrad, "זָקֵן," *TDOT* 4:126–31; J. McKenzie, "The Elders in the Old Testament," *Bib* 40 (1959) 522–40; C. Van Dam, *The Elder* (Explorations in Biblical Theology; Phillipsburg, NJ: Presbyterian & Reformed, 2009) 41–60.

national stage, where they could act as counselors (Judg 9:2; 1 Kgs 12:6), elect kings (1 Sam 8:4; 1 Kgs 12:1–15), and represent the people in cultic service (Lev 9:1–2; 1 Kgs 8:3).[49] Further, elders had the most connection to traditional knowledge and thus could both affirm the incomparability of the current situation and inaugurate a new tradition of passing down this scenario.[50] The phrase יֹשְׁבֵי הָאָרֶץ 'dwellers of the land' encompasses the rest of the inhabitants, signifying that the whole collective group is the implied audience (cf. Jer 10:18; Hos 4:1). Thus, the scope of Joel's call deliberately stretches out across the entire people, attempting to garner the largest possible audience.

After making the broad appeal for everyone living in the land to view themselves as part of the implied audience, the text then seeks to draw this audience into the message by employing a strategy of delay that increases the tension. The text first uses a rhetorical question in 1:2b, asking הֶהָיְתָה זֹּאת בִּימֵיכֶם וְאִם בִּימֵי אֲבֹתֵיכֶם 'Has this been in your days or in the days of your fathers?', which refers to the event only through the demonstrative pronoun זֹאת. A rhetorical question is an effective device to command the attention of the audience despite the ambiguity of the question, since a rhetorical question "invites active participation in the dialogue, whether spoken out or silent, on the part of the hearer, thus arousing his attention and interest in the matter under discussion."[51] The participation that the question in Joel 1:2b invites draws upon the call to the elders in the previous clause and emphasizes their age; on account of their many years, they can affirm the incomparability of the described events.[52] By urging them to participate in this process of reflection, this rhetorical question engages the implied audience and guides them toward accepting the perspective that the text will present.[53] Joel 1:2b thus establishes the exceptional nature of

---

49. Ahlström, *Joel*, 35. Some commentators take notice of the lack of reference to a king in this call and use it to place Joel in a time after the end of kingship, though again an approach of this sort is an argument from silence.

50. Linville, "Day of Yahweh," 105. Van Dam further notes the instructing function of the elders in the phrase "counsel of the elders" that occurs alongside the vision of the prophets and the teaching of the priests (Jer 18:18; Ezek 7:26). See Van Dam, *The Elder*, 60.

51. T. Muraoka, *Emphatic Words and Structures in Biblical Hebrew* (Leiden: Brill, 1985) 118.

52. Garrett, *Hosea, Joel*, 313. Garrett also detects an echo of Deut 4:32–34 in the way that Joel 1:2b uses rhetorical questions to set up the incomparability of the present situation. Deuteronomy 4:32–34 uses similar rhetorical questions to emphasize the uniqueness of Yʜᴡʜ's selecting Israel as the deity's own people. Thus, for Garrett, Joel's use of a similar form challenges Yʜᴡʜ's claim over the audience. Crenshaw, however, notes that "appeal to the unprecedented" seems to be a literary *topos* of the ancient world. He cites Sumerian texts that employ incomparability as a strategy to gain an audience (Crenshaw, *Joel*, 86). Thus, while Joel 1:2 may employ a rhetorical device similar to Deut 4:32–34, one cannot conclude that this verse is explicitly reversing a claim found in Deuteronomy.

53. Y. Gitay, "Rhetorical Criticism and Prophetic Discourse," in *Persuasive Artistry: Studies in New Testament Rhetoric in Honour of George A. Kennedy* (ed. D. Watson; JSNTSup

the current situation and calls the audience to listen to the forthcoming prophetic word.

The text then delays the revelation of the event again in Joel 1:3, when it gives the injunction for the witnesses to communicate this message to their children and for their children to carry it down to the next generation and for that generation to retell it yet again to a fourth generation. The reference to future generations in Joel 1:3 works in tandem with the reference to prior generations in the final clause of 1:2. These references set apart the current situation for continual remembrance. The text thus stresses the incomparability of what is occurring by using intergenerational appeals that look both to the past and to the future.

The rhetorical strategy of Joel 1:3 also draws from exodus traditions in its use of the motif of instructing the children and the retelling of the deeds of YHWH for the people of Israel.[54] The call to tell this story to multiple generations sets up the prophet's desire for the community to retell this prophetic word unfailingly throughout its existence. By engaging in this preliminary conversation, the prophet heightens its impact when he finally reveals the exact nature of this momentous event. The text's rhetoric of delay is effective since it draws in the implied audience with its depiction of a unique occasion but requires the implied audience to continue listening if it wants to learn the exact nature of the event in question.[55]

Joel 1:4 finally reveals the specific nature of the devastation. This verse introduces the image-world of locusts that plays such an important role.[56] Joel 1:4 is connected to what precedes since the text again uses a pattern of repetition involving succeeding generations. In this case, it is not a command to relate the message to future generations but, rather, a description of the severity of the event that the text makes evident by referring to multiple "generations" or waves of locusts. The stylized way in which Joel 1:4 describes the onslaught of multiple waves of locusts intensifies the magnitude of the disaster.[57] Joel 1:4 uses four synonyms for locusts (הֶחָסִיל; הַגָּזָם; הָאַרְבֶּה; הַיֶּלֶק) in a pattern that is repeated three times. Each clause of this verse begins with the construct noun יֶתֶר 'remainder' followed by one

---

50; Sheffield: Sheffield Academic Press, 1991) 137. Gitay argues for the importance of finding a common perspective as a key feature in the effectiveness of a given text. Joel's invitation for the implied audience to dwell on the incomparability of the situation begins the process of convincing the implied audience to adopt the same point of view.

54. Sweeney, *Twelve*, 155. Sweeney draws parallels to Exod 12:26–27; 13:8, 14; and Deut 6:20–23.

55. Crenshaw, *Joel*, 88.

56. See under "rhetorical situation" for a discussion of the potential historicity of the locust plague. At the very least, what Joel presents is a plausible depiction of a locust infestation. In the discussion of the rhetorical strategy, the focus is on the way in which the prophet used this imagery.

57. Van der Merwe and Wendland, "Word Order," 117.

of the four words for locust. The verb אָכַל 'it ate' occurs next, followed by
the next locust synonym.

The intended effect of the repetitious clauses is to paint a picture of total
destruction.[58] Joel 1:4 creates an image in which whatever remains after the
first wave of locusts is eaten by the second, third, and fourth waves in succession, dramatically emphasizing that nothing will escape this rapacious
horde. Sellers speculates that the different terms for locust refer to various
stages in the development of the desert locust, which was the species most
likely to visit Israel.[59] This claim is dubious, however, since it is difficult to
identify the text's words for locust with particular stages of locust development.[60] Fortunately, the text's lack of concern for insect entomology does
not detract from its rhetorical power, since the three clauses in Joel 1:4
effectively emphasize the nature and scope of the situation. The combination of the rhetoric of delay in Joel 1:2–3 and the description of the locusts'
devastation in Joel 1:4 is potent, and the gravity of the situation as portrayed in Joel 1:2–4 provides the foundation for the prophet's forthcoming
calls to response.[61]

Joel 1:5–14: Calls to Lament

Joel 1:5–7: Call to Lament I

A series of subunits that begin with imperative verbs follow this depiction of the locust infestation (Joel 1:5–7, 8–10, 11–12, 13–14). The prophet
issues commands to various groups within the implied audience, com-
municating the prophet's intent to evoke the proper response to the crisis created by the locust invasion. The preponderance of imperatives in
Joel 1:5–14 is part of the text's broader rhetorical strategy. Perelman and
Olbrechts-Tyteca suggest that imperatives are as effective as the degree of
adherence that the rhetor can command from the audience; if the adherence is lacking, an imperative assumes the tone of a plea or a prayer.[62] In
the case of the imperatives found in Joel 1:5–14, the text constructs the
prophet's authority over the implied audience through the identification of
the divine source of this communication (Joel 1:1) and through the incomparability of the situation (Joel 1:2–3). The text portrays the locust infestation as being so grave that a response articulated by YHWH is appropriate.

---

58. J. Thompson, "The Use of Repetition in the Prophecy of Joel," in *On Language,
Culture and Religion* (ed. M. Black and W. Smalley; The Hague: Mouton, 1974) 106.

59. O. Sellers, "Stages of Locust in Joel," *AJSL* 52 (1935–36) 81–95.

60. See the detailed discussion of locust development in Simkins, *Yahweh's Activity*,
101–20. Thompson ("Joel's Locusts," 54) argues that the desert locust has six stages of
development instead of four.

61. Perelman and Olbrechts-Tyteca, *New Rhetoric*, 21. Perelman and Olbrechts-Tyteca
indicate that the rhetor's first duty is to reinforce a sense of shared understanding of the
situation between the speaker and the audience. Establishing the nature and scope of the
devastation in Joel 1:2–4 admirably performs this function.

62. Ibid., 158.

Thus, when the text begins to issue imperatives calling for a response, the authority that it has established over the implied audience should increase its persuasive potential.

Wolff helpfully characterizes the various imperative-led subunits as stages in an elaborate call to lament that contains three elements: (1) the call to lament, (2) a vocative describing who is to lament, and (3) clauses detailing the reasons for lament.[63] The first stage of the call is found in Joel 1:5–7. Joel 1:5 begins with a series of imperatives commanding drunkards and wine-drinkers to awake (הָקִיצוּ) and then to weep (וּבְכוּ) and wail (וְהֵילִלוּ). The proximity of multiple imperatives adds emphasis, with command following command in a staccato rhythm.[64]

The content of the imperatives reveals the rhetorical strategy of this verse. Beginning with an appeal for the drunkards and wine-drinkers to awaken and lament might appear to be a rather unlikely strategy, but it is appropriate in two ways. First, the drunkards or wine-drinkers are the individuals who are most affected by the lack of wine mentioned in the latter half of Joel 1:5 and the destruction of the vine in 1:7.[65] There may be a further cultic connection in this appeal, given that the lack of wine renders it impossible to engage in cultic celebrations properly, thus strengthening the reason to lament since what should be a joyous celebration will lack the fruit of the harvest.[66] Second, the use of the imperative הָקִיצוּ 'awake' pushes the idea of drunkenness into the metaphorical realm, where it denotes inability to comprehend the situation.[67] Although הָקִיצוּ typically refers to waking from sleep (1 Sam 26:12; Isa 29:8; Pss 3:6; 7:20), it also appears in Prov 23:25, where it denotes waking from a drunken stupor.[68]

One might ask if using derisive terminology to address a subset of the implied audience is a commendable rhetorical strategy. This approach,

---

63. Wolff, *Joel and Amos*, 21–22.

64. Prinsloo, *Theology*, 16.

65. Simkins, *Yahweh's Activity*, 125.

66. K. Nash, *The Palestinian Agricultural Year and the Book of Joel* (Ph.D. diss., Catholic University of America, 1989) 84. Kapelrud tries to connect the calls for weeping and wailing to the mourning rites of the Tammuz/Baal fertility cult (Kapelrud, *Joel Studies*, 17–30). Others, however, note the ubiquity of calls to weep and wail in many contexts surrounding death, suggesting that Kapelrud's interpretation is unnecessary (Crenshaw, *Joel*, 94; Dillard, "Joel," 258).

67. Stuart, *Hosea–Jonah*, 242. In this case, it is also possible that the text is not referring to a specific subset within the community but is, rather, classifying the entire audience as those who refuse to comprehend the situation. Jemielity adopts this perspective when he refers to Joel's audience as "indolent, lolling drunken elders" (T. Jemielity, *Satire in the Hebrew Prophets* [Louisville: Westminster John Knox, 1992] 89). The difficulty with this universal extension of "drunkards" is that the following verses refer to specific subsets within the community including agriculturalists and priests. Consequently, the exact identification of the "drunkards" remains ambiguous, but its rhetorical effect lies in its shock value of commencing the prophetic call to response with an apparently pejorative term.

68. Dillard, "Joel," 258.

however, effectively combines punitive and persuasive elements of prophetic speech. Ridiculing drunkards reinforces the necessity for the majority of the implied audience to insist that they are not part of that category and may increase the likelihood that they will respond as the prophet requires in order to avoid this demeaning classification.[69] Consequently, calling for drunkards and wine-drinkers to awake is appropriate and even necessary for the audience to come to grips with the gravity of the situation. Once the prophet goads these drunkards and wine-drinkers to "awaken," the calls to weep and wail provide the appropriate response to the situation.

Following the triad of imperatives, the latter half of Joel 1:5 explores the reasons for lamentation. The text commands the drunkards and wine-drinkers to weep and wail עַל־עָסִיס 'on account of the sweet-wine', which is probably a beverage that is slightly less fermented, though still potentially intoxicating (Isa 49:26). The final clause of Joel 1:5 indicates that this beverage has been נִכְרַת 'cut off' from those who desire it on account of the activities of the locusts. The object of this verb is מִפִּיכֶם 'from your mouths', and the antecedent of the object suffix relates to the imperatives that began this verse. The text commands the drunkards and wine-drinkers to lament since the locust infestation is going to affect them directly. They must emerge from drunkenness and note what is metaphorically occurring right in front of their faces.

Joel 1:6–7 provides a more detailed picture of the need for lament by going into greater depth concerning the nature of the destruction. The first clause of Joel 1:6 personifies the locusts as an invading nation attacking Yhwh's chosen land.[70] The first-person pronominal suffix on אַרְצִי 'my land' is somewhat confusing considering that this unit also refers to Yhwh in the third person (Joel 1:9, 14–15), but referring to Yhwh in the first person identifies Yhwh with the implied audience as targets of the locust infestation.[71] This brief snippet of divine speech reminds the drunkards that Yhwh also suffers loss because of the locusts' depredations, a reminder that reinforces the relationship between Yhwh and this facet of the implied audience. The locusts have cut off the wine from its drinkers and, in doing so, they wreak havoc on the land that Yhwh claims.

---

69. Jemielity, *Satire*, 81. Jemielity does excellent work in demonstrating how punitive and persuasive strategies can coexist in prophetic literature, linking it to the *pathos* of the prophet. He claims, "Satire and prophecy thus seek and despair of reform at the same time, urge change and yet expect none." The intermingling of motives and expectations demonstrates that, while the prophet may employ a derisive term to describe part of the implied audience, the prophetic intent is still to persuade this group to follow the prophet's program.

70. See the discussion in the "Rhetorical Situation" section above concerning the metaphorical use of "nation" in this verse.

71. Crenshaw, *Joel*, 96.

The remainder of Joel 1:6 focuses on heightening the locusts' destructive potential. Not only are the locusts a גּוֹי 'nation', they are a nation that is עָצוּם וְאֵין מִסְפָּר 'mighty and without number'. The verse next compares their power and might to the devouring teeth and jaws of a lion and lioness, emphasizing the ferocity with which locusts devour crops. These two images poetically describe the two most distinctive features of locust infestations: vast numbers and voracious appetite.[72]

Joel 1:7 moves from describing the locusts to detailing the actual results of their assault on the land.[73] In doing this, the prophet also again invokes YHWH's claim to the land through first person suffixes on גַּפְנִי 'my vine' and תְאֵנָתִי 'my fig tree'. In combination with the reference to אַרְצִי 'my land' in Joel 1:6, these suffixes suggest that YHWH remains connected to the people and the land, which suggests that YHWH will respond if the audience adopts the prophet's call to lament.[74] Around the first-person suffixes, Joel 1:7 paints a vivid picture of the savagery of the locusts' attack.

The choice of vine and fig tree is significant since an abundance of these two crops often symbolizes security and prosperity (1 Kgs 5:5; 2 Kgs 18:3; Mic 4:4; Zech 3:10). Consequently, the destruction of the vines and fig trees points to catastrophic circumstances.[75] Joel 1:7 emphasizes the destruction through the paranomastic construction חָשֹׂף חֲשָׂפָהּ 'fully stripped bare', which describes removing bark from the branches.[76] The bare branches are then the subject of the verb הִלְבִּינוּ 'turn white', which indicates that they are bleached by the sun as a final sign of their death. Thus, the first call to lament in Joel 1:5–7 builds the implied audience as it commands the attention of those who may be oblivious to the situation. It then employs vivid imagery to emphasize the severity of this locust infestation while offering subtle reminders of YHWH's continued presence in the land.

Joel 1:8–10: Call to Lament II

The next call to lament is found in Joel 1:8–10. The feminine-singular imperative אֱלִי 'wail!' introduces this next call to lament. The referent of this verb is not immediately apparent, although it does agree in gender with the call for the community to mourn in the manner of a בְּתוּלָה 'young

---

72. Simkins, *Yahweh's Activity*, 129. Simkins points to contemporary examples that show that locust swarms can have upwards of a billion members and can consume vast quantities of grain in a very short period.

73. Van der Merwe and Wendland, "Word Order," 118.

74. Prinsloo, *Theology*, 17.

75. Crenshaw, *Joel*, 87. Wendland argues for an underlying irony that becomes visible to the reader when the text reverses these images of supposed blessing; cf. Wendland, *Prophetic Rhetoric*, 251.

76. B. Waltke and M. O'Connor, *An Introduction to Biblical Hebrew Syntax* (Winona Lake, IN: Eisenbrauns, 1990) 584. Waltke and O'Connor refer to this construction as an "intensifying infinitive." See also Muraoka on the emphatic sense of the paranomastic infinitive absolute. He asserts that this grammatical structure guides the reader to give special attention to the verbal idea (Muraoka, *Emphatic*, 87–92).

woman/virgin' who has lost her betrothed. This proximity suggests that the simile affects the gender of the imperative. The lack of specific vocative addressee to the imperative verb is unique in Joel 1:5–14, although it is possible to argue that a likely referent is Jerusalem itself, personified in female form (Isa 51:7; 52:1; Jer 4:14; 6:8; Zeph 3:14).[77] The potential invocation of Jerusalem in Joel 1:8 prefigures the text's transition to the temple as the location of mourning in the following verse.

Following the imperative call to lament, Joel 1:8 employs the simile of a virgin mourning the loss of her husband to express the manner in which the implied audience should lament. This simile creates an evocative image of distress through reversed anticipation as the command to חִגְרִי-שָׂק 'put on sackcloth' cruelly replaces the prospect of marriage and entry into a new family unit.[78] The image of widowhood is devastating since being a widow threatened a woman's standard role in society as one who bore and reared children for the advancement of the family unit (Gen 30:1; 1 Sam 2:5; Pss 127:3–5; 128:3–4).[79] The loss of a husband left a woman facing an uncertain future, unable to guarantee social or economy stability.

After opening with the call to wail in this manner, Joel 1:9 begins to articulate the reasons for lament. On account of the devastation of the landscape, the tithe of the nation's crop of drink and grain offerings is no longer being offered to YHWH. Consequently, the temple and the priests who depend on those offerings are cut off from their primary source of sustenance (cf. Lev 27:30–33; Num 18:12; Deut 14:22–29; 18:1–8; 26:1–15).[80] Further, the cessation of these offerings indicates that the means of sacrificial communion with YHWH has come to a standstill, which is a frightening prospect.[81]

---

77. Dillard, "Joel," 261; Simkins, *Yahweh's Activity*, 131–35. Wolff attempts to deal with the lack of referent by proposing an elaborate textual reconstruction in which he places 1:9b in front of 1:8 in order to specify that the priests are the ones commanded to wail; Wolff, *Joel and Amos*, 18. However, his construction is unnecessary since the text is still eminently readable as it occurs in the Masoretic Text.

78. Crenshaw, *Joel*, 98.

79. L. Perdue et al., *Families in Ancient Israel* (Louisville: Westminster John Knox, 1997) 181–82. Perdue aptly summarizes the social and economic threat that Joel 1:8 borrows, stating, "Divorce and widowhood before any children were born were especially threatening to women, if they did not later remarry . . . Pragmatically speaking, the mother produced the children who would provide the labour and the heirs for the household's (and her) survival." The potential for remarriage is not an issue that this verse intends to address. Its focus is to transpose the devastation of widowhood into the situation of the locust infestation.

80. Sweeney, *Twelve*, 158. Sweeney notes that, since the priests and Levites could not hold land of their own, the cessation of sacrifices would quickly have a deleterious effect on their level of sustenance.

81. Prinsloo, *Theology*, 20. Prinsloo here emphasizes the continuity between the cultic and agricultural realms, noting that serving YHWH and gathering crops cannot be placed in separate compartments.

This subunit concludes in Joel 1:10 with five agricultural images that emphasize the scope of the destruction. Alliteration and concatenation characterize this verse because each of the five descriptions contains only two words. Each of the five images begins with an affix verb describing destruction or lament, followed by its subject. Only the explanatory particle כִּי between the second and third sequence interrupts the hammering rhythm of this verse. The structure of these short, staccato phrases helps to paint a thorough picture of the devastation wrought by the locust infestation.

The content of the images also emphasizes the gravity of the situation. The first two images, שֻׁדַּד שָׂדֶה אָבְלָה אֲדָמָה 'the field withers, the ground mourns', are woven together through the use of similar words and sounds.[82] The first image is passive, with the unmentioned agency of the locusts destroying the fields, while the second image is active, with the earth mourning in response. There is an interweaving of human and natural responses to the destruction, since the text employs the same verb of mourning in Joel 1:9 to describe the response of the priests.[83] Invoking the natural realm alongside its human inhabitants demonstrates the overwhelming nature of the devastation; nothing living, whether human, animal, or agricultural product, can escape the scope of the disaster. The final three images then detail the specifics of the destruction that has caused the earth to mourn. Following the כִּי, the text describes the devastation of דָּגָן 'grain', תִּירוֹשׁ 'new wine', and יִצְהָר 'oil'. These three crops represent the three primary types of agricultural produce in ancient Israel, and their inclusion here articulates the totality of the destruction and reinforces that the people cannot offer appropriate sacrifices to Yhwh because sacrifices would require these crops.[84]

---

82. Crenshaw, *Joel*, 99. Mallon attaches critical significance to the use of aural repetition here and argues for the existence of a subunit that stretches from Joel 1:10–12 based on shared agricultural imagery and grammatical structure (E. Mallon, "A Stylistic Analysis of Joel 1:10–12," *CBQ* 45 [1983] 541). While the images of agricultural products certainly occur in these three verses, this theory of textual division ignores the governing role that imperatives play throughout Joel 1:5–14.

83. K. Hayes, *The Earth Mourns: Prophetic Metaphor and Oral Aesthetic* (SBLAB 8; Leiden: Brill, 2002) 192. There is some discussion over whether there is a second root אָבַל with the meaning 'to dry up' related to an Akkadian cognate *abālu* when this verb has a nonhuman subject. There are several passages (Jer 12:4; 23:10; Joel 1:10; Amos 1:2) where אָבַל occurs in proximity or parallelism to the verb יָבֵשׁ 'to wither'. Clines, however, points to texts where the nonhuman subject is clearly portrayed as mourning (Isa 3:26; Jer 12:10–11; Lam 1:4; 2:8), which weakens the case for positing a separate root (D. Clines, "Was There a *'bl* II 'be dry' in Classical Hebrew?" *VT* 42 [1992] 1–11). Instead, it is better to conclude that the primary meaning, 'to mourn', encompasses the sense of 'drying up', as an activity that the earth performs amidst dire circumstances (K. Hayes, "When None Repents, Earth Laments: The Chorus of Lament in Jeremiah and Joel," in *Seeking the Favor of God*, vol. 1: *The Origins of Penitential Prayer in Second Temple Judaism* [SBLEJL 21; ed. M. Boda, D. Falk, and R. Werline; Atlanta: Society of Biblical Literature, 2006] 128).

84. Dillard, "Joel," 262.

Joel 1:11–12: Call to Lament III

The third call to lament in this section appears in Joel 1:11–12. Again, the text shifts focus to a different segment of the implied audience that it identified in Joel 1:2. It is now the אִכָּרִים 'farmers' and כֹּרְמִים 'vine growers' whom the text calls to lament on account of the loss of their crop. In this section, the text expands the range of the destruction that has come upon the land. Joel 1:11 lists a series of both cereal and fruit crops that the locust invasion has destroyed. Specifically, the text mentions grain and barley, along with the previously mentioned vines and fig trees. Joel 1:12 expands on the list and adds other fruit crops, including the pomegranate, date palm, and apple trees. Joel 1:11–12 may reflect the progression of a year of agricultural failure based on the times when the crops should have been harvested, moving from the period of winter rains to the summer harvest and climaxing around the time of the celebration of Sukkot.[85] By referring to crops from different stages of the agricultural cycle, these examples indicate the all-encompassing nature of the devastation.

Lexeme repetition and an elaborate wordplay further characterize the rhetorical strategy of these verses. Joel 1:11 begins with an imperative from the root בּוּשׁ 'to be ashamed', while the first two lines of 1:12 contain affix forms of a root that is similar in appearance (יָבֵשׁ 'to dry up'). Joel 1:12 then concludes with an affix form of the root יָבֵשׁ.[86] The meanings of these two roots fuse together in the final line of Joel 1:12, כִּי־הֹבִישׁ שָׂשׂוֹן 'indeed rejoicing dries up'. This connects the ideas of shame and withering with the cessation of expressions of joy that should emerge from the community in its celebration of the cult.[87]

The joy mentioned in Joel 1:12 probably has cultic connotations. The cessation of these sacrifices indicates that the community cannot properly engage in required festivals to celebrate the collection of a bountiful harvest. Essentially, the withering of agricultural produce leads to shame because of the community's seeming inability to offer the necessary sacrifices to YHWH.[88] The similarity of the two roots is another facet of how the text

---

85. Nash, "Palestinian," 68.

86. The previous call to lament foreshadows this dual root rhetorical strategy when it also employs a verbal form of שׁ יָבֵ (דָּגָן הוֹבִישׁ) in Joel 1:10.

87. Prinsloo, *Theology*, 20.

88. Simkins, *Yahweh's Activity*, 144–45. Frankfort puts forward a somewhat contrarian argument, claiming that the final clause of Joel 1:12 (כִּי־הֹבִישׁ שָׂשׂוֹן מִן־בְּנֵי אָדָם) indicates that the previously mentioned fruit trees wither because "joy" has departed from those who should be tending the trees. Frankfort roots this argument in the scarcity of fruit-bearing trees in Israel and the necessity for almost daily solicitous care; if depression over the locusts' destruction of the grain crops afflicts those who take care of the trees, then the trees will suffer (T. Frankfort, "Le כִּי de Joël 1:12," *VT* 10 (1960) 445–48. This argument, however, seems to overread the evidence of Joel 1:11–12. Images of the devastation wrought by the locusts and the subsequent threat of drought (developed in Joel 1:15–20) are more than sufficient to explain the loss of fruit trees.

draws together the natural and human realms since both realms lament what they have lost.[89] Consequently, Joel 1:11–12 effectively persuades another element of the community to enter into mourning while stressing the pervasive nature of the destruction on both human and natural realms.

Joel 1:13–14: Call to Lament IV

The final subunit of Joel 1:1–14 again shifts the context of the call to lament. It moves from the agricultural world to the world of cultic ritual in Joel 1:13–14. The text employs three imperatives from the realm of lament in the first half of 1:13, in which the prophet explicitly calls for the religious leaders of the people to cry out (חִגְרוּ וְסִפְדוּ הַכֹּהֲנִים הֵילִילוּ מְשָׁרְתֵי מִזְבֵּחַ). The first command is חִגְרוּ 'gird on', which is missing its object. The subsequent imperatives that call for mourning activities and the presence of sackcloth in Joel 1:13b suggest that חִגְרוּ calls the priests to put on their own mourning garb. This command may reflect the gravity of the situation since often priests were not permitted to mourn for the dead without compromising their ritual purity (Lev 10:4–7; 21:10–12).[90]

The following two imperatives (וְסִפְדוּ 'lament'; הֵילִילוּ 'wail') are synonymous, and they indicate that the prophet is calling for audible sounds of lament. The objects of these imperatives explicitly identify cultic personnel. Joel 1:13 sets the common word הַכֹּהֲנִים 'priests' in parallel with the unique phrase מְשָׁרְתֵי מִזְבֵּחַ 'ministers of the altar'. This phrase echoes similar titles in Joel 1:9, which calls on the מְשָׁרְתֵי יְהוָה 'ministers of YHWH', and Joel 1:13b, which appeals to the מְשָׁרְתֵי אֱלֹהָי 'ministers of my God'. The mention of the altar in this phrase has the effect of reinforcing the declarations of the previous verses concerning the cessation of sacrifices; the priests who minister at the altar have nothing to offer to YHWH.

Joel 1:13b draws a parallel to 1:8 since the text commands the priests to don the same garb of mourning as the young woman. This verse commands the priests to spend the night in sackcloth in the temple, emphasizing the gravity of a situation that requires continual lament (cf. 2 Sam 12:16; 1 Kgs 21:27).[91] The text again describes the situation as so grave that there is a cessation of the מִנְחָה וָנָסֶךְ 'grain and drink offering'.[92] This phrase

---

89. Hayes, *The Earth Mourns*, 194. See the discussion of Joel 1:8–10.

90. Sweeney, *Twelve*, 159–60.

91. Crenshaw, *Joel*, 103; Barton, *Joel*, 55. Crenshaw suggests that this command is for the priests to keep a ceaseless vigil at the temple, voicing their lamentation. In contrast, Barton proposes that it simply means that the priests are not to take off their sackcloth garments while the need for lamentation continues. In either case, the essential point is that the call to spend the night in lamentation reflects the severity of the situation and the necessity for the priests to commit themselves fully to the response that the prophet proposes.

92. Hurowitz identifies an interesting parallel to the devastation that the locusts create in an Assyrian hymn to the goddess Nanaya that is attributed to Sargon II. Notably, the hymn also describes the cessation of sacrifices on account of the locusts' activity. Hurowitz does not claim that Joel depends on the Assyrian text, but he does posit the potential

is found at the end of Joel 1:13, well removed from the verb נִמְנַע 'withheld' for which it is the subject.[93] Consequently, this separation marks the מִנְחָה וָנֶסֶךְ for constituent focus, which is especially appropriate given that the greatest crisis facing the religious leaders was the inability to sacrifice correctly.[94] Besides the cessation of sacrifice, commanding the religious leaders to don sackcloth emphasizes the gravity of the situation: it is a powerful symbol of the failure of proper cultic ritual for them to set aside their usual garments of service and dress symbolically to lead the community into mourning.[95]

Joel 1:14 pushes forward the calls to lament by trying to evoke a response from the implied audience to the devastation of the situation. Joel 1:14 articulates a plan of action that calls for the priests to sanctify a fast and call a sacred assembly that encompasses the entire community. Fasting is a standard element of both private and communal cultic expressions; thus, it is typically associated with other cultic terms to give it context.[96] In this case, Joel links the call to fast with the noun עֲצָרָה 'solemn assembly', which refers to ritual observance in general terms that gain specificity from the surrounding context.[97]

The unifying element in these calls to response is that the command to call a sacred assembly requires a cessation of all normal activity to concentrate on the cultic observance (Lev 23:36; Num 29:35; Deut 16:8; Neh

---

existence of a body of shared liturgical literature that could be employed in the wake of locust infestations (V. Hurowitz, "Joel's Locust Plague in Light of Sargon II's Hymn to Nanaya," *JBL* 112 [1993] 597–603).

93. Some see a contrast between the claim that sacrifices are 'withheld' (נִמְנַע) in Joel 1:13 and the declaration that they are 'cut off' (הָכְרַת) in Joel 1:9. Simkins suggests that there is a volitional aspect here, given that the community refuses to part with the meager provisions that have escaped the locusts (Simkins, *Yahweh's Activity*, 145). In contrast, Barton suggests that the implied subject of the verb is Yhwh, a construction that would mirror 1:9 (Barton, *Joel*, 55). The verb נִמְנַע is in the Niphal, which helps to render its subject ambiguous. The root מָנַע appears in the Niphal in three other locations (Num 22:16; Job 38:15; Jer 3:3). The Jeremianic reference is interesting since it refers to withholding rain in the wake of Judah's iniquity. Although no subject is identified, the context seems to indicate that Yhwh is the one doing the withholding. In Joel 1:13, the context reflects the cessation of sacrifice as a result of the ravages of the locusts. Consequently, it makes the most sense to attribute the "withholding" of sacrifices to the situation that the community faces. It is not necessary to import a sense of reluctance to offer sacrifice to capture the gravity of the situation.

94. Van der Merwe and Wendland, "Word Order," 120.

95. Sweeney, *Twelve*, 159.

96. H. Preuss, "צום," *TDOT* 12:298.

97. D. Wright and J. Milgrom, "עצר," *TDOT* 11:314; M. Haran, *Temples and Temple-Service in Ancient Israel: An Inquiry into the Character of Cult Phenomena and the Historical Setting of the Priestly School* (Oxford: Clarendon, 1978) 296–97 (repr. Winona Lake, IN: Eisenbrauns, 1995). References to a "sacred assembly" range from prophetic condemnation of Israel's religious festivals in general (Isa 1:13) to non-Yahwistic cultic gatherings (2 Kgs 10:20). These "sacred assemblies" seem to imply communal convocations, which may refer to established gatherings (see Lev 23:36 and the Feast of Booths) but also can refer to the apparently ad hoc gatherings that Joel commands (cf. Joel 1:14, 2:15).

8:18).[98] Joel's command to call an עֲצָרָה thus calls the implied audience to focus its activities and attentions on appealing to Yhwh. Interestingly, Joel's call for a sacred assembly contrasts with other prophetic perspectives, especially in Amos 5:21 and Isa 1:13.[99] Those passages castigate the ritualized nature of sacred assemblies when they are not performed in the correct spirit. In contrast, Joel 1:14 requires sacred assemblies as the proper means of response to a crisis that threatens continued cultic functions.

This verse describes the recipients of these commands by using the same merismus of זְקֵנִים 'elders' and יֹשְׁבֵי הָאָרֶץ 'dwellers of the land' that it used in calling them to hear the prophetic message in Joel 1:2. Essentially, the text has come full circle, with all of those whom it summoned to hear now being implored to respond as the text commands. There is a strong element of irony at work here in the call to fast since Joel 1:11–12 claims that the lack of agricultural produce is so severe that it ends cultic offerings at the temple. The community and the temple are engaged in fasting whether they wish to or not, but the text adds another layer to this description of want in order to create a call for cultic sanctification of the people's hunger.[100]

Joel 1:14 spells out explicitly the purpose of this assembly in the final clause of the verse with the imperative clause וְזַעֲקוּ אֶל־יְהוָה 'and cry out to Yhwh'. This final imperative is "the emotive climax" and "the thematic peak" of Joel 1:1–14 since all of the devastation mentioned in these verses leads to only one possible response, which the prophet requires: crying out to Yhwh for relief.[101] The calls to fasting and sacred assembly provide the context for crying out to Yhwh since they emphasize the communal nature of the cry.[102] Essentially, this final call to lament sets the tone for the appropriate response. It commands the community to go to the house of Yhwh and submit itself to the cultic guidance of the priests, hoping that their lament cries can elicit a response from Yhwh.

Overall, Joel 1:5–14 provides a series of calls to lament in the wake of the announcement of the locust invasion and the commands to preserve the memory of this event throughout the following generations. Each of these calls draws in a different subset of the implied audience and provides them with reasons to lament. Joel 1:14 then draws together all of these different groups since it addresses the priests but calls on them to lead the elders and inhabitants of the land in crying out to Yhwh. One can detect a strategic parallel between Joel 1:4 and 1:5–14 since both rely on "cumulative

---

98. Sweeney, *Twelve*, 160.

99. Coggins, *Joel*, 32–33.

100. Linville, "Day of Yahweh," 107. Linville notes how the sanctification of the community's hunger returns it to ritual space and time, where it becomes a symbol of communion, rather than a sign of devastation and destruction.

101. Van der Merwe and Wendland, "Word Order," 120.

102. J. Muddiman, "Fast, Fasting," *ABD* 2:773. Muddiman notes that fasting can be conjoined with supplicatory prayer to emphasize the commitment to seeking divine response (Ps 35:13; 1 Kgs 21:27).

overkill."[103] The multiple waves of locusts and the variations in the calls to lament emphasize repeatedly the severity of the situation that the implied audience faces. It also begins to establish the necessity of responding in the manner that the text directs.

Summary

Joel 1:1–14 employs a broad range of rhetorical strategies in order to heighten the impact of the message and to urge the audience to respond. The text introduces the prophet in Joel 1:1 as one who communicates the word of Yhwh. Then, Joel 1:2–14 exhorts the implied audience through the regular use of imperatives, calling on different elements of the community to respond. The text first calls the entire community to listen before detailing the locust infestation that has afflicted the land. It then calls upon those most affected within the community to lament, beginning with the drunkards or wine-drinkers, who desperately need to realize the gravity of the situation. It then addresses the agriculturalists, whose livelihoods are threatened. After this, the text calls out to the priests and charges them with leading the community in lament to Yhwh in spite of the fact that the regular cultic communion with Yhwh has ceased in the wake of the locusts' devastation. The final imperative encapsulates the only possible response; under priestly leadership, the implied audience must cry out to Yhwh.

Rhetorical Effectiveness

The final step of the rhetorical-critical model is an investigation of the unit's rhetorical effectiveness. As chap. 1 articulates above, I will consider the rhetorical effectiveness of the text in view of its audiences, noting particularly the text's implied audience and the idea of a universal audience. The root of the text's rhetorical strategy is to take the image-world of a locust infestation and link this natural disaster with the workings of the divine world. This approach could persuade the text's implied audience since an ancient Judahite context would not maintain rigid barriers between the natural and the cosmological worlds. Simkins argues that "Yahweh acts in the totality of the natural world in order to achieve his purposes in the history of creation."[104] Simkins's observations reveal the potential effectiveness of the text's approach. Essentially, the persuasive potential of Joel 1:1–14 hinges on the text's ability to link images drawn from the realm of natural catastrophes to the working of Yhwh in the world.

Identifying the connection between events in the natural world and Yhwh's own actions reveals the rhetorical effectiveness of Joel 1:1–14. The call in Joel 1:14b to cry out to Yhwh fits this world view (cf. Joel 1:19),

---

103. Linville, "Bugs," 294. The declaration that four waves of locusts overwhelmed the land and the repeated appeals for every social group in the community to enter into lament make evident the text's fixation on the gravity of the situation it describes.

104. Simkins, "God, History and the Natural World," 436.

guiding the implied audience to seek divine causality for its current circumstances, even though the events are rooted in natural phenomena. In doing so, the implied audience ought to follow the prophet's repeated exhortations to lament and cry out to YHWH in the midst of these circumstances.

Another facet of rhetorical effectiveness involves reflecting on the understanding of Patrick and Scult concerning the appropriate stances that interpreters can take, discussed in detail in chap. 1 above on methodology. They argue that, from the perspective of a "hermeneutics of affirmation," interpreters can receive truth from the text since they acknowledge the possibility that it could be true.[105] This permits them to construct a picture of the audience that is both specific to the situation and also interested in the universal nature of a text's truth-claims.[106]

Adopting Patrick and Scult's hermeneutics of affirmation, we find that this passage paints a powerful picture of destruction and devastation for its implied audience. It binds the activity of the natural world to the activity of YHWH and demonstrates that YHWH does act discernibly in the broader world. YHWH's power is visible in destructive occurrences in the natural realm as he demonstrates his power and authority over nature. It is also significant to note that the prophet's call in this situation is for the community to attempt to return to YHWH and to go to YHWH's house in order to cry out, even though the regular form of communication through daily sacrifice is no longer operational. In spite of the seeming distance between YHWH and the implied audience, the prophet urges the community to gather in the place of YHWH's presence and speak the lament that is on its lips.

The rhetorical effectiveness of this realization is also significant to a universal audience, who affirms the possibility that this text can communicate truth. It reveals that there is space for protest and lament within the confines of worship of YHWH.[107] The fact that the prophet calls the people to lament in response to his depiction of the natural world as presaging the coming day of YHWH suggests that YHWH is interactive and might hear and respond to these cries of lament. Although YHWH's response does not appear in this rhetorical unit, later parts of the book bear witness to the validity of crying out in this manner.

Rhetorical effectiveness thus functions on two levels. First, it requires a consideration of the ability of the given text to persuade its implied audience in the suggested rhetorical situation to adopt its point of view. Secondly, rhetorical effectiveness can also address the ability of the text to

---

105. D. Patrick and A. Scult, *Rhetoric and Biblical Interpretation* (JSOTSup 92; Sheffield: Almond, 1990) 77.

106. Ibid., 79.

107. Ibid., 204. Brueggemann also notably develops the idea of speaking back to a sometimes-silent YHWH in the context of lament (W. Brueggemann, *Theology of the Old Testament: Testimony, Dispute, Advocacy* [Minneapolis: Fortress, 1987] 333–72).

affect a universal audience who grants the premise that the text can contain truth that speaks across audiences and contexts. In the case of Joel 1:1–14, the repeated calls to lament reflect its intention to gather all elements of the implied audience and persuade them to listen and adopt the text's perspective of the climactic events that it describes. On the level of the universal audience, Joel 1:1–14 demonstrates that Yhwh acts in the natural world and that appealing to Yhwh even in times of weakening worship is still the most appropriate course of action.

Conclusion

Joel 1:1–14 provides an excellent point of departure for studying the persuasive potential of the entire book. Although there are other proposals, delineateing Joel 1:1–14 as the first rhetorical unit for study is the best interpretation of the text's structure and content. This unit establishes the threat to the community's continued existence through the exigence of locust infestation and ensuing agricultural disasters. It identifies its implied audience both generally through the merismus in Joel 1:2 and by highlighting subsections through the various imperatives found in Joel 1:5–14. This unit's rhetorical strategy is deliberative in genre, using imperatives to persuade its implied audience to note the scope of the disaster and to respond in lament. Notably, the rhetorical strategy of this unit brings its audience under the aegis of the priests, who are to lead the community in lament and fasting, crying out to Yhwh for restoration. The text demonstrates its effectiveness by establishing that divine action affects the natural world and also by guiding Joel 1:1–14 to a climactic conclusion when the prophet implores the implied audience to beseech Yhwh, hoping for divine intervention.

Chapter 3

"To You, O Yhwh, I Cry":
Rhetorical Analysis of Joel 1:15–20

Introduction

Joel 1:15–20 moves away from the repeated appeals for the implied audience to gather and cry out to Yhwh. Instead, these verses provide actual lament speech that reflects on the situation. Key to this transition in Joel 1:15–20 is the cessation of imperative verbs to the implied audience. Instead, the text brings together the perspectives of the prophet and the implied audience in the laments. These laments also function to communicate that what the implied audience is experiencing is nothing less than a harbinger of the day of Yhwh. This presents the implied audience with another reason to embrace the prophet's appeals and call out to Yhwh. The text concludes by appealing for divine response, indicating that Yhwh alone can ameliorate the situation.

Rhetorical Unit

Joel 1:15–20 opens with a powerful expression, אֲהָהּ לַיּוֹם 'Alas for the day', which sets the stage for the following verses. This exclamatory utterance is a sign of aperture, particularly since it shifts the tone of the discourse away from calling people to lament to beginning the process of crying out to Yhwh (cf. Hos 5:1; 8:1).[1] It also marks a shift in the perspective of the prophet, who now identifies with the implied audience and speaks in the first-person plural in Joel 1:16, describing how food is cut off from עֵינֵינוּ 'our eyes' and joy and gladness מִבֵּית אֱלֹהֵינוּ 'from the house of our God'. Thus, while Joel 1:15–20 continues to portray scenes of devastation, it changes its approach sufficiently to warrant separate consideration.

At the end of this rhetorical unit, Joel 1:19–20 contains two significant features that indicate closure. In Joel 1:19a, there is a shift in addressee when the prophet ceases calling the implied audience to lament over the devastation that has occurred. He now turns his cry to Yhwh and again describes the devastation using first-person language. In a study of boundary markers in prophetic discourse, Wendland argues that inserting a snippet of direct address has a dramatizing effect and demonstrates that the

---

1. Wendland helpfully demonstrates how exclamatory utterances and shifts in the type of discourse mark the aperture of a rhetorical unit (E. Wendland, *The Discourse Analysis of Hebrew Prophetic Literature* [MBPS 40; Lewiston, NY: Edwin Mellen, 1995] 38–41).

rhetorical unit has reached a peak (Hos 2:1; 8:2; 14:3).[2] The prophet's cry to Yhwh is a signal that the rhetorical unit is closing, having reached the peak of its appeal with this interjection of the prophet's own voice.

Second, following the cry to Yhwh, the next clause in Joel 1:19 and the final clause of Joel 1:20 are almost identical (Joel 1:19b reads כִּי אֵשׁ אָכְלָה נְאוֹת מִדְבָּר 'for fire consumes the pastures of a wilderness'). This phrase differs from Joel 1:20 only by placing a definite article in front of מִדְבָּר. This is an example of epiphora, a literary device that uses the repetition of key words or phrases to signal the end of a text unit.[3] Buttressing this identification of epiphora is the evidence that it probable recurs to conclude other discourse units, most notably Joel 2:26–27 (cf. Hos 1:9; 2:25).[4] Thus, the repeated clause and the first-person interjection of the prophet indicate that this rhetorical unit closes at Joel 1:20.

Rhetorical Situation

The rhetorical situation of Joel 1:15–20 changes slightly from that portrayed in Joel 1:1–14. In these verses, the text no longer concentrates on assembling the implied audience by appealing to its individual subgroups. Instead, the prophet strategically identifies himself with the implied audience of Joel 1:1–14, indicating that he is suffering alongside it.[5] This eventually culminates in the prophet's direct address to Yhwh in Joel 1:19–20, which draws Yhwh into the audience of this unit. Thus, the text fuses the prophet and the implied audience created by Joel 1:1–14 and reveals that the proper response for this audience is to implore Yhwh to act restoratively.

One key element of the rhetorical situation of Joel 1:15–20 is its introduction of the day of Yhwh.[6] The exclamatory utterance that the day of Yhwh is near adds a sense of urgency to the exigence of this rhetorical unit. Joel 1:15–20 begins to tie the devastation mentioned in 1:2–14 into the broader theological context of Yhwh's relationship with the implied audience. This relationship is in view because the announcement of the day of Yhwh targets those whom the text commands to assemble at the house of Yhwh and cry out to Yhwh. This heightens the exigence of the locust infestation and gives it another, more terrifying layer. The remainder of the book will develop the concept of the day of Yhwh in greater detail as it progresses.

Alongside the announcement of the day of Yhwh, the specter of a devastating drought also plays a part in creating the exigence of the rhetorical

---

2. Ibid., 54–55.

3. J. Thompson, "The Use of Repetition in the Prophecy of Joel," in *On Language, Culture and Religion* (ed. M. Black and W. Smalley; The Hague: Mouton, 1974) 107.

4. Wendland, *Discourse Analysis*, 50.

5. L. Allen, *The Books of Joel, Obadiah, Jonah and Micah* (NICOT; Grand Rapids: Eerdmans, 1976) 61.

6. I address the day of Yhwh to a greater extent in the discussion of the rhetorical strategy of Joel 1:15.

situation in Joel 1. Joel 1:17–20 makes reference to the withering of crops in significant detail by describing fields aflame and animals suffering from the lack of water. This may reflect a connection between the imagery of Joel 1:17–20 and the effects of a sirocco wind following a period without rain. Nash suggests that this combination could lower the water table to such an extent that it would be possible for fires to rage unchecked.[7] The images of drought and flame thus appear to reflect what would have been a conceivable situation for the implied audience.

I diverge from Nash in that she uses the drought imagery to try to establish the "world behind the text" and to suggest a time for Joel's oracles when a drought ravaged the land.[8] Her proposal is highly speculative, however, and what is of greater significance for the purposes of my study is the way that the image-world of drought contributes to the rhetorical situation of this prophetic communication. The images of drought build on the lengthy description of the locusts' ravaging the land in the previous rhetorical unit. This combination heightens the threat to the community's survival.[9] The earlier mentions of the locusts and the vivid images of drought in this rhetorical unit establish the exigence of an unfolding catastrophe that provides the motivation for the actions that the text proposes.

Rhetorical Strategy

Joel 1:15 begins with the cry אֲהָהּ 'Alas!' which is the standard particle used to indicate lament or mourning (Josh 7:7; 2 Kgs 3:10; 6:5; Jer 4:10; 14:13; Ezek 9:8; 11:13). This interjection is especially appropriate given the repeated commands in Joel 1:5–14 for the community to cry out to Yhwh. This cry breaks the sequence of imperatives that introduced the various lament calls in Joel 1:1–14 and begins to provide the content of the lament.[10] Joel 1:15–20 adds further detail to its description of the ruin of the land, emphasizing the lack of food and water for both human and animal.[11]

---

7. K. Nash, *The Palestinian Agricultural Year and the Book of Joel* (Ph.D. diss., Catholic University of America, 1989) 56.

8. Ibid., 59. Specifically, Nash suggests that the prophet uttered his oracles at the end of summer, just prior to the autumn rains; insufficient winter rains combined with a dry summer would create powerful drought conditions.

9. Simkins addresses the issue of whether locust and drought imagery are likely companions. He suggests that, while locusts require a certain amount of vegetation in order to support the growth of a swarm, the aftermath of a locust infestation could easily be thought to resemble that of a devastating drought, since the various plants and vines would be devoid of foliage. He posits that the locust invasion coincided with the coming of the hot, dry summer, which would have created a connection between the locust and drought imagery (R. Simkins, "God, History and the Natural World in the Book of Joel," *CBQ* 55 [1993] 441–42). While my study is less concerned with determining a specific time for these calamities, Simkins's theory does help to explain why the text may fuse locust and drought imagery in this chapter.

10. Wendland, *Discourse Analysis*, 42; idem, *Prophetic Rhetoric: Case Studies in Text Analysis and Translation* (Longwood, FL: Xulon, 2009) 18.

11. D. Ellul, "Introduction au livre de Joël," *ETR* 54 (1978) 428.

The lack of imperative verbs in this section distinguishes Joel 1:15–20 from Joel 1:1–14 and suggests a change in rhetorical genre. Joel 1:15–20 is primarily descriptive, detailing the state of the land and its inhabitants before issuing a first-person appeal to Yhwh in Joel 1:19–20. Probably the most appropriate way to classify the rhetorical genre of Joel 1:15–20 is to categorize it in the educational function of epideictic rhetoric. Perelman and Olbrechts-Tyteca see epideictic discourse as the means of strengthening adherence to an accepted set of beliefs and reinforcing a disposition to act.[12] In this case, Joel elaborates on the well-attested prophetic theme of day of Yhwh, providing the implied audience with a picture of its devastation. This leads to the prophet's own cry in Joel 1:19–20, which may provide a model that the implied audience ought to follow, especially in the wake of the direct command to cry out in Joel 1:14.

Joel 1:15–20 contains three short prayers (Joel 1:15–16, 17–18, 19–20): the first two are communal cries, in which the prophet joins the implied audience; the concluding prayer is an appeal from an individual, namely, the prophet.[13] These cries elaborate on the appeal to call out to Yhwh, providing the next step in persuading the implied audience to respond properly to the prophetic exhortations. Alongside the shift in verbal mood, these verses shift the image-world to drought and desiccation, no longer mentioning the locust infestation. The situation described in Joel 1:15–20 is, however, equally grave.

Joel 1:15–16: First Communal Cry

Joel 1:15 ties the disaster to the theologically rich concept of the day of Yhwh, a topic that continues to occasion much discussion about its origins, development, and meaning.[14] Joel is indisputably an important

---

12. C. Perelman and L. Olbrechts-Tyteca, *The New Rhetoric: A Treatise on Argumentation* (Notre Dame, IN: Notre Dame University Press, 1969) 54.

13. C. van der Merwe and E. Wendland, "Mark Word Order in the Book of Joel," *JNSL* 36 (2010) 120. See the first-person plural suffixes in Joel 1:16a (עֵינֵינוּ) and 1:16b (אֱלֹהֵינוּ) and the first-person singular verb in 1:19 (אֶקְרָא).

14. Most of the research related to the day of Yhwh focuses on tracing its origins and transmission in the traditions of the Old Testament. Mowinckel and von Rad offer the two most discussed views, with Mowinckel locating the day of Yhwh in a cultic enthronement festival, while von Rad proposes an original setting of holy war (S. Mowinckel, *He That Cometh* [trans. G. Anderson; Oxford: Blackwell, 1956] 130–45; G. von Rad, "The Origin of the Concept of the Day of Yahweh," *JSS* 4 [1959] 97–108). Other proposals interact with these foundations in different ways, with Černý questioning the existence of a cultic enthronement festival, and Cross attempting to find points of contact between Mowinckel and von Rad (L. Černý, *The Day of Yahweh and Some Relevant Problems* [Prague: Nákl. Filosofické fakulty Univ. Karlovy, 1948] 35–103; F. Cross, "The Divine Warrior in Israel's Early Cult," in *Biblical Motifs: Origins and Transformations* [ed. A. Altmann; Cambridge: Harvard University Press, 1966] 11–30). Stuart also emphasizes the militaristic nature of the day of Yhwh and connects it to ancient Near Eastern traditions that describe the victory of a sovereign over an enemy in a single day (D. Stuart, "The Sovereign's Day of Conquest," *BASOR* 221 [1976] 159–64). Fensham and Weiss criticize von Rad's assertion that holy war

resource for discussing the day of Yʜᴡʜ, given the frequency with which the exact phrase יוֹם יְהוָה 'day of Yʜᴡʜ' appears (Joel 1:15; 2:1, 11; 3:4; 4:14), while also using other expressions that probably invoke the day of Yʜᴡʜ (Joel 3:2; 4:1, 18).[15] Although it is beyond the purview of my study to delve deeply into questions of origin and development, the rhetorical purpose of invoking the realms of imagery related to the day of Yʜᴡʜ is worth considering.

The reasons for which prophetic literature invokes the day of Yʜᴡʜ are multifaceted, although they all relate to a time in which Yʜᴡʜ intervenes in human events.[16] Speaking about the Minor Prophets, Nogalski aptly notes that Yʜᴡʜ's intervention "does not fall neatly into a single, systematic

---

lies behind the day-of-Yʜᴡʜ tradition, with Fensham viewing it as a day of judgment, possibly with covenantal overtones, and Weiss arguing that the key point is the appearance of Yʜᴡʜ, who may act in a variety of fashions (C. Fensham, "A Possible Origin of the Concept of the Day of the Lord," in *Biblical Essays: Proceedings of the Ninth Meeting of die Ou-Testamentiese Werkgemeenskap in Sud-Afrika* [Bepeck: Potchefstroom Herald, 1966] 90–97; M. Weiss, "The Origin of 'The Day of the Lord,'" *HUCA* 37 [1966] 29–60). Another contribution to the discussion comes from Hoffman, who sees theophany as the guiding image behind the day of Yʜᴡʜ (Y. Hoffman, "The Day of the Lord as a Concept and a Term in Prophetic Literature," *ZAW* 93 [1981] 37–50). Everson advances the discussion by noting that the temporal orientation of the day of Yʜᴡʜ can vary, with certain passages pointing to past events (Lam 1:12; 2:22; Isa 22:1–14; Jer 46:2–20; Ezek 13:1–9) and the remainder looking toward a future day (J. Everson, "The Days of Yahweh," *JBL* 93 [1974] 329–37). The result of these studies is that there is no established consensus about the origin and transmission of the idea of the day of Yʜᴡʜ. These studies, however, do effectively convey the range of images invoked by this day. On the day of Yʜᴡʜ, Yʜᴡʜ appears, announces both judgment and salvation, and causes the cosmos to tremble in response. For additional consideration of the development of scholarship relating to the day of Yʜᴡʜ, see Boase's thoughtful and thorough summary (E. Boase, *The Fulfillment of Doom: The Dialogic Interaction between the Book of Lamentations and the Pre-exilic/Early Exilic Prophetic Literature* [LHB/OTS 437; New York: T. & T. Clark, 2006] 105–39).

15. Scholars usually refer to the repeated use of the exact phrase יוֹם יְהוָה in Joel when debating the range of what should be considered a "day-of-Yʜᴡʜ" text. The exact phrase occurs 15 times, 12 of which are in the Minor Prophets (Isa 13:6, 9; Ezek 13:5; Joel 1:15; 2:1, 11; 3:4; 4:14; Amos 5:18, 20; Obad 15; Zeph 1:7, 14 [2×]; Mal 3:23). Hoffman, most notably, seeks to restrict study of the day-of-Yʜᴡʜ motif to these passages, suggesting that interpreters should consider related phrases only as a secondary step (Hoffman, "Day of the Lord," 38). Weiss takes the opposite approach, arguing that related phrases invoke the same concept and should be considered. This has the potential of greatly expanding the pool of available texts (Weiss, "Day of the Lord," 64–65). Rendtorff and Nogalski continue this trend, while focusing specifically on the Minor Prophets, arguing that any text that refers to a day in which Yʜᴡʜ acts is worthy of consideration (R. Rendtorff, "How to Read the Book of the Twelve as a Theological Unity," in *Reading and Hearing the Book of the Twelve* [ed. J. Nogalski and M. Sweeney; SBLSymS 15; Atlanta: Society of Biblical Literature, 2000] 75–87). Nogalski explicitly includes the phrases בַּיּוֹם הַהוּא 'on that day' and בַּיָּמִים הָהֵמָּה 'in those days', which are found in Joel (J. Nogalski, "The Day[s] of Yʜᴡʜ in the Book of the Twelve," *SBL 1999: Seminar Papers* [SBLSP 38; Atlanta: Society of Biblical Literature, 1999] 619–21).

16. Ibid., 621. Nogalski captures the flexibility of the day of Yʜᴡʜ, suggesting that it can be "anticipated, recounted or interpreted."

view."[17] Instead, the day of Yhwh can serve purposes ranging from announcing Yhwh's judgment on Israel to promising Israel's restoration and enduring security. To communicate these messages, the day of Yhwh can employ
multiple motif complexes, including covenant, holy war, and theophany.[18]

The range of communicative purposes that the day of Yhwh can serve is
evident even within Joel. The text first uses it in the context of a locust infestation that sets off a cycle of liturgical laments among people in Judah/
Jerusalem that hopefully leads to divine restitution (Joel 1–2), while also
invoking the day of Yhwh as a time when Judah and Jerusalem stand aside,
allowing Yhwh their God to preserve their security and destroy the foreign
nations who threaten them (Joel 3–4).[19] Bourke concludes that the day of
Yhwh that targets Judah and Jerusalem in Joel 1–2 is a microcosm of the day
of Yhwh that affects foreign nations in Joel 3–4.[20] Other texts demonstrate
a similar creative range, with Zephaniah invoking the day of Yhwh to describe Yhwh's sovereignty, judgment, and salvation; and Obadiah using the
day of Yhwh to announce judgment, while making Judah the agent that
executes Yhwh's verdict.[21] I will continue to explore the effects of invoking
the day of Yhwh in conjunction with the specific passages where it occurs.

The rhetorical effect of employing the day of Yhwh in Joel 1:15 relates
to the tradition of announcing judgment against the people of Yhwh

---

17. J. Nogalski, "Recurring Themes in the Book of the Twelve: Creating Points of Contact for a Theological Reading," *Int* 61 (2007) 126. Nogalski categorizes the varied uses
of the day of Yhwh according to differences in target, time, and means. He effectively
develops the differences in target (Israel or foreign nations) and time (past, near future, or
distant future), while briefly mentioning some of the various means through which the
day of Yhwh is described.

18. K. Leung, *An Intertextual Study of the Motif-Complex Yom Yahweh in the Book of Joel*
(Ph.D. diss., Fuller Theological Seminary, 1987) 78–96. Leung finds examples of the covenant motif in the connection between the curses of Deut 28 and the calamities that afflict
the audience in Joel. The theophany motif is found in the cosmic upheaval that surrounds
the day-of-Yhwh descriptions in Joel 2, 3, and 4. Leung also draws in the holy-war motif in
her discussion of the day of Yhwh in Joel 2 and 4, arguing that these passages show Yhwh
appearing to engage in warlike activity. I do not agree with all of Leung's identifications of
motif complexes, but her work is significant for demonstrating the breadth of images that
the day of Yhwh can employ.

19. R. Rendtorff, "'Alas for the Day!' The 'Day of the Lord' in the Book of the Twelve,"
in *God in the Fray: A Tribute to Walter Brueggemann* (ed. T. Linafelt and T. Beal; Minneapolis:
Fortress, 1998) 19. See also J. Bourke, "Le jour de Yahvé dans Joël," *RB* 66 (1959) 5–6.

20. Ibid., 22. Bourke comments on the shared terminology between different uses of
the day of Yhwh in Joel and argues, "Il emploie systématiquement les mêmes termes selon
deux dimensions entièrement différentes."

21. G. King, "The Day of the Lord in Zephaniah," *BSac* 152 (1995) 16–32; S. Snyman,
"Yom (Yhwh) in the Book of Obadiah," in *Goldene Äpfel in silbernen Schalen: Papers from
the 13th Congress of the International Organization for the Study of the Old Testament* (ed.
K. Schunck and M. Augustin; Frankfurt am Main: Peter Lang, 1992) 81–91. Although the
exact phrase "day of the Lord" is only found in Zeph 1:7 and 14, King employs a methodology similar to Nogalski's and treats all of Zephaniah's references as a day in which Yhwh
acts. This brings out the full range of Zephaniah's understanding of Yhwh's intervention
in human affairs.

themselves (cf. Amos 5:18). The reference to the day of YHWH in Joel 1:15 also has a nearly exact parallel in Isa 13:6. Both verses stress the imminence of the day through the phrase כִּי קָרוֹב יוֹם יְהוָה 'for the day of YHWH is near'. They also employ phonological wordplay in the shared *šin-dalet* sounds found in the phrase כְּשֹׁד מִשַּׁדַּי יָבוֹא 'it will come like destruction from the Almighty', which highlights the power of that day.[22] One important difference between Isa 13:6 and Joel 1:15 is that the Isaianic passage targets Babylon while Joel 1:15 is directed at YHWH's own community. This demonstrates the adaptability of this concept to warn of YHWH's wrath toward any target.[23] Further, Isa 13:6 presents a picture of inescapable judgment surrounding the announcement that the day of YHWH is approaching, while the announcement in Joel 1:15 ties into later passages (specifically Joel 2:12–17) that appear to offer a way to avoid judgment.[24] Thus, while the image of the day of YHWH resonates across the prophetic canon, one must examine how individual texts nuance the motif.

Joel 1:15 declares that the day of YHWH will bring destruction through divine agency. Joel 1:15 views this day as a day that is coming, because it describes the day as קָרוֹב 'near'. Essentially, the situation described in these verses is a precursor to this coming day.[25] Joel only briefly introduces the day of YHWH in Joel 1:15, effectively foreshadowing further discussions of the motif. In later chapters, the text will elaborate and expand on its theophanic and cosmological ramifications.[26] Joel 1:15 makes it clear, however, that the day of YHWH is a day of woe for the community of YHWH.[27] The land has experienced a terrible locust plague, and the text wants to make it evident that the community cannot interpret it as occurring simply due to natural causes.[28] In effect, announcing the imminence of the day of YHWH strengthens the text's appeal to cry out to YHWH in Joel 1:14. The implied audience is suffering the ravages of the locust infestation, which

---

22. R. Mason, *Zephaniah, Habbakuk, Joel* (OTG; Sheffield: Sheffield Academic Press, 1994) 117; A. Müller, *Gottes Zukunft: Die Möglichkeit der Rettung am Tag JHWHs nach dem Joelbuch* (WMANT 119; Neukirchen-Vluyn: Neukirchener, 2008) 79.

23. R. Coggins, *Joel and Amos* (NCBC; Sheffield: Sheffield Academic Press, 2000) 34.

24. Rendtorff, "Alas for the Day," 188.

25. Ellul, "Introduction," 428. This is contrary to the interpretive tradition that M. Vernes inaugurated (*Le peuple d'Israel et ses espérances relative à son avenir depuis les origines jusqu' à l'epoque persane Ve siècle avant J. C.* [Paris: Sandos & Fischbacher, 1872]), in which Joel 1–2 refers to a day of YHWH, in the past while Joel 3–4 speaks of a day of YHWH to come. See the above discussion regarding theories of Joel's literary unity, in the introduction.

26. G. Ahlström, *Joel and the Temple Cult of Jerusalem* (VTSup 21; Leiden: Brill, 1971) 64–65. A broad overview of the day-of-YHWH texts in Joel reveals a progression from wrath directed at Judah to wrath directed against Judah's enemies. See Bourke, "Jour de Yahvé," 5–30, 191–212. For the various thematic resonances of the day of YHWH, see Leung, "Intertextual," 71–97.

27. A. Kapelrud, *Joel Studies* (UUÅ 4; Uppsala: Lundequist, 1948) 58.

28. R. Simkins, *Yahweh's Activity in History and Nature in the Book of Joel* (ANETS 10; Lewiston, NY: Edwin Mellen, 1991) 153.

provides many reasons to cry out, but the text heightens the gravity of the situation by briefly invoking the day of Yhwh and implying that Yhwh lies behind the devastation.

The destructive nature of the day of Yhwh ties Joel 1:15 back to 1:10, which uses the same root to describe the destruction of agricultural produce.[29] The שֻׁדַּד 'destruction' that the locusts bring in Joel 1:10 thus is connected to the שֹׁד 'devastation' wrought by the day of Yhwh in 1:15. In doing this, the text invokes the presence of Yhwh, not only as the one to whom the people cry, but also as the agency behind their current circumstances. The text brings Yhwh into the foreground and creates a new understanding of the situation's gravity.[30] In establishing that the current situation is potentially a precursor for additional hardship brought on through divine agency, the text presents a powerful case for the implied audience to engage in the actions it prescribes in the earlier calls to lament.[31]

After the announcement of the day of Yhwh, Joel 1:16 adds greater detail in describing the crisis that points to the proximity of that day. Joel 1:16 again declares that the cult is unable to function properly. The text refers again to the cessation of daily sacrifices in Joel 1:16 through two rhetorical questions that connect the day of Yhwh, the locust plague, and the cultic crisis.[32] Joel 1:16a reads: הֲלוֹא נֶגֶד עֵינֵינוּ אֹכֶל נִכְרָת 'Has not the food been cut off from before our eyes?' This clause commences with a negative interrogative particle followed by the adjunct of place (נֶגֶד עֵינֵינוּ) and the subject of the verb (אֹכֶל).[33] In fronting the adjunct of place, Joel emphasizes the helplessness of the situation because the community is powerless to stand against what is happening, even though it is occurring right in front of them.[34]

Joel 1:16b reads, מִבֵּית אֱלֹהֵינוּ שִׂמְחָה וָגִיל 'from the house of our God, joy and mirth', with the verb נִכְרָת 'it is cut off' also governing this half of the verse. Joel 1:16b ties the cessation of cultic practice to the description of inescapable want in Joel 1:16a. This clause focuses on the house of Yhwh, from where שִׂמְחָה וָגִיל 'joy and mirth' are cut off. Joy and mirth in this instance have cultic connotations, reflecting the attitude that making offer-

---

29. Van der Merwe and Wendland, "Word Order," 120.

30. On the role of presence in the construction of an argument, see Perelman, *New Rhetoric*, 116–17, which states that one of the rhetor's tasks is "to make present, by verbal magic alone, what is actually absent but what [the rhetor] considers important to his argument."

31. M. LaRocca-Pitts, *The Day of Yahweh as Rhetorical Strategy among the Hebrew Prophets* (Ph.D. diss., Harvard University, 2000) 290.

32. Simkins, *Yahweh's Activity*, 149.

33. Van der Merwe and Wendland, "Word Order," 120.

34. J. Crenshaw, *Joel* (AB 24c; New York: Doubleday, 1995) 107. Crenshaw further connects this image with covenant futility curses in places such as Deut 28:31, where again the community will be powerless to stand against Yhwh's judgment.

ings to Yнwн ought to create (cf. Deut 12:5–7).[35] The structure of Joel 1:16b also highlights the cultic connection since it parallels the structure of the final clause of 1:13, which speaks to the interruption of the מִנְחָה וָנֶסֶךְ 'grain offering and drink offering' in the house of Yнwн. Ultimately, Joel 1:16 is a reminder that there can be no cultic celebrations of joy in the context of the tremendous want within the community that makes it impossible to follow the sacrificial system.

Joel 1:17–18: Second Communal Cry

Following the reference to the day of Yнwн and its cultic ramifications, Joel 1:17–18 again paints a vivid picture of natural disaster that focuses on images drawn from the realm of drought and desiccation. Some interpreters use the shift in imagery to argue for different layers of composition, with Ahlström claiming that the drought images "cannot be in harmony with the damaging ravages of the locusts."[36] On the other hand, it is possible to demonstrate the congruity of the two image-worlds: both locusts and droughts can draw from the realm of fire to describe their effects (cf. Joel 2:3, 5), and the destruction of foliage in the aftermath of a locust invasion could resemble the effect of a devastating drought.[37] For the purposes of this study, what is of greater interest is how the strategy of shifting image-worlds contributes to the rhetorical strategy of the text. Primarily, the development in imagery reinforces the hammering rhythm of attack after attack against the implied audience, resulting in total devastation. Joel 1:1–14 portrays wave after wave of locusts devastating the land, rendering inoperative the sacrificial system and requiring the community to call out in lament. If that were not enough, the text now adds the image of a desiccating drought, heightening the despair by introducing yet another calamitous threat.

Joel 1:17–18 delves into the specifics of the drought and again reinforces the desperate straits of the community. Joel 1:17 first portrays seeds that are unable to sprout because of the lack of moisture.[38] This effectively adds

---

35. Ibid. Anderson also uses this verse to illustrate the connectedness of the community and the divine presence. Yнwн's absence and the presence of lament and fasting indicate that it is impossible to preserve communal joy or rejoicing in this context (G. Anderson, *A Time to Mourn, A Time to Dance: The Expression of Grief and Joy in Israelite Religion* [University Park, PA: Pennsylvania State University Press, 1991] 109–10).

36. Ahlström, *Joel*, 51–52. Bergler also argues in this vein when he attempts to isolate the references to the drought and identify them as the kernel of the prophetic book; S. Bergler, *Joel als Schriftinterpret* (Frankfurt am Main: Peter Lang, 1988) 275.

37. Simkins, *Yahweh's Activity*, 149–53.

38. Joel 1:17 is one of the most difficult verses of the book to decipher since 1:17a contains three hapax legomena. The MT reads עָבְשׁוּ פְרֻדוֹת תַּחַת מֶגְרְפֹתֵיהֶם (the only word that is not a hapax legomenon is תַּחַת), which is usually rendered 'the seeds have been shriveled up in their clods' based on an understanding of פְּרֻדוֹת as 'seeds' from Aramaic and Syriac cognates. Since the remainder of the verse refers to the destruction of granaries because of the absence of crops, this at least seems to fit the context. The LXX offers little in the way

to the imagery of famine that is prevalent in this chapter because reading it together with the destruction of the locusts shows that the few stalks and seeds that the locusts did not devour will succumb to the drought that follows.[39] The remainder of Joel 1:17 refers to the disrepair of the storage houses for the crops. The widespread crop failure means that there is no need for these storehouses and that the disasters have erased any prior surplus. In the last clause of the verse, Joel engages in lexical repetition, again referring to the loss of grain by using verbs derived from יָבֵשׁ 'to wither', which recalls the elaborate description of crops withering in Joel 1:11–12 that calls agricultural workers into lament. Consequently, one can see continuity in the way that the text describes the effects of the locust infestation and the drought.

Joel 1:18 adds a new element to the imagery of drought and suffering. Not only have the locusts and the drought affected the community; they have also affected their livestock. Joel 1:18 introduces the animal realm, using an emphatic phrase with three rhyming words מַה־נֶּאֶנְחָה בְהֵמָה 'how the beasts groan!'[40] In this first clause, the text personifies the בְהֵמָה 'beasts' by giving them the capacity to groan. The text provides the reason for this in an explanatory כִּי clause that declares אֵין מִרְעֶה לָהֶם 'there is no pasture for them'. Joel 1:18 then concludes by adding an extra detail to the description of the animals' suffering. The final clause reads, גַּם־עֶדְרֵי הַצֹּאן נֶאְשָׁמוּ 'even the flocks of sheep suffer', and is notable for fronting the subject of the verb. This fronting emphasizes that even the flocks of sheep—which are presumably accustomed to foraging in drier areas—find this situation devastating.[41] Overall, Joel 1:18 expands the scope of those affected by the series of disasters. The preceding verses vividly communicate the effects of the current catastrophes on people and crops, while this verse adds extra weight by detailing the effects on livestock.

---

of clarification. It reads δαμάλεις 'heifers' for פְּרָדוֹת (which would be פָּרוֹת) and then refers to them as ἐσκίρτησαν 'skipping about', potentially due to hunger pangs. No solution to this issue has garnered significant support. Barton suggests that there is little hope of ever restoring the original Hebrew or of fully comprehending the sense of the MT, should it be the correct text, while Simkins declines to offer a translation and skips this clause in his analysis (J. Barton, *Joel and Obadiah: A Commentary* [OTL: Louisville: Westminster John Knox, 2001] 58; Simkins, *Yahweh's Activity*, 146–47). Given the lack of reasonable alternatives, I follow the general scholarly consensus about what the Masoretic Text seems to mean, on the grounds that this meaning best fits with the latter half of the verse.

39. Simkins, "God, History and the Natural World," 442.

40. Although the noun and verb in this phrase are both singular, the rest of the verse suggests that the meaning is collective, indicated by a plural object suffix and a reference to flocks of sheep.

41. Van der Merwe and Wendland, "Word Order," 121. Van der Merwe also suggests that this fronting is to be expected, because גַּם + constituent tends to be the focus of an utterance (C. van der Merwe, "Another Look at the Biblical Hebrew Focus Particle גַּם," *JSS* 54 [2009] 330).

Joel 1:19–20: The Cry of the Prophet

Joel 1:15–20 concludes in Joel 1:19–20 with the text's changing its rhe-torical voice from the first-person plural identification with the implied audience to a first-person appeal from the prophet to Yʜᴡʜ. This shift in voice highlights the prophet himself as he adds his own voice to the pic-ture of devastation and drought. In Joel 1:19, the prophet declares, אֵלֶיךָ יְהוָה אֶקְרָא 'To you, O Yʜᴡʜ, I cry'—appealing to Yʜᴡʜ as the sole source of suc-cor in the face of the onslaught of overwhelming catastrophes.[42] The prophet's personal interjection is a natural progression from the earlier appeals to different groups within the implied audience to call out to Yʜᴡʜ. The text uses the prophet as a model for the way the community ought to respond to the preceding descriptions of disaster; they are to follow his lead and call out to Yʜᴡʜ. This appeal also makes Yʜᴡʜ into a part of the audience that the text addresses. While this appeal to Yʜᴡʜ may intend to draw the implied audience to cry out amidst their circumstances, it also opens up the expectation for divine response.

The prophet's cry is also powerful due to the fact that it deepens the picture of destruction. Joel 1:19–20 introduces the image of fire burning the pastures and trees, which forcefully points to impending devastation (cf. Amos 7:4–6). The image-world imagined here reflects a full-fledged drought that drops the water table to such an extent that wildfires could ravage the region.[43] As mentioned in the discussion of rhetorical unit, the phrase אֵשׁ אָכְלָה נְאוֹת מִדְבָּר occurs in both Joel 1:19 and 1:20, functioning epiphorically to indicate that this imagery of fire brings this rhetorical unit to a close.[44] The text further heightens the gravity of this cry to Yʜᴡʜ through personification in Joel 1:20. The beasts of the field add their voice of longing as they תַּעֲרוֹג 'pant' for Yʜᴡʜ. The only other appearance of this verbal root is in Ps 42:2, which places the panting of the deer for streams of water in parallel with the psalmist's longing for Yʜᴡʜ. Thus, alongside the audience and the prophet, the beasts add their voice to the appeal to Yʜᴡʜ because of the lack of water (cf. Job 38:41; Ps 104:21).[45]

Joel 1:20 also contains another parallel to Ps 42:2: both verses use the phrase אֲפִיקֵי מָיִם 'streams of water'. This term probably refers to water sources that are seasonal in nature and derive from the underground water table (cf. Ps 126:4).[46] In Ps 42, the psalmist uses the example of the deer seeking

---

42. Van der Merwe and Wendland, "Word Order," 121.

43. Nash, *Palestinian*, 57. Additionally, Simkins suggests that the description of fire may refer to the destructive capacity of the locusts in that their rapacious consumption could resemble a building fire; Simkins, *Yahweh's Activity*, 149–50. It is difficult to untangle the image-worlds of this reference, and it may also be unnecessary. The idea remains that fire is ravaging the landscape, adding yet another level to the distress pictured in Joel 1.

44. Wendland, *Discourse Analysis*, 50–51.

45. Ellul, "Introduction," 429; Allen, *Joel*, 63.

46. Simkins, *Yahweh's Activity*, 151–52.

the אֲפִיקֵי מָיִם to illustrate the urgency of the quest for Yʜᴡʜ. Joel 1:20, however, suggests that, just as the אֲפִיקֵי מָיִם are dried up, those who pant in their search for Yʜᴡʜ will come away unsatisfied.[47] The lack of water goes beyond its effects on both humans and animals. It is also likely that the disappearance of this water source is symbolic of the removal of divine favor.[48] This idea gains strength from the end of the book, where Yʜᴡʜ's enthronement in Zion will cause abundant streams of water to flow in Judah. Both Joel 1:20 and 4:18 use the same construct noun אֲפִיקֵ to refer to water or its lack in the context of divine favor. Water, the precious commodity necessary for life, is thus promised when Yʜᴡʜ is restoring Judah but is lacking when it seems that Yʜᴡʜ is either silent or angered.

Overall, Joel 1:20 expands the effects of the drought imagery. It is not only the different varieties of domesticated beasts of 1:18 that cry out; wild animals accustomed to foraging on their own fare no better since the pastures of the wilderness, on which grazing animals depend, also succumb to the fires (cf. Ps 65:13; Jer 9:9; 23:10).[49] As a result, those suffering from the conditions, whether they are human or animal, join their voices to cry out to Yʜᴡʜ. These intermixed cries appear to play on the cultic lament by offering only the first element of crying out to Yʜᴡʜ; they do not include a petition, vow, or confession of trust.[50] Instead, the text leaves the burden of action with Yʜᴡʜ, who is the only agent capable of answering. The cries of the people and animals are not answered in Joel 1:15–20. Instead, they await further resolution in the remainder of the book.

There is a connection between the descriptions of devastation in these cries to Yʜᴡʜ and the destruction caused by the locusts in Joel 1:5–14 in that the text uses both to set up the statement that the day of Yʜᴡʜ is near.[51] Consequently, the present emergency is an act of Yʜᴡʜ, and it foreshadows the potential of an even greater catastrophe to come in succeeding rhetorical units. The prophet thus attempts to persuade the implied audience that Yʜᴡʜ is at work in all of the circumstances that he has so intricately detailed throughout the course of Joel 1:1–14 and 1:15–20. The prophet's cry to Yʜᴡʜ reflects on the current devastation and points the community to the one whose day is coming.

---

47. Ibid., 153–54. Simkins attempts to get behind the metaphorical references to streams of water by detailing how the devastation of a locust plague would be compounded in the dry heat of early summer. Whether or not his hypothetical reconstruction of the circumstances that led to this text is correct, he articulates a chilling picture of the level of devastation and desperation that these circumstances could create.

48. Ibid., 153.

49. Crenshaw, *Joel*, 111.

50. Ibid., 115.

51. W. Prinsloo, *The Theology of the Book of Joel* (BZAW 163; Berlin: de Gruyter, 1985) 38.

Summary

Joel 1:15–20 ties the imagery of the locust plague together with a picture of the coming day of Yhwh, which it portrays as a day of destruction and devastation for the implied audience. Joel 1:15–20 uses additional pictures of cultic and agricultural crisis to heighten the community's awareness of this fateful day. These images come from the realm of drought, and they combine with the pictures of the ravages of the locusts from Joel 1:1–14, indicating the severity of the situation. Joel 1:15–20 concludes with the prophet rhetorically crying to Yhwh, modeling the cry that the implied audience ought to adopt. This cry is not answered in this section, leaving the implied audience in suspense about whether Yhwh will hear and respond.

Rhetorical Effectiveness

The discussion of rhetorical effectiveness in Joel 1:15–20 begins with the text's progression from calls to lament in Joel 1:5–14, to the actual cries of lament, which culminate in a direct appeal from the prophet to Yhwh in Joel 1:15–20. The steps that the text takes toward crying out to Yhwh may indicate the effectiveness of the prophetic word.[52] This movement reflects the text's potential effectiveness since it fits with the claim of Perelman and Olbrechts-Tyteca that an effective deliberative argument achieves a decision to act.[53] By providing these laments, the text indicates that the call to cry out to Yhwh in Joel 1:14 is effective. Essentially, Joel 1:15–20 presents a prophet who reflects on the situation and responds appropriately by drawing Yhwh into the discussion. This should galvanize the implied audience and direct the individuals to the house of Yhwh, where they should follow the prophetic lead and offer up these cries to Yhwh.[54]

Joel 1:15–20 further reflects an effective strategy of identification between the prophet and the implied audience. Joel 1:1–14 begins with appeals to the community to hear the prophetic word, followed by more specific commands to various subsections to take up the prescribed cries of lamentation. Joel 1:15–20, however, does not leave the person of the prophet aloof from the situation. When the laments are issued in Joel 1:15–20, the text draws the prophet and the implied audience together

---

52. Simkins, "God, History and the Natural World," 436; R. Dillard, "Joel," in *The Minor Prophets: An Exegetical and Expository Commentary* (ed. T. McComiskey; Grand Rapids: Baker, 1992) 266; Coggins, *Joel*, 33. Coggins specifically refers to Joel 1:15 as the verse where the text switches from a "summons *to* the assembly, to a cry apparently uttered *by* the assembly."

53. Perelman and Olbrechts-Tyteca, *New Rhetoric*, 54.

54. Looking ahead, the great reversal of all the elements of deprivation in Joel 2:18–27 potentially indicates a scenario in which the people faithfully followed the course of action that the prophet prescribed. Of course, the text never explicitly makes this claim, leaving the situation ambiguous.

in Joel 1:16–18, before placing the final cry in the mouth of the prophet himself in 1:19–20. Thus, Joel 1:15–20 effectively connects its rhetor with the implied audience, whom it seeks to persuade. When the implied audience gathers to "cry out to Yhwh," the text places the prophet among the people, uttering similar cries for respite and relief from the exigences that drive the rhetorical situation.

This strategy of identification is also effective given the rhetorical genre of Joel 1:15–20. Perelman and Olbrechts-Tyteca indicate that one of the aims of epideictic discourse is to establish a sense of communion between the rhetor and the audience based around a shared value or belief.[55] In Joel 1:15–20, the prophet draws from the tradition of the day of Yhwh and uses this to establish his connection with the implied audience. By identifying with the implied audience as someone who cries out as the day of Yhwh nears, the prophet can effectively persuade the implied audience that it ought to respond in a similar manner.

Conclusion

Joel 1:15–20 begins with a powerful exclamatory cry that marks the transition from calls to lament in Joel 1:5–14 to the uttering of lament cries. It also develops the rhetorical situation by introducing the exigence of the day of Yhwh, while further portraying the level of devastation through images drawn from the realm of drought. Joel 1:15–20 also reflects a development in the rhetorical genre of the text, trying to educate the implied audience that it ought to follow the prophet's lead in responding to the exigences that the text presents. Joel 1:15–20 continues to use the desperate circumstances that it powerfully describes to draw the implied audience into response, which opens the door for evoking a response from Yhwh, who is the one who can remedy the situation. Ultimately, Joel 1:15–20 permits the prophet to identify more closely with the implied audience, urging it to follow the prophet's leadership in crying out to Yhwh.

---

55. Ibid., 51. Perelman and Olbrechts-Tyteca argue that the rhetor attempts to emphasize the value that the rhetor and the audience share, so that this sense of communion can remain intact even when conflicting values come into play.

Chapter 4

Despair in the Great and Dreadful Day of YHWH: *Rhetorical Analysis of Joel 2:1–11*

Introduction

Joel 2:1–11 follows the prophet's cry to YHWH and takes the text in a startling direction. It again announces the day of YHWH as a day of destruction for the Judahite community, evidenced by the command to blow a trumpet in Zion and the description of an invading army. Joel 2:1–11 culminates in the shocking revelation that YHWH leads the invaders against Zion. This heightens the crisis articulated in Joel 1:1–14 and 1:15–20, indicating that the initial appeals to cry out to YHWH and the prophet's own lament have not successfully persuaded YHWH to act salvifically. This revelation establishes the need for the more detailed call to response that follows in Joel 2:12–17. By threatening the community's continued existence, the text lays the foundation for another attempt to evoke from the people the response of appealing to YHWH in Joel 2:12–17.

Rhetorical Unit

Following the descriptions of fire and drought, Joel 2 commences with further imagery related to devastation and destruction. The first discrete unit in this chapter is Joel 2:1–11. An inclusio using the theologically rich phrase "day of the Lord" demarcates the boundaries of this particular rhetorical unit.[1] The latter half of Joel 2:1 declares that this day is coming and that the inhabitants of the land should tremble, while 2:11 concludes by detailing the magnitude of that day and posing a rhetorical question about the miniscule likelihood of surviving it. Joel 2:1–11 differentiates itself from what precedes by shifting away from the laments and prophetic entreaties to YHWH that characterize Joel 1:15–20. Instead, this passage re-addresses the implied audience with a series of imperatives and presents an additional picture of disaster. Joel 2:1–11 concludes by returning to the idea of the day of YHWH, ending with an exclamatory rhetorical question concerning the possibility of surviving its onslaught. The climactic conclusion

---

1. J. Crenshaw, *Joel* (AB 24c; New York: Doubleday, 1995) 128. Crenshaw also points to the threefold repetition of the suffixed noun פָּנָיו in Joel 2:1–11 as a feature that binds it together (לְפָנָיו in Joel 2:3, 10; מִפָּנָיו in 2:6).

to the rhetorical unit summarizes all that precedes and asks an overarching question that the following unit (Joel 2:12–17) begins to answer.[2]

Within Joel 2:1–11, the text breaks into several subunits. Joel 2:1–2a introduces the day-of-Yhwh inclusio and describes the devastating darkness that this day brings. Joel 2:2b–5 shifts to describing the advance of an invading army. This army leaves the landscape devastated in its wake and arrives at the gates of Zion to launch its assault. Joel 2:6 provides a brief shift of scene, focusing on the reactions of those who fall victim to the invader. Joel 2:7–9 then describes the assault on Zion and the invader's ability to overcome any defenses. Finally, Joel 2:10–11 closes the day-of-Yhwh inclusio, describing the cosmos-rending effects of Yhwh's leading the invaders against Zion.

Rhetorical Situation

The rhetorical situation created by the text shifts from Joel 1:1–14 and 1:15–20. The situation of Joel 1:1–14 revolves around the announcement of a locust invasion and subsequent agricultural disasters, while pointing the audience to cultic observances to appeal for relief. Joel 1:15–20 continues to describe agricultural hardships through imagery drawn from the realm of drought. Joel 2:1–11 makes no additional references to agricultural products such as grain, wine, and oil. Instead, it focuses on an army ravaging the surrounding landscape before besieging Zion.[3] This militaristic picture provides the setting for Joel 2:1–11; following the detailed description of an army ravaging the landscape in Joel 2:2b–5, attention turns to Zion as the one stronghold where the implied audience can hope to find succor. The references to the temple found in Joel 1:9, 13, and 14 do bring Zion into view, but Joel 2:1–11 crystallizes the text's focus on this location, beginning with the first warning to blow the ram's horn.

This is a significant transition, given the importance of Zion throughout the book. Joel explores the relationship between Yhwh and Zion and returns to this theme for its conclusion (Joel 2:23; 3:5; 4:16, 17, 21).[4] The key aspect of Zion's role in the rhetorical situation of Joel 2:1–11 is its relationship with Yhwh in the wake of the day of Yhwh. The text first situates Zion as one would expect, by referring to it in Joel 2:1 with the phrase בְּהַר קָדְשִׁי 'my holy mountain', but by the end of Joel 2:1–11 the relationship between Zion and Yhwh is under severe threat.

---

2. E. Wendland, *The Discourse Analysis of Hebrew Prophetic Literature* (MBPS 40; Lewiston, NY: Edwin Mellen, 1995) 44. Wendland lists rhetorical questions principally as signals of aperture for new rhetorical units, but he also acknowledges the possibility of using them as signals of closure. See Hos 9:14.

3. J. Barton, *Joel and Obadiah: A Commentary* (OTL; Louisville: Westminster John Knox, 2001) 70.

4. Crenshaw, *Joel*, 128.

The imagery that the text uses to construct the rhetorical situation is reminiscent of an imminent military invasion that also contains powerful theophanic overtones.[5] The exigence driving the situation of Joel 2:1–11 is the arrival of the invading horde and its assault on Zion. The description of the invader in Joel 2:2b–5 uses its effects on the landscape to emphasize the power of its assault and highlight its invulnerability, while 2:6–9 details the assault itself and demonstrates that Zion, the supposedly inviolable fortress, cannot withstand this assault. The overwhelming nature of the threat heightens the tension of the rhetorical situation in Joel 1:1–14 and 1:15–20. Whereas Joel 1:1–14 points to a locust infestation that threatened the agricultural and sacrificial systems, Joel 2:1–11 threatens the survival of Y<small>HWH</small>'s covenant people as it describes an invader capable of penetrating Zion's defenses and wreaking havoc.[6]

---

5. Leung highlights the theophanic resonances of Joel 2:1–2a (K. Leung, *An Intertextual Study of the Motif-Complex* Yom Yahweh *in the Book of Joel* [Ph.D. diss., Fuller Theological Seminary, 1997] 176–77). Leung detects the presence of theophany in Joel's prophetic rereading of the day of Y<small>HWH</small> from Joel 1:15. Whereas that reference to the day of Y<small>HWH</small> focused on the locusts, the image associated with the day of Y<small>HWH</small> in Joel 2:1–2a is cosmic darkness, reflecting the presence of Y<small>HWH</small> (cf. Deut 4:11). Darkness is a common theme in day-of-Y<small>HWH</small> texts, reflective of the divine authority over the natural order (cf. Isa 13:10; Amos 5:18–20; Zeph 1:15). As I argue below, the locusts are still part of the image-world in Joel 2:1–11, but the text locates them in the middle of an inclusio composed of references to the cosmos-rending power of Y<small>HWH</small>.

6. The term *covenant* is a central metaphor that describes the relationship between Y<small>HWH</small> and Israel/Judah. The key idea is that a covenant is a complex enactment of a relationship created between the covenanted parties. The covenant to which I am referring in this book is the Mosaic covenant at Sinai, which codified the relationship between Y<small>HWH</small> and Israel. Many, following Mendenhall, note the similarities between the covenant language of the Old Testament and suzerain-vassal treaties of the ancient Near East, specifically as illustrated in Deuteronomy. Features common to both include: (1) the identity of the covenant giver, (2) a historical prologue, (3) stipulations, (4) a list of witnesses, and (5) a list of blessings and curses. Also significant to the Old Testament concept of covenant is the acknowledged inequality between the parties; Y<small>HWH</small> takes the initiative in establishing covenant relationship with the Israelites, who are called to serve Y<small>HWH</small> faithfully. The tension in much of the prophetic literature of the Old Testament concerns whether or not Israel/Judah will uphold the stipulations of its covenant with Y<small>HWH</small>, including faithfully worshiping Y<small>HWH</small> alone and living in accordance with Y<small>HWH</small>'s decrees. If the people do uphold it, the prophets indicate that Y<small>HWH</small> will bring blessing; but if they fail, Y<small>HWH</small> will bring curses, including exile. The term *covenant community* in this book reflects the relationship between Y<small>HWH</small> and the implied audience that Joel constructs. Pronominal suffixes that refer to "your God" (Joel 1:13, 14; 2:13, 14, 23, 26, 27; 4:17), "our God" (Joel 1:16), "my people" (Joel 2:26, 27; 4:2), and "your people" (Joel 2:17) suggest the depth of this relationship. The responses of the implied audience and Y<small>HWH</small> are intertwined throughout the book, reflecting the covenantal connection between them. For additional reading on covenant and the Old Testament, see G. Mendenhall and G. Herion, "Covenant," *ABD* 1:1179–1202; G. Mendenhall, *Law and Covenant in Israel and the Ancient Near East* (Pittsburgh: Biblical Colloquium, 1955) 20; D. Hillers, *Covenant: The History of a Biblical Idea* (Baltimore: Johns Hopkins University Press, 1969); M. Kline, *Treaty of the Great*

The text heightens this exigence through theophanic imagery revealed in the day-of-Yhwh inclusio that brackets this unit. On top of imagery related to a military invasion, this unit creates the cosmological backdrop in which the heavenly lights dim and the earth shakes, before revealing Yhwh's claim to lead the invading horde.[7] Thus, the exigence of the threat to Zion's survival comes not only from a military threat but also from the theophanic realm, where Yhwh as sovereign ruler of the cosmos is the one bringing this threat against Zion.

The way in which this unit establishes its implied audience is also worthy of comment. The text addresses the implied audience directly in Joel 2:1, locating it in Zion, which is also Yhwh's holy mountain.[8] The text describes the audience as כֹּל יֹשְׁבֵי הָאָרֶץ 'all dwellers of the land', which echoes one-half of the initial prophetic call in Joel 1:2. In Joel 2:1, the text makes no reference to elders, which may reflect the impending gravity of the situation; there is no command for the implied audience to pass on its knowledge of this time to future generations since the approach of this invader may herald final doom. Consequently, the term "all dwellers of the land" gathers all of the elements of the implied audience in Joel 1:1–14.

The text instructs this implied audience through a sequence of three imperatives, beginning with a call to תִּקְעוּ 'blow' the warning horn, and then commands the audience to וְהָרִיעוּ 'sound an alarm' and יִרְגְּזוּ 'tremble'. These commands create the context of an attack warning, with the prophet functioning as the watchman, calling for the alarm to sound (Isa 21:11–12; Jer 6:17; Ezek 3:17).[9] The command for the implied audience to tremble suggests that this call to alarm is likely to have serious consequences.[10] In-

---

King: *The Covenant Structure of Deuteronomy* (Grand Rapids: Eerdmans, 1963); P. Williamson, *Sealed with an Oath: Covenant in God's Unfolding Purpose* (NSBT 23; Downers Grove, IL: InterVarsity, 2007) 94–119; S. McKenzie, *Covenant* (UBT; St. Louis: Chalice, 2000) 25–40, 53–64; S. Hahn, *Kinship by Covenant: A Canonical Approach to the Fulfillment of God's Saving Promises* (YABRL; New Haven, CT: Yale University Press, 2009) 49–92.

7. Wendland discusses in detail the metaphorical blend of imagery that combines the locust invasion, military assault, and theophanic phenomena (E. Wendland, *Prophetic Rhetoric: Case Studies in Text Analysis and Translation* [Longwood, FL: Xulon, 2009] 34). Wendland correctly notes the reuse of locust imagery in Joel 2:3–9, which fleshes out the detail of the divinely sanctioned assault on Zion in Joel 2:1–2, 10–11.

8. See the section on rhetorical strategy in Joel 2:1–11 for further discussion of the effect of referring to Zion as Yhwh's holy mountain.

9. R. Dillard, "Joel," in *The Minor Prophets: An Exegetical and Expository Commentary* (ed. T. McComiskey; Grand Rapids: Baker, 1992) 271. Dillard suggests that "Joel is in effect giving another battle oracle—but it is the Lord's army coming against Israel on the day of the Lord." This reverses the expectation that the prophet will articulate the way in which the battle ought to proceed (cf. 2 Kgs 3:14–19; 6:8–7:2; 13:14–20. See 1 Kgs 20 and 2 Chr 11:1–4 for examples of the prophet's declaring that the battle ought not to occur).

10. G. Vanoni, "רגז," *TDOT* 13:304–8. The root רָגַז has a semantic range that suggests that its subject is moved powerfully, both inwardly and outwardly. The causes of such reactions tend to be negative for humanity, such as announcement of death (2 Sam 19:1; Isa 32:10–11), injustice (Ps 45:5), or cosmic turmoil (Isa 14:9, 16; Job 3:26). The root רָגַז also

terestingly, this is the final occasion on which Joel 2:1–11 addresses its implied audience as active agents. Joel 2:2–11 describes the day of Yhwh and the advance of the invader without once mentioning any action on the part of those living in Zion to resist the onslaught. This stands in distinct contrast to the previous rhetorical unit, which first constructed its implied audience in broad strokes (Joel 1:2), before highlighting specific groups within the larger community (Joel 1:5–14), and calling on them to gather at the temple to cry out to Yhwh.

The only additional action that the text allows the audience is to writhe in abject terror in the face of the invader's advance (Joel 2:6).[11] The text's focus on the invader's activities and silence concerning those who dwell in Zion creates a situation in which the rhetor seeks to emphasize the implied audience's inability to ameliorate their situation. The implied audience and rhetor may share the same degree of interest in the situation, but establishing the implied audience's powerlessness is the primary purpose.[12] The call to alarm in Joel 2:1 is ironic because the progression of this rhetorical unit reveals that the sounding alarm has no effect on the implied audience's fate. Essentially, the situation governing this rhetorical unit is not calling its audience to a response that can modify the exigence; instead, it emphasizes that there is no viable response other than terror and fear. This lays the foundation for the implied audience to respond through an appeal to Yhwh to remedy the situation in Joel 2:12–17.

In summary, the rhetorical situation of Joel 2:1–11 is based on the exigence of an invading horde that reflects the day of Yhwh. Joel 2:1–11 details the inexorable advance of the invader as it makes its way across the countryside (Joel 2:3–5) to the city walls, which it penetrates with ease (Joel 2:7–9). The implied audience of this rhetorical unit consists of the "dwellers of the land" who hear the command to blow the trumpet in Zion and who can only tremble as the invader draws near. Joel 2:1–11 essentially eliminates their ability to modify the exigence directly, indicating that its intent is to persuade the audience that they are helpless before the unleashed power of Yhwh.

Rhetorical Strategy

The overaching theme of Joel 2:1–11 connects with the preceding rhetorical units. Again, the text provides a detailed depiction of disaster falling

---

describes trembling of bodies in the natural world, usually as the result of Yhwh's moving and acting as divine warrior (1 Sam 14:15; Pss 18:8; 77:19; Isa 64:1; Mic 7:17). Joel 2:1–11 makes use of both elements since the description of the earth's response in Joel 2:10 mirrors the command for the implied audience to tremble here.

11. For more on the effect of commanding the implied audience to respond by writhing, see the discussion below on the rhetorical strategy of Joel 2:1–11.

12. G. Hauser, *Introduction to Rhetorical Theory* (2nd ed.; Long Grove, IL: Waveland, 2002) 57–58.

on Yнwн's covenant people, this time focusing on the destruction of Jerusalem. One of the key questions guiding scholars' discussion of Joel 2:1–11 is the connection between this disaster and the disaster articulated in Joel 1:1–20. Three prominent streams of interpretation can be discerned from previous research.[13] First, the commentators who argue that the locusts of Joel 1 represented a human army carry this argument through Joel 2:1–11, again pointing to the Babylonian army that carried the Jerusalem community into captivity.[14] Second, some argue that Joel 2:1–11 makes a transition from a literal locust plague in Joel 1:1–14 to an evocative description of an apocalyptic enemy that cannot be identified with an earthly foe.[15] Third, others view Joel 2:1–11 as another depiction of a locust plague such as the one that dominated the image-world of Joel 1:1–14.[16]

Taking these different views in turn—there are relatively few who hold to the "literal-enemy" interpretation for this passage. Stuart attempts to make the case for this point of view by arguing that the language and imagery of Joel 1:1–2:17 are appropriate to descriptions of the devastation that can be wrought by human armies and are not characteristic of locusts.[17] He associates this army with a looming Babylonian threat. This interpretation fits the militaristic tone of Joel 2:1–11, with its images of armies, chariots, and horses. Simkins and Linville challenge Stuart by noting the prevalence of the preposition כְּ, which precedes many of these images, and suggest that this indicates the presence of simile (cf. Joel 2:2, 3, 4, 5, 7, 9).[18] If the

---

13. R. Simkins, *Yahweh's Activity in History and Nature in the Book of Joel* (ANETS 10; Lewiston, NY: Edwin Mellen, 1991) 159. Nash puts forward a different proposal and argues that the referent of this section is a sirocco windstorm that could dry out the land and drive dust into everything (K. Nash, *The Palestinian Agricultural Year and the Book of Joel* [Ph.D. diss., Catholic University of America, 1989] 136–56). This idea, however, has not gained much traction because it fails to deal sufficiently with the images of individual warriors found in Joel 2:4–9.

14. See D. Stuart, *Hosea–Jonah* (WBC 31; Waco, TX: Word, 1987) 233; G. Ogden and R. Deutsch, *Joel and Malachi: A Promise of Hope—A Call to Obedience* (ITC; Grand Rapids: Eerdmans, 1987) 27. Ogden argues that Joel is borrowing the imagery of the Babylonian invasion and using it here to call the community to hear his message concerning the coming of the day of Yнwн.

15. See H. Wolff, *Joel and Amos* (Hermeneia; Philadelphia: Fortress, 1977) 41–42; M. Sweeney, *The Twelve Prophets*, vol. 1 (Berit Olam; Collegeville, MN: Liturgical Press, 2000) 162–64; Crenshaw, *Joel*, 118–25.

16. See Simkins, *Yahweh's Activity*, 163–69.

17. Stuart, *Hosea–Jonah*, 233. Ogden asserts a similar position, arguing that the text is reflecting back on the experience of the Babylonian invasion and treating it as occurring in the present in order to direct the nation to seek Yнwн; Ogden, *Promise of Hope*, 27. This position is dependent on successfully identifying Joel's time of composition, which continues to prove challenging.

18. For the comparative function of כְּ, see B. Waltke and M. O'Connor, *An Introduction to Biblical Hebrew Syntax* (Winona Lake, IN: Eisenbrauns, 1990) 202–3; C. van der Merwe, J. Naudé, and J. Kroeze, *A Biblical Hebrew Reference Grammar* (Sheffield: Sheffield Academic Press, 1999) 283; GKC 375–76.

invader is said to be "like a mighty people arrayed for battle" or "like men of war," it would be surprising for the referent of the simile actually to be an invading army.[19]

One response to Simkins's and Linville's critique is that Joel 2:1–11 is employing the *kap veritatis*, which would indicate that the invader is "in every respect like" the images it presents (cf. Num 11:1; Neh 7:2; Joel 1:15).[20] The presence of *kap veritatis* in Joel 2:1–11, however, is debatable. The description in Joel 2:2 of the invader's arriving כְּשַׁחַר פָּרֻשׂ עַל־הֶהָרִים 'like dawn spread over the mountains' is most likely a simile comparing the arrival of the invader to the sudden appearance of light. Similarly, the description of the landscape's being כְּגַן־עֵדֶן הָאָרֶץ 'like the garden of Eden' before the approach of the invader seems to be hyperbolic simile rather than indicating that the landscape is Edenic in every respect. The other occurrences of כְּ in Joel 2:1–11 are more ambiguous but, given that the first two occurrences are most likely similes, it is defensible to see similes in the rest of the unit.

Further, as I mentioned while discussing the rhetorical situation of Joel 1:1–14, Stuart's attempt to dismiss the locusts as the foundation of the imagery in Joel 1:2–2:11 is unconvincing. His argument that the ravages of locusts were transient and would not generate this level of alarm does not take into account the presence of YHWH at the head of the invader. Locusts alone may not generate this level of threat, but the climactic image of YHWH leading the invader contributes to the gravity of the situation. The explicit mention of locusts in Joel 1:4 activates this particular image-world, and it is worth considering whether this image-world continues to resonate in the present chapter.

The apocalyptic interpretation of the invader is the next option to consider. This proposal, championed by Wolff, is stronger at first glance. Wolff's arguments include his assertion that the prayer of Joel 2:17, which calls for divine redress of the circumstances described in this unit, presupposes a Jerusalem overwhelmed by "nations," which he does not think could refer to locusts. Further, Joel 2:1–11 does not contain references to

---

19. Simkins, *Yahweh's Activity*, 160; J. Linville, "Bugs through the Looking Glass: The Infestation of Meaning in Joel," in *Reflection and Refraction: Studies in Biblical Historiography in Honour of A. Graeme Auld* (ed. R. Rezetko, T. Lim, and W. Aucker; Cambridge: Cambridge University Press, 2006) 290. Linville captures the apparent tautology, stating, "of course an army is like an army."

20. R. Chisholm, *Interpreting the Minor Prophets* (Grand Rapids: Zondervan, 1990) 58. On the general use of *kap veritatis*, see Waltke and O'Connor, *Introduction*, 203; van der Merwe, Naudé, and Kroeze, *Biblical*, 283; GKC 376. Andiñach also relies on this understanding of *kap*, even though he does not use the technical term (P. Andiñach, "The Locusts in the Message of Joel," *VT* 42 [1992] 439). Joel 1:15 is probably an example of *kap veritatis*. It states that the day of YHWH will come כְּשֹׁד מִשַּׁדַּי 'like destruction from the Almighty', which prefigures YHWH's powerful activity. Essentially, divinely ordained destruction is an integral part of the day of YHWH.

typical devastations caused by locusts, such as hunger and blight.[21] Instead, the references to fire and the shaking of the heavenly bodies suggest a cosmological interpretation. Additionally, Wolff argues that Joel 2:1–11 describes the enemy as unique, standing outside the course of natural events. Meanwhile, in his view Joel 1:2b describes the locusts and the severity of their attack as being unusual but not out of the realm of possibility.[22] Wolff draws a parallel concerning their uniqueness to the reign of locusts found in Rev 9:2–11, suggesting that Joel 2:1–11 is an apocalyptic form prefiguring the Revelation passage.[23] Wolff also notes that in Joel 1 the majority of the verbs are in affix form, representing completed action, while in Joel 2:1–11, the majority of the verbs are in prefix form, reflecting incomplete or future action.[24] According to his argument, this indicates that the two passages cannot refer to the same event.

Further scrutiny, however, reveals significant weaknesses in Wolff's proposal. Wolff's appeal to the heightened description of the disaster in

---

21. Wolff, *Joel and Amos*, 42.

22. Ibid. Wolff mentions two other arguments that are not as strong. He states that: (1) locusts are not mentioned in Joel 2:1–17 but have disappeared from the scene in 1:8–12; (2) Yʜᴡʜ is mentioned as the commander of the army in 2:11 but is not mentioned as commanding the locusts in Joel 1. The problem with the first argument is that, while the word "locust" is not found in Joel 2:1–17, this does not prove that the metaphors and similes of the passage are not referring to locusts. The second argument is also problematic because it does not leave room for the possibility that the prophet could use the same locusts to put forward different facets of his argument.

23. Ibid. The relationship of Joel to apocalyptic literature requires some discussion. Collins offers the seminal definition of apocalyptic literature as "a genre of revelatory literature with a narrative framework, in which a revelation is mediated by an otherworldly being to a human recipient, disclosing a transcendent reality which is both temporal, insofar as it envisages eschatological salvation, and spatial insofar as it involves another, supernatural world." Joel may reflect some of the characteristics of apocalyptic with its visions of cosmos-rending divine activity, but it lacks the otherworldly mediator that is integral to the genre (J. Collins, "Introduction: Towards the Morphology of a Genre," *Semeia* 14 [1979] 9; idem, "The Jewish Apocalypses," *Semeia* 14 [1979] 29). Grabbe criticizes the attempt to distinguish between prophetic and apocalyptic literature, suggesting that both are scribal products. He proposes viewing apocalyptic as a subset of prophetic literature (L. Grabbe, "Prophetic and Apocalyptic: Time for New Definitions—and New Thinking," in *Knowing the End from the Beginning: The Prophetic, the Apocalyptic and Their Relationships* [ed. L. Grabbe and R. Haak; JSPSup 46; London: T. & T. Clark, 2003] 107–33). This proposal takes into account the difficulty of arriving at the world behind the text, but it glosses over distinctions in the ways that texts construct their eschatological visions. Collins rightly claims that one can find differences in eschatology in the Old Testament between a *prophetic* book such as Joel and an *apocalyptic* book such as Dan 7–12, including the presence of an intermediating figure (J. Collins, "Prophecy, Apocalypse and Eschatology: Reflections on the Proposal of Lester Grabbe," in *Knowing the End from the Beginning: The Prophetic, the Apocalyptic and Their Relationships* [ed. L. Grabbe and R. Haak; JSPSup 46; London: T. & T. Clark, 2003] 49). Consequently, while Joel may put forward a vision of Yʜᴡʜ's dramatic intervention in the affairs of this world, the most appropriate category to understand it remains *prophetic literature*.

24. Wolff, *Joel and Amos*, 41–42. See also Crenshaw, *Joel*, 129.

Joel 2 does not necessarily require that it reference a different event.[25] The multigenerational command to commemorate this incident in Joel 1:2–3 and the identification of the uniqueness of this moment in Joel 2:2 are more similar than dissimilar.[26] Both bring the crisis into stark relief, and it is equally likely that the text uses slightly different language and imagery to describe the phenomenon in these chapters. Simkins also discusses the potential parallel to Rev 9:2–11 and finds some similarities related to the appearance and the organization of the invaders. Simkins, however, notes a significant discrepancy that renders Wolff's parallel less apt. In Rev 9:2–11, the locusts are explicitly forbidden to act like locusts—that is, they are expressly commanded not to harm the foliage but to afflict humans with scorpion-like tails that real locusts do not possess (Rev 9:3–4, 10). Clearly, the locusts of Revelation are an apocalyptic creation and not a reflection of actual locusts. By way of contrast, Simkins demonstrates that, by and large, the invaders mentioned in Joel 2:1–11 do behave as one would expect from locusts. Their destructive activity ravages the earth and in the aftermath it looks as though a fire has burned the land clean.[27] The descriptions found in Joel 2:1–11 may be hyperbolic, but they do resemble descriptions of actual locusts.

Finally, the question of affix versus prefix verb forms ultimately does not bear the weight that Wolff places on it. While the preponderance of prefix verbs in Joel 2:1–11 may suggest an imminent threat, this does not necessitate that the threat be derived from a different source than Joel 1:1–14. Joel 2:1–11 reflects an imperfective situation in which the text portrays the advance of the invading army as a continual series of overlapping events that builds toward YHWH's climactic intervention in Joel 2:10.[28] Dillard suggests that this situation is an extended metaphor that builds on the locust invasion of Joel 1:1–14.[29] In this view, Joel 2:1–11 appropriates the locusts of Joel 1:1–14 and transforms them into harbingers of the day of YHWH, which is again described as *near* in Joel 2:1. The prevalence of imperatives and affix forms in Joel 1:1–14 may contrast with the prefix forms of Joel 2:1–11, but both passages could equally articulate different approaches to a threat drawn from the same image-world.

---

25. Barton, *Joel*, 69.
26. Wolff, *Joel and Amos*, 42. Wolff tries to make a distinction between Joel 1:2–14 and 2:1–11, suggesting that the events of 1:2–14 were unusual, while those of 2:1–11 were unique. This level of precision is difficult to claim when dealing with the potential for prophetic hyperbole.
27. Simkins, *Yahweh's Activity*, 163. See also his discussion of contemporary accounts of locust attacks and the resulting descriptions of the land.
28. Waltke and O'Connor, *Introduction*, 504–5. Interestingly, the text reverts to predominantly affix verbs in Joel 2:10–11 when describing YHWH's intervention. This may indicate the inevitability of YHWH's actions, reflecting an example of the prophetic perfect (ibid., 490).
29. Dillard, "Joel," 278.

The third and most likely possibility to explain the image-world governing the rhetorical strategy of Joel 2:1–11 is that the text again draws from
the realm of a locust invasion. The most common theory is that the text is
referring back to the same infestation from which it drew its imagery for
Joel 1, though some have proposed that the text is constructing a second
infestation that prompts the heightening of the rhetoric.[30] This attempt to
look behind the imagery of the text is ultimately irresolvable and detracts
from considering the rhetorical effect of returning to the image-world of
locust activities. To this end, one can effectively argue that the activities
of the invading horde are appropriate to the expected activities of locusts,
especially concerning the seeming discipline with which bands of locusts
advance across a landscape.[31] Similarly, the image of landscape devastated
by fire in Joel 2:3 can reflect the aftermath of the advance of locusts.[32] Consequently, the imagery that forms the backdrop of Joel 2:1–11 is a locust
invasion, which the text describes using "magnificent poetic hyperbole,"
combining it with overtones of an invading army.[33] The grandiose effects
on the heavenly bodies noted in Joel 2:10 do not reduce to observable locust phenomena, but one can argue effectively that the function of these
phenomena is to transition the text from the image-world of the locusts
toward the portrayal of powerful divine action.[34]

While it is most plausible to find locust imagery at the core of Joel 2:1–
11, it is clear that the text enhances its portrayal of the locusts. Whereas
the locusts in Joel 1:1–14 function as one would expect by devouring crops,
which leads to devastating privation, the text fuses locust imagery in Joel
2:1–11 with imagery reflecting an invader. The locusts continue to ravage the landscape (Joel 2:3), but the description of their assault against
Zion also evokes a military assault (Joel 2:7–9). This metaphorical blend
heightens the sense of threat against the implied audience. Not only are
the people facing agricultural devastation, they must also face the reality
of an invader who gravely threatens their physical security.[35] Thus, the text

---

30. See Simkins, *Yahweh's Activity*, 154. Simkins draws from the promise of restora-
tion found in Joel 2:25, where Y<small>HWH</small> states that he will restore the 'years' (הַשָּׁנִים) that the
locusts have devoured. Mason offers a trenchant critique, noting that, according to Simkins's own fusion of mythic and historical elements in Joel's understanding of the world,
the idea of a divinely inspired locust infestation should be available for use in various
crises. Consequently, there is no need to posit a second wave of locusts to explain Joel's
reuse of this particular image-world (R. Mason, *Zephaniah, Habbakuk, Joel* [OTG; Sheffield:
Sheffield Academic Press, 1994] 122).
31. Simkins, *Yahweh's Activity*, 164–65.
32. Ibid., 165.
33. Barton, *Joel*, 70.
34. Simkins, *Yahweh's Activity*, 167.
35. Wendland, *Prophetic Rhetoric*, 32–34. Wendland goes into further detail discussing the elements that make up the metaphorical blend in Joel 2:1–11, noting that the
text strengthens its militaristic tint by employing theophanic imagery, especially in Joel

reuses the locust imagery of Joel 1 and transforms it to announce another, greater threat against the implied audience.

Joel 2:10 then moves from powerful descriptions of locusts to cosmos-rending divine activity. The way in which locust imagery fuses with descriptions of the day of Y<small>HWH</small> permits the text to communicate an additional message. The text creatively places the locust army in the middle of the day-of-Y<small>HWH</small> inclusio that frames Joel 2:1–11. After announcing the day of Y<small>HWH</small>, the text describes the advance of the invading locusts, intermingling images derived from an attacking army. The locusts, however, are only a precursor to the climactic conclusion to Joel 2:1–11. The power and irresistibility of their assault against Zion sets the stage for Y<small>HWH</small> to return and establish that the locust invasion has dramatic, cosmos-rending significance because it occurs under divine aegis.

After discussing the developments of the image-world of Joel 2:1–11, we turn to look closely at the text to see how this unit constructs its persuasive arguments. While Joel 2:1–11 returns to the image-world of the locusts that governs Joel 1:1–14, this rhetorical unit has its own unique features and techniques that merit analysis.

Joel 2:1–2a: Announcing the Day of Y<small>HWH</small>

Joel 2 begins with a series of three commands in which the text issues additional warnings concerning the imminent arrival of the day of Y<small>HWH</small>. As in Joel 1:15, Y<small>HWH</small>'s covenant people are the targets of the day of Y<small>HWH</small>, since Zion is under attack. The text places the warning call in the mouth of Y<small>HWH</small>, evidenced by the first-person pronominal suffix on the phrase בְּהַר קָדְשִׁי 'on my holy mountain'.[36] In constructing Y<small>HWH</small> as the one who sounds the alarm, the text is quite possibly engaging in irony, because the remainder of this rhetorical unit reveals that Y<small>HWH</small>'s actions render the alarm futile.

The parallel construction with which Joel 2:1a begins is a strident warning call that lays the foundation for the attack described in this rhetorical unit. Its first act is to issue the command תִּקְעוּ שׁוֹפָר 'blow a trumpet' in Zion. This is a command that is used elsewhere in the Old Testament to warn

---

2:11, which portrays Y<small>HWH</small> as a military leader, commanding the activities detailed in the preceding verses.

36. Crenshaw, *Joel*, 117. Crenshaw suggests that Y<small>HWH</small>'s persona persists in this section through the end of Joel 2:10, with 2:11 providing the response in the voice of the prophet. Joel 2:1b does mention the "day of Y<small>HWH</small>," however, which is a third-person reference. Crenshaw argues that the "day of Y<small>HWH</small>" is a fixed form. Consequently, one does not need to posit a change in speaker. It is also possible, in Fleer's opinion, to posit a change of speaker in Joel 2:1b to the prophet, who then carries the discourse through Joel 2:1 (D. Fleer, "Exegesis of Joel 2:1–11," *ResQ* 26 [1983] 152). Resolution of this issue is unlikely, but it does not greatly affect the understanding of the text's rhetorical power, since the prophet and Y<small>HWH</small> both appear to adopt the same perspective on the situation in Joel 2:1–11.

people of attacks (Jer 4:5; 6:1; Hos 8:1), summon people to war (Judg 3:27; 6:34; 7:8; Jer 51:27), or summon them to cultic observance (Lev 25:9; Pss 47:6; 81:4; 2 Chr 15:14).[37] The progression of this rhetorical unit supports the idea that Joel 2:1 is drawing mainly on the warning-of-attack motif, since what follows is a detailed description of an invader's assault on Zion.

There is additional support for the call-to-alarm setting of Joel 2:1–11 through its connections with the call to blow the trumpet in Jer 4:5–8 and the description of the day of YHWH in Zeph 1:14–16. Jeremiah calls for the trumpet to sound and for the people to gather in Zion and other fortresses because YHWH is sending an invader from the north (Jer 4:6b). This connection with Joel is strengthened when one considers Joel 2:20, which explicitly refers to the invading force of Joel 2:1–11 as הַצְּפוֹנִי 'the northerner'.[38] These parallels suggest that Joel 2:1 echoes the statement of threat to Zion's continued security in Jer 4:6.[39] Zephaniah 1:14–16 further resonates with this passage since it also stresses the nearness of the day of YHWH and the darkness that it brings. Zephaniah 1:16 additionally places the day of YHWH in the context of an assault against fortified cities, including Jerusalem, with the trumpet sounding the alarm (cf. Zeph 1:12).[40] Thus, the shared motif of a city under assault unites Jer 4:6 and Zeph 1:16 with Joel 2:1 and suggests that the command to sound the trumpet in Joel 2:1 emphasizes a call to alarm.

Beyond the dominant call to alarm, cultic resonances of blowing the trumpet may also be present, given the cult-based program that the prophet puts forward in Joel 2:12–17, both to lament the destruction found in Joel 1:14 and hopefully to turn aside YHWH's wrath. This exact command recurs in Joel 2:15 in the context of a gathering at the house of YHWH to try to avoid the realization of the destruction forewarned in Joel 2:1–11. Consequently, while the call to blow the trumpet in Joel 2:1 presages the forthcoming assault, it may also begin to prepare a cultic remedy.[41]

---

37. Sweeney, *Twelve*, 162.

38. There is a significant amount of research on the identity and function of the northern enemy in prophetic literature. I will explore this in more detail in conjunction with analysis of the explicit use of this tradition in Joel 2:20.

39. J. Strazicich, *Joel's Use of Scripture and the Scripture's Use of Joel: Appropriation and Resignification in Second Temple Judaism and Early Christianity* (BIS 82; Leiden: Brill, 2007) 115–16.

40. The passage in Zephaniah differs slightly in that there is no command to blow a trumpet; rather, Zeph 1:16 describes the day of YHWH as a 'day of the trumpet' (יוֹם שׁוֹפָר). The close connection between the descriptions of the day of YHWH in Joel and Zephaniah suggests, however, that both passages employ the sounding of the trumpet to warn of coming, divinely sanctioned assault.

41. Ibid., 117. Strazicich also rightly points out that Joel preserves the cultic resonance of the trumpet blast since, although it is here used as a call to alarm, the prophet does not call for the implied audience to resist the forthcoming assault, since no one can stand in the face of YHWH's appearance (Joel 2:11).

The second command, which calls for sounding an alarm on Y~HWH~'s holy mountain, echoes and enhances the first while introducing imagery that resonates with ancient Near Eastern traditions of mountains as the dwelling place of deities.[42] The first-person suffix on בְּהַר קָדְשִׁי 'on my holy mountain' makes evident Y~HWH~'s claim to this location. Clifford draws intriguing parallels between the Canaanite idea of Mount Zaphon and the Old Testament descriptions of Mount Zion. In both locations, the deity dwells in the temple on the mountain, and while the mountain may be a scene of battle, it is ultimately impregnable since the power of the deity preserves it.[43] The theme of inviolability concerning Mount Zion is also found in several locations in the Psalter, notably Ps 48:2–7 and Ps 2. In both instances, attackers approach Zion, only to go down to defeat at the hands of the deity who dwells in Zion.[44] Consequently, it is all the more shocking when Joel 2:1–11 dramatically overturns the idea of inviolability by depicting a force that experiences little difficulty in overcoming the defenses of the place where Y~HWH~ is supposed to dwell.[45]

A third command directing the dwellers of the land to tremble (יִרְגְּזוּ) follows these first two imperatives in Joel 2:1.[46] This reconstitutes the implied audience, since it echoes Joel 1:2 and probably covers all the subsections of the implied audience created in Joel 1:5–14. The command to tremble heightens the dire nature of the situation, implying that the previous commands to blow the trumpet and sound the alarm will not lead to rescue.[47] The call to tremble leads to the reasons why the audience should tremble.

---

42. Barton, *Joel*, 70–71.

43. R. Clifford, *The Cosmic Mountain in Canaan and the Old Testament* (Cambridge: Harvard University Press, 1972) 131. See also Hoppe's work on Ps 48, which draws out the psalmist's intent to claim Mount Zaphon for Y~HWH~ by placing it parallel to Zion. This psalm goes beyond borrowing the imagery of a holy mountain. It intends to place a rival location under the aegis of Y~HWH~ (L. Hoppe, *The Holy City: Jerusalem in the Theology of the Old Testament* [Collegeville, MN: Liturgical Press, 2000] 26).

44. Clifford, *Cosmic*, 153. Ollenburger correctly emphasizes that the reason for Zion's inviolability is rooted foremost in the presence of Y~HWH~. Zion is only impregnable insofar as the deity who claims this location is present to protect the city (B. Ollenburger, *Zion the City of the Great King: A Theological Symbol of the Jerusalem Cult* [JSOTSup 41; Sheffield: JSOT Press, 1987] 66. Further, Hayes connects the theme of inviolability to pre-Israelite conceptions of Jerusalem and helpfully points to prophetic passages that attach the condition of obedience to the guarantee of security in Zion (cf. Isa 10:5–6; 29:1–8; Jer 7:13–15; 26:4–6; J. Hayes, "The Tradition of Zion's Inviolability," *JBL* 82 [1963] 419–26).

45. The issue of the inviolability of Zion has been raised in attempts to date this book. If the majority opinion that this book is post-Babylonian captivity is correct, one wonders how strongly the concept of inviolability would resonate in Zion traditions. Crenshaw argues that it still held sway, inasmuch as Y~HWH~ was thought to have commandeered the Babylonian army to punish sinful Judah (Crenshaw, *Joel*, 118).

46. Whether יִרְגְּזוּ is in imperative mood must be determined from context, since the prefix and jussive have the same form. The proximity of this verb to the preceding imperatives, however, suggests that the jussive reading is more likely in this context.

47. See n. 10 above for a discussion of the semantic range of רָגַז.

This verse uses two synonymous clauses beginning with causal כִּי, stating that the day of Yʜᴡʜ is imminent. The first clause reads כִּי־בָא יוֹם־יְהוָה 'for the day of Yʜᴡʜ is coming', while the second elides the day of Yʜᴡʜ and states, כִּי קָרוֹב 'for [it is] near'.[48] The second clause echoes Joel 1:15b in stressing the imminence of the day, since both passages use the adjective קָרוֹב.[49] The lack of detail that the text gives to the day of Yʜᴡʜ in Joel 1:15 begins to be remedied in the day-of-Yʜᴡʜ inclusio of Joel 2:1–11, which details all the frightening ramifications of that day for the implied audience.

There is an interesting structural parallel between Joel 2:1 and 1:5–6a since both passages employ a sequence of three imperatives followed by two כִּי clauses.[50] Joel 1:5–6a follows the description of the locust invasion and begins the process of calling for lament from the drunkards while detailing the consequences of the infestation through כִּי clauses. Joel 2:1 builds off the previous unit's description of the ravages of locust invasion, sounding the alarm, through its imperatives, and claiming that the day of Yʜᴡʜ necessitates this alarm, through its כִּי clauses. It is also possible that the second כִּי clause in Joel 1:6, which introduces the locusts as a גּוֹי 'nation', resonates with the characterization of the invaders as עַם רַב וְעָצוּם 'a people great and numerous' who come against Zion in Joel 2:2.[51] Thus, one element of the rhetorical strategy in Joel 2:1–11 is to echo a previously established rhythm for detailing the nature of the devastation and calling for response. The use of this pattern in Joel 2:1–2a stands out even more starkly since these are the only imperatives that the text directs toward the implied audience in this unit.

---

48. The verb בָא is either an affix or a participial form, but the presence of a qualifying statement that stresses the nearness of Yʜᴡʜ's day suggests that a participial translation is more appropriate.

49. Carroll suggests that the phrase קָרוֹב כִּי in Joel 2:1 is an editorial insertion, indicating that the editor intended for this verse to refer to a future day of Yʜᴡʜ rather than a day in the past or present. This downplays the resonance between Joel 2:1 and other texts that describe the day of Yʜᴡʜ as "near" (Isa 13:6; Joel 1:15, 4:14; Zeph 1:14). These parallels suggest that Joel 2:1 fits into a broader prophetic conception of the day of Yʜᴡʜ. Carroll also comments on the ambiguous nature of describing the day of Yʜᴡʜ as "near," suggesting that this is a rhetorical strategy to reduce potential dissonance between prophetic expectations and a historical reality in which these expectations were not realized (R. Carroll, *When Prophecy Failed: Cognitive Dissonance in the Prophetic Traditions of the Old Testament* [New York: Seabury, 1979] 124–28, 171–72). Chisholm challenges Carroll's perspective, suggesting helpfully that one ought to consider the contingent nature of prophetic language. Prophetic language is functional (or rhetorical) in that it intends to persuade its audience to respond in certain ways. It can employ a wide variety of strategies to achieve this purpose. Consequently, describing the day of Yʜᴡʜ as "near" in Joel 1:15 and 2:1 is not necessarily a sign of later hedging but, rather, is language that intends to heighten the urgency of the audience's response (R. Chisholm, "When Prophecy Appears to Fail, Check Your Hermeneutic," *JETS* 53 [2010] 561–78).

50. Van der Merwe and Wendland, "Word Order," 122.

51. Ibid.

Joel 2:2a employs two short, verbless clauses headed by יוֹם 'day' in order to describe what will happen when the day of Yнwн comes. Both clauses use word pairs describing it as יוֹם חֹשֶׁךְ וַאֲפֵלָה 'a day of darkness and gloom', and יוֹם עָנָן וַעֲרָפֶל 'a day of clouds and thick darkness', which reinforces the somber nature of impending calamity. These are stock images in day-of-Yнwн literature, probably reflecting Amos's depiction of the day of Yнwн as one of darkness and not light (Amos 5:18–20; cf. Zeph 1:15–16).[52] The occurrence of these word pairs also emphasizes theophanic imagery of the day of Yнwн because the combination of horn blasts, dark clouds, and the trembling of the people recalls manifestations of Yнwн's presence (Exod 19:16; Deut 4:11; Ps 97:2).[53] The brevity of these clauses, each containing only the word יוֹם in addition to the word pairs, also emphasizes the stark nature of what is about to befall. These descriptions of the darkness of the day of Yнwн convey Yнwн's imminent appearance and reinforce the calls to sound the alarm in Joel 2:1. The descriptions of darkness also prefigure the return to the day of Yнwн in Joel 2:10–11, where the theophany affects the heavenly bodies and makes the heavens and earth tremble. The effect is to create a sense of impending doom that the remainder of this unit explores.

Joel 2:2b–5: The Advance of the Locust Army

In Joel 2:2b–5, this rhetorical unit moves from declaring the imminence of the day of Yнwн to a detailed description of its harbingers. These verses also introduce the dominant genre of persuasion that Joel 2:1–11 employs. While the beginning imperatives found in Joel 2:1–2a seem to call the implied audience to respond to the unfolding situation, the course of action that the text proposes is ultimately futile. Instead, the bulk of Joel 2:1–11 is descriptive rather than prescriptive, since it focuses on detailing the full gravity of the devastation that the implied audience will face.[54] The revelation in Joel 2:11 that Yнwн commands this army identifies the principal persuasive genre of this passage as epideictic since its emphasis is to reveal

---

52. Barton, *Joel*, 72. Barton also suggests that the darkening refers to the sight of locusts covering the landscape with their mass.

53. Wolff, *Joel and Amos*, 44. Klein notes that עֲרָפֶל in particular presages the presence of Yнwн since it "is used almost exclusively elsewhere in the Old Testament to describe the appearance of Yahweh"; cf. Exod 20:21; Deut 4:11; 2 Sam 22:10; Ps 97:2; Job 22:13 (R. Klein, "The Day of the Lord," *CTM* 39 [1968] 518). Ringgren emphasizes the connection between this verse and Deut 4:11, which describes the manifestation of Yнwн's presence at Sinai using three of the four words for darkness found in Joel 2:2 (חֹשֶׁךְ; עָנָן; וַעֲרָפֶל) (H. Ringgren, "חשׁך," *TDOT* 5:257).

54. The text returns overtly to prophetic prescription in the following rhetorical unit. Joel 2:1–11, however, thoroughly details the power and authority of Yнwн and the invading horde that is under divine control. Thus, the locutionary intent of Joel 2:1–11 is to describe the power of Yнwн in full detail. There may be, however, an illocutionary intent here through which the prophet tries to persuade the implied audience that the only potential means of response will come in the program detailed in Joel 2:12–17.

the nature of the deity who is threatening to unleash this day. Focusing on the nature of Yʜwʜ then ties Joel 2:1–11 into the next unit, which provides the text's solution to the situation that it describes here.

Joel 2:2b–5 depicts the arrival of the עַם רַב וְעָצוּם 'people great and numerous' who bring only destruction and ruin. In accordance with the above discussion, I think that this invader probably originates from the realm of the locust invasion that dominated the imagery of Joel 1; however, in Joel 2:1–11, the locusts take on new, frightening traits because they also have the characteristics of a military force. As I argued above, Joel 2:1–11 frequently employs simile to describe the appearance and activities of the invading locusts. Joel 2:2b contains the first simile of this unit, describing the arrival of the invading army as being "like dawn spreading out upon the mountains." This image is meant to emphasize the suddenness of the invader's arrival since a mountain sunrise can quickly bring places of shadow into blindingly vivid light.[55] The invader's swift, sudden appearance emphasizes the dread that it brings. This simile relating to light stands in vivid contrast to the four synonyms related to darkness that are found in the previous clause.[56] The rapidity of this shift from images of darkness to an image of light also contributes to the disorienting quickness with which the invading horde appears.

After this simile, Joel 2:2b once again uses the incomparability of the situation to add emphasis, echoing the use of rhetorical questions pointing to the past and future that are found in Joel 1:2b. In this case, the prophet states that the size and power of the invader have not been seen previously and will never be seen again.[57] The strategy of incomparability again calls to mind the temporal progression found in Joel 1:2–3, where the prophet invokes both the past and future to describe the gravity of the unfolding situation. There is even some overlap in vocabulary since both Joel 1:3 and 2:2b refer to the necessity of informing the דּוֹר 'generation' that follows about these incidents.[58] In Joel 1:2–3, the prophet asks rhetorically whether such an event had occurred in the past and then commands the audience to tell of this event to succeeding generations. In Joel 2:2, the text looks before and after the event being described and stresses its incomparability. In both cases, the rhetorical strategy is to express the singular significance of the situation.

---

55. T. Finley, *Joel, Amos, Obadiah* (WEC; Chicago: Moody Press, 1990) 43.

56. Wolff and Allen take issue with this switch from darkness to light and have suggested repointing שַׁחַר 'dawn' to read שְׁחוֹר 'darkness', which is found in Lam 4:8 (Wolff, *Joel and Amos*, 44; Allen, *Joel*, 68–69). This seems to fit better with the imagery of the preceding verse; however, the lack of textual support for this change renders it speculative.

57. Barton, *Joel*, 72.

58. Fleer, "Exegesis," 151. The way in which the text constructs its multigenerational audience is slightly different since Joel 1:3 uses imperatives to command the implied audience to tell about this to their children, a process that is to be generationally repeated. Joel 2:2b is more succinct, employing repetition (דּוֹר וָדוֹר) to indicate continuing generations.

Following the invader's appearance, the text focuses on the activities of the locust army. Helpfully, Alter examines the verbs that the text uses to describe this locust invasion and proposes that they reflect a strategy of "incremental repetition."[59] The verbs principally describe the activities of the invading force and in doing so they overlap and occasionally even repeat. The net effect is to describe a steady advance of the invading force that ravages the landscape and moves from the mountains down to the city, over the walls, and into the houses. The locust army's advance is inexorable, and the powerful concentration of verbs of movement devoted to describing its activities make that point throughout Joel 2:1–11.

Joel 2:3a begins to describe the activities of the invading horde. This verse evokes a level of destruction reminiscent of the passing of a large locust swarm. The two clauses in this verse again employ a "before-and-after" strategy that describes the locusts' geographical progression across the landscape.[60] Joel 2:3a uses two parallel phrases to construct the "before-and-after" statement. The first clause is לְפָנָיו אָכְלָה אֵשׁ 'before it a fire consumes', which begins with a locative phrase, followed by the verb and its subject. The second clause, וְאַחֲרָיו תְּלַהֵט לֶהָבָה 'and after it, a flame blazes', mirrors this construction. The fronting of the locative phrases underscores the magnitude of the devastation. It shifts focus from the temporal dimension of the day of Yнwн to the spatial dimension, where the invading horde leaves behind only ruin and destruction.[61] Again, one can connect this imagery to actual descriptions of locust invasions, where the aftermath of their ravaging can make it appear that a fire gutted the entire landscape, leaving behind only charred ruins.[62]

Joel 2:3b expands on the devastation by again employing a simile and another "before-and-after" scheme. The simile creates an extreme contrast because the land is like the Garden of Eden before the arrival of the invaders and like a desert after they pass.[63] The syntax of this half of the verse differs, because this phrase is arranged as a chiasm, with the two prepositions of location (לְפָנָיו 'before it', אַחֲרָיו 'after it') appearing in the middle positions. The reference to Eden is notable because the image of a paradise garden plays a surprisingly limited role in the Old Testament.[64] Obviously, it draws

---

59. R. Alter, *The Art of Biblical Poetry* (New York: Basic Books, 1985) 42. Alter separates the verbs related to the advance of the army and lays them out together, which effectively makes his point. These verbs read (according to his translation) "they run, they dance, they run, they scale a wall, they go, indeed they go, they swarm, they run, they scale, they come in at the windows like thieves."

60. Ogden, *Promise of Hope*, 28–29.

61. Wendland, *Prophetic Rhetoric*, 24.

62. Simkins, *Yahweh's Activity*, 150.

63. A. Karp, "A Comparative Analysis of Stylistic Embellishment in the Speeches of Hosea and Joel," in *Biblical Literature* (ed. F. Francis; Ithaca, NY: Snow Lion, 2002) 62.

64. Crenshaw, *Joel*, 120. Kapelrud lists Gen 2:8, 10, 15; 3:23; 4:16; Isa 51:3; Ezek 31:9, 16, 18; and 36:35 as the only other passages that employ either גַּן־עֵדֶן or עֵדֶן; Kapelrud, *Joel Studies*, 76.

on the idyllic description of the early chapters of Genesis, but this theme also appears elsewhere in prophetic literature, although in the opposite direction from Joel 2:3. Isaiah 51:3 and Ezek 36:35 are both relevant since they describe how Yʜwʜ will act to undo destruction and desolation and to restore the land to an Edenic state.[65]

Joel 2:3 essentially uses this image in a contrary fashion since the coming of the day of Yʜwʜ, shown through the activities of the invading locusts, changes the land from paradise to wasteland. The simile comparing the land to Eden and then to a wasteland may go beyond merely describing the enormity of the change that the locust invasion brings. Instead, the use of Eden and its "uncreation" opens up the image-world of the earth returning to a pre-creation chaotic state.[66] Strengthening this association, Deut 32:10 parallels the term מִדְבָּר that Joel 2:3 uses for wasteland with the term תֹהוּ, which describes the uncreated state from which Yʜwʜ formed the earth (Gen 1:2). At minimum, the switch from Eden to a מִדְבַּר שְׁמָמָה 'wasteland of devastation' graphically expresses the totality of the destruction and may invoke the prospect of complete ruin and a return to chaos.

The final phrase of Joel 2:3 again reinforces the totality of the event, articulating that it is impossible to avoid what is coming. This clause summarizes the "before-and-after" constructions that precede it, employing an emphatic וְגַם that links this clause with the preceding phrases.[67] This final clause in Joel 2:3 foregrounds the subject פְּלֵיטָה 'escape' before the negated verb לֹא־הָיְתָה 'there is not', emphatically dashing any potential of avoiding the unfolding catastrophe.[68] The invading locust horde that follows the announcement of the day of Yʜwʜ in Joel 2:1 is both incomparable and inescapable.

Joel 2:4 again uses two similes to describe the invaders as having both equine appearance and mobility. The first clause is verbless, and it twice uses the noun מַרְאֵה 'appearance' to bracket סוּסִים 'horses'. The first occurrence is prefixed by כְ in order to construct the simile, and the second occurrence has the third-person-masculine-plural suffix attached (מַרְאֵהוּ), in order to establish that the antecedent of this comparison is the invading horde. The comparison with horses may also point to locusts as the intended referent of the imagery since there are noted similarities between the shapes of the heads of both creatures.[69] The second clause of Joel 2:4

---

65. Crenshaw, *Joel*, 120; see also R. Scoralick, "Jʜwʜ als Quelle der Fruchtbarkeit und das Motiv vom Gottesgarten in der Prophetie: Beobachtungen anhand des Zwölfprophetenbuches," in *Mythisches in biblischer Bildsprache* (ed. H. Irsigler; Freiburg: Herder, 2004) 334–37.

66. Simkins, *Yahweh's Activity*, 167.

67. On the summarizing function of גַם, see Waltke and O'Connor, *Introduction*, 663–64.

68. Van der Merwe and Wendland, "Word Order," 122.

69. Crenshaw (*Joel*, 121) refers to the German *Heupferd* and Italian *cavaletta* as modern languages that preserve the idea of the equine appearance of locusts. Barton also mentions that Rev 9:7 describes locusts as horses equipped for battle (Barton, *Joel*, 73).

constructs a simile related to the movement of the invading horde. It uses כְּפָרָשִׁים 'like steeds' as a word pair with סוּסִים and it is the subject of the verb יְרוּצוּן 'they run'. This verb is the first of several verbs in this rhetorical unit to employ the paragogic *nun* ending.[70] This feature may deepen the gravity of the situation and bring out the full sense of terror and awe since in poetic passages one potential function of the paragogic *nun* is to indicate certainty.[71] The verbs that show the paragogic *nun* in Joel 2:1–11 refer to the invading army. Consequently, this ending heightens the idea that their attack is unstoppable. Since this alternative ending is relatively rare, its repeated occurrence in this particular passage is noteworthy.[72]

Joel 2:5 maintains the militaristic theme of the previous verse but shifts from visual to audial phenomena.[73] Through them, the text invites the implied audience to engage another one of their senses as it articulates the nature of this invading force. This verse first describes the sound of the invaders as being like that of chariots on the hilltops. Chariots are mentioned in the Old Testament to indicate a powerful military force (Exod 14:6–7; Judg 4:3; 5:28; 1 Sam 13:5). Further, chariots occur in theophanic passages, which resonates with the revelation of this host's divine leadership in Joel 2:11 (2 Kgs 2:11–12; 6:17; Ezek 1).[74] These chariots move frenetically, emphasized by the verb יְרַקֵּדוּן 'skip about', which points to the swift approach of the invader against Zion (Nah 3:2; cf. 1 Chr 15:29; Job 21:11; Isa 13:21).

The location in which Joel 2:5 places the chariots is surprising since they are weapons of the plains, not of the hilltops (Judg 1:19; 4:3). The text, however, is drawing on shock value be first engaging the audience's aural senses, referring to the invaders' approach as כְּקוֹל מַרְכָּבוֹת 'like the sound of chariots'. The sound precedes their appearance, and the rumble of the chariot wheels conveys a sense of impending dread, brought to life when these weapons burst into view. It may suggest further the power of the

---

70. See also יְרַקֵּדוּן in Joel 2:5; יְרֻצוּן; יֶחֱבֹטוּן; יֵלֵכוּן; יְרֻצוּן in Joel 2:7; יֵלֵכוּן; יְדָּחָקוּן in Joel 2:8 and יְרֻצוּן in Joel 2:9.

71. Prinsloo, *Theology*, 42; Waltke and O'Connor, *Introduction*, 517. Waltke and O'Connor distinguish between the uses of the paragogic *nun* in prose and poetry. They note that in prose, this ending usually denotes contrastivity (cf. Num 11:19), while in poetry this ending typically indicates either certainty or the lack of a volitional sense. See also Joüon and Muraoka, who confirm this use of the paragogic *nun* and state that the typical reason for employing a paragogic *nun* is for a "fuller and more emphatic or expressive form" (P. Joüon and T. Muraoka, *A Grammar of Biblical Hebrew: Revised English Edition* [Rome: Pontifical Biblical Institute, 2006] 126). For a more detailed study on the phenomenon of the paragogic *nun*, see J. Hoftijzer, *The Function and Use of the Imperfect Forms with nun paragogicum in Classical Hebrew* (Assen: Van Gorcum, 1985) 1–93.

72. Joüon and Muraoka claim that there are 305 occurrences of the paragogic *nun* in the Old Testament. Deuteronomy contains the most (56), while Isaiah (37), Job (23), and Psalms (104) contain the next highest number of examples (Joüon and Muraoka, *Grammar*, 126).

73. Crenshaw, *Joel*, 121; Allen, *Joel*, 71.

74. Dillard, "Joel," 275.

invader since, if it can bring chariots over the mountains, city walls will be no barrier. Joel 2:5 thus combines aural and visual imagery and gives a picture of a portent that is first heard before appearing in all of its stunning reality.[75] The sound of the chariots' wheels and the horses' hooves inspires fear and dread, setting the stage for their frightening effect on the implied audience (cf. Joel 2:6).

Joel 2:5 then uses two more similes to describe the invader. The second simile of Joel 2:5 compares the invaders to the sound of a rampaging fire devouring the stubble of the fields. This recalls Joel 2:3, which employs fire as an image for the aftermath of the passage of a locust horde. This time, the text focuses on the sound; the blaze creates crackling hisses and explosions as it devours everything in its path, the sound preceding and warning of the onrushing flames and their heat. The idea of fire's consuming stubble may also foreshadow YHWH's appearance in Joel 2:10–11 since this image often describes divinely ordained judgment against both Judah and foreign nations (cf. Isa 5:24; 33:11; Obad 18; Nah 1:10).[76] This simile again emphasizes the totality of the destruction, declaring that the invader will even devour the stubble, which reemphasizes the "scorched-earth" nature of the invader's march.

Finally, Joel 2:5 refers to the invaders through a third simile as being כְּעַם עָצוּם 'like a mighty people'. This simile departs from the aural focus of the previous two and recalls Joel 2:2, which refers to the great and mighty people who are attacking (Num 20:20; 21:33; Judg 5:13; 2 Kgs 18:26).[77] The passive participle עָרוּךְ 'being set up' follows the simile and demonstrates that this force is arrayed to achieve maximum fighting capability (Gen 14:8; 1 Sam 4:2; Jer 6:23; 50:9).[78] The third simile encapsulates the threats created through the first two. The threatening sounds of approaching chariots and flames coalesce into an image of a great army preparing to attack. By the end of Joel 2:5, the text has detailed the advance of the invading locust army to the gates of Zion and slowed to engage in a detailed description of its power and appearance. The assault forewarned in Joel 2:1 is imminent.

---

75. Fleer, "Exegesis," 157. Fleer states, "One listens as the locusts make the noise of chariots. Then one watches as they leap on the tops of mountains."

76. Dillard, "Joel," 275. Beyse notes that there are two typical judgment metaphors that use stubble. First, as in Joel 2:5, fire can burn stubble, which suggests total consumption and devastation; nothing remains in the wake of judgment. Second, wind can scatter stubble, suggesting impermanence (cf. Jer 13:24; K. Beyse, "קַשׁ," *TDOT* 13:180–82). The association of stubble with fire in Joel 2:5 reveals the image-world from which it is drawn.

77. E. Lipiński, "עַם," *TDOT* 11:176. This word can refer to an army or levy, which suggests that the mention of a "mighty people" again emphasizes the militaristic aspect of the metaphor blend describing the locust army.

78. Crenshaw, *Joel*, 122. The active participle is used to describe the military capability of David's forces in 1 Chr 12:33, 35.

Joel 2:6: The View of the Victims

Joel 2:6, however, delays the unfolding of the invader's assault. This verse first stops the flow of similes describing the invaders. Instead, it articulates the reaction of their victims. The verse signals the shift toward the victims with the fronted constituent מִפָּנָיו 'from its face' preceding the specific action of the victims, which is to יָחִילוּ 'writhe in anguish'.[79] This writhing is indicative of a loss of control over the body's movements, reflecting the level of fear. Interestingly, those who writhe are not specifically identified as Zion dwellers. The text instead uses a generic term עַמִּים 'peoples' and an anarthrous construction כָּל־פָּנִים 'all faces' to describe the victims. This is slightly confusing since Joel 2:2 and 2:5 refer to the invading locust horde with the singular form עַם, but the purpose of using עַמִּים is to emphasize the immense power of the invaders since their approach sends reverberations through surrounding lands even as they prepare to attack Zion (cf. Isa 2:3; 8:9; 12:4).[80]

As a result of the invaders' arrival, the victims stare in anguish, and their faces are transformed as they contemplate their fate. The description of the victims also begins with the fronted constituent כָּל־פָּנִים, echoing מִפָּנָיו in Joel 2:6a. Joel 2:6 plays with the word "faces": the appearance of the face of the invader leads to a visible transformation of the victims' faces.[81] This is powerful because it provides a close-up of the victims' reaction, which

---

79. Wendland, *Prophetic Rhetoric*, 24. Dille and Baumann discuss the metaphorical range of חִיל, which can include the idea of writhing in childbirth (Isa 13:8; Jer 4:31; 6:24). Dille categorizes Joel's use of חִיל as a dead metaphor: the allusion to childbirth is not active. Instead, what remains is a generic sense of anguish or dismay (S. Dille, *Mixing Metaphors: God as Mother and Father in Deutero-Isaiah* [London: T. & T. Clark, 2004] 28–29). helpfully fleshes out the image of חִיל, suggesting that it externally evokes an "involuntary and uncontrolled spasmodic movement, to which the body is surrendered, accompanied by a sense of weakness and heat," and internally evokes "a state of trembling, panic, fear" (A. Baumann, "חִיל," *TDOT* 4:344–47). This sense of all-pervasive terror and loss of bodily control is the image-world that the text is trying to access in describing the wake of the army's march.

80. Barton, *Joel*, 73.

81. The exact nature of this transformation is difficult to determine since the translation of the remainder of Joel 2:6b is debated. The issue hinges on the rare word פָּארוּר, which concludes the verse. Most commentators understand this word to mean 'glow' or 'grow pale'. The word is found only here and in Nah 2:11, which does not provide much context on which to base an interpretation. In the LXX tradition, this phrase is πᾶν πρόσωπον ὡς πρόσκαυμα χύτρας, which is usually understood as faces becoming darkened like soot on a pot (Barton, *Joel*, 58). This may have resulted from reading פָּארוּר as פָּרוּר 'cooking pot' (Wolff, *Joel and Amos*, 38). Probably the best solution is to argue that the nuance of color change in a face to represent fear or terror may vary from society to society; thus, both traditions could well be trying to communicate a similar phenomenon of faces showing the emotive response that the invaders evoke (C. Dogniez, "Fautes de traduction, ou bonnes traductions: Quelques examples pris dans la LXX des Douze Petits Prophetes," in *X Congress of the International Organization for Septuagint and Cognate Studies* [ed. B. Taylor; Atlanta: Scholars Press, 2001] 253).

creates fear in the implied audience by seeking to draw it into the description being offered.[82] Further, the change of perspective from the activities of the invader to the reactions of the victims heightens the persuasive potential of Joel 2:1–11. The text can highlight the powerlessness of those whom this army is about to attack. The destructive activities of the invader and the terror-struck response of the victims point toward the inevitability of the invader's victory, which again helps to provide the foundation for the call to response in Joel 2:12–17.

Joel 2:7–9: The Attack of the Locust Army

Joel 2:7–9 articulates additional reasons that the reactions of Joel 2:6 are entirely appropriate. These verses shift the perspective back to the invaders now that they have completed their march across the countryside. They are now prepared to overwhelm the defenses and break into the besieged city in order to unleash terror and destruction. Joel 2:7a accelerates the pace and employs two similes that describe the invaders as being כְּגִבּוֹרִים 'like warriors' and כְּאַנְשֵׁי מִלְחָמָה 'like men of battle', who move quickly and breach the city's walls. Both similes are the first term in their respective clauses, which means they have been foregrounded for emphasis.[83] Joel 2:7b then emphasizes the discipline of the attacking force by means of two parallel clauses that indicate that all of the invading army's members follow their allotted path.[84] This again has resonances with locust imagery

---

82. Kalmanofsky does excellent work in considering the connections between the genre of horror and prophetic rhetoric in Jeremiah. Although her work does not mention Joel, the description of the "victims" in Joel 2:6 resonates with her understanding of "indirect horror," in which the implied audience looks on the state of the victim with a sense of fear and disgust. She suggests that the rhetorical effectiveness of such horrific imagery lies in its ability to make the audience into participants who struggle to maintain emotive distance from the images unfolding before them. The horrific images dynamically engage the implied audience, causing it to identify with the victims, while struggling to preserve itself by maintaining a certain distance (A. Kalmanofsky, *Terror All Around: The Rhetoric of Horror in the Book of Jeremiah* [LHB/OTS 390; New York: T. & T. Clark, 2008] 91–103).

83. Van der Merwe and Wendland, "Word Order," 123.

84. The second parallel clause contains the negated verb וְלֹא יְעַבְּטוּן, which has been the subject of some discussion. The root עָבַט appears in the Qal or Hiphil in a legal sense of giving or taking in pledge (Deut 15:6, 8; 24:10). Joel 2:7 would be the only time that this root occurs in the Piel, in which case it seems to require the meaning 'exchange' or 'change'. Whitley instead proposes that there was an interchange of gutturals and that the root should be חָבַט 'to decline'. He points to evidence from an Arabic cognate *hbt*. This would explain the reading in some of the ancient versions, such as the LXX, which reads ἐκκλίνωσιν (C. Whitley, "*'bt* in Joel 2:7," *Bib* 65 [1984] 101–2). Ahlström, however, notes a chiastic structure in the four verbs that Joel 2:7b–8a comprises. The first and fourth verbs are both יֵלֵכוּן 'they go', while the second and third verbs are וְלֹא יְעַבְּטוּן and לֹא יְדְחָקוּן, respectively. This grammatical structure leads Ahlström to suggest that the second and third verbs are synonymous and, since לֹא יְדְחָקוּן clearly refers to the locust army's maintaining ranks, וְלֹא יְעַבְּטוּן does likewise (Ahlström, *Joel*, 11–13; see also Dillard, "Joel," 275).

since they are noted to move in a seemingly organized manner in both biblical (Prov 30:27) and nonbiblical accounts.[85]

Joel 2:8 begins with the same word as 2:7b (וְאִישׁ) and continues the description of the attackers' relentlessness and discipline.[86] Interestingly, the preposition כְּ disappears, indicating that the text is now employing metaphor, rather than simile. This draws the implied audience more deeply into the textually constructed world; no longer is the locust horde "like" an army, it *is* an army that breaches Zion's walls. Joel 2:8b develops the scene, painting a picture of this army continuing its inexorable advance.[87] This clause indicates that the weapons of the defenders are ineffectual with Allen noting the futility of employing regular weaponry against this foe.[88] Joel 2:8 concludes with a final clipped phrased לֹא יְבַצֵּעוּ 'they do not break ranks' that summarizes all of the preceding descriptions; the invaders penetrate all of the defenses without having to slow down or break formation. Their overwhelming power is ultimately unchallenged and they are free to wreak havoc anywhere they choose.

Joel 2:9 describes the outcome of the assault. After penetrating all the defenses, the locust army has free reign to run about the city. It can run along the top of the walls and even enter people's dwellings.[89] The "short staccato rhythm" of this verse emphasizes the overwhelming nature of the attack.[90] Joel 2:9a creates this rhythm by constructing a threefold repetition of the pattern preposition + geographical location + verb of motion, with the locust army as the implied subject of all of the verbs. The locations grow progressively more intimate as the locust army is the subject of three verbs of action beginning with יָשֹׁקּוּ 'they rush about' the city, to יְרֻצוּן 'they

---

85. See the survey of modern descriptions of a locust swarm in Simkins, *Yahweh's Activity*, 164–65. He notes numerous descriptions of locusts moving like members of a cohesive, disciplined military force.

86. Wolff, *Joel and Amos*, 46.

87. The phrase is וּבְעַד הַשֶּׁלַח יִפֹּלוּ. The preposition בְּעַד is used here with a verb of motion יִפֹּלוּ. According to Waltke and O'Connor this usually means that the preposition will indicate motion away from a given object, Waltke and O'Connor, *Introduction*, 201–02. הַשֶּׁלַח then probably is referring to the defensive weapons being fired at the invaders and by moving through or away from them, the image is one of their failure to slow this army. Crenshaw argues instead that this verse is actually employing a second meaning of הַשֶּׁלַח, which is a tunnel or aqueduct. In this instance the poem would be describing the route through which the army breached the defenses (Crenshaw, *Joel*, 124).

88. Allen, *Joel*, 72.

89. The image of locusts invading homes may echo the plague of locusts invading Egyptian houses in Exod 10:5–6. In this instance, the rhetorical effect of this identification would be to inform the implied audience that it now stands in place of Egypt as the target of divine wrath. This adds further reason for the implied audience to adhere to the prophetic plan of response articulated in the following rhetorical unit. See Stuart, *Hosea—Jonah*, 251; Dillard, "Joel," 276; Strazicich, *Joel's Use of Scripture*, 132; S. Bergler, *Joel als Schriftinterpret* (Frankfurt am Main: Peter Lang, 1988) 140.

90. Crenshaw, *Joel*, 124–25.

run upon' its walls, to יַעֲלוּ 'they ascend' upon the houses.[91] There is a parallel between "this way of dramatically stacking the threatening advance of the destroying army" and the description of locust waves in Joel 1:4.[92] In both instances, the clipped, repeated syntactic structures stress the totality of the devastation.

The final clause of Joel 2:9 slows down the previously mentioned rhythm by adding an extra element. Its geographical location is the most intimate yet, describing the invaders with the words בְּעַד הַחַלּוֹנִים יָבֹאוּ 'through the windows they enter', after they climb onto houses. In addition, this final clause uses a simile to compare their mode of entry to that of a thief. There is an intriguing parallel between this description and Jer 9:21, which describes death as entering through the window.[93] In both instances, the undesired intruder easily enters into the dwelling and demonstrates that there is no sanctuary available.

Overall, Joel 2:7–9 portrays the power of the locust army as so overwhelming that there is nothing that can stop it from breaching the defenses of the city. This again portrays the nature of the threat against the implied audience graphically, allowing no hope for escape at this stage. In the following verses, Joel 2:10–11 will strengthen this sense of impending doom by revealing that this invasion has divine sanction.

Joel 2:10–11: Return to the Day of Yhwh

The final two verses of this unit reach a climactic crescendo while returning the audience back to the concept of the day of Yhwh mentioned in Joel 2:1. The image-world returns to cosmological heights from the blend of locust and military imagery.[94] Joel 2:10 begins with the fronted spatial constituent לְפָנָיו 'before it', which has an ambiguous pronominal suffix. The suffix could refer to the invader, envisioning it as a collective entity, which is an approach that the text adopts when it refers to the invader with the collective noun עַם in Joel 2:2 and 2:5. The other possibility is that this suffix points forward, foreshadowing the explicit appearance of Yhwh in the next verse (cf. Joel 1:2–3, 5, 11).[95] The first possibility preserves the strongest rhetorical effect, the sudden revelation that Yhwh is at the head of the invading army, making it the most likely option. The ambiguity of the referent is fitting, however, given the transition toward cosmological

---

91. Joel 2:9 is also notable for lexeme repetition. Two of the verbs of motion (יְרֻצוּן; יַעֲלוּ) are also found in 2:7a, while 2:7 and 2:9 both make reference to the army breaching a wall (חוֹמָה). This lexeme repetition combines with the syntactic repetition to describe the capture of the city in dramatic fashion (Prinsloo, *Theology*, 43).

92. Van der Merwe and Wendland, "Word Order," 123.

93. Barton, *Joel*, 74.

94. Crenshaw, *Joel*, 125–26.

95. Van der Merwe and Wendland, "Word Order," 124. See also J. Jeremias, *Die Propheten Joel, Obadja, Jona, Micha* (Göttingen: Vandenhoeck & Ruprecht, 2008) 26–27.

imagery that follows the introductory לְפָנָיו, which leaves the implied audience in anticipation of a forthcoming revelation to clarify the antecedent.[96]

Following the introductory spatial constituent לְפָנָיו, Joel 2:10 employs
dramatic cosmological phenomena to heighten the power of the invader.
These images also draw from the realm of theophany, where the trembling
and darkening of heavenly bodies prefigure the appearance of Yhwh (cf.
Ps 77:16; Isa 13:10, 13; Mic 1:4). This is especially evident because Yhwh
appears on the scene in Joel 2:11.[97] When Yhwh arrives, nature cannot
help but react powerfully.[98] Joel 2:10a uses רָגְזָה 'it trembles' and רָעֲשׁוּ 'they
shake' to describe the response of the earth and the heavens. When the
verb רָעַשׁ has an impersonal subject or object, its meaning is usually hyperbolic in nature, suggesting that objects of permanence such as stars or
mountains quake before the one doing the shaking (Judg 5:4; Pss 18:8;
77:18–19; Jer 10:10; Ezek 26:10).[99] Further, the root רָגַז 'to tremble' also
occurs as an imperative in Joel 2:1, calling on the dwellers of the land to
tremble.[100] The fact that the earth trembles in Joel 2:10 suggests that all the
dwellers of the land have good reason to heed the command of Joel 2:1.

---

96. Crenshaw, *Joel*, 126.

97. Allen, *Joel*, 73. Allen notes that the standard effect of Yhwh's interventions is
an earthquake and other related cosmological phenomena. For more on the theophanic
realm as it relates to the day of Yhwh, see Leung, "Intertextual," 88–92, 193–97. Leung
rightly claims that the effects on the heavenly bodies usher theophany into the image-
world of Joel 2:10–11. Leung also understands Joel's use of theophany in Joel 2:1–11 as a
combination of the day-of-Yhwh traditions put forward in Isa 13:10–13, Amos 5:18–20,
and Zeph 1:14–16. Amos and Zephaniah focus on the element of darkness, while Isaiah
describes tremendous cosmic disturbances. Joel combines these image-worlds, presenting
the appearance of Yhwh through both darkness (Joel 2:1–2a) and the effects on the heavenly luminaries (Joel 2:10).

98. The presence of thunderstorm imagery informs many prophetic references to
theophanies, which is especially notable in references to dark clouds and precipitation
(Isa 28:2; 30:30; Nah 1:2–4; Zeph 1:14–16). It is evident, however, that the prophetic
descriptions of theophany also rely on other activities in the natural world, including the
trembling of the earth (Isa 29:6; Amos 1:2). See T. Hiebert, "Theophany in the OT," *ABD*
6:509–10.

99. J. Kessler, "The Shaking of the Nations: An Eschatological View," *JETS* 30 (1987)
161.

100. Interestingly, Isa 13:13, another day-of-Yhwh passage, describes the convulsing
of the earth and the heavens using the same verbal roots. Isaiah, however, applies רָגַז
'to tremble' to the heavens and רָעַשׁ 'to quake' to the earth, which may reveal that they
share a common vocabulary and tradition regarding Yhwh's appearance. There remains
a significant degree of flexibility, however, in the use of these images since the target
of the day of Yhwh in Isa 13 is clearly Babylon, while in Joel 2:1–11 the heavenly bodies shake as the day of Yhwh comes against Yhwh's own people. See S. Matthews, "The
Power to Endure and Be Transformed: Sun and Moon Imagery in Joel and Revelation," in
Imagery and Imagination in Biblical Literature: Essays in Honour of Aloysius Fitzgerald, F.S.C.
(ed. L. Boadt and M. Smith; Washington, DC: Catholic Biblical Association, 2001) 38–39.
Matthews notes the connection between Joel and Isaiah by stating, "Joel's description of
the Day of the Lord corresponds to that of Isaiah, in theme and imagery, but not in slav-
ish vocabulary." See also Müller's additional discussion of all of the elements connecting

If the earth trembles when this army approaches, then surely the implied audience ought to heed the command to tremble as it experiences the assault of this army.

Joel 2:10b changes from imagery of trembling to description of the darkening of the heavenly bodies. This half-verse emphasizes that all of these luminaries are going to be affected. The text declares that the sun and the moon קָדָרוּ 'darken', while using the idiom אָסְפוּ נָגְהָם 'they gather their brightness' to describe the dimming of the stars.[101] Ordinarily, this idiom would suggest an augmentation of light, but the presence of the previous clause points toward its diminishment.[102] The descriptions of darkening in Joel 2:10b recall the announcement of the day of Yhwh in Joel 2:2, which emphasizes that it is a day of darkness, gloom, and cloud. Beyond the boundaries of Joel 2:1–11, descriptions of the darkening of heavenly luminaries are a significant part of the expected lexicon of day-of-Yhwh imagery.[103] They are harbingers of the imminent arrival of Yhwh's presence (Amos 5:8–10; Zeph 1:15–16).[104] Overall, Joel 2:10 returns the image-world of Joel 2:1–11 to a theophanic plane. The text provides imagery, no longer of an assault, but instead of convulsing and darkening heavenly luminaries, suggesting that the entire cosmos is going to be affected.[105]

Joel 2:11 further contributes to the climax of this unit by stating what Joel 2:10 foreshadows. It reveals the stunning detail that Yhwh leads the invader, which is made even more shocking when we recall that Joel 2:1 identifies Zion as Yhwh's holy mountain. Joel 2:11 reverses this picture and portrays Yhwh as the one authorizing the assault. This is an even greater example of the rhetoric of delay than the text employs in Joel 1:2–3. The

---

Isa 13 to Joel 2:1–11 (K. Müller, *Gottes Zukunft: Die Möglichkeit der Rettung am Tag Jhwhs nach dem Joelbuch* [WMANT 119; Neukirchen-Vluyn: Neukirchener Verlag, 2008] 79–81).

101. The root קָדַר is typically associated with divine judgment when its objects are the heavenly bodies. The judgment can be enacted by Yhwh (Ezek 32:7–8; Isa 50:3) or by a force standing in for Yhwh (see the "foe from the north" in Jer 4:27–28). See S. Schmoldt, "קדר," *TDOT* 12:518–20.

102. Crenshaw, *Joel*, 127. Crenshaw suggests that a parallel use can be found in 1 Sam 14:19, where Saul commands a priest to 'withdraw' (אֱסֹף) his hand.

103. M. Weiss, "The Origin of the 'Day of the Lord,'" *HUCA* 37 (1966) 59. Weiss argues for a metaphorical interpretation of the darkening, which is correct to the extent that it does not try to locate actual times and places of cosmic phenomena that agree with this imagery. Instead, the darkening of the luminaries reflects the imminent arrival of Yhwh, which introduces the final climactic crescendo, building on the fear that was inspired by the invasion detailed in Joel 2:3–9.

104. Crenshaw, *Joel*, 127.

105. Although there are descriptions of locust infestations that seem to darken the sun, it is hard to see how this could also apply to the darkening of the moon and stars. Further, this statement concerning the heavenly luminaries recurs in Joel 4:16, where there is no surrounding context of locusts. Consequently, it is most likely that the text has moved beyond the image-world of locusts and now focuses on laying the foundation for the appearance of Yhwh in the following verse. See Dillard, "Joel," 276; Simkins, *Yahweh's Activity*, 167.

preceding verses use theophanic imagery and describe a powerful invader, but they conceal the fact that Y<small>HWH</small> leads the assault against Zion. Rhetorically, this creates a moment of abject despair; there is little hope of escape from an attack that Y<small>HWH</small> leads against a location that Y<small>HWH</small> is supposed to defend.

After all of these vivid pictures of destruction, the prophet's voice refers to Y<small>HWH</small> in the third person, declaring starkly that Y<small>HWH</small> utters קוֹלוֹ 'his voice' before חֵילוֹ 'his army'.[106] Referring to Y<small>HWH</small> in the third person only adds to the shock, since Y<small>HWH</small>, who calls for the sounding of the alarm in Joel 2:1, is also the reason why the alarm needs to be sounded in Joel 2:11.[107] Thus, the leader of the host sent against them here is the implied audience's own covenant partner and the one whose presence in Zion should guarantee security and protection. The rhetorical strategy of Joel 2:1–11 peaks at this moment, when Y<small>HWH</small> is no longer protector but attacker.

Following the revelation that Y<small>HWH</small> leads the invading horde, three successive clauses in Joel 2:11 describe Y<small>HWH</small>'s army and emphasize its invincibility. They are linked together since they all commence with an asseverative כִּי.[108] The first two כִּי clauses operate in parallel, describing Y<small>HWH</small>'s encampment as רַב מְאֹד 'very great' and referring to the ones obeying his commands as עָצוּם 'mighty'. Y<small>HWH</small> thus comes against his own people at the head of an attacking force that is both numerically overwhelming and physically capable. Then, the final כִּי clause explicitly announces the day of Y<small>HWH</small> and declares that it is גָּדוֹל וְנוֹרָא מְאֹד 'great and very terrifying'.[109]

---

106. The shock of the text's revelation that Y<small>HWH</small> is the leader of a force overrunning Zion is hard to overstate. Y<small>HWH</small>'s constant presence should guarantee Zion's security since, unlike Baal, Y<small>HWH</small> is not a deity who suffers seasonal or periodic defeats by opposing forces. See L. Dow, *Images of Zion: Biblical Antecedents for the New Jerusalem* (New Testament Monograph 26; Sheffield: Sheffield Phoenix, 2010) 80. In Joel 2:11, however, Y<small>HWH</small> has removed the divine presence and instead has brought destruction to the former sanctuary. Ollenburger provides excellent detail on the function of Zion as a refuge from enemies thanks to Y<small>HWH</small>'s presence. He notes both Ps 46 and Ps 48 as passages that declare that Zion is a refuge from foes ranging from the forces of chaos to foreign attackers. In this prophecy, however, the place that should provide refuge loses its security because the text places the deity who guarantees refuge outside the walls, directing the assault (Ollenburger, *Zion*, 75).

107. S. Loewenstamm, "The Trembling of Nature during Theophany," in *Comparative Studies in Biblical and Ancient Oriental Literature* (AOAT 24; Neukirchen-Vluyn: Neukirchener Verlag, 1980) 173–89. Joel 2:11 associates Y<small>HWH</small>'s military leadership with the theophany described in the previous verse. The fusion of these image-worlds should not be too surprising, since there is a close link between the trembling of nature and the portrayal of the divine warrior (Job 26:10–12; Isa 13:6–13; Nah 1:4–6; Hab 3:8–15).

108. Sweeney, *Twelve*, 164.

109. The combination of the adjectives הַגָּדוֹל וְהַנּוֹרָא appears to have two different connotations. On one hand, these adjectives can refer to the power of Y<small>HWH</small> in positive terms, usually calling on Y<small>HWH</small> to intervene in strength on a supplicant's behalf (cf. Neh 1:5; 4:8; 9:32; Dan 9:4). On the other hand, these adjectives can carry a more threatening overtone, when the implied audience seeks to avoid having the power of Y<small>HWH</small> unleashed against

Yhwh's leadership of the army may reflect a modification of the expected function of the Zion tradition mentioned in Joel 2:1. Instead of proclaiming salvation, the Zion tradition now sounds an alarm as the day of Yhwh approaches, full of portents of doom and disaster.[110] The one who is supposed to dwell in Zion and guarantee its impregnability is now depicted as the one leading the attacking force. This depiction of Yhwh is in conflict with the prophet's previous messages. Joel 1:6–7 uses three first-person-singular nominal suffixes ("my land," "my vine," "my fig trees"), the antecedents of which are Yhwh.[111] In that passage, the prophet portrays Yhwh as bewailing the invasion, whereas in this passage (Joel 2:11), Yhwh is the guiding force behind it. Yhwh's care and concern for the land are now juxtaposed with Yhwh's leadership of the invading army.

The day-of-Yhwh inclusio in these verses is significant to the understanding of this rhetorical unit. This concept is essentially a day of divine appearance, when the deity intervenes in unmistakable power. Prophetic literature often portrays it as a day in which Yhwh's judgment will fall on his own covenant community (cf. Amos 5:18–20; Zeph 1:16; Ezek 13:5), although it can also have a salvific element when Yhwh directs divine wrath against foreign nations (cf. Isa 13:6–22; Joel 3:4; 4:14; Obad 15).[112] This inclusio in Joel 2 reflects an intensification of the concept from Joel 1. Whereas Joel 1:15 suddenly transforms the discussion from a relatively literal description of locust invasion, Joel 2:1 and 2:11 bracket a scene that, on its own, transitions from earthbound to cosmological imagery.[113]

The locusts in Joel 2:1–11 are essentially harbingers of the day of Yhwh, and their purpose is to provoke a response from the implied audience. By describing this day as "near," in Joel 2:2 the text leaves open the possibility that the full effects of the day can be mitigated if the community responds in the ways that the text will reveal.[114] The following mention of the day of Yhwh in Joel 2:11, however, indicates that time is drawing short because it is described as though it has arrived. It is no longer "near." Instead, the day of Yhwh is "great and very terrible."[115] The locust invasion has caused

---

it. The latter connotation seems to obtain in the texts that use these adjectives to describe the day of Yhwh (cf. Joel 2:11; Mal 3:23). Consequently, while Yhwh's attributes of greatness and fearfulness are celebrated when Yhwh and the implied audience are in accord, the same attributes can evoke consternation when the context suggests that Yhwh will unleash his power against the implied audience.

110. Prinsloo, *Theology*, 48.

111. Sweeney, *Twelve*, 157.

112. Finley, *Joel*, 40. This element will come out in the discussion of later references to the day of Yhwh in this book.

113. M. LaRocca-Pitts, *The Day of Yahweh as Rhetorical Strategy among the Hebrew Prophets* (Ph.D. diss., Harvard University, 2000) 290–91.

114. Finley, *Joel*, 41.

115. LaRocca-Pitts, *Day of Yahweh*, 291.

much grief and destruction, but the text uses it to indicate that this is only a foretaste of what could occur when the day of Y<small>HWH</small> comes in full.

The overall effect of this stunning revelation in Joel 2:11 lies in creating an overwhelming sense of despair and desperation. If Y<small>HWH</small> leads this invading host that prefigures the ominous day of Y<small>HWH</small>, to whom can the community turn for salvation? Joel 2:11 is the "emotive psychological nadir of the entire prophecy," since at this point it appears that there is no escaping this catastrophe.[116] Y<small>HWH</small>'s presence among the invaders sets up the final summation, כִּי־גָדוֹל יוֹם־יְהוָה וְנוֹרָא מְאֹד 'for great is the day of Y<small>HWH</small>, very terrifying', and the poignant rhetorical question וּמִי יְכִילֶנּוּ 'and who can withstand it?' that follows.[117] This rhetorical question evokes the full power of Y<small>HWH</small> and the inescapable eventuality of this day since the implied answer to this question is "no one" (cf. Mal 3:2). This sense of despair sets up the prophet's portrayal of a proper response that follows, in Joel 2:12–17.

Summary

Joel 2:1–11 heightens the sense of threat found in Joel 1, with Linville referring to it as the rhetorical "coup de grace," implying that the appeals found in 1:15–20, even those uttered by the prophet, have not been positively answered.[118] The ease with which the invading army penetrates Zion further depicts the implied audience's inability to withstand what is coming. This unit culminates with the shocking declaration that the one leading the invader is none other than Y<small>HWH</small>. Y<small>HWH</small> thus personally controls the portents of the day and makes it clear that, behind the onslaught of these invaders, there is divine agency.[119] The brief mention of עַמִּים 'peoples' in Joel 2:6 may foreshadow the international effects of the day of Y<small>HWH</small> that later chapters explore, but the focus of Joel 2:1–11 is to establish that the day of Y<small>HWH</small> will not be a day of salvation. Instead, it is persuasively presented as a day of doom and disaster for the implied audience that it cannot escape based on its own strength, a fact that the plaintive rhetorical question that ends this unit emphasizes.[120]

---

116. Wendland, *Prophetic Rhetoric*, 25.

117. Wuellner comments on the effectiveness of rhetorical questions, suggesting that they seek to evoke an established reality or social value while guiding the audience toward the implied proper response (W. Wuellner, "The Rhetorical Genre of Jesus' Sermon in Luke 12.1–13.9," in *Persuasive Artistry: Studies in New Testament Rhetoric in Honour of George A. Kennedy* [ed. D. Watson; JSNTSup 50; Sheffield: Sheffield Academic Press, 1991] 110). It is also interesting to note that the verb in this final rhetorical question is in the prefix form, following affix verbs associated with divine action. This emphasizes the imperfective aspect of the question about whether it is possible to withstand the day of Y<small>HWH</small>, which is an appropriate position to adopt since Joel 2:12–17 addresses this issue in detail.

118. Linville, "Bugs," 296.

119. Prinsloo, *Theology*, 48.

120. Ibid.

Rhetorical Effectiveness

The effectiveness of Joel 2:1–11 is rooted in its potential to gain a hearing from the implied audience so that the text can garner the people's assent and guide them to respond in the ways that it proposes in the next rhetorical unit. The effect of this unit is to indicate beyond doubt that Yhwh's power is irresistible and that there is nothing that the implied audience can do that might restrain the unleashing of the day of Yhwh. The text creates significant tension in the implied audience as it announces their doom that must be relieved through action, preferably the action prescribed by the prophet, as the messenger of Yhwh.[121] The powerful rhetorical question with which this unit concludes sets up the necessity for the response that the text articulates in Joel 2:12–17. At the very least, by tapping into the powerful day-of-Yhwh tradition and directing its wrath at the very community that it intends to influence, the text has created a circumstance in which the prophet would have the opportunity to present his solutions to the issue at hand. Part of the rhetorical effectiveness of this unit is the way it creates the necessity for the prophet's program of response in Joel 2:12–17.

Beyond the effect of Joel 2:1–11 in setting up the text's proposed response, the rhetorical power of this unit is incredibly striking. The text's portrayal of Yhwh as one who can come in power against his own covenant people is one that would certainly seem to garner the attention of any member of any audience. Wendland suggests that part of the effect of this unit is to pose the question of whether the reading/hearing audience is ready to experience Yhwh's day or whether the full weight of its power still needs to permeate the audience's consciousness.[122] Similarly, one can ponder the effect of the text's portraying Yhwh as someone who employs powerful symbols of destruction, such as locusts and invading armies, to threaten the order of creation.[123] Joel 2:1–11 ought to evoke feelings of uneasiness and potential questions about the nature of the divine as constructed in the imagination of the text.

This sense of disquiet is undoubtedly part of the rhetorical effect of Joel 2:1–11 on its implied audience and any later audiences. It raises dramatic questions about the nature of Yhwh and the divine's relationship with humanity. This text portrays Yhwh as having the freedom to adopt whatever posture Yhwh chooses toward the implied audience, even if it seemingly threatens their continued existence. To experience this text as Patrick and Scult require—that is, to read it in such a way that its truth claims are active on the interpreter—brings the interpreter to a place of concern about

---

121. Kapelrud, *Joel Studies*, 81.
122. Wendland, *Prophetic Rhetoric*, 35.
123. R. Coggins, *Joel and Amos* (NCBC; Sheffield: Sheffield Academic Press, 2000) 42.

or even questioning of the divine character.[124] Moments like these that undercut familiar and expected norms require intensive activity on the part of the reading audience to comprehend the text.[125] If this is the case, then Joel 2:1–11 creates a paradoxical situation in which the passivity of the implied audience in the wake of Yhwh's actions requires greater activity on the part of the reader(s) to bring it into line with the expectations of the divine character—which is a challenging process. Of course, Joel 2:1–11 is one unit in a broader rhetorical discourse that paints a many-hued perspective of Yhwh; however, this unit's rhetorical effects certainly include a sense of disquiet.

Another aspect of considering the rhetorical effectiveness of Joel 2:1–11 is reflecting on its position in the broader development of the book. Although the implied audience of the text and the broader reading/hearing audience struggle with the portrayal of Yhwh and the threat of devastation, one must recognize that this unit represents the book's greatest moment of disorientation. The text attains this status given its relationship with the preceding rhetorical unit. Joel 1:19–20 offers up a passionate plea placed in the mouth of the prophet to Yhwh to come and act because of the devastation unleashed on the land and its people. In response to the appeal to Yhwh in Joel 1:19–20, Joel 2:1–11 indicates that Yhwh will indeed come, but the nature of his appearance portends further devastation and destruction. Joel 2:1–11 seems to indicate that the calls to lament issued throughout Joel 1:1–14 and the lament cries of Joel 1:15–20 did not receive a positive response and that Yhwh is actually moving against his own covenant community. Consequently, Joel 2:1–11 is the nadir of the text. This unit's rhetorical effect is to delay the hope of salvation and to deepen the community's fear as the rhetorical situation threatens to become overwhelming.

After the shocking revelation of Joel 2:11, the remaining rhetorical units offer a way out of misery and despair. They grapple with the issues that Joel 2:1–11 raises and they present a more fully developed picture of Yhwh and the implied audience. The rhetorical effect of Joel 2:1–11 is to provoke the implied audience to greater action and consideration about how to respond to this shocking revelation and, as this response is being provoked, the text transitions into a passage (Joel 2:12–17) where it offers its own vision of response. Thus, this unit is effective in provoking challenging questions, but it is also effective in pushing the implied audience to continue on through the remainder of the book, where it seeks to provide resolution to the tension.

---

124. D. Patrick and A. Scult, *Rhetoric and Biblical Interpretation* (JSOTSup 82; Sheffield: Almond, 1990) 24.

125. W. Iser, *The Act of Reading: A Theory of Aesthetic Response* (London: Routledge & Kegan Paul, 1978) 85.

Conclusion

Joel 2:1–11 continues the trajectory established in the previous chapter, building on the devastation of the locust plague and the introduction of the day of Yhwh. Joel 2:1–11 delves deeper into the day of Yhwh, using it as an inclusio to demarcate the boundaries of this unit. It emphasizes the power of the day by employing cosmos-rending imagery that leads to the final, despairing, rhetorical question of Joel 2:11. Between the boundaries of the inclusio, Joel 2:1–11 raises the level of threat against the implied audience by describing the advance and assault of an unstoppable force against Zion. Joel 2:1–11 again draws from the realm of locust imagery to describe the voracity of the invaders, but it adds militaristic images, transforming the locusts into disciplined soldiers who easily breach all defenses. The rhetorical strategy of this unit reaches its climax in the stunning revelation that Yhwh is at the head of the invaders, uttering the divine voice to command them in their assault against Zion. This revelation pushes this prophetic text to its nadir, indicating that there is no escape for the implied audience from the unleashed day of Yhwh. Joel 2:1–11 effectively demonstrates to the implied audience that it cannot stand against Yhwh and modify the exigence that it faces on its own. Instead, the only effective response is to continue to listen to the prophetic word and hope that it provides a means of escaping the day of Yhwh.

Chapter 5

Signs of Hope:
Rhetorical Analysis of Joel 2:12–17

Introduction

Joel 2:12–17 is key to the persuasive power of this book. In this rhetorical unit, the text attempts to construct an appropriate response for the implied audience to the devastating situations that it details in Joel 1:1–2:11. Joel 2:12–17 intertwines human and divine perspectives, calling on the implied audience to return to Yʜᴡʜ and even providing the prayer that the people should offer, while indicating Yʜᴡʜ's desire for the implied audience to respond appropriately. Further, Joel 2:12–17 uses its appeal for the implied audience to turn to motivate Yʜᴡʜ to turn in response. This interplay and the prophet's construction of the implied audience's cry establish the foundation for the turn from devastation to restoration that begins with Yʜᴡʜ's actions in Joel 2:18. Joel 2:12–17 offers renewed hope, indicating that it is possible to avoid the imminent destruction detailed in the day of Yʜᴡʜ. This hope is rooted in the prophet's construction of the implied audience's response and in Yʜᴡʜ's sovereign and gracious character.

Rhetorical Unit

Joel 2:12–17 commences with a phrasal hapax legomenon, וְגַם־עַתָּה 'even now'. This most likely reflects a disjunctive use of וְ since it is attached to a non-verbal constituent.[1] Van der Merwe and Wendland compare וְגַם־עַתָּה with the deictic phrase וְעַתָּה 'and now'. They argue that the two phrases are not synonymous, suggesting that the addition of גַם indicates that the focus of Joel 2:12 is this fronted phrase.[2] In other words, וְגַם־עַתָּה does not merely reflect a logical continuation from Joel 2:11; instead, the use of גַם helps to focus attention on עַתָּה.[3] In this instance, עַתָּה is best understood as a temporal adverb that shifts the implied audience from the announcement of the day of Yʜᴡʜ to their own response.

---

1. W. Prinsloo, *The Theology of the Book of Joel* (BZAW 163; Berlin: de Gruyter, 1985) 49. Waltke and O'Connor discuss the disjunctive function of *waw* when attached to a non-verbal constituent (B. Waltke and M. O'Connor, *Introduction to Biblical Hebrew Syntax* [Winona Lake, IN: Eisenbrauns, 1990] 650–52). On the uniqueness of וְגַם־עַתָּה, see C. van der Merwe and E. Wendland, "Marked Word Order in the Book of Joel," *JNSL* 36 (2010) 125.

2. Ibid., 126.

3. Ibid. "It is reasonable to regard 2:12 as a clause which has a fronted adjunct as its focus. This means that the appeal in 2:12 would be interpreted as follows: 'And even now, says Yahweh, return to me.'"

139

A change in speaker marked by the formula נְאֻם־יְהוָה 'declaration of
YHWH' also marks the beginning of this rhetorical unit. The voice of YHWH
breaks in to call for the community to return and to demonstrate this
through lament activities such as fasting and weeping. Alongside the
change in speaker, there is also a shift in tone as the text changes from descriptions of the invader in Joel 2:1–11 to directives addressed to the implied audience throughout Joel 2:12–17.[4] This provides an appropriate
response to the revelation of Joel 2:1–11, which emphasizes YHWH's leadership of the army that assaults Zion.[5] It also demonstrates its distinctiveness
from Joel 2:1–11 since that unit establishes the inadequacy of any human
response to the exigence of the divinely sanctioned assault. Joel 2:12–17
builds on that situation and begins to provide prophetic guidance to the
implied audience regarding the response they ought to make.

Joel 2:12–17 also begins to offer answers to the climactic rhetorical question that ended 2:1–11. The ability to withstand the onslaught of YHWH's
power on the coming day of YHWH is linked to the people's willingness to
respond in lament and return to YHWH. This unit then uses the same signal
for closure as Joel 2:1–11. It concludes with another poignant rhetorical
question in 2:17, in the context of a prayer that the prophet instructs the
implied audience to offer to YHWH. In this prayer, the prophet places the
question אַיֵּה אֱלֹהֵיהֶם 'where is their God?' on the lips of the other nations,
who look upon Judah's plight and question YHWH's sovereignty. This rhetorical question creates significant tension, and it sounds an ominous note
for the future of God's people, who are left hanging in the balance.

The identification of Joel 2:12–17 as a rhetorical unit has the support of
most interpreters, but there are objectors.[6] Sweeney, in particular, argues
that the major division of the book occurs within this proposed rhetorical
unit. He detects the aperture of the second half of the book in Joel 2:15
rather than in 2:18 or 3:1, as is usually thought.[7] This argument has some
credibility since Joel 2:15 begins with the same imperative phrase (תִּקְעוּ

---

4. T. Finley, *Joel, Amos, Obadiah* (WEC; Chicago: Moody Press, 1990) 51. Finley also
notes the shift in topic that goes alongside this shift in tone since Joel 2:12–17 changes
from announcing judgment to offering a program of escape.

5. E. Wendland, *Prophetic Rhetoric: Case Studies in Text Analysis and Translation* (Longwood, FL: Xulon, 2009) 20. Joel 2:1–11 concludes with YHWH uttering the divine voice
against Zion, while Joel 2:12–17 shifts the point of view so that YHWH now speaks directly
to the implied audience.

6. Those who identify Joel 2:12–17 as a cohesive textual unit include Finley, *Joel*, 51;
Prinsloo, *Theology*, 49–50; R. Simkins, *Yahweh's Activity in History and Nature in the Book of
Joel* (ANETS 10; Lewiston, NY: Edwin Mellen, 1991) 172–74; J. Crenshaw, *Joel* (AB 24c; New
York: Doubleday, 1995) 132–33; J. Barton, *Joel and Obadiah: A Commentary* (OTL: Louisville:
Westminster John Knox, 2001) 75–77; L. Allen, *The Books of Joel, Obadiah, Jonah and Micah*
(NICOT; Grand Rapids: Eerdmans, 1976) 76–77.

7. M. Sweeney, *The Twelve Prophets*, vol. 1 (Berit Olam; Collegeville, MN: Liturgical
Press, 2000) 166–67. See also Ogden, who divides the text using the repeated calls to blow
a trumpet in Zion in Joel 2:1, 15 (G. Ogden and R. Deutsch, *Joel and Malachi: A Promise of
Hope—a Call to Obedience* [ITC; Grand Rapids: Eerdmans, 1987] 29–31).

שׁוֹפָר בְּצִיּוֹן 'blow a *shofar* in Zion!') that introduces the previous rhetorical unit (cf. Joel 2:1). Following this command, Joel 2:15 contains two imperative phrases (קַדְּשׁוּ־צוֹם קִרְאוּ עֲצָרָה 'Sanctify a fast! Call a sacred assembly!') which also occur in Joel 1:14. These quotations of previous imperatives push Sweeney to argue that, since these quotations come from previous rhetorical units (Joel 1:2–20 and 2:1–14 in his understanding), this verse summarizes all that comes before.[8] Further, he notes that Joel 2:18 begins with a *waw*-consecutive form, which suggests to him that it is tied to the preceding verse and does not begin its own rhetorical unit. This last concern is valid, and the question of the relationship between Joel 2:17 and 2:18 is potentially problematic.[9]

This understanding of the rhetorical unit, however, has flaws that render it unlikely. It diminishes the transitional nature of Joel 2:12–14, which moves from a prophetic declaration of disaster toward a divinely offered hope for restoration.[10] Sweeney also points to the imperatives in Joel 2:15 as markers of disjunction, commencing a new unit. This assertion, however, overlooks the presence of imperatives (וְקִרְעוּ; שֻׁבוּ) that govern the call to response in Joel 2:12–13. Consequently, imperative verbs containing instructions for the implied audience from the prophet or from YHWH dominate both Joel 2:12–14 and 2:15–17, suggesting continuity between these verses rather than disjunction. It is not until Joel 2:18 that the text changes from prophetic commands to cry out to YHWH to promises of restoration and revitalization. Further, Joel 2:12–17 contains a large concentration of cultic terminology that binds the whole of the rhetorical unit together, terms describing lament activities, names of cultic sacrifices, and specific references to the priests.[11] There is also an element of lexical cohesion between Joel 2:12 and 2:17, which both call for weeping and use nominal (וּבְכִי) and verbal (יִבְכּוּ) forms from the same root to do so.[12] In light of this, it is quite appropriate to regard 2:12–17 as a coherent rhetorical unit that seeks to provide an appropriate response to the threat articulated in Joel 2:1–11.

Rhetorical Situation

This unit is pivotal in the development of the rhetorical situation within Joel. Joel 1:1–2:11 describes the threat of the locust invasion and ultimately

---

8. Sweeney, *Twelve*, 167.
9. See the discussion in chap. 6 for reasons why Joel 2:18 is best understood as the aperture of the next rhetorical unit.
10. R. Dillard, "Joel," in *The Minor Prophets: An Exegetical and Expository Commentary* (ed. T. McComiskey; Grand Rapids: Baker, 1992) 280.
11. Prinsloo, *Theology*, 49. This terminology includes the triad of fasting, weeping, and mourning in Joel 2:12b, the promise of blessing in the form of renewed sacrifices in 2:14, the calls to fast and gather in sacred assembly in 2:15–16, and the identification of cultic locales and personnel in 2:17.
12. Finley, *Joel*, 51.

reveals its divine sanction. These passages establish the exigence that drives the whole of the prophetic message; the land and its inhabitants are under an overwhelming assault led by Yʜᴡʜ that threatens all aspects of their existence. Joel 2:12–17 drives the life cycle of the rhetorical situation forward by building from the evidence of the exigence and moving toward a detailed program of response for the implied audience. There is an initial element of response in Joel 1:15–20, but the assault described in Joel 2:1–11 indicates the necessity for a more detailed program of response. In Joel 2:12–17, the text finally presents a comprehensive plan for the implied audience to react properly to the exigences of locusts, drought, and an invading army. In essence, Joel 2:12–17 attempts to work through the implied audience to correct the exigence. This unit intends to affect them with its discourse so that they will act appropriately.[13]

The description of Yʜᴡʜ in previous rhetorical units significantly affects the rhetorical situation of Joel 2:12–17. Joel 1:1–14 and 1:15–20 portray Yʜᴡʜ as the one to whom the prophet personally calls out for relief and respite (Joel 1:19) while urging the implied audience, through the means of an all-encompassing sacred fast, to do likewise (Joel 1:13–14). Yʜᴡʜ's answer in Joel 2:1, however, only worsens the situation by threatening the very existence of Zion. The capstone comes in the statement that Yʜᴡʜ himself leads the invader in Joel 2:11. This deepens the gravity of the rhetorical situation by revealing to the implied audience that the one to whom they are instructed to cry out is threatening to unleash a day of powerful divine intervention upon them.[14] Thus, it is striking when Joel 2:12 begins with וְגַם־עַתָּה 'even now', since the text combines the imagery of the locust invasion, drought, military threat, and finally, divine wrath in order to build the exigence of the situation to its highest point.

When considering the discussion of the overwhelming nature of the exigence in Joel 2:1–11, we must note that the response that the prophet presents does not provide direct resolution. The implied audience does not have the capacity to remedy these exigences directly by removing the locusts or resisting the invading army. Instead, Joel 2:12–17 creates a rhetorical situation in which the audience needs to accept its constraints and call out to the one with the authority to ameliorate the situation.

Rhetorical Strategy

As mentioned above, Joel 2:12–17 adopts a different orientation from the preceding unit. Whereas Joel 2:1–11 focuses on description, ultimately

---

13. D. Patrick and A. Scult, *Rhetoric and Biblical Interpretation* (JSOTSup 82; Sheffield: Almond, 1990) 34.

14. Joel 1:15 foreshadows Yʜᴡʜ's opposition when it briefly mentions the day of Yʜᴡʜ in the context of the locust invasion and drought. Yʜᴡʜ, however, remains silent in Joel 1. Joel 2:1–11 increases the level of threat when Yʜᴡʜ speaks and "utters his voice" to assert command over the force threatening Zion (Joel 2:11).

leading to the revelation that Yʜᴡʜ leads the attackers, Joel 2:12–17 employs many direct commands. In Joel 2:12–17, both Yʜᴡʜ and the prophet issue imperatives that call this audience to act in accordance with their prescriptions for remedying the exigence of the rhetorical situation (Joel 2:12, 13, 15, 16, 17). This unit thus demonstrates the features of deliberative rhetoric.[15] Joel 2:1–11 provides the reason for issuing imperatives since it reveals that this disaster has divine sanction. Joel 2:12–17 now offers an appropriate response.

Significantly, Joel 2:12–17 is the final unit in which the text commands the implied audience to act in order to ameliorate the situation. The following unit (Joel 2:18–27) employs three imperatives directed toward the land, the livestock, and the people, but these call for rejoicing and celebration in the wake of Yʜᴡʜ's powerful actions. Succeeding units continue to describe Yʜᴡʜ's restorative actions for Judah and his punitive actions against foreign nations. The imperatives in the following units are directed toward foreign nations (Joel 4:9–13), emphasizing the futility of the nations' actions. The text's venture into deliberative rhetoric here is pivotal. The description of the exigence in Joel 1:1–2:11 leads to this call for response, and the focus on Yʜᴡʜ's actions in 2:18–4:21 flows out of what the text calls the implied audience to do.

Within this deliberative orientation, Joel 2:12–17 has two distinct subunits that move from generality to specificity. The first is Joel 2:12–14, and it is a call to return to Yʜᴡʜ uttered by the prophet that is rooted in a description of the character of Yʜᴡʜ. Two imperatives from the root שׁוּב 'to turn/return' govern these verses. There is some potential confusion involved in identifying the speaker in Joel 2:12–14, since it shifts from first-person divine address in the first imperative, שֻׁבוּ עָדַי 'return to me', in 2:12 to third-person prophetic address in the second imperative, וְשׁוּבוּ אֶל־יְהוָה אֱלֹהֵיכֶם 'return to Yʜᴡʜ your God', in 2:13. This fusion of the identities of the messenger and his or her divine commissioner is a common feature in prophetic literature.[16] In this case, it helps to confirm that the prophet's proposed remedy also has divine sanction.

---

15. G. Kennedy, *New Testament Interpretation through Rhetorical Criticism* (Chapel Hill: University of North Carolina Press, 1984) 20.

16. See Overholt's discussion on the nature of prophetic authority and the necessity for close identification with a deity (T. Overholt, *Channels of Prophecy: The Social Dynamics of Prophetic Activity* [Minneapolis: Augsburg Fortress, 1989] 69–70). Concerning the juxtaposition of human words and the divine word in prophetic proclamation, see Moberly's discussion of Jeremiah's commissioning (W. Moberly, *Prophecy and Discernment* [CSCD 14; Cambridge: Cambridge University Press, 2006] 43–47). In this particular situation, this fusion may also reflect the text's use of Exod 34:6 in its description of the divine character since there is a similar potential for confusion in identifying the speaker in that passage (J. Crenshaw, "Who Knows What Yʜᴡʜ Will Do? The Character of God in the Book of Joel," in *Fortunate the Eyes That See: Essays in Honour of David Noel Freedman in Celebration of His Seventieth Birthday* [ed. A. Beck et al.; Grand Rapids: Eerdmans, 1995] 191).

The second subunit, Joel 2:15–17, expands on the initial calls to return to Yʜᴡʜ that govern the preceding imperatives. Joel 2:15–17 offers a specific picture of response, which includes identifying the place of response, the words of response, and even the composition of the audience. This second subunit assumes the establishment of an attitude of turning that permits it to describe in greater detail the interaction that it should create between the community and its God.

Joel 2:12–14: A Call to Turn

Joel 2:12–14 introduces the general parameters of the "turn" that the text proposes. It reads like a prophetic "call to repentance," which consists of an appeal for repentance, followed by statements that should motivate repentance (cf. Isa 1:19–20; Jer 3:12–13; 4:1–2; 22:3–5; 25:5–6; Ezek 14:6–11).[17] The text's apparent use of this form in Joel 2:12–14, however, gives rise to some interesting questions, given the preceding units of this book. The most pressing issue concerns the text's silence regarding the "sin" from which the community needs to repent. Commentators propose many different possibilities ranging from lack of regard for the prophetic word (Wolff), to critique of the Jerusalem cult (Redditt), and the possibility of syncretistic or idolatrous worship (Ahlström).[18] Unfortunately, the lack of explicit reference in the text to any specific form of wrongdoing renders these informed speculations.[19]

Nogalski tries to nuance the portrayal of the implied audience's guilt by using his understanding of *Stichwort* connections in the broader Book of the Twelve to argue that Joel's proximity to Hosea brings in the perspective of guilt.[20] Nogalski also tries to reverse the argument from silence and claim

---

17. R. Simkins, "'Return to Yahweh': Honour and Shame in Joel," *Semeia* 68 (1994) 42; Prinsloo, *Theology*, 53. Raitt attempts to break this category down further, suggesting that the appeal for repentance can incorporate a divine messenger formula, a vocative address, and admonitions. The admonitions are essential to the form, while the other two criteria are optional. The motivating factors include promises that Yʜᴡʜ will respond, accusations of guilt, and threats of punishment. Accusations of guilt are the most common motivating feature, with Joel 2:12–13 and Isa 55:6–7 being the only passages in which Raitt does not find such an accusation (T. Raitt, "Prophetic Summons to Repentance," *ZAW* 83 [1971] 30–49).

18. See H. Wolff, *Joel and Amos* (Hermeneia; Philadelphia: Fortress, 1977) 40–42; P. Redditt, "The Book of Joel and Peripheral Prophecy," *CBQ* 48 (1985) 225–40; and G. Ahlström, *Joel and the Temple Cult of Jerusalem* (VTSup 21; Leiden: Brill, 1971) 26.

19. J. Crenshaw, "Joel's Silence and Interpreters' Readiness to Indict the Innocent," in *Lasset uns Brücken bauen—: Collected Communications to the XVth Congress of the International Organization for the Study of the Old Testament, Cambridge 1995* (BEATAJ 42; ed. K. Schunck and M. Augustin; Frankfurt am Main: Peter Lang, 1998) 255–59. Crenshaw addresses the perspectives of Wolff, Redditt, and Ahlström and effectively locates the assumptions that they must make in order to support their theories. This brief critique reveals the lack of textual standing for their assumptions.

20. J. Nogalski, *Redactional Processes in the Book of the Twelve* (BZAW 218; Berlin: de Gruyter, 1993) 19–22. Nogalski claims that "Joel deliberately picks up where Hos 14:2ff. leaves off. . . . In addition, further connections to images of guilt from Hosea's message

that, since there is no explicit statement that this is unjust suffering, Joel assumes that the people are guilty.[21] Similarly, House argues that reading Joel "canonically" means that Joel's announcement of catastrophe comes as a natural response to Hosea's warnings of impending judgment.[22] Requiring the interpreter to draw from Hosea, however, at least partially invalidates reading Joel as its own discrete literary unit. As discussed above, one can defend the practice of reading prophetic books on their own by citing the presence of features that provide evidence of a book's essential integrity. These include titles and incipits, unique conclusions, and unique systems of cross-references and idioms.[23] Further, one can challenge Nogalski's list of *Stichworter* connecting Hosea and Joel and argue that they are common words that do not necessarily require borrowing from one prophetic work to the other.[24] Ultimately, the ability to read prophetic books as prophetic books and the critique of the Hosea–Joel catchword phenomenon render Nogalski and House's strategy of importing the guilt of the community from Hosea to Joel less persuasive.

---

to Israel imply that Joel transfers this guilt to his own message to Jerusalem." Schart appeals to Iser's theory of an "information gap" to suggest that readers must import Hosea's understanding of Israel's guilt in order to place this call to return in proper context (A. Schart, "The First Section of the Book of the Twelve Prophets: Hosea-Joel-Amos," *Int* 61 [2007] 142; cf. W. Iser, *The Act of Reading: A Theory of Aesthetic Response* [London: Routledge & Kegan Paul, 1978] 168–69). Clendenen follows a similar line of argument, suggesting that Joel relies on the implied audience's knowledge of traditions related to repentance to establish that there is sin for which the individuals need to repent (E. Clendenen, "Text-linguistics and Prophecy in the Book of the Twelve," *JETS* 46 [2003] 395–96).

21. Nogalski, *Redactional Processes*, 17. Nogalski buttresses his approach by appealing to Solomon's temple-dedication speech in 1 Kgs 8:37–39. That speech refers to the necessity for an individual who is appealing to Y<small>HWH</small> to know "the affliction of his own heart" in order for Y<small>HWH</small> to act to alleviate disasters, including locusts and drought.

22. P. House, *The Unity of the Twelve* (JSOTSup 27; Sheffield: Almond, 1990) 130. House's theory regarding the narrative structure of the Twelve struggles when it addresses the issue of sin in Joel. He considers Hosea and Joel to be the books that start the downward trajectory of the Twelve, since he claims that these books focus on sin against Y<small>HWH</small>. As mentioned above, he can only establish this in Joel on the basis of inference, since Joel never mentions the sin of the community. Joel's silence on sin stands in marked contrast to books such as Hosea and Amos, which delve into great detail concerning the community's transgressions.

23. E. Ben Zvi, "The Prophetic Books or 'The Twelve': A Few Preliminary Considerations," in *Forming Prophetic Literature: Essays on Isaiah and the Twelve in Honour of John D. W. Watts* (ed. J. Watts and P. House; JSOTSup 235; Sheffield: Sheffield Academic Press, 1996) 152–53; E. Ben Zvi and J. Nogalski, *Two Sides of a Coin: Juxtaposing Views on Interpreting the Book of the Twelve / the Twelve Prophetic Books* (Analecta Gorgiana 201; Piscataway, NJ: Gorgias, 2009) 47–83.

24. R. J. Coggins, "Interbiblical Quotations in Joel," in *After the Exile: Essays in Honour of Rex Mason* (ed. J. Barton and D. Reimer; Macon, GA: Mercer University Press, 1996) 77. The list consists of זֹאת ('this'), יֹשְׁבֵי ('dwellers'), יַיִן ('wine'), גֶּפֶן ('vine'), דָּגָן ('grain'). Coggins does not dispute some level of connection between Hosea and Joel, but he argues that this relationship should be placed in the broader context of Joel's quotations from and allusions to the rest of the Old Testament.

The question of the community's potential guilt in Joel 2:12–14 requires further exploration, especially when one considers the consternation created among interpreters by the lack of an explicit statement articulating the community's guilt. Shapiro writes that this passage does not give us "sinners in the hands of an angry God; rather they are people in the hands of a megalomaniacal God."[25] This perspective stands in tension with the text's own description of Yʜwʜ's character in Joel 2:13, but the idea of Yʜwʜ's acting against the implied audience without an explicit statement of their guilt hovers uncomfortably over this passage.

One attempt to explain this tension is to question whether Joel's call should fit into a scheme that reflects a pattern of sin-judgment-repentance-blessing. Commenting on the need to find an appropriate sin, Simkins states, "[I]f Joel calls the people to return to Yahweh, surely they had sinned! Like Eliphaz, Bildad, and Zophar, we must search out and identify that sin."[26] Allen even suggests that the lack of reference to a specific sin is a strategy to draw the people into self-reflection to see where they had erred (cf. Lam 3:40).[27] This search, however, is not the only framework in which to understand the rhetorical strategy of Joel 2:12–14. It is possible to make the argument instead that the language of Joel 2:12–14 is oriented toward lament and not repentance in the wake of sin. According to this formulation, Joel 2:12–14 would then continue the stream of lament cries found throughout Joel 1 (Joel 1:5, 8, 11, 13, 14, 18, and potentially 2:15–17).[28] Joel 1 urges the community to cry out, and the lament activities of "fasting, weeping, and mourning" found in 2:12–14 are part of the text's strategy to call the community to respond to the exigence of the rhetorical situation by acknowledging that only Yʜwʜ can restore the implied audience.

The lack of an identifiable charge against the community appears to fit with cries of lament, since they do not require a preexisting sin but may even contain protestations of innocence (Pss 7:3–5; 59:3–4). In the case of lament, the call to turn to Yʜwʜ is intended to express the community's utter dependence on Yʜwʜ in the face of crisis.[29] This perspective may free the interpreter from speculation about a sin that occasioned the events described in Joel 1:1–2:11. This permits the argument that the text's silence on the issue should be taken at face value rather than provoking a search for intertexual inferences to establish the community's sinfulness.[30] Given

---

25. H. Shapiro, "Joel," in *Congregation: Contemporary Writers Read the Jewish Bible* (ed. D. Rosenberg; San Diego: Harcourt, Brace, Jovanovich, 1987) 201.

26. Simkins, "Return to Yahweh," 43.

27. Allen, *Joel*, 79.

28. G. Ogden, "Joel 4 and Prophetic Responses to National Laments," *JSOT* 26 (1983) 97.

29. Ibid., 105. Ogden suggests that the fact that the suffering is undeserved is what gives rise to the anguish evident in the cries to Yʜwʜ.

30. Crenshaw, "Who Knows," 188. "In times of trouble, whether deserved or undeserved, turning to Yʜwʜ was the appropriate response inasmuch as he alone could remove the adversity."

the prophetic propensity to identify the sins from which they are calling the nation to repent in other passages (cf. Isa 5:8–30; Jer 5:1–17; 44:1–14; Ezek 8:1–18; Amos 4:4–11; Zech 1:1–6), the absence of an explicit sin in Joel suggests that it is worthwhile to seek an alternative explanation.[31]

In place of equating calamity with guilt, Simkins interprets the call to return in Joel 2:12–14 against the background of an honor/shame model derived from cultural anthropology. Bechtel offers a working definition of shame in an Old Testament context:

> The feeling of shame is a response to failure or inability to live up to internalized ideals, social identifications, and roles inculcated by parents and society, which dictate expectations of what a person "should" be able to do, be, know or feel.[32]

This proposal is controversial since the expected vocabulary of shame does not govern this passage, although it does surface in Joel 2:17 with the use of the term חֶרְפָּה 'scorn' in a plea for Yhwh not to let the community fall into this state.[33] Simkins argues, however, that the disasters described earlier in the book create an appropriate context for considering the community's shame. Essentially, the devastation mentioned in the previous pericopes causes the Judahite community to experience shame, since it was unable to live up to its expected religious duties.[34] The cessation of sacrifices mentioned in the previous chapter is evidence of this situation (cf. Joel 1:9, 13). The text's call to the Judahite community in this model directs the

---

31. Clendenen, "Textlinguistics," 393–95. Clendenen provides a useful chart that examines the Minor Prophets according to a fourfold scheme: (1) indictment; (2) instruction; (3) judgment; (4) incentive/salvation. He notes that Joel and Nahum are the two books that are missing explicit mention of the first element. He imports indictment into Joel through the command to "return to me," potentially echoing Ahlström's identification of improper worship. Clendenen's chart, however, also highlights the oddity of Joel's seeming silence concerning the guilt of the implied audience in contrast to the rest of the Minor Prophets, who explicitly state their indictment.

32. L. Bechtel, "The Perception of Shame within the Divine-Human Relationship in Biblical Israel," in *Uncovering Ancient Stones: Essays in Memory of H. Neil Richardson* (ed. L. Hopfe; Winona Lake, IN: Eisenbrauns, 1994) 80. Bechtel attempts to maintain a distinction between shame and guilt but acknowledges that both states can arise from similar circumstances. Bechtel also provides useful commentary on the internal and external societal pressures that lead to shame and guilt, noting that shame relies more on external sanction, while guilt relies more on internal conscience (L. Bechtel, "Shame as a Sanction of Social Control in Biblical Israel: Judicial, Political and Social Shaming," *JSOT* 49 [1991] 47–76).

33. Stiebert notes the absence of typical shame terminology in Joel 2:12–14 (J. Stiebert, *The Construction of Shame in the Hebrew Bible: The Prophetic Contribution* [JSOTSup 346; London: Sheffield Academic Press, 2002] 78–79). Huber compiles this terminology, identifying the roots בוש 'be ashamed', כלם 'be humiliated', חפר 'be abashed', קלה 'be dishonored', and חרף 'reproach' (L. Huber, *The Biblical Experience of Shame/Shaming: The Social Experience of Shame/Shaming in Biblical Israel in Relation to Its Use as Religious Metaphor* [Ph.D. diss., Drew University, 1983] 53). None of these terms appears in Joel 2:12–14.

34. Simkins, "Return to Yahweh," 51–52.

community to engage in worship with actions of mourning and, in return, the prophet offers the potential that Y[HWH] might turn and restore their honor.[35]

Simkins's proposal has been challenged since there are questions concerning whether he oversteps the applicability of an honor/shame model by giving it an international focus.[36] Stiebert states that the anthropological studies that discuss honor/shame models focus on small-scale societies and do not necessarily translate into the broader context of international relations.[37] One can challenge this critique, however, by appealing to examples of what appears to be communal shaming activity within the context of warfare or diplomacy (2 Sam 10:1–5; Isa 20:1–5).[38] Consequently, the question whether the Judahite community would care that it was shamed in the eyes of other nations remains open. Simkins would need to claim that the concept of shame was similar for both the implied audience and these unnamed "nations."[39] Similarly, there are questions as to whether the category of *honor* is appropriate to describe what the community experiences when it worships Y[HWH] by sacrificing properly, or *shame* to describe the lack of sacrifices.[40] Conceivably, one could understand the cessation of sacrifice as a grave situation without introducing the loaded terminology of honor and shame.

These critiques are important reminders of the necessity for methodological rigor when appropriating models from other disciplines, but it is possible to retain the idea of the Judahite community's shame to consider how the text constructs the rhetorical strategy of Joel 2:12–17. There are other examples in which the Old Testament rhetorically takes into account the way foreigners would perceive Y[HWH] and the Judahite community as a valid motivation for Y[HWH]'s actions. On two occasions, Moses constructs a hypothetical Egyptian reaction to Israel's destruction as a means of persuading Y[HWH] to relent from sending punishment (Exod 32:11–14; Num 14:11–16). Further, Ps 79 pleads for Jerusalem's restoration as a matter of Y[HWH]'s glory since the city's destruction allows the nations to question Y[HWH]'s power (Ps 79:10). The usefulness of these examples for advancing the honor/shame perspective, however, is mitigated by the fact that they

---

35. Ibid., 52.

36. J. Chance, "The Anthropology of Honour and Shame: Culture, Values and Practice," *Semeia* 68 (1996144.

37. Stiebert, *Construction*, 79.

38. Bechtel, "Shame as Sanction," 65–70. Both texts reflect examples of attempts to bring shame on the community as a whole. Isaiah mimics the fate of captives, and the Ammonite king mistreats David's envoys to express a change in status that eventually requires a communal response.

39. Chance, "Anthropology," 145.

40. Stiebert, *Construction*, 79. Stiebert suggests that Simkins's social values of honor and shame are rather generic if he intends to argue that honor consists of joyful activity while shame consists of the inability to perform the correct sacrifices.

all occur in contexts responding to Israel's sinful behavior.[41] Yʜwʜ may act
to restore Israel and preserve the divine reputation, but in these examples
Israel merits the punishment from which Yʜwʜ relents.

A stronger example is found in 2 Kgs 18–19, where Sennacherib's taunt-
ing of Hezekiah includes equating Yʜwʜ with the impotent gods of other
nations whom the Assyrians conquered (2 Kgs 18:35).[42] If the Judahite
community falls, then Yʜwʜ is vulnerable to shame because he failed to
protect what he claimed. Yʜwʜ, however, responds to this foreign perception and asserts divine authority over this king, reaffirming supremacy over
a mortal ruler (2 Kgs 19:28). This example contains no explicit mention
of Judah's or Hezekiah's sin but, rather, focuses on Yʜwʜ's response to the
hubris of the Assyrian ruler.

Within Joel itself, the idea of restoring communal honor may manifest
itself after we consider other overt references to the community's shame
found in Joel 1–2. Joel 1:11 uses the imperative הֹבִישׁוּ 'be ashamed!' which
explicitly calls on the farmers to experience the ignominy of the agricultural failure, since this could be an example of Yʜwʜ's lack of regard for the
community. This reference and the threefold occurrence of the similar root
יָבֵשׁ 'be dried up' in Joel 1:12 create a wordplay in which the shame of the
people is tied to the withering of joy.[43] Looking ahead to Joel 2:18–27, we
can see that 2:19 promises that Yʜwʜ will not allow his people to be a חֶרְפָּה
'reproach' or an object of scorn among foreign nations. This same word
occurs in Joel 2:17 in the context of the people's plea to Yʜwʜ. Further, Joel
2:26 and 27 both contain the phrase וְלֹא־יֵבֹשׁוּ עַמִּי לְעוֹלָם 'and my people will
not be ashamed again' in summarizing Yʜwʜ's restorative activity. According to Joel 2:18–27, one of the most notable results of Yʜwʜ's intervention
will be to restore the community after its shame, which is detailed in the
breakdown of the sacrificial system in Joel 1:5–14. Yʜwʜ's intervention in
Joel 2:18–27 may also imply that the prophet's call to "return to Yʜwʜ"
sparks the implied audience to call out to Yʜwʜ in hopes of divine
intervention.

In summary, this discussion considers the possibility of the honor/
shame interpretation of Joel 2:12–17 but also reveals the difficulty of separating Yʜwʜ's actions for the purpose of maintaining Yʜwʜ's divine reputation from the potential sin of the community. Consequently, it is
necessary to once again consider the possibility of the implied audience's
guilt in the rhetorical flow of Joel 2:12–17. A stronger case for importing

---

41. Exodus 32:11–14 describes the aftermath of the Golden Calf incident, Num 14:11–
16 records Moses' plea for Yʜwʜ to spare Israel in the wake of the Israelites' refusal to enter
the land, while Ps 79:5 pleads with Yʜwʜ to forgive the sins of former generations and
restore the current generation.

42. Bechtel, "Perception of Shame," 87–89. See the discussion of Yʜwʜ's vulnerability
to shame as a counterpart of the requirement to offer praise and honor to Yʜwʜ.

43. See the discussion of the rhetorical strategy of Joel 1:11–12.

guilt is found in Joel's conversations with other Old Testament texts. As many interpreters note, Joel is replete with references to other texts, which it uses in the course of its rhetorical strategies.[44] Specifically, the list of calamities that the implied audience faces in Joel may reflect elements of Solomon's dedicatory prayer for the temple in 1 Kgs 8:37–39, which mentions famine, pestilence, blight, mildew, locusts, or enemy invasions as reasons for the community to reflect on its potential errors.[45] A few verses later, 1 Kgs 8:48 uses language similar to Joel 2:12 in constructing its response, suggesting that, if the people of the community return to Yhwh with all their hearts (וְשָׁבוּ אֵלֶיךָ בְּכָל־לְבָבָם) in the wake of their sin, then Yhwh may act restoratively (cf. Deut 30:2; 2 Chr 6:38; Jer 24:7). This resonance with Solomon's prayer may suggest the presence of guilt in Joel 2:12–14.

The connection between Joel and Jonah may also suggest the presence of guilt in Joel. The declaration of Yhwh's character in Joel 2:13 echoes the same statement in Jonah 4:2, where the citizens of Nineveh clearly acknowledge their guilt before Yhwh and seek divine forgiveness. Jonah 3:8 also expresses the Ninevites' desire for repentance through the injunction וְיָשֻׁבוּ אִישׁ מִדַּרְכּוֹ הָרָעָה 'let each turn from his wicked way'.[46] In this instance, the command to שׁוּב 'turn/return' clearly indicates repentance. The question מִי יוֹדֵעַ 'who knows?' how Yhwh might respond also links the context of Joel and Jonah, when the Ninevites ask the question concerning the utility of repenting before Yhwh (Joel 2:14; Jonah 3:9). In Joel's assertion that the day of Yhwh is near, there may also be a connection with the identical announcement in Isa 13:6–9 that clearly punishes guilty Babylon.[47] In effect, while agreeing with Ben Zvi's perspective on reading prophetic books as discrete literary units, I think that it is still possible to see the resonances with other biblical literature that may inform proper interpretation and suggest the context of guilt for this rhetorical unit.

Overall, there are two strong, competing perspectives on this issue. The lack of an explicit statement of guilt suggests an interpretation grounded in the realm of lament and turning to Yhwh as the only hope for restoration

---

44. Mason identifies some of these parallels, suggesting the presence of "stock" oracles concerning divine activity, while also drawing attention to the parallels in thought between Joel and Zech 9–14 (R. Mason, *Zephaniah, Habbakuk, Joel* [OTG; Sheffield: Sheffield Academic Press, 1994] 117–21). See also the chart in Crenshaw, *Joel*, 27–28, which identifies potential verbal parallels.

45. J. Strazicich, *Joel's Use of Scripture and the Scripture's Use of Joel: Appropriation and Resignification in Second Temple Judaism and Early Christianity* (BIS 82; Leiden: Brill, 2007) 156.

46. See below for a more detailed analysis of the resonance between Joel 2:13 and Jonah 4:2 and the ways in which they employ this description of the divine character.

47. H. Schmitt, "'Reue Gottes' im Joelbuch und in Exodus 32–34," in *Schriftprophetie: Festschrift für Jörg Jeremias zum 65. Geburtstag* (ed. F. Hartenstein, J. Krispenz, and A. Schart; Neukirchen-Vluyn: Neukirchener Verlag, 2004) 300–301. The parallel with Isa 13:6–9 is useful but not convincing on its own since the target of the day of Yhwh in Isa 13 is clearly Babylon. While Joel may borrow some of the same phraseology, it does not necessarily import the context of a guilty nation whom Yhwh judges for its oppression.

amid desperate circumstances. Conversely, the circumstances described in Joel 1:1–2:11 and the actions commanded in Joel 2:12–13 suggest intertextual resonances that activate the concept of guilt and the need for repentance before Yhwh will act restoratively. This issue yields no simple resolution, but the intertextual connections and the presence of sin in passages where Yhwh acts restoratively to preserve Yhwh's own reputation tilts the balance toward the presence of guilt in Joel 2:12–17.[48]

The next step is to move beyond the broad discussion of the nature of the call in Joel 2:12–14 and consider the persuasive power of the text itself. The specific wording reveals the text's emphasis on the concept of turning to Yhwh in hopes of restoration. Joel 2:12 begins with וְגַם־עַתָּה and the divine-pronouncement formula נְאֻם־יְהוָה. The initial וְגַם־עַתָּה focuses the situation, suggesting that, in the wake of the declaration of the day of Yhwh, immediate response is required.[49] The divine-pronouncement formula places the imperative that follows in the mouth of Yhwh. The use of this formula is a rhetorical move that underscores the fact that the upcoming offer of salvation comes from Yhwh. While it is a formula frequently employed to conclude prophetic oracles, this is its only occurrence in Joel, which adds to its emphatic impact.[50]

The divine word is also particularly powerful since it follows directly after the declaration in Joel 2:11 that Yhwh is the one leading the invading host. Yhwh may utter his voice at the head of the army that comes against Zion, but before all hope fades, the text portrays Yhwh as speaking once again to the implied audience and providing a way to avoid the foretold devastation. The text first creates the context in which it is Yhwh who comes in wrath and judgment, but before judgment occurs, Yhwh calls the community to turn, with the understanding that this may avert the approaching disaster (cf. Joel 2:14).[51]

The command in Joel 2:12 is for the implied audience to "return to me with all your hearts." It relies on an imperative form of the root שׁוּב. This verb is common in the Old Testament, and its semantic range extends from simply turning around physically to meanings laden with theological significance. The use of שׁוּב in Joel 2:12–14 clearly falls into the theological

---

48. C. Dempsey, "'Turn Back, O People': Repentance in the Latter Prophets," in *Repentance in Christian Theology* (ed. M. Boda and G. Smith; Collegeville, MN: Liturgical Press, 2006) 58–59. Dempsey admirably captures the ambiguous nature of the question of the community's guilt by noting that, in Joel, ill fortune brings about responses of pain, suffering, and lamentation, while the prophetic call of Joel 2:12–13 seems to use the vocabulary of penitence and prayer.

49. A. Kapelrud, *Joel Studies* (UUÅ 4; Uppsala: Lundequist, 1948) 81.

50. Barton, *Joel*, 77. Crenshaw draws a distinction between the paucity of prophetic oracular formulas in Joel, and Haggai and Zechariah who "peppered" their messages with formulas of this sort. The scarcity of the formulas in Joel maintains the rhetorical effect of emphasizing that what follows is a divine word. See Crenshaw, "Who Knows," 187–88.

51. Dillard, "Joel," 280.

category and precipitates a discussion of the relationship between YHWH and the implied audience. The typical use of this root in "covenantal" contexts is to call for repentance or a return to YHWH (2 Chr 30:6; Isa 1:27; 6:10; 9:12; 10:21; 19:22; 31:6; Jer 3:1, 7, 10, 12, 14, 22; 24:7; Hos 3:5; 5:4; 6:1; Amos 4:6, 8–11; Zech 1:3; Mal 3:7).[52] Essentially, this verb calls for the reestablishment of the disrupted relationship between YHWH and his people.[53] In the context of Joel 2:12, which lacks an explicit statement of guilt, the idea of returning to YHWH at the very least requires the implied audience to reorient its thoughts toward YHWH, whose manifestation is near (Joel 1:15; 2:1).[54] If the intertextual activation of guilt and sin is correct, then this command also carries the nuance of calling the community to return to YHWH in repentance. Interestingly, YHWH can also be the subject of שׁוּב, denoting a change in the divine disposition about a particular course of action.[55] This phraseology typically appears in reciprocal relationship with a turning back to YHWH on the part of the community (2 Chr 30:6; Zech 1:3; Mal 3:7).[56]

The use of an imperative form of the root שׁוּב in Joel 2:12 sets up a triad of activities indicative of an appropriate response in the conclusion of the verse: fasting (וּבְצוֹם), weeping (וּבִבְכִי), and mourning (וּבְמִסְפֵּד). These are stock responses to situations in which the community needs to demonstrate commitment to its deity, hoping for a divine reversal of the circumstances.[57] Examples of these terms abound in the Old Testament, including David's fasting for the life of the child conceived in adultery (2 Sam 12:16), prophetic calls to weep (Isa 22:12; Jer 31:9), and descriptions of mourning (Jer 6:26; Amos 5:16, 17; Mic 1:8). Engaging in this triad of activities reflects the community's "utter dependence on Yahweh the faithful and compassionate deliverer."[58] It is also notable that the only other occurrence of these three terms together in the Old Testament is Esth 4:3, where the exiled Jewish community engages in these activities in the wake of learning about Haman's plot. This parallel is interesting since it is a context of lamentation without a description of a specific previous sin; however, Esther's lack of a command to return to YHWH means that interpreters ought not to

---

52. W. Holladay, *The Root ŠÛBH in the Old Testament* (Leiden: Brill, 1958) 147.

53. Ibid., 120, 147.

54. Wolff, *Joel and Amos*, 52–53; see also H. Fabry, "שׁוּב," *TDOT* 14:507–8. Wolff and Fabry suggest here that the rhetorical effect of the command to return to YHWH is to acknowledge the divine sovereignty and submit to judgment.

55. R. Pratt, "Historical Contingencies and Biblical Predictions," in *The Way of Wisdom: Essays in Honour of Bruce K. Waltke* (ed. J. Packer and S. Soderlund; Grand Rapids: Zondervan, 2000) 186.

56. Holladay, *Root*, 148–49.

57. Wolff, *Joel and Amos*, 49. Ogden suggests that these activities are expressions of the implied audience's total dependence on aid from YHWH; Ogden, *Promise of Hope*, 30.

58. Idem, "Joel 4," 105.

draw too emphatically on this parallel.[59] Overall, Joel 2:12 extends hope for salvation and calls on the implied audience to hear and respond with appropriate activities.

In the first clause, Joel 2:13 implores its audience to "rend" their hearts and not simply their clothes. In doing so, the text resonates with a broader prophetic tradition that calls for genuine turning as opposed to rote genuflection to correct rituals and formulas. Amos is an exemplar of this tradition as seen in Amos 4:4–5 and 5:21–23, where the prophet castigates the religious observances that the community does not offer in the proper spirit (cf. Isa 58:1–12; Jer 7:1–8; Hos 6:6; Mic 6:1–8). Joel, however, is not engaging in "anticultic" prophecy since the remedy that the text proposes is rooted in the cultic context (cf. Joel 2:15–17).[60] Instead, the text's call in Joel 2:12 is for deep inner response to the crisis.[61] The prophet's prescription to "rend" hearts is for the community to engage in fasting and weeping under cultic leadership in the temple. Thus, this imperative is a call for the people's internal states to match their external actions. Joel 2:12 concludes with calls for the people to use expected forms in their responses, while Joel 2:13 implores the audience to have their hearts mirror their outward actions.

The next phrase in Joel 2:13 restates the command to return to Yhwh, again using an imperative form from the root שׁוּב. At this point, the tone shifts from first to third person so that the voice of the prophet breaks in and implores the audience to "return to Yhwh your God." This second imperative from the root שׁוּב develops the concept of turning further, moving from the initial appeal to turn, to supplying a reason for turning that is firmly rooted in the character of Yhwh. Following the imperatival שׁוּב, the

---

59. The ambiguity about whether the calls to fasting, weeping, and mourning necessitate repentance continues when one looks at these terms individually. The word for 'fasting' (צוֹם) occurs 26 times in the Old Testament and, while certain fasts are in response to sin or guilt (2 Sam 12:16; Neh 9:1; Jer 36:6, 9; Jonah 3:5), others seem to reflect an appeal to Yhwh in the midst of desperate circumstances, where sin may not be involved (2 Chr 20:3; Ezra 8:21; Pss 35:13; 69:11; 109:24; Dan 9:3). Isaiah 58:1–12 calls for repentance to replace fasting, suggesting that the community's fasts do not necessarily imply a repentant attitude (J. McKenzie, *Second Isaiah* [AB 20; New York: Doubleday, 1968] 166–67). Similarly, the word for 'weeping' (בְּכִי) can reflect contexts of both repentance (Isa 22:12; Jer 3:21; Mal 2:13) and sorrow over lament-worthy events (Deut 34:8; 2 Sam 13:36; 2 Kgs 20:3; Ezra 3:13; Jer 31:16). Finally, the word for 'mourning' (מִסְפֵּד) can also reflect contexts of both repentance (Isa 22:12; Jer 6:26; Zech 12:10) and lamentation over difficult circumstances (Gen 50:10; Ps 30:12; Ezek 27:32; Amos 5:16). Consequently, the use of these terms is not conclusive in indicating whether or not the prophet is trying to evoke repentance in this context.

60. Barton, *Joel*, 80.

61. Ogden, *Promise of Hope*, 30. Essentially, this verse intends to call the implied audience into wholehearted, united pleading for divine assistance in the wake of the many crises detailed throughout the early sections of the book.

text draws from the divine "character credo" of Exod 34:6–7.[62] These verses describe the character of Yhwh as Moses receives the second copy of the stone tablets in the aftermath of the golden calf incident, where Israel's sin is on full display. They claim that Yhwh is compassionate and gracious, slow to anger, abounding in lovingkindness, and one who both forgives iniquity and punishes the unrepentant. This summary of Yhwh's character appears in other Old Testament passages in a variety of literary genres, suggesting its pervasiveness in the Hebrew understanding of its deity (Num 14:18, Pss 86:15; 103:8; 145:8; Nah 1:3; Jonah 4:2; and Neh 9:17, 31b).[63]

The use of this creed in Joel 2:13b is not an exact citation, since it does not include the declaration that Yhwh visits punishment on the generations following those who disobey.[64] The final phrase in Joel's use of this credo is וְנִחָם עַל־הָרָעָה 'he relents from evil', which is not derived from Exod 34:6–7. The verbal root נָחַם 'to relent' with Yhwh as its subject occurs several times in the Old Testament. Typically, it implies that Yhwh changes his mind or relents concerning punishment that he was going to visit upon either his people or foreign nations (Jer 4:28; 15:6; 20:16; Amos 7:3, 6; Zech 8:14).[65] This same credo with the additional phrase also appears in Jonah 4:2, where Jonah uses it as an accusation against Yhwh for showing mercy to Nineveh.[66] While Joel 2:13 shows the character of Yhwh primarily in

---

62. Concerning Joel's use of Exod 34:6–7, see M. Lang, "Das Exodusgeschehen in der Joelschrift," in *Führe mein Volk heraus: Zur innerbiblischen Rezeption der Exodusthematik: Festschrift für Georg Fischer* (ed. S. Paganini, C. Paganini, and D. Markl; Frankfurt am Main: Peter Lang, 2004) 68–74. Lang suggests that Joel imports the broader context of Exodus through this citation, especially in its potential to activate a divine turning toward mercy.

63. Crenshaw, *Joel*, 136–37. Ahlström suggests that this phrase is part of a temple liturgy, arguing that its praising phraseology is at home primarily in the center of religious observance; cf. Ahlström, *Joel*, 24–25. For a chart marking the variations in the reuse of Exod 34:6–7, see G. Clark, *The Word* Hesed *in the Hebrew Bible* (JSOTSup 157; Sheffield: Sheffield Academic Press, 1993) 248.

64. M. Fishbane, *Biblical Interpretation in Ancient Israel* (New York: Clarendon, 1985) 342–47. Fishbane notes other passages that use this formula without the final declaration of intergenerational punishment, including Deut 7:10 and Jonah 3:9.

65. See also Jer 20:16 and Ezek 24:14 for negated examples of נחם where Yhwh claims that his punishment cannot be averted.

66. Coggins, "Interbiblical," 79. Zapff notes the differing directions in which the books of Joel and Jonah take the same phrase, stating, "On the one hand, it functions as a reason to motivate Israel to return to Yahweh; while on the other hand, it functions as a reproach to Yahweh because of his patience with Nineveh, put in the mouth of Jonah with satiric intent" (B. Zapff, "The Perspective on the Nations in the Book of Micah as a 'Systematization' of the Nations' Role in Joel, Jonah and Nahum? Reflections on a Context-Oriented Exegesis in the Book of the Twelve," in *Thematic Threads in the Book of the Twelve* (ed. P. Redditt and A. Schart; BZAW 325; Berlin: de Gruyter, 2003) 299. The question of which text borrows from the other remains open. For the priority of Jonah, see J. Magonet, *Form and Meaning: Studies in Literary Technique in the Book of Jonah* (Frankfurt: Peter Lang, 1976) 77–79; T. Bolin, *Freedom beyond Forgiveness: The Book of Jonah Reexamined* (JSOTSup 236; Sheffield: Sheffield Academic Press, 1997) 171–72. For the priority of Joel, see Allen, *Joel*, 228; Fishbane, *Biblical Interpretation*, 345–46; Nogalski, *Redactional Processes*, 273.

relationship with his own covenant people, Jonah 4:2 moves outward and demonstrates that YHWH's gracious and compassionate character has universal ramifications. It even offers the possibility of restoration to Israel and Judah's enemies, much to Jonah's chagrin.[67] Thus, the different prophetic reuses of the character credo demonstrate the flexibility of the motif, with Joel and Jonah both considering the implications of YHWH's character as it applies to their distinct situations.[68]

Interestingly, verbal forms of the root נָחַם occur in Exod 32:12 and 14, where Moses and YHWH debate the fate of idolatrous Israel during the golden calf episode. In Exod 32:12, Moses uses an imperative form of נָחַם (וְהִנָּחֵם), directed at YHWH, while in Exod 32:14, the text employs an indicative form (וַיִּנָּחֶם), stating that YHWH will not destroy Israel. Based on this verbal parallel, it is likely that the addition of this piece onto the character credo in Joel and Jonah draws in the conversation between Moses and YHWH in Exod 32:7–14 alongside Exod 34:6–7.[69]

The rhetorical effect of combining this earlier piece with the established character credo is well worth considering. The text declares that YHWH relented (וַיִּנָּחֶם) in Exod 32:14, which purchased Israel a stay of execution,

---

Wöhrle proposes a "grace-corpus" redactional layer in the Book of the Twelve that encompasses both Joel 2:12–13 and Jonah 4:2, while also including Mic 7:18–20, Nah 1:2b–3a, and Mal 1:9a, since they may employ snippets of Exod 34:6–7 (J. Wöhrle, "A Prophetic Reflection on Divine Forgiveness: The Integration of Jonah into the Book of the Twelve," *JHS* 9 [2009], http://www.jhsonline.org/Articles/article_109.pdf). The weakness of this proposal is in how little of Exod 34:6–7 is found in the latter three passages. Malachi 1:9a shares with Exod 34:6 only the root חנן, while Nah 1:2b–3a only shares the phrase אֶרֶךְ אַפַּיִם 'slow to anger'. It is unlikely that this minimal verbal correspondence indicates an intentional redactional strategy. Dozeman offers the most appropriate approach and leaves the question open in order to offer readings of Joel in light of Jonah and vice versa (T. Dozeman, "Inner-biblical Interpretation of Yahweh's Gracious and Compassionate Character," *JBL* 108 [1989] 213–18). Strazicich suggests that Joel repatriates the character credo away from Jonah's universalized application (Strazicich, *Joel's Use of Scripture*, 154).

67. Ibid., 222–23. Dozeman does see a universalizing element in the Joel passage. He draws on the question of how catastrophes might affect YHWH's credibility in Joel 2:17 and Exod 32:12 in order to argue that YHWH's actions toward his own covenant community are intertwined with the actions of foreign nations. This potential universalizing element, however, is subsumed in Joel under the concern for the fate of Judah, which involves judgment on the nations in Joel 4.

68. R. Schultz, "Ties That Bind: Intertextuality, the Identification of Verbal Parallels, and Readings Strategies in the Book of the Twelve," in *Thematic Threads in the Book of the Twelve* (BZAW 325; ed. P. Redditt and A. Schart; Berlin: de Gruyter, 2003) 39–40. Schultz notes that variations of Exod 34:6–7 also appear in Mic 7:18–19 and Nah 1:3.

69. Dozeman, "Inner-biblical," 221. Dozeman rightly suggests that the addition of the phrase declaring that YHWH can turn from evil in the character credo that Joel and Jonah employ is "anchored in the same narrative context in which the formula is introduced in the Torah." Clark also works through the narrative context of Exod 32–34 and notes how it brings together YHWH's kindness and severity, presenting these characteristics as complementary and suggesting that YHWH has the sovereign freedom to invoke them at the time of his choosing (Clark, *The Word* Hesed, 247–52).

but according to the narrative, the community had to be cleansed of its guilt through the actions of Exod 32:19–29 before YHWH would reissue the Ten Commandments and make the creedal statement of Exod 34:6–7. This parallel may help with the reading of guilt in Joel 2:12–14 since, in the Exodus narrative, Moses must act as intercessor in order to preserve the community and call on YHWH to relent. Only his pleading with YHWH spared them complete devastation (cf. Exod 32:30–35).

In Joel 2:12–17, there is an opportunity for the community itself to respond appropriately to the announcement of YHWH's character in Joel 2:13. The placement of the character credo is quite apt since what follows in Joel 2:15–17 is a detailed program about how the community should appeal for YHWH's salvation and restoration. YHWH may 'relent' (וְנִחָם) from his intention, but Joel 2:12–14 reminds the community that there are actions that it should undertake in order to demonstrate proper turning to YHWH, even if the text does not provide an indictment against the people.

In the wake of Joel's adaptation of the character credo, the prophet puts forward a question emphasizing the inscrutability of YHWH's character. In asking "who knows?" whether YHWH will turn at the beginning of Joel 2:14, the text provides an open door for an amelioration of the present dire circumstances. This question is a prophetic "perhaps," leaving open the possibility of reprieve since the implied answer to this question is negative, emphasizing humanity's inability to comprehend the mind of YHWH (cf. 2 Sam 12:22; Esth 4:14; Ps 90:11; Qoh 2:19; 3:21; 6:12; 8:1; Jonah 3:9).[70] The text does not guarantee that the above-mentioned acts of penitence will change YHWH's mind so that YHWH will act restoratively on their behalf, but it does suggest that this possibility is worth considering.[71]

---

70. J. Crenshaw, "The Expression MÎ YÔDĒA in the Hebrew Bible," *VT* 36 (1986) 274–75; D. Reimer, "An Overlooked Term in Biblical Theology: Perhaps," in *Covenant as Context: Essays in Honour of Ernest Nicholson* (ed. A. Mayes and R. Salters; Oxford: Oxford University Press, 2003) 341. Crenshaw identifies two categories of מִי יוֹדֵעַ texts. The first (including Joel 2:14) provides for the possibility of reprieve, while the second seems to close the door to redemptive action. The second category reflects a skeptical world view, in which the inability to know what YHWH will do leads to resignation. Reimer correctly identifies the impossibility of knowing all facets of God's behavior as being at the core of both categories of מִי יוֹדֵעַ texts.

71. Dempsey, "'Turn Back,'" 56–57. Fishbane aptly states, "[A]lthough YHWH 'relents' he does so for his own reasons. Thus, like oracles, the words and acts of repentance are also not magical: YHWH does not relent *because* of them" (Fishbane, *Biblical Interpretation*, 346–47). Pratt presents a similar view, arguing that this question indicates that those who turn to YHWH can have no specific expectation of divine turning; Pratt, "Historical Contingencies," 193. In contrast, Cooper overstates the case by suggesting that Joel's perspective is that YHWH is forced to turn because of this description of the divine character. He tries to make this claim in a comparison with Jonah 4:2, which, he suggests, preserves divine freedom by confounding the expectations of the prophet (A. Cooper, "In Praise of Divine Caprice: The Significance of the Book of Jonah," in *Among the Prophets: Language, Image and Structure in the Prophetic Writings* [ed. P. Davies and D. Clines; JSOTSup 144; Sheffield: Sheffield Academic Press, 1993] 161–63). This approach devalues the power of the ques-

Interestingly, the question מִי יוֹדֵעַ is also found in Jonah 3:9 and 2 Sam 12:22 in contexts where showing penitence before YHWH can hopefully reverse dire circumstances.[72] Significantly, the key verb שׁוּב appears once again in Joel 2:14, this time in an indicative form (יָשׁוּב). YHWH is its subject, and the wordplay is introduced whereby the "turning" of the community through fasting, weeping, and mourning may establish the context for YHWH to "turn" in response. Joel 2:14 pairs יָשׁוּב with וְנִחָם, a verb repeated from the previous verse.[73] Reusing נִחָם plays off the description of YHWH's character in 2:13b since Joel 2:14 offers an opportunity to test YHWH's ascription as someone who relents from punishing in the wake of calling the implied audience to respond.

The hope that the community's response to the commands to שׁוּב in Joel 2:12–13 could lead to a divine שׁוּב in 2:14 establishes the context for the remainder of the verse. The sign of this divine turning will be for YHWH to leave behind a blessing that the verse then further breaks down as מִנְחָה וָנֶסֶךְ 'a grain offering and a drink offering'. This phrase reveals yet another example of the text's use of "momentary suspense," since it refers first to the general blessing before breaking it down into its constituent parts.[74] These two offerings recall Joel 1:9, 13 where the locust infestation destroys the crops so that the priests cannot make these sacrifices. The promise of a restored מִנְחָה וָנֶסֶךְ is a synecdoche implying a full turning of YHWH from

---

tion "who knows?" in Joel 2:14. The fact that YHWH turns in Joel 2:18 does not negate the tension that this question creates. Fretheim helpfully reverses the argument and suggests instead that the potential for divine turning stands in contrast to claims of arbitrariness in divine action. Instead, YHWH's ability to turn away from destruction reflects the extent of YHWH's intention to execute YHWH's salvific intentions (T. Fretheim, "The Repentance of God: A Key to Evaluating Old Testament God-Talk," *HBT* 10 [1988] 60–61).

72. Dillard, "Joel," 280–81. In keeping with the theme of YHWH's sovereignty, it is interesting to note that, in the case of Jonah 3:9, the ones posing the question and engaging in penitence (Ninevites) did see YHWH change his mind while, in 2 Sam 12:22, David's penitence did not reverse the curse on the child born out of his adultery with Bathsheba. Bolin argues that, even in Jonah 3:9, the question מִי יוֹדֵעַ has a negative answer since, even on occasions when YHWH does change his mind, there is still typically an episode of punishment (cf. 2 Sam 12:22; Ps 90:11). This allows the audience of Jonah to read YHWH's change of mind through the lens of Nahum, in which Nineveh is guaranteed destruction (Bolin, *Freedom beyond Forgiveness*, 143–47). While this intertextual linkage is interesting, this approach robs the Jonah narrative of some of its dramatic tenor. The tension in the dialogue between Jonah and YHWH in Jonah 4 depends on YHWH's granting full pardon to Nineveh because of its repentance. This emphasizes YHWH's freedom to show mercy to whomever YHWH chooses.

73. The first verb, יָשׁוּב, is in the prefix conjugation, and the following two verbs, וְנִחָם וְהִשְׁאִיר, are in the form of the *waw*-relative + affix conjugation. In this case, they take on the sense of the preceding prefix verb, which is appropriate given that they follow the question מִי יוֹדֵעַ. This preserves YHWH's freedom by describing potential divine action using the verb form that expresses modality. On the modal use of the prefix conjugation, see Waltke and O'Connor, *Introduction*, 506–8. On the *waw*-relative + affix conjugation, see p. 527.

74. Van der Merwe and Wendland, "Word Order," 125.

wrath to mercy.[75] In order for the community to make these offerings, Yʜwʜ must replace the destroyed harvest and restore agricultural prosperity. The text thus portrays blessings and the offering of sacrifices as two sides of the same coin, both indicating a restored relationship between Yʜwʜ and the implied audience.[76] The hope of Joel 2:14 is that Yʜwʜ's abundant provision will permit the implied audience to offer these signs of restored relationship.

In summary, Joel 2:12–14 establishes the general parameters of the prophetic argument for the proper response to the situation previously described. The call is for the implied audience to "turn" to Yʜwʜ with appropriate actions, including fasting, weeping, and mourning. In response, the text points to the possibility of a divine "turning," rooted in its description of Yʜwʜ's character. The text does not guarantee what Yʜwʜ will do, but it indicates that appropriate activity on the part of the implied audience is the first step in evoking a divine response that will change the situation from devastation to restoration.

Joel 2:15–17: Detailing the Turn

Joel 2:15–17 delves more deeply into the specifics of the desired response and how it places pressure on Yʜwʜ in return. Joel 2:15 links this unit back to the preceding units by reusing imperatives. The first command is תִּקְעוּ שׁוֹפָר בְּצִיּוֹן 'blow a trumpet in Zion', which echoes Joel 2:1. In Joel 2:15, the context suggests that the prophet employs this command not to warn of invasion but rather to call for a communal gathering to appeal to Yʜwʜ in a cultic context (Lev 25:9; 2 Sam 6:15; 1 Chr 15:28; 2 Chr 15:14; Pss 81:4; 98:6). Reissuing this imperative reestablishes the exigence of the invading army that has led the text to call for sacral gathering.

The subsequent two imperatives in Joel 2:15 make evident the cultic orientation of the call to sound the trumpet. The prophet reissues commands first found in Joel 1:14, calling on the community to קַדְּשׁוּ־צוֹם קִרְאוּ עֲצָרָה 'sanctify a fast, call a sacred assembly'.[77] The reuse of these commands also helps to identify the target of these imperatives. Joel 2:15 does not identify to whom the text directs these imperatives, but when they occur in Joel 1:14 they are clearly directed toward the priests mentioned in Joel 1:13. Consequently, Joel 2:15 anticipates 2:17 and issues directives to the priests who lead the community in calling out to Yʜwʜ.

---

75. Crenshaw, *Joel*, 139.

76. Kapelrud, *Joel Studies*, 85.

77. Sweeney, *Twelve*, 166–67. As noted, Sweeney sees the reuse of commands from Joel 2:1 and 1:14 as a signal that the new rhetorical unit commences with the call to sound the trumpet in 2:15 since it recalls elements from the preceding rhetorical units. Notably, however, this still holds true if one posits Joel 2:12–17 as a rhetorical unit, since the imperatives found in 2:15 could be said to derive from 1:1–14 and 2:1–11.

The use of these imperatival phrases differs slightly since Joel 1:14 simply issues the calls to assemble and lament while Joel 2:15–17 expands further on these imperatives and gives much more detail concerning who is supposed to assemble and what should be the nature and content of their lament.[78] Thus, the reuse of imperatives in Joel 2:15 invokes exigences from both Joel 1:1–14 and 2:1–11, lending significant weight to the program of action that the text describes in the following verses.

The next verse begins to expand the calls to lament by first issuing additional commands to assemble. Joel 2:16 commands the gathering of the people, followed by a generational merismus that details the intended scope of the congregation. The summons is all-encompassing, calling on everyone from זְקֵנִים 'elders' to עוֹלָלִים 'children' and יֹנְקֵי שָׁדָיִם 'nursing infants' to attend.[79] The latter half of Joel 2:16 again echoes images from 1:8 by commanding even those about to be married to leave their preparations and join the rest of the community in sacred assembly before YHWH. Unlike 1:8, the bride in 2:16 has not lost her partner. The text, however, calls the bridal couple to depart from their private chambers and join in the communal cry to YHWH, emphasizing the primacy of the call to assemble.[80] Newly married couples were supposed to be exempt from elements of cultic service (Deut 20:7; 24:5), and thus the prophetic call for them to join in the fast further indicates the totality of the commitment to "turning" that the text requires.[81] Every member of the community must respond to the situation, which effectively details what the implied audience must do to return to YHWH with all their hearts (cf. Joel 2:12).

Joel 2:17 moves from enumerating who is called to attend this assembly to explaining how it is supposed to proceed. This verse displays great attention to detail, as the prophet states precisely who is to offer up the petitions, the location from where they should do so, and the exact wording of the petition.[82] Concerning who is supposed to utter the petition, the

---

78. Prinsloo, *Theology*, 54–55.

79. Unlike Joel 1:2, 14, the elders are not paired with the inhabitants of the land, which would indicate a merism of leaders and the rest of the people. Instead, the focus is generational, suggesting that everyone from the oldest to the youngest is required to attend this cultic gathering. The gravity of the situation is such that only a full response from the entire community is sufficient, because everyone from oldest to youngest is probably feeling its effects (Crenshaw, *Joel*, 140).

80. The two nouns used to describe the chamber are חֶדֶר and חֻפָּה. Both most likely refer to a private location where the marriage could be consummated (for חֶדֶר as the bridal chamber, see Song 1:4; Judg 15:1; 2 Sam 13:10; for the only other use of חֻפָּה, see Ps 19:6). Calling on the bridal couple to leave this chamber and join the assembly communicates the urgent necessity of the prophet's call to assemble.

81. Ibid., 141. Crenshaw draws parallels to Jer 7:34; 16:9; and 25:10, which use the plight of the bride and bridegroom during enemy invasions to describe the totality of the foretold destruction.

82. Ibid.

prophet commands the priests to lead the community in this time of lament and crying out to YHWH. This recalls the similar command of Joel 1:13 for the priests to don sackcloth and cry out to YHWH from the temple. Both of these passages offer responses that require priestly leadership—responses to the ominous day of YHWH and its threat to the covenant people. This reflects a prophetic concern to create cohesion out of seeming chaos; the priests retain their leadership role in the community even at a time when the sacrificial system is in disarray (cf. Joel 1:9, 13).[83] This creates a time and space for sanctuary where the community can remember and reflect on YHWH's character, as mentioned above, even with the looming threat of the day of YHWH.

On this occasion, the command to the priests is more specific, calling on them to weep in the space בֵּין הָאוּלָם וְלַמִּזְבֵּחַ 'between the porch and the altar'. This is a reference to the open area immediately in front of the temple that was the normal place for offering sacrifices.[84] This location was a buffer zone separating the people from the holy place, but it was also considered sanctified space devoted to YHWH.[85] Identifying this location precedes the command to let the priests weep, which foregrounds the setting of the petitions. Through this first half of the verse, the text places the responsibility for appropriate response in the hands of the priests, whom the text calls to lead the sacral assembly. They are the ones who are to lead the people to gather in the place of worship and to cry out to YHWH.

The latter half of this verse provides the words that the priests are to utter in their prayer to YHWH. These begin with two short petitions for YHWH to act in a restorative manner and conclude with a plaintive question appealing for divine intervention.[86] It is at this stage where the prophet's articulation of the community's "turning" now makes the rhetorical move toward calling for a divine "turning." The prophet employs the jussive וְיֹאמְרוּ 'let them say' in order to introduce these petitions and place them in the mouths of the priests. The first petition begins with the imperative חוּסָה 'have compassion!' followed by a vocative use of the divine name. It concludes with the prepositional phrase עַל־עַמֶּךָ 'upon your people', which

---

83. J. Linville, "The Day of Yahweh and the Mourning of the Priests in Joel," in *The Priests in the Prophets: The Portrayal of Priests, Prophets and Other Religious Specialists in the Latter Prophets* (ed. L. Grabbe and A. Bellis; JSOTSup 408; London: T. & T. Clark, 2004) 106. Interestingly, Linville views the call to gather as essential to reestablishing social cohesion in the context of failed sacrifices articulated in Joel 1. Reengaging in ritual, even rituals of mourning and crying out to YHWH acknowledges YHWH's authority over the implied audience.

84. Sweeney, *Twelve*, 168. See 1 Kgs 8:64 for a description of sacrifices occurring in this location.

85. Crenshaw, *Joel*, 141–42. This is made evident in Ezek 8:16–18, where priests appear to be engaging in idolatry in this space, causing YHWH to state that he will no longer listen to them.

86. Allen, *Joel*, 83.

functions as the object of the imperative directed toward Yнwн. The second-person pronominal suffix on עַמֶּךָ is a useful strategy for putting the
onus on Yнwн to respond since it refers to the divine claim of ownership
of this community (1 Sam 10:1; 1 Kgs 8:53; 2 Kgs 21:14; Isa 19:25; Mic 7:18;
Pss 33:12; 68:10; 106:5). The parallel term נַחֲלָתְךָ 'your inheritance' in the
second petition reinforces this perspective since it reflects the tradition of
land belonging to Yнwн. By paralleling עַמֶּךָ with נַחֲלָתְךָ, the prophet employs covenant terminology to stress the intimate relationship among
Yнwн, the community, and the land promised to their forefathers.[87]

The second petition of Joel 2:17 moves from the positive imperative
"spare!" to a negated imperative וְאַל־תִּתֵּן 'do not give' the community over
to disgrace. Joel 2:17 expresses this desire twice, first with the phrase לְחֶרְפָּה
'into reproach'. The second word, which follows immediately after לְחֶרְפָּה,
is the infinitive construct לִמְשָׁל, which in this case is probably a synonym
for the preceding word.[88] Typically, חֶרְפָּה appears in the Old Testament in
contexts indicating the disgrace and shame that rest on a given individual
or group.[89] Consequently, Joel 2:17's use of חֶרְפָּה relates to the concept of
outside observation that informs the latter half of 2:17. This verse identifies
the nations as the ones who will see the community in this light if Yнwн
does not intervene.

Again, the text employs a strategy of momentary delay, first referring to
those observing the state of the Judahite community with a generic pronoun בָּם 'among them' before identifying these onlookers as גוֹיִם 'nations'.
Outside observation of Judah's state worsens the situation since it turns
Judah into a public spectacle among foreign and hostile nations. By extension, this image also challenges Yнwн since Yнwн is the one who permits
the community to fall into this state. The double reference to reproach and
shame in the first half of Joel 2:17 emphasizes the urgency of the petition.
The prophet tells the priests and people to offer up this prayer in order to
place pressure on Yнwн to "turn" and rectify the situation. The text
carefully constructs the plea so that Yнwн's divine character is at issue if
Yнwн does not choose to respond.

---

87. Prinsloo, *Joel*, 56.

88. The root מָשַׁל can also mean 'to rule over'. The LXX tradition follows this interpretation (τοῦ κατάρξαι αὐτῶν ἔθνη 'of being ruled over by nations'). However, the proximity of
this word to לְחֶרְפָּה suggests that the meaning of לִמְשָׁל is probably synonymous. Linville
argues for a polysemic interpretation, claiming that interpreters ought to invoke both
meanings here. He understands both the concepts of 'reproach' and being 'ruled over' by
foreigners as challenges to God's sovereignty and ability to protect his chosen inheritance
(J. Linville, "Letting the 'Bi-Word' Rule in Joel 2:17," *JHS* 5 [2004], http://www.jhsonline
.org/Articles/article_32.pdf, §§12–14).

89. A. Kalmanofsky, *Terror All Around: The Rhetoric of Horror in the Book of Jeremiah*
(LHB/OTS 390; New York: T. & T. Clark, 2008) 39; E. Kutsch, "חרף," *TDOT* 5:203–15. See
Jer 23:40; 31:19; 51:51.

Similar to the previous unit, this section ends with a climactic rhetorical question in Joel 2:17. The last phrase of Joel 2:17 follows the entreaties not to let the community experience the scorn of its neighbors. It envisions the surrounding nations as looking at the distress of the Judahite community and disparaging both the people and their deity. The final question is directed at Yʜᴡʜ, asking why these nations should be able to say among themselves, אַיֵּה אֱלֹהֵיהֶם 'where is their God?'[90] This question raises the stakes by putting Yʜᴡʜ among those whom the nations are mocking. This question resonates with the Sinai tradition and Moses' pleas to preserve Israel in spite of its apostasy after the golden calf incident (Exod 32:12; Deut 9:26–28).[91] Both of these scenarios share in their identification of Israel's destruction with the perceived powerlessness of Yʜᴡʜ.

The rhetorical strategy at work in Joel 2:17 constructs the voice of the "nations" as a means of broaching potentially blasphemous thoughts concerning Yʜᴡʜ's character. If these unnamed "nations" suggest that Yʜᴡʜ is powerless, the community itself cannot be charged with turning from Yʜᴡʜ. The text thus issues an appeal to Yʜᴡʜ to act in a salvific manner to preserve his people but also to preserve his own divine reputation from being besmirched by outsiders.[92] Overall, the "turning" of the people is expressed through engaging in activities described in Joel 2:12–13 and in their utterance of the plea found in 2:17. Now, the prophet effectively places the onus on Yʜᴡʜ to "turn" in response and to act to reverse the dire circumstances that Yʜᴡʜ has previously permitted.

Summary

This rhetorical unit develops the depiction of Yʜᴡʜ and the relationship with the implied audience. Joel 2:1–11 focuses on the approach of the great and terrible day of Yʜᴡʜ, with Yʜᴡʜ leading the invading army that overruns Mount Zion. In contrast, Joel 2:12–17 urges the community to beseech Yʜᴡʜ to intervene on their behalf and not to unleash the full power of that day against those who cannot withstand it.[93] Yʜᴡʜ is the source of devastation in Joel 2:1–11, but 2:12–17 reverses the perspective and portrays Yʜᴡʜ as the means of salvation. Joel 2:12–17 tries to persuade the implied audience to respond so that Yʜᴡʜ will act and move the situation from devastation to restoration. Essentially, these verses petition Yʜᴡʜ to

---

90. The final phrase of Joel 2:17 reuses the term עַמִּים 'peoples' that also occurs in Joel 2:6. On that occasion, the עַמִּים trembled in the wake of the approaching invader, while in this instance they turn and disparage Yʜᴡʜ and the community that he claims.

91. Crenshaw, *Joel*, 143.

92. Barton considers it odd that the rationale employed in this cry to Yʜᴡʜ does not restate the attributes of Yʜᴡʜ's character mentioned in 2:12–14. It is not because Yʜᴡʜ is gracious or merciful that he is called to respond here but, rather, on the basis of preserving his reputation; Barton, *Joel*, 84.

93. Prinsloo, *Joel*, 56.

reinstate relationship with the implied audience by acting to restore rather than destroy.

The text opens up the possibility of restoration's occurring with its call to return to Yhwh and its reuse of Exod 34:6–7, but it does not presume too much, since it asserts the impossibility of knowing what Yhwh will do. The strategy of earlier rhetorical units emphasizes the overwhelming nature of the exigences that the community faces, while offering little hope. Joel 2:12–17 represents a significant development in the life cycle of this prophetic book since it both creates the potential for hope rooted in the divine character and then explicitly lays out how the community can act to realize this hope. The rhetorical strategy of Joel 2:12–17 is to require a complete commitment from all members of the community to respond by turning back to Yhwh. The text commands them to gather under the leadership of the priests and cry out, beseeching Yhwh to remember that they are Yhwh's inheritance and that Yhwh's divine reputation is caught up with their fate.

Rhetorical Effectiveness

Of all the units in Joel, this particular passage may offer the most hope for gauging its rhetorical effectiveness on the level of the text's implied audience. Joel 2:12–17 sets out a plan of action rooted in its understanding of the divine character. The call is to "return to Yhwh" and engage in appropriate acts demonstrating the sincerity and gravity of this return. The hope is that, in doing so, Yhwh will make a similar turn and will become the Judahite community's covenant partner and protector. This identity would hopefully trump Yhwh's identity as the leader of the locust army. This stands in stark contrast to Joel 2:1–11, which offers no possible modification of the exigence. Joel 2:12–17 adopts a different perspective, however, and while not denying Yhwh's authority to unleash the day of Yhwh, it opens up the possibility of response that the implied audience can make to modify the exigence.

Joel 2:12–17 is admirably constructed to try to evoke this response. It begins by offering a window of hope in the wake of Joel 2:11 and then puts forward a plan to realize it. The prophet's reuse of Exod 34:6–7 strengthens the possibility of restoration by reinforcing Yhwh's willingness and desire to act on the implied audience's behalf, even after one of Israel's most egregious periods of apostasy. The specificity of Joel 2:15–17 is potentially effective since the prophet guides the implied audience toward fully crying out to Yhwh, using the words that the prophet commands. On account of his intermediating function, the prophet has the authority to detail what actions may cause Yhwh to respond positively. Consequently, the prophet's presentation should be effective in persuading the implied audience to adopt this course of action. Following Joel 2:11, a detailed plan of response to the crises at hand that is rooted in the acknowledgment of Yhwh's character should persuade the implied audience that its hope for survival rests in its willingness to act in the manner that the prophet requires.

The potential for effective response to Joel 2:12–17 is also tied into the broader conception of prophetic oracles of woe and doom. Specifically, Joel 2:12–17 operates under the assumption that an appropriate response can turn back pronouncements of judgment. A classic example occurs in the aftermath of the prophecy of Jonah 3:4, whose language and portrayal of Yнwн resonate quite closely with Joel 2:12–17. The words of Jonah's prophecy did not appear to allow any room for hope (עוֹד אַרְבָּעִים יוֹם וְנִינְוֵה נֶהְפָּכֶת 'yet forty days and Nineveh will be overthrown'); however, the overwhelming response of the Ninevites persuaded Yнwн to withhold destruction. Eagleton approaches this issue by appealing to speech-act theory and arguing that, while Jonah's prophetic declaration might appear to be constative, it actually functions as a performative—that is, speech that creates conditions for actions.[94] Ironically, Jonah's response to Yнwн's decision to spare Nineveh reveals his hope that his prophetic word would be constative and that Nineveh would meets its doom.

Another contribution to the discussion of rhetorical effectiveness in Joel 2:12–17 comes from drawing a distinction between the illocutionary intent and perlocutionary effects of judgment oracles. Essentially, the illocutionary intent is to announce and activate potential judgment which could provoke a variety of perlocutionary responses, including lament and penitence from the audience addressed by the oracles.[95] Houston differentiates between illocution and perlocution in order to explain what happens when a prophetic pronouncement of doom is averted, arguing that it is still a valid oracle since its illocutionary intent was to activate the announcement of divine judgment; the perlocutionary responses it creates in its audiences do not invalidate its illocutionary force, even if these responses cause the judgment to be turned aside (cf. Jer 18:7–10).[96] One can even apply this perspective to oracles proclaiming unconditional judgment and understand that they might have the perlocutionary effect of leading their audiences to respond in hopes of avoiding the declared punishment.[97]

---

94. T. Eagleton, "J. L. Austin and the Book of Jonah," in *The Book and the Text* (ed. R. Schwartz; Cambridge: Blackwell, 1990) 233. Möller also welcomes the move to the performative level of prophetic language, claiming that it forces the interpreter to move beyond the surface level of the text and to engage with its deeper communicative strategy (K. Möller, "Words of (In-)evitable Certitude? Reflections on the Interpretation of Prophetic Oracles of Judgement," in *After Pentecost: Language and Biblical Interpretation* [ed. C. Bartholomew, C. Greene, and K. Möller; SHS 2; Grand Rapids: Zondervan, 2001] 370).

95. W. Houston, "What Did the Prophets Think They Were Doing? Speech Acts and Prophetic Discourse in the Old Testament," *BibInt* 1 (1993) 187.

96. Ibid., 184.

97. Möller, "Words," 368–69. Möller also points to the reaction of the Ninevites in Jonah 3 and David's response to Nathan's oracle in 2 Sam 12 as evidence of the perlocutionary effect of oracles of doom.

In the case of Jonah, the text portrays a prophet who does not want there to be room for a divine change of heart, yet it occurs despite the fact that the prophetic speech does not open this door. In Joel 2:12–17, the capacity for averting prophesied disaster is even stronger, since on this occasion the prophet explicitly makes this option available. The text establishes the imminence of doom in the preceding rhetorical units, but Joel 2:12–17 provides the proper perlocutionary response. The exigences of locust plague, drought, and invasion establish the potential of devastation, but proclamation of these threats is not the final word. The text urges the implied audience to act in a way that could turn aside these threats based on its portrayal of Yhwh's character. Consequently, it is possible to see that Joel 2:12–17 has the capacity to effect change in its implied audience based on how it establishes the possibility of Yhwh's turning and changing Yhwh's course of action alongside the appropriate actions of Yhwh's people.

Ideally, the text would record that the community to whom Joel prophesied either heeded this call and engaged in the prescribed activities or refused to obey. The text remains silent on the subject, however, just as it remains silent on the specific identity of the "sin" that seems to provoke this prophetic call to return to Yhwh.[98] One can argue, however, that the conceptual gap between Joel 2:17 and 2:18 opens up room to consider how the text might construct the implied audience's response to this particular unit.[99] Essentially, readers may need to supply "transitional material" and assume that the implied audience did as the text commands (uttered the proposed prophetic responses) in order to understand the progression of the text.[100]

---

98. Interesting, Beal finds a potential secondary audience for Joel 2:12–17 in the Jonah narrative. She suggests that Jonah takes Joel's call to turn to Yhwh and the description of Yhwh's character and shows that the Ninevites actually obeyed it. Essentially, a pagan nation responds to a Judahite prophet in the terms that Joel calls for in 2:12–14. This proposal requires Jonah's dependence on Joel, which remains an open debate, but it is valuable to consider the idea that Joel's rhetorical effectiveness is found in a different audience's interaction with the text. See Anna Sieges Beal, "The Twelve Quoting Itself: Jonah's Critique of Joel" (paper presented at the annual meeting of the SBL, Chicago; Nov 18, 2012) 8–9.

99. On the function of gaps in literature, see W. Iser, "Indeterminacy and the Reader's Response in Prose Fiction," in *Aspects of Narrative: Selected Papers from the English Institute* (ed. J. Miller; New York: Columbia University Press, 1971) 1–46. Iser suggests that gaps of this sort are what invite the reader to participate in the text, adding to its esthetic quality and its ability to affect the reader. Iser discusses this theory of gaps with reference to serialized novels, which tended to stop at a point of climax, ensuring the involvement of the reader in considering how the tension might be resolved. One can see a similar climactic moment at the conclusion of Joel 2:17, with its unanswered rhetorical question that draws the audience in to consider whether Yhwh will respond to the people's appeal.

100. Barton, *Joel*, 87. Barton notes that, when an audience followed a prophetic command, the text typically made this fact explicit. He draws a parallel to Mal 3:16–17, where the claim that "those who revered Yhwh spoke to one another" stands in for obedience to previous prophecy.

In the space between these verses, the text moves from a cry to Yʜᴡʜ to act so that foreign nations will not mock Yʜᴡʜ's name, to a statement of jealousy and pity for the land and the people. The character of Yʜᴡʜ described in Joel 2:13 comes to the forefront when the deity who leads an assault against Zion transforms into the deity who enacts total restoration. It is conceivable that hidden here in the transition between Joel 2:17 and 2:18 is the implication of an appropriate response by the implied audience that created the conditions for Yʜᴡʜ to act restoratively. Therefore, the rhetorical effectiveness of Joel 2:12–17 comes to light as the remainder of the book moves from announcements of doom to promises of restoration for its implied audience.

Conclusion

Joel 2:12–17 commences the process of advancing the rhetorical situation in order to turn this prophetic text away from scenes of devastation and offers the potential of restoration rooted deeply in the character of Yʜᴡʜ. This rhetorical unit interacts with Exod 34:6–7 and Jonah 4:2 to illustrate the potential for restoration on account of Yʜᴡʜ's gracious and compassionate nature. It calls the implied audience to respond by committing itself to Yʜᴡʜ through its actions and its innermost beliefs, in hopes that it may avoid the situation described in Joel 2:1–11. Joel 2:12–17 not only calls the implied audience to return to Yʜᴡʜ but also details who should gather and what they should declare. It employs wordplay on the verb שׁוּב to suggest that the implied audience's actions of turning to Yʜᴡʜ should in turn lead Yʜᴡʜ to שׁוּב 'turn'. The prophet's portrayal of Yʜᴡʜ's character and the detail of the program of response reflect an effective appeal to the implied audience that it ought to cry out to Yʜᴡʜ amidst the crises that it is facing. Joel 2:12–17 does not record an explicit response from the implied audience, but it appears to imply through the gap between Joel 2:17 and 2:18 that the community responds in obedience, prompting Yʜᴡʜ to respond by enacting restoration. This is evident in the forthcoming rhetorical units, which highlight the reversal of circumstances because of Yʜᴡʜ's actions.

Chapter 6

Reversing the Crisis: Rhetorical Analysis of Joel 2:18–27

Introduction

Joel 2:18–27 is one of the key points of transition in the text. At this juncture, the text moves from appealing to the human audience to declaring the responses of Yhwh. The tenor of the text changes from threat and exhortation to promises of presence and provision. Joel 2:18–27 again uses the exigences of locust infestation and agricultural hardship as the backdrop against which it portrays Yhwh's restorative activity. Joel 2:18–27 continues to reveal the interconnected nature of the text as it refers to specific crises in Joel 1:1–2:17 that it reverses. The rhetorical purpose of this passage is to persuade the implied audience that Yhwh intends to act on its behalf and that its proper response is to rejoice. This builds to the final promise that Yhwh dwells in the midst of the people, which should further persuade them to trust the promises of restoration.

Rhetorical Unit

Joel 2:18–27 provides the divine response to the call to cry out to Yhwh that governs Joel 2:12–17. As mentioned in the initial discussion concerning Joel's compositional unity, Joel 2:18 (along with Joel 3:1) is a primary point of perceived disjunction. Some who view the book as containing two distinct halves make this their point of primary division.[1] Breaking the book into halves between Joel 2:17 and 2:18 can be described as a "division according to form," in which 2:18–4:21 articulates Yhwh's response to the prophetic call to lament in 1:2–2:17.[2] The switch to restoration in Joel 2:18 does reflect a major shift in the tenor of the book. Similarly, there is a major division in the gap between Joel 2:27 and 3:1, where the text changes from addressing an immediate and urgent exigence to looking toward an indeterminate future.[3] Nogalski refers to this as a "division according to content."[4] It is also undeniable that the book's outlook distinctly broadens

---

1. R. Dillard, "Joel," in *The Minor Prophets: An Exegetical and Expository Commentary* (ed. T. McComiskey; Grand Rapids: Baker, 1992) 285–86; R. Coggins, *Joel and Amos* (NCBC; Sheffield: Sheffield Academic Press, 2000) 45; L. Allen, *The Books of Joel, Obadiah, Jonah and Micah* (NICOT; Grand Rapids: Eerdmans, 1976) 42–43.

2. J. Nogalski, *Redactional Processes in the Book of the Twelve* (BZAW 218; Berlin: de Gruyter, 1993) 2.

3. T. Finley, *Joel, Amos, Obadiah* (WEC; Chicago: Moody Press, 1990) 68–69.

4. Nogalski, *Redactional Processes*, 2.

in Joel 3–4, moving from speaking primarily about the Judahite community to discussing in detail the fate of foreign nations who oppose Yʜᴡʜ.[5]

Against such theories of textual division, one should also remember
Prinsloo's caution against overemphasizing the discontinuity between Joel
2:18–27 and preceding units since it can be argued that 2:18–27 fulfills
the hope raised in 2:12–17.[6] The question "who knows?" from the previous unit opens up the potential for Yʜᴡʜ to perform the restorative acts
that characterize this unit. Yʜᴡʜ answers this question powerfully in the
affirmative, promising to guarantee the future survival and prosperity of
Yʜᴡʜ's people. The division between Joel 1–2 and 3–4 also should not be
stated too strongly. There is also significant lexical overlap between the
two "halves," especially related to the day of Yʜᴡʜ.[7] Phrases referring to
"the great and terrible day of Yʜᴡʜ" (Joel 2:11; 3:4), "the day of Yʜᴡʜ
is coming" (Joel 2:1; 3:4), "the heavens and the earth quake" (Joel 2:20;
4:16), and "Yʜᴡʜ gives forth his voice" (Joel 2:11; 4:16) occur in both
"halves" of Joel. These connectors are useful reminders of the value of
reading this text in its entirety; noting and exploring these connections
help the interpreter to consider the rhetorical power of the imagery and
prophetic declarations.

If one focuses specifically on Joel 2:18–27, the text provides sufficient
indicators to determine the boundaries of the rhetorical unit.[8] The content
helps to determine the aperture of this unit since the text ceases to instruct
the community in how to cry out to Yʜᴡʜ, which is the prevalent mode
of address in Joel 2:12–17. Instead, Joel 2:18–27 shifts toward reporting and
mediating the divine word. While some argue that Joel 2:18 concludes the
previous unit,[9] others note that the *waw*-consecutive chain of four verbs
(וַיְקַנֵּא; וַיַּחְמֹל; וַיַּעַן; וַיֹּאמֶר) in 2:18–19 makes a compelling case for linking 2:18
with 2:19 since it would be odd to see a unit break in the middle of a *waw*-
consecutive chain.[10] Thus, following the climactic rhetorical question that
ends Joel 2:17, it is more in keeping with the syntax of the text to understand Joel 2:18 as the beginning of a new rhetorical unit.

---

5. R. Simkins, *Yahweh's Activity in History and Nature in the Book of Joel* (ANETS 10;
Lewiston, NY: Edwin Mellen, 1991) 203.

6. W. Prinsloo, *The Theology of the Book of Joel* (BZAW 163; Berlin: de Gruyter, 1985)
64. This search for continuity characterizes Prinsloo's approach to the book of Joel since he
is one of the few interpreters who refuses to divide the book into two "halves."

7. Simkins, *Yahweh's Activity*, 203.

8. Prinsloo, *Theology*, 62.

9. A. Merx, *Der Prophetie des Joel und ihrer Ausleger, von den Ältesten Zeiten bis zu den
Reformatoren: Eine exegetisch-kritische und hermeneutisch-dogmengeschichtliche Studie* (Halle:
Waisenhauses, 1879) 106–7. According to this reading, the proposed unit of Joel 2:12–18
would include the divine response to the communal lament.

10. J. Crenshaw, *Joel* (AB 24c; New York: Doubleday, 1995) 143; R. Dillard, "Joel," in
The Minor Prophets: An Exegetical and Expository Commentary (ed. T. McComiskey; Grand
Rapids: Baker, 1992) 286.

After the elaborate description of Yʜᴡʜ's response, the text signals the close of this rhetorical unit through the use of epiphora.[11] The same phrase וְלֹא־יֵבֹשׁוּ עַמִּי לְעוֹלָם 'my people will never be ashamed' concludes both Joel 2:26 and 2:27, bringing the description of Yʜᴡʜ's restorative acts to a ringing crescendo. The remainder of Joel 2:27 further indicates that its function is to close the rhetorical unit. It contains a modified formula of divine recognition introduced by וִידַעְתֶּם 'you will know' that states that Yʜᴡʜ's actions are proof of both his power and his relationship with the community.[12] The text adds a statement of Yʜᴡʜ's presence in the midst of Israel to the use of the formula in Joel 2:27. The use of this relatively well-established formula in conjunction with the use of epiphora in the final clause effectively signals the end of this rhetorical unit.[13]

Within these boundaries, Joel 2:18–27 contains several subunits. Joel 2:18–20 describes Yʜᴡʜ's restorative actions, including the removal of the invading army described in Joel 2:1–11. It commences with a narrative introduction (Joel 2:18–19a) followed by a series of first-person indicative verbs with which the voice of Yʜᴡʜ breaks in and promises restoration (Joel 2:19b–20). Joel 2:21–24 presents prophetic commands to the implied audience to rejoice in response, providing lavish descriptions of all that Yʜᴡʜ promises to do on behalf of the people. These commands stand in marked contrast to the imperatives calling for fear and lamentation in the previous units. Finally, Joel 2:25–27 again reverts to the voice of Yʜᴡʜ, providing divine reassurances of Yʜᴡʜ's commitment to restore and promises of his presence among the members of the implied audience.

Rhetorical Situation

Joel 2:18–27 continues to develop the life cycle of the rhetorical situation. In previous units, the text establishes its implied audience through the merismus of elders and inhabitants of the land and further delineates it through the sequence of imperatives addressed to specific subgroups (Joel 1:1–14). It again stresses the intended extent of the implied audience in the commands for everyone from the elders to the children to attend the assembly of Joel 2:16. The text also describes at great length the exigence of a locust infestation that ultimately reflects the unleashing of the day of Yʜᴡʜ against this implied audience in Joel 2:1–11. The text constrains the implied audience by indicating that it cannot resist these catastrophes and that its only hope is to cry out to Yʜᴡʜ in hopes of divine intervention.

---

11. E. Wendland, *The Discourse Analysis of Hebrew Prophetic Literature* (MBPS 40; Lewiston, NY: Edwin Mellen, 1995) 50–51.

12. For a fuller discussion of the divine-recognition formula and its rhetorical impact in Joel 2:27, see the following discussion of rhetorical strategy.

13. E. Wendland, "The Discourse Analysis of Hebrew Poetry: A Procedural Outline," in *Discourse Perspectives on Hebrew Poetry in the Scriptures* (ed. E. Wendland; United Bible Societies Monograph Series 7; New York: United Bible Societies, 1994) 5.

The rhetorical situation changes in Joel 2:12–17 with the text adopting a motivating tone, urging the implied audience to respond and cry out to YHWH in hopes of alleviating the exigence directed against it. Joel 2:18–27 continues the transition. The locust army provides the primary exigence, but this rhetorical unit details in depth the final resolution of that threat.

The most dramatic shift in the rhetorical situation of Joel 2:18–27 concerns the text's positioning of YHWH. In previous rhetorical units, YHWH has either not acted or, worse, has been revealed as the one driving the exigence that threatens the existence of the Judahite community (Joel 2:10–11). In this rhetorical unit, YHWH finally acts to remedy the exigence rather than to exacerbate it further (Joel 2:20). The locust army that ravages the land and even penetrates the sanctity of Zion meets its demise beyond the borders of the land. This is an important moment of transition in the text's rhetorical situation since YHWH's actions, both salvific and destructive, dominate the remainder of the prophetic book. Interestingly, the text does not explicitly claim that the community responded as directed by the previous rhetorical unit; instead, it focuses on the actions of YHWH.[14]

The text signals YHWH's change of position within the life cycle of the rhetorical situation in several ways. First, the narrative snippet found in Joel 2:18–19 provides YHWH's motivation for the actions that unfold in the remainder of the rhetorical unit. Second, the text provides significant portions of direct address: YHWH speaks in first person to the implied audience, indicating YHWH's actions on their behalf (Joel 2:19–20; 2:25–27). Third, the text employs a preponderance of pronominal suffixes that link YHWH to the implied audience. Throughout Joel 2:18–27, YHWH has pity on "his land" and "his people" (Joel 2:18), for whom he is "YHWH your God" (Joel 2:23, 26, 27), while also laying claim to them in the first person through the phrase "my people" (Joel 2:26, 27). All of these linkages between YHWH and the implied audience signal YHWH's change of position.

Joel 2:18–27 maintains the same implied audience as in previous rhetorical units, which the reference to the "children of Zion" makes apparent (Joel 2:23). As mentioned above, in this rhetorical unit, the key point of emphasis for the implied audience is its relationship to YHWH. Prior references to Zion commanded either a warning (Joel 2:1) or a summons to sacred assembly (Joel 2:15) to respond to the threat of the day of YHWH. Now, the text commands the implied audience to rejoice because its relationship with YHWH is restored. The text expands the scope of the audience slightly with imperatives directed toward the land and its creatures (Joel 2:21–22). These references cohere with the threats against the land and its creatures in prior rhetorical units (cf. Joel 1:10, 17–20; 2:3).[15] These examples of per-

---

14. J. Strazicich, *Joel's Use of Scripture and the Scripture's Use of Joel: Appropriation and Resignification in Second Temple Judaism and Early Christianity* (BIS 82; Leiden: Brill, 2007) 163.

15. In Joel 2:21–24, the text calls on the land (אֲדָמָה), the beasts of the field (בַּהֲמוֹת שָׂדָי), and the children of Zion (בְּנֵי צִיּוֹן) to respond to YHWH's actions. These groups reflect some of those called to fear in previous descriptions of devastation (cf. Joel 1:8, 18; 2:1).

sonification lead into the address to the people of Zion in Joel 2:23, adding further weight to its call to rejoice since the prophet commands the people to follow the lead of the land and its creatures.

Finally, I do not claim that the prophet uttered these words against the backdrop of an actual year of agricultural recovery, just as I do not claim that Joel 1:1–2:17 reflects an actual locust invasion or drought.[16] In the "world of the text" that informs this rhetorical unit, however, there is a strong sense that exigences of invasion and divine threat have been turned on their heads. The image-world of Joel 2:18–27 reflects on the catastrophes mentioned in previous rhetorical units and deliberately reverses them.[17]

Rhetorical Strategy

Broadly speaking, Joel 2:18–27 inaugurates a programmatic turnaround of the catastrophes found in Joel 1:1–2:17. It culminates in the assurance וְלֹא־יֵבֹשׁוּ עַמִּי לְעוֹלָם 'And my people will not be ashamed again', found in the final clauses of both Joel 2:26 and 2:27. The previous rhetorical unit concludes in Joel 2:17 with a call for a sacred assembly in which the prophet urges the community to make entreaty to YHWH to avoid becoming objects of scorn and derision among foreign nations. The rhetorical question of the nations, אַיֵּה אֱלֹהֵיהֶם 'where is their God?' remains unanswered and bears the full weight of the catastrophes described in Joel 1:1–2:17. The text has thus far articulated the gravity of the situation while proposing a course of action by calling the implied audience to lament and cry out, using language that recalls the character of YHWH. These cries rhetorically entreat YHWH to respond in mercy lest inactivity sully the divine reputation.

Joel 2:18 then begins the transition from calling the implied audience to cry out, focusing instead on divine response. There is a conceptual ellipsis between Joel 2:17 and 2:18, perhaps leading to the inference that the sacred assembly gathered and spoke as the prophet required.[18] Unfortunately, it is impossible to make this claim in the "world behind the text" with any

---

16. For an attempt to locate the promises of restoration within the framework of the Israelite agricultural calendar, see K. Nash, *The Palestinian Agricultural Year and the Book of Joel* (Ph.D. diss., Catholic University of America, 1989) 117–35.

17. For the fullest detailing of the elements of reversal, see F. Deist, "Parallels and Reinterpretation in the Book of Joel: A Theology of *Yom Yahweh*?" in *Text and Context: Old Testament and Semitic Studies for F. C. Fensham* (ed. W. Claasen; JSOTSup 48; Sheffield: Sheffield Academic Press, 1988) 63–69.

18. Nash, *Palestinian*, 115. Allen states that it was "Joel's privilege" to present an oracle of salvation in this rhetorical unit since the appeals in Joel 1:1–2:17 are presumed to have been successful (Allen, *Joel*, 86–87). Simkins takes a different approach and argues that Joel 2:18–27 is related epexegetically to the preceding material, claiming that "the oracle of salvation logically precedes and becomes the motivation behind Joel's summons for the people to return to Yahweh." Simkins builds this case off a parallel to Isa 44:21–23, where a proclamation of salvation seems to precede a call to return (Simkins, *Yahweh's Activity*, 191). This interpretation, however, reads against the most common grammatical usage of *waw*-relative + prefix forms, which as Simkins himself admits, is to indicate temporal succession. Therefore, since there is a logical and coherent case for interpreting Joel 2:18–19

degree of certainty, but it is possible to view this passage as presenting a picture of the "rhetorical effectiveness" of Joel 2:12–17. The prophetic appeal to the implied audience essentially prompts the response that reverses YHWH's prior orientation toward the implied audience.[19] The great promise of reversal continues all the way through Joel 2:27, which concludes this rhetorical unit by offering comfort and assurance of YHWH's presence.

This unit puts forward a different type of argument from the preceding rhetorical unit's argument. Instead of direct address to the implied audience, Joel 2:18–27 focuses on YHWH and the actions that YHWH takes in response to the implied audience's presumed reaction to the prophet's entreaties. This unit builds off the hope offered in the description of the divine character in Joel 2:13. YHWH is no longer the one leading the invaders against Zion as in Joel 2:11, nor is YHWH the inscrutable figure who may turn and have mercy in 2:12–17. Instead, YHWH becomes the implied audience's stalwart protector and provider. The focus on YHWH and his powerful, positive acts causes this passage to fit most readily into the category of epideictic rhetoric, which Kennedy defines as rhetoric that intends to persuade its audience to hold or affirm a point of view in the present, such as celebrating or denouncing a person or quality.[20] In this case, Joel 2:18–27 focuses on YHWH as the deity of the implied audience and celebrates YHWH's ability and willingness to act on its behalf.

As mentioned in the discussion of Joel 1:15–20, Perelman and Olbrechts-Tyteca claim that epideictic discourse frequently has an educational function, serving to strengthen the adherence of the target audience to a given set of generally accepted principles or beliefs.[21] This resonates with Joel 2:18–27 since this unit focuses on the idea of YHWH as the one who acts mightily to preserve the covenant community. This is an important element of the Old Testament's understanding of covenant relationship with YHWH (Exod 7:3–5; 15:1–18; Judg 6:13; Isa 29:14; Jer 21:2; Mic 7:15).[22] In detailing how YHWH can enact salvation and restoration, this passage offers reasons why remaining faithful to YHWH in all circumstances is so vital to

---

in temporal succession to previous material, this is probably the most appropriate course to follow.

19. For more detail, see the discussion of "rhetorical effectiveness" that follows.

20. G. Kennedy, *New Testament Interpretation through Rhetorical Criticism* (Chapel Hill: University of North Carolina Press, 1984) 19.

21. C. Perelman and L. Olbrechts-Tyteca, *The New Rhetoric: A Treatise on Argumentation* (Notre Dame, IN: Notre Dame University Press, 1969) 51–54. Interestingly, Perelman and Olbrechts-Tyteca note that employing epideictic rhetoric requires the strongest qualifications to speak to the subject at hand since the rhetor is upholding the views of the entire community. In this instance, one who speaks through the office of the prophet would seem to be most qualified to make known the actions of YHWH that strengthen the connection to the implied audience.

22. See Lind on the tradition that, for Israel, faithfulness and trust in the ability of YHWH to act decisively were at the core of its proper relationship with YHWH (M. Lind, *Yahweh Is a Warrior* [Scottdale, PA: Herald, 1980] 171).

the community's continued existence. In other words, this unit does not introduce anything surprising or shocking into its description of Yhwh; rather, its focus on Yhwh's restorative activities reminds its implied audience of the core concepts of protection and provision that should characterize its relationship with Yhwh.

The focus on the character and direct actions of Yhwh is an interesting development in the rhetorical approach of this book.[23] In praising Yhwh and promising restorative acts the text potentially adds greater persuasive power to its previous calls to cry out and return. The text promises total restoration without indicating whether the community acted on the previous call to lament and return. However, by reminding the implied audience of the character of Yhwh as a deity who is powerful and who cares for the community, the text strengthens adherence to its program of calling its implied audience to return to Yhwh. It is possible to see how the implied audience would be more likely to follow the prophet's lead in acknowledging the sovereignty of Yhwh in the wake of revelations that Yhwh is going to act powerfully on its behalf.

Joel 2:18–20: Yhwh Enacts Restoration

Joel 2:18–20 clearly establishes from the outset that Yhwh is the agent who brings about the great changes revealed throughout this rhetorical unit. Yhwh's activity is the subject of four successive verbs in 2:18–19a. The fact that this verbal sequence is in the *waw*-consecutive + prefix conjugation is somewhat problematic since this verbal conjugation is typically the backbone of narrative accounts of past action.[24] The temporal orientation of this passage, however, looks beyond the locust invasion and drought report in Joel 1:1–2:17 and offers Yhwh's response to these threats. Probably the most helpful way to consider this issue is to suggest that these verses provide the promise of future reversal presented in a familiar prophetic

---

23. Griffin aptly notes that Yhwh's direct actions are typically positive for the implied audience, bringing about recovery and blessing. Meanwhile, the expressions of disaster are attributed to Yhwh indirectly, especially through the vehicle of the locusts as an invading army (cf. Joel 2:1–11). Thus, when the text presents Yhwh as the primary actor in a rhetorical unit, one expects positive repercussions for the implied audience (W. Griffin, *The God of the Prophets: An Analysis of Divine Action* [JSOTSup 249; Sheffield: Sheffield Academic Press, 1997] 166).

24. P. Joüon and T. Muraoka, *A Grammar of Biblical Hebrew: Revised English Edition* (Rome: Pontifical Biblical Institute, 2006) 361. The difficulties of interpreting a *waw*-consecutive chain at this point have led to some suggestions for alternative readings. Merx, for example, suggests repointing the *waw*-consecutives and understanding them instead as jussives ('May Yhwh become jealous for his land . . . may he say, "I am sending you grain"'). In this case, everything from 2:18 to the end of the book is attached to the prayer of Joel 2:15–17 uttered by the priests (Merx, *Prophetie*, 91). This approach looks like an attempt to smooth over a difficult syntactical problem. Prinsloo also helpfully notes the difficulties inherent in joining Joel 2:17, which refers to Yhwh in the second person, to Joel 2:18, which refers to Yhwh in the third person (Prinsloo, *Theology*, 64).

style whereby they appear to foretell what has already happened.[25] Against the backdrop of the devastation portrayed in Joel 1:1–2:17, this style strengthens the sense of relief that the implied audience would experience. Consequently, the calls for rejoicing that follow in Joel 2:21–23 may fall upon more-receptive ears.

The occurrence of narrative in conjunction with prophetic oracles also has parallels elsewhere in the Old Testament. Zechariah 1:6 records the response of the immediate audience to that text's call for a return to Yhwh (cf. Hag 2:12–15; Mal 3:16). Zechariah 1:6 answers the injunction to "return to me" that Zech 1:3 places in the mouth of Yhwh with two *waw*-consecutive + prefix conjugation verbs detailing the response. The text records that the community repented (וַיָּשׁוּבוּ) and spoke (וַיֹּאמְרוּ) words accepting the validity of the prophetic oracle. Joel 2:18 differs since its series of *waw*-consecutive + prefix conjugation verbs reflects the actions of Yhwh, rather than those of the community, but this difference is understandable since the conclusion of Joel 2:17 effectively challenges Yhwh to act. Whereas Zech 1:6 is a response to the command to "return to me," Joel 2:18 begins to answer the question "where is their God?" In both cases, the occurrence of a narrative structure in a prophetic passage points to a response that generates additional prophetic declarations.

The appearance of the four verbs in such short order provides the answer to the rhetorical question lingering from Joel 2:17. That passage concludes by imploring Yhwh to preserve his divine reputation by acting powerfully. Yhwh as the subject of the verbal sequence in Joel 2:18–19a demonstrates that the desired response is forthcoming. The two verbs of Joel 2:18 describe characteristics of God that lead to the desired restorative actions. The first verb, וַיְקַנֵּא 'he was jealous', describes the relationship between Yhwh and the implied audience. It has a dual significance: first Yhwh's jealousy indicates that the deity brooks no rivals and promises punishment when Israel fails to worship Yhwh alone (cf. Exod 20:3–5; 34:14; Deut 4:24; 5:9; Josh 24:19). Notably, both instances of the Decalogue highlight Yhwh's jealousy (Exod 20:5; Deut 5:9), suggesting that the use of וַיְקַנֵּא in Joel 2:18 recalls this foundational creed.[26]

---

25. J. Barton, *Joel and Obadiah: A Commentary* (OTL; Louisville: Westminster John Knox, 2001) 87. Barton suggests further that ultimately this problem of temporal orientation fades into insignificance in the transmission history of the text since the value of these words is rooted in their ability to provide assurance of divine concern in the midst of calamity.

26. Strazicich, *Joel's Use of Scripture*, 167. Strazicich suggests that the use of the character credo from Exod 34:6–7 strengthens the possibility of allusion to this part of the Decalogue in Joel 2:18. Joel creatively employs these descriptions, using Yhwh's graciousness and compassion to motivate the implied audience to return to Yhwh, while using Yhwh's zeal to introduce promises of divine restoration. Further, Brueggemann offers a discussion of the dual-pronged reality of Yhwh and קַנָּא. Brueggemann notes both Yhwh's

The second aspect of Yʜᴡʜ's jealousy refers to the deity's passionate commitment to the people and the deity's refusal to allow anyone to wrest them away (Isa 9:7; Ezek 39:25; Zech 1:14). These two senses coalesce around the concept of Yʜᴡʜ's unique relationship with the implied audience; Yʜᴡʜ demonstrates wrath when it turns away, but Yʜᴡʜ is also committed to its well-being and will intercede when the people sincerely cry out.[27] Joel 2:18 invokes the latter sense of קָנָא, with the idea that in the wake of the community's cries from Joel 2:12–17, Yʜᴡʜ will again demonstrate commitment and the ability to save. This strengthens the covenantal bond between Yʜᴡʜ and the implied audience.

The object of וַיְקַנֵּא in Joel 2:18 is לְאַרְצוֹ 'for his land', which parallels the object עַמּוֹ 'his people' attached to the following verb. These two objects together emphasize that Yʜᴡʜ's restorative activity covers the totality of both the people and the land on which they live. This is fitting since previous rhetorical units highlight threats against both the covenant people and their land, especially their argricultural produce. The second verb, וַיַּחְמֹל, 'he had compassion', echoes and emphasizes Yʜᴡʜ's zeal. It highlights Yʜᴡʜ's mercy, which is necessary in this situation given the deprivations described previously (Jer 15:5; Ezek 16:5; Zech 11:5, 6; Mal 3:17).[28] The attribution of these characteristics to Yʜᴡʜ provides the orientation for reading the remainder of this unit, where divine jealousy and compassion move Yʜᴡʜ to act restoratively.

Joel 2:19 begins to detail the elements of Yʜᴡʜ's promised restoration. The verse commences with the latter two verbs of the waw-consecutive sequence (וַיַּעַן; וַיֹּאמֶר). Joel 2:19 reuses the divine name as the explicit subject of both וַיַּעַן and וַיֹּאמֶר, and reuses לְעַמּוֹ as the object of Yʜᴡʜ's response. These repetitions draw Yʜᴡʜ's connection to the implied audience to the forefront, highlighting both the one who acts in this rhetorical unit and those who benefit from Yʜᴡʜ's actions. The two verbs in Joel 2:19 also introduce first-person divine speech, which continues through 2:20. Shifting the implied speaker here is a potentially powerful rhetorical strategy since

harsh responses when Israel strays (Deut 32:16, 21) and Yʜᴡʜ's passionate commitment to Israel when circumstances dictate (Zeph 3:8; W. Brueggemann, *Theology of the Old Testament: Testimony, Dispute, Advocacy* [Minneapolis: Fortress, 1997] 293–97). There is similar rhetorical force expended in detailing the depths of Yʜᴡʜ's קָנָא in both its positive and negative senses for Israel. Reuter traces the trajectory of this verb across the Old Testament before concluding that Yʜᴡʜ's concern for his people defines its highest level of passionate commitment (E. Reuter, "קנא," *TDOT* 13:56–57).

27. Barton, *Joel*, 88.

28. D. Hubbard, *Joel and Amos* (TOTC 25; Downers Grove, IL: InterVarsity, 2009) 66. Hubbard looks to the story of an Egyptian princess's rescuing Moses from the river for an example of the compassion described by חָמַל (Exod 2:6). See also the examples of negated חָמַל to describe Yʜᴡʜ's lack of compassion over Judah's sins (Ezek 5:11; Lam 2:2, 17, 21). See Crenshaw, *Joel*, 149.

it pushes past the mediation of the prophet in presenting the divine word. YHWH speaks in the first person, demonstrating to the implied audience the depth of the divine commitment to its restoration.

The first element of YHWH's speech is the promise to restore agricultural prosperity. YHWH's speech commences with הִנְנִי שֹׁלֵחַ 'Behold I am sending', which is an emphatic particle with a first-person singular suffix followed by a participle. This syntactic construction occurs mostly in prophetic literature or in narrative accounts of prophecy. It stresses imminent action, usually performed by YHWH.[29] The subject of this syntactic construction is typically YHWH, and it normally introduces divine promises or threats (cf. 1 Sam 25:19; 2 Sam 12:11; 1 Kgs 5:19; 11:31; Jer 1:15; 2:35; 6:21; 35:17; Ezek 4:16; 11:3; 22:19; 23:22; Hos 2:8; Amos 6:14; 7:8).[30] Crenshaw eloquently describes the rhetorical effect of the construction הִנְנִי שֹׁלֵחַ by stating, "The promised event is on the verge of taking place; YHWH is poised to inaugurate a new era."[31] This sense of anticipation drives the promises that the text proclaims in Joel 2:18–27.

Joel 2:19 then proclaims that YHWH is restoring a trio of agricultural crops to the land. These are הַדָּגָן וְהַתִּירוֹשׁ וְהַיִּצְהָר 'grain, new wine, and fresh oil'. These crops were both staples of the community's diet and essential to people's worship offerings to YHWH (Deut 14:22–23; Neh 13:12; Hos 2:8).[32] Significantly, Joel 1:9–10 mentions these same three crops when describing the devastation of the locust plague and the cessation of offerings at the temple. YHWH's act of restoring these three crops to the community thus reverses the description of deprivation and despair. The next phrase in Joel 2:19 succinctly emphasizes the efficacy of YHWH's activity on the com-

---

29. T. Muraoka, *Emphatic Words and Structures in Biblical Hebrew* (Leiden: Brill, 1985) 137–40. For further discussion of the participial function of introducing imminent action, see Joüon, *Grammar*, 381–82. Also, note that הִנֵּה can introduce an important change of perspective (C. van der Merwe, J. Naudé, and J. Kroeze, *A Biblical Hebrew Reference Grammar* [Sheffield: Sheffield Academic Press, 1999] 329–30). This is evident in Joel 2:19 since this phrase commences the description of YHWH's restorative action whereas previously YHWH has either been silent or acted against the implied audience.

30. P. Humbert, "La formule hebraique en hineni suivi d'un participle," *Revue des Etudes Juives* 97 (1934) 58–64. Humbert tallies 125 examples of this syntactic construction and asserts that 118 of them introduce either a divine promise or threat. This syntactic construction is most prevalent in Jeremiah and Ezekiel which account for over half of the occurrences, but it is also sprinkled throughout other prophetic books as well as occurring in narrative contexts.

31. Crenshaw, *Joel*, 150.

32. M. Sweeney, *The Twelve Prophets: Vol. 1* (Berit Olam; Collegeville, MN: Liturgical Press, 2000) 169. The mention of these three crops in Neh 13:12 combines their value as sustenance and as worship offerings. Nehemiah reinstitutes tithing of the grain, wine and oil to the temple so that the Levites can return to ministering there without having to go find food. Consequently, restoring grain, wine and oil in Joel 2:19 indicates both sated appetites and renewed cultic worship.

munity's behalf through the verb וּשְׂבַעְתֶּם 'you will be satisfied'.[33] YHWH's promised actions in Joel 2:19 banish the specter of famine from Joel 1:1–14 and 1:15–20, replacing calls to fast (Joel 1:14; 2:15) with assurances of feasts.

The final phrase of Joel 2:19 begins to reverse an element of the cry that the text prescribes for the community in 2:17. One of the pleas in Joel 2:17 is for YHWH to prevent his people from becoming a חֶרְפָּה 'reproach'. In Joel 2:19, YHWH states that this will not occur, declaring וְלֹא־אֶתֵּן אֶתְכֶם עוֹד חֶרְפָּה בַּגּוֹיִם 'and I will not give you again [over to] reproach among the nations'. YHWH's speech indicates that the restoration of the community's standing among the nations will match restoration of agricultural prosperity. These signs of the divine presence answer the question "where is their God?" In essence, the full stomachs that YHWH promises to the people in Joel 2:19 are representative of the divine commitment to eliminate their vulnerability to the mockery of foreign nations.[34] YHWH thus promises to alleviate fully both the physical and the psychological distress created in Joel 1:1–2:17.

The divine speech of Joel 2:19–20 also reverses the threat of invasion in Joel 2:1–11. Joel 2:20 describes how YHWH will push the invading host out of the land. Joel's use of the term הַצְּפוֹנִי 'the northerner' to refer to the invader in this verse raises some interesting interpretive issues. This term is an example of what Dillard refers to as the text's "almost studied ambiguity" since it appears to be applicable equally to locusts, an apocalyptic army, and a foreign invader.[35] Although the noun is singular, its reference is most likely to the invading horde of Joel 2:1–11 as a collective entity. Some attempt to apply the term *northerner* to a literal locust invasion, arguing that the locusts in this invading horde arrived from the north, even if the standard direction from which they would enter Israel is south or east.[36] This assertion, however, cannot be proven, and it does not capture the full significance of the concept of *the northerner*.

The term הַצְּפוֹנִי has a broader significance than simply identifying the direction of attack used by the invading horde of Joel 2:1–11. The Old Testament employs the idea of the north or the northerner to refer to Israel's great historical enemies, whose invasions typically came from the north

---

33. Crenshaw, *Joel*, 150. Crenshaw correctly notes that this single verb summarizes everything that YHWH promises to accomplish in Joel 2:18–27.

34. Ibid.

35. Dillard, "Joel," 286.

36. Allen, *Joel*, 88, argues for locusts from the north. Kapelrud makes the counter-argument that locusts would typically enter from the south or east (A. Kapelrud, *Joel Studies* [UUÅ 4; Uppsala: Lundequist, 1948] 96–107). Garrett suggests that locusts may not be in view here since the text justifies this force's destruction because of its pride (D. Garrett, *Hosea, Joel* [NAC 19A; Nashville: Broadman & Holman, 1997] 357). See the discussion below on the meaning of הִגְדִּיל לַעֲשׂוֹת in this passage.

due to the implausibility of attack across the eastern desert (Isa 41:25; Jer 1:13–15; 4:6; 6:22; 10:22; Ezek 26:10; 38:6, 15; Zech 2:10).[37] The attempt to pin down a specific identity for this foe in all cases has proven futile, but the image of the northerner as a great enemy remains.[38] The identity of the north in Canaanite mythology as the abode of deities, typically on Mount Zaphon, provides another element to this term.[39] The concept of a northern dwelling for deity occasionally finds its way into the Old Testament (Job 37:22; Ps 48:3; Isa 14:13; Ezek 1:4).[40] Given this complexity, the designation of this invading host as הַצְּפוֹנִי is probably a reference to its significance, not to a specific marker of geographical provenance.

In the case of Joel 2:20, it is possible that this verse represents a fusion of the latter two concepts: an invincible invader coming from the abode of the divine.[41] This makes sense in light of Joel 2:10, which introduces theophany into its description of the invading force. Joel 2:10 describes the 'shaking' (רָעֲשׁוּ) of the heavens, a word that developed associations of announcing the return of chaos as part of a suprahistorical cataclysm.[42] This

---

37. Dillard, "Joel," 287.

38. There are several options suggested by scholars for identifying the northern enemy, beginning with Cazelles, who posits a Scythian incursion around the time of Josiah (H. Cazelles, "Zephaniah, Jeremiah and the Scythians in Palestine," in *A Prophet to the Nations: Essays in Jeremiah Studies* [ed. L. Perdue and B. Kovacs; Winona Lake, IN: Eisenbrauns, 1984] 129–50). Whitley links this enemy to Babylonians on account of the threat they posed to Judah after the battle of Carchemish (Whitley, "Carchemish and Jeremiah," in ibid., 163–73). Childs attempts to loosen the historical moorings of this foe, attaching it to the idea of a chaos myth that threatens creation (B. Childs, "The Enemy from the North and the Chaos Tradition," *JBL* 78 [1959] 187–98). Reimer offers the best way forward, explaining that one ought not to look for a monolithic tradition of the northern foe but, rather, view it as a motif complex that could be employed creatively to speak of judgment coming against both Israel and other nations (D. Reimer, "The 'Foe' and the 'North' in Jeremiah," *ZAW* 101 [1989] 223–32). This helps to make sense of passages such as Jer 50:1–3 that speak of the northern enemy coming against Babylon, which is often identified as the northern enemy itself. Kapelrud adopts essentially the same perspective in his detailed excursus, suggesting that Joel is alluding to Jeremiah and emphasizing a mythic element of a motif complex (Kapelrud, *Joel Studies*, 93–108).

39. R. Clifford, *The Cosmic Mountain in Canaan and the Old Testament* (Cambridge: Harvard University Press, 1972) 57–73.

40. Dillard, "Joel," 286.

41. G. Ahlström, *Joel and the Temple Cult of Jerusalem* (VTSup 21; Leiden: Brill, 1971) 32–34. Ahlström rightly cautions against trying to parse the image too closely, claiming that "logic and symbols should not be played against each other." In this case, the multiple hues of the "northerner" build on each other to construct a powerful enemy against whom Yʜᴡʜ will act.

42. Childs, "Enemy from the North," 197. Childs performs a diachronic survey of the use of שׁער, arguing that it became associated with the "enemy-from-the-north" tradition when this enemy began to take on suprahistorical characteristics. He specifically connects Ezek 38:18–20 with Joel 2:10 and 20 on the grounds that a cataclysmic shaking of the cosmos is the result of the battle with the "enemy from the north."

shaking occurs because of the great revelation of Joel 2:11 that this invasion has divine sanction; none other than Yhwh thunders at the head of this army. Therefore, according to Simkins, "For Joel the locusts were the enemy from the north; they were the enemy army brought up by Yahweh from his dwelling in the north against Judah."[43] The text transforms the idea of a divinely sanctioned locust invasion and reads it against the traditions of the enemy from the north in Joel 2:18–27. The locust army is the "northerner" of Joel 2:20 inasmuch as its invasion in Joel 2:1–11 culminates in the declaration that Yhwh leads the army and threatens the created order.

After identifying the enemy as the "northerner" with all of its theological ramifications, Joel 2:20 details its destruction. Yhwh, the one who sanctioned the invasion, promises to return and drive out the great foe. This is a rather shocking role reversal since Yhwh now turns on the invading force that was formerly under divine leadership.[44] The description of Yhwh's actions resonates with divine warrior traditions since the text makes Yhwh the primary actor; the role of the people is only to rejoice in Yhwh's victory.[45] Again, this reversal points back to the efficacy of the text's calls in Joel 2:12–17; from the nadir of Joel 2:11, the implied audience is now assured that Yhwh will not abandon it. Instead, its potential turn to Yhwh helps to inaugurate Yhwh's promises of protection.

Joel 2:20 claims that Yhwh will push this powerful invading horde into a parched and desolate land incapable of fulfilling its needs. There is poetic justice at work in this description since Yhwh declares that the invader will suffer the fate of thirst and deprivation that it threatened to inflict on Yhwh's covenant community in previous rhetorical units. Joel 2:3 articulates how the invader turned the Edenic landscape into a wasteland using the adjective שְׁמָמָה 'desolate', which now recurs in Joel 2:20 to describe the final fate of this invader. The attacking horde that left devastation in its wake will ultimately find itself suffering the fate of its victims.

---

43. Simkins, *Yahweh's Activity*, 197. See also Van Leeuwen, who supports the idea that Joel is portraying the locusts as "the northerner" since they are both a great enemy and have divine sanction for their activities in Joel 1:2–2:11 (C. Van Leeuwen, "The 'Northern One,' in the Composition of Joel 2,19–27," in *The Scriptures and the Scrolls: Studies in Honour of A. S. van der Woude on the Occasion of His 65th Birthday* [ed. F. Martínez, A. Hilhorst, and C. Labuschagne; VTSup 49; Leiden: Brill, 1992] 98–99). Conflating the locusts with the image of the northern enemy heightens their threat and consequently strengthens the power of Yhwh's restorative activity.

44. Note that the text states that Yhwh leads this invader in Joel 2:25.

45. C. Sherlock, *The God Who Fights: The War Tradition in Holy Scripture* (Rutherford Studies in Contemporary Theology 6; Lewiston, NY: Edwin Mellen, 1993) 31. Sherlock notes that Yhwh could intervene in a variety of fashions ranging from military to miraculous; however, any response from Israel that did not exude trust and faithfulness could lead to the renewal of threat.

The verb describing Yнwн's action, וְהִדַּחְתִּיו 'and I will drive it', evokes images of an enemy scattering in defeat, which effectively reverses the descriptions of the invaders' rigid discipline in Joel 2:7–8 (cf. Jer 8:3; 24:9; Dan 9:7; Ezek 4:13).[46] No longer does this invading horde maintain ranks. Instead, Yнwн's actions disrupt its activities, culminating in its destruction at Yнwн's hands. The force of the verb וְהִדַּחְתִּיו continues into the following verbless clauses, which the definite-object marker introduces.[47] These clauses create a geographical merismus, describing how Yнwн's actions will push the head of the invading army into the Dead Sea in the east and its tail into the Mediterranean to the west. This merismus indicates that Yнwн's actions will cleanse the land by pushing the enemy to the periphery and accomplishing its destruction in the waters that form the natural boundaries of the land.

Joel 2:20 concludes its description of destruction by employing olfactory imagery. It consists of two parallel clauses, both beginning with *waw*-consecutive affix verbs from the root עָלָה that are followed by a noun referring to the invaders' odor (בָּאְשׁוֹ 'stench', צַחֲנָתוֹ 'foul smell') as the enemies are destroyed.[48] Many ancient and modern commentators note the putrefaction of locust bodies when the swarm dies, suggesting that the stench may once again point to the locusts as a key part of the image-world that governs the description of the invader.[49] The effect of these images is to create a vivid picture of utter destruction by describing the smell of the rotting corpses as being the remains of the formerly invincible enemy.

The final clause of Joel 2:20 provides the reason for the punishment that Yнwн inflicts in the earlier clauses of this verse. This clause reads כִּי הִגְדִּיל לַעֲשׂוֹת 'for it has done great things'. The subject of the verb הִגְדִּיל is unexpressed, which leads to interpretive confusion since a similar phrase concludes the following verse. The sole difference is that the final phrase of Joel 2:21 identifies Yнwн as the subject (כִּי־הִגְדִּיל יְהוָה לַעֲשׂוֹת). Based on this close parallel, it is possible to see Yнwн as the subject of the clause in 2:20 and to argue that either the divine name was elided during the process

---

46. Crenshaw, *Joel*, 151–52.

47. There is a text-critical issue here. The Septuagint uses the verbal form ἀφανιῶ to translate the adjectival form שְׁמָמָה. The Septuagint is probably reading שממתי in this instance. The septuagintal reading appears to reflect an attempt to smooth out the reading by supplying a verb just before a phrase marked by the definite-object marker. The Masoretic Text is probably preferable since it is the more difficult but still comprehensible reading.

48. The term צַחֲנָתוֹ is a hapax legomenon; however, the repetition of the verb and the exactly parallel syntax between the two clauses push the interpreter to understand the word as a synonym of בָּאְשׁוֹ.

49. Simkins cites the example of Augustine, who described the death of a locust swarm as something with enough stench and toxicity to spark a pestilence; Simkins, *Yahweh's Activity*, 195.

of transmission,[50] or the verb is part of Yʜᴡʜ's speech and should instead read in the first person as אַגְדִּיל.[51] This would make evident Yʜᴡʜ's agency as the one who performs "great things." Neither eliding the divine name nor emending the verb has any textual support, however, and thus the two ideas remain conjectural.[52]

There is another, preferable solution that does not require changing the Masoretic Text. It is possible to argue instead that the "northerner" from earlier in the verse is the unexpressed subject of הִגְדִּיל לַעֲשׂוֹת in Joel 2:20.[53] Accordingly, it is a result clause, giving justification for Yʜᴡʜ's acting to destroy it. The term "great deeds" refers to its self-aggrandizement.[54] This clause may have a parallel in Isa 10:5–19, which is another prophetic passage that describes a foreign invader as a divine agent of punishment. Similarly, when the invading host (Assyria) exceeds its commission, Yʜᴡʜ directs his wrath toward it (cf. Hab 2:16–19).

A parallel in Ps 35:26–27 further suggests that the "northerner" is the subject of הִגְדִּיל in Joel 2:20.[55] This passage uses a participial form of the root גָּדַל (הַמַּגְדִּילִים) to describe the overly proud enemies of the psalmist in Ps 35:26. Psalm 35:27 then uses a jussive form of the root (יִגְדַּל) to call the audience to magnify Yʜᴡʜ for vindicating the psalmist.[56] Consequently, it is conceivable that this final clause of Joel 2:20 is the first part of an intricate wordplay. It promises that Yʜᴡʜ will destroy the invading army completely on account of the "great deeds" that it has done, but it also sets up the attribution of "great deeds" to Yʜᴡʜ in Joel 2:21. Yʜᴡʜ's "great deeds" overwhelm the "great deeds" of the invading horde.

Overall, Joel 2:18–20 inaugurates Yʜᴡʜ's programmatic reversal of the destruction described in Joel 1:1–2:17. It announces Yʜᴡʜ's change of heart and introduces first-person divine speech in which Yʜᴡʜ promises to

---

50. H. Wolff, *Joel and Amos* (Hermeneia; Philadelphia: Fortress, 1977) 55.

51. E. Sellin, *Das Zwölfprophetenbuch übersetzt und erklärt* (KAT 12/1; Leipzig: Deichert, 1929) 166.

52. See also Miller's work on the linguistics of ellipsis. The direction of the potential ellipsis in Joel 2:20 and 21 is backward since the extra constituent occurs in v. 21. Miller claims that "backward ellipsis" of this sort only occurs when the elided constituent is in the final position in line (cf. Ps 20:8; C. Miller, "A Linguistic Approach to Ellipsis in Biblical Poetry [or, What to Do When Exegesis of What's There Depends on What Isn't]," *BBR* 13 [2003] 263–65). This may help argue against the presence of ellipsis in Joel 2:20, 21, since Yʜᴡʜ is not the final constituent of Joel 2:21. One cannot make this argument too firmly, however, since Miller focuses solely on the elision of verbs, but the position of the supposedly missing constituent in Joel 2:20, 21 may suggest that ellipsis is not occurring here.

53. See Simkins, *Yahweh's Activity*, 192; Prinsloo, *Theology*, 77; Allen, *Joel*, 89–90; Crenshaw, *Joel*, 152; Dillard, "Joel," 287.

54. Prinsloo, *Theology*, 77.

55. Allen, *Joel*, 89.

56. See also Zeph 2:8, 10 for additional examples of texts that employ גָּדַל in a pejorative sense.

restore agricultural abundance to the land and destroy the foreign invader. Whereas Yʜwʜ thunders at the head of the army in Joel 2:11, the text now has the deity speak in the first person to signify the divine commitment to restoring the implied audience. The rhetorical strategy of Joel 2:18–20 also draws deeply from previous rhetorical units. Yʜwʜ's promises to send sustenance including grain, new wine, and oil reverse what was lacking in Joel 1:1–14 and 1:15–20. Further, the text claims that Yʜwʜ's actions signify that the community is no longer a reproach among the nations, directly answering the plea that the text constructs for the implied audience in Joel 2:17.[57]

Joel 2:21–24: Calls to Rejoice

Joel 2:21 begins a new subunit in which the text switches from first-person divine speech to imperatives from the prophet. These imperatives provide the prophet's evaluation of the preceding description of Yʜwʜ's actions, which is to call on the implied audience to rejoice. The prophet creatively first addresses the land, followed by the animals, and finally the children of Zion. This progression from inanimate object to animals to humans demonstrates the fullness of the restoration brought about by Yʜwʜ's actions since Yʜwʜ restores everything that was devastated in Joel 1:1–2:17. The delay in referring to the children of Zion also heightens the climactic effect. By first addressing the land and the animals, the prophet builds up to the commands addressed to the implied audience as the culmination of the sequence. The implied audience shares in the positive repercussions for the land and the animals, ultimately rejoicing in the fullness of Yʜwʜ's actions.

The flow of Joel 2:21–24 resembles that of a thanksgiving psalm containing (1) a command or exhortation; (2) vocative addressee; (3) reason for jubilation introduced by כִּי; and (4) designation of the divine basis of the rejoicing (cf. Pss 117; 135).[58] Joel 2:21 begins with the command אַל־תִּירְאִי

---

57. Deist, "Parallels," 64.

58. Crenshaw, *Joel*, 153; Prinsloo, *Theology*, 71. Allen differentiates between thanksgiving psalms and their prophetic adaptations on the grounds that the Psalms tend to reflect on an attribute of Yʜwʜ or specific deed that Yʜwʜ accomplished, while the prophets use the form to point toward an event that Yʜwʜ will create (cf. Isa 44:23; 54:1–3; Zeph 3:14–15; Zech 2:14; 9:9–10); Allen, *Joel*, 90. Joel 2:21–24 may also resonate with the literary form of an *Aufruf zur Freude* ('summons to joy'). Boda examines nine prophetic texts, including Joel 2:21–24, that seem to reflect this form. Boda notes that the texts that address a female city figure reflect military victory as the reason for celebration (Isa 12:6; 54:1; Zeph 3:14–15; Zech 2:14; 9:9–10; Lam 4:21) while those that do not use the metaphor of a female city figure reflect harvest contexts, with some potential for invocation of military imagery (Hos 9:1; Joel 2:21–24; see M. Boda, "The Daughter's Joy," in *Daughter Zion: Her Portrait, Her Response* [SBLHB/OT; ed. M. Boda, C. Dempsey, and L. Snow Flesher; Atlanta: Society of Biblical Literature / Leiden: Brill, 2013] 321–42). This is an appropriate form of response for the text to require since the threats portrayed in Joel 1:1–2:17 were oriented around locusts that ravage the landscape and have the attributes of a military force.

'be not afraid!' followed by a vocative identification of the land as the object of the imperative.[59] It then echoes the first command when it employs the imperatives גִּילִי וּשְׂמָחִי 'shout and rejoice!' before using כִּי to introduce YHWH's actions as the reason for adopting this attitude.[60] These two imperatives point to a reversal of Joel 1:16; a verse that employed nominal forms of these roots (שִׂמְחָה וָגִיל) to describe the results of the cessation of sacrificial worship at the temple.[61] The commands to the earth to shout and rejoice essentially reverse the elimination of "gladness and joy" in Joel 1:16.

The final phrase of Joel 2:21 is כִּי־הִגְדִּיל יְהוָה לַעֲשׂוֹת 'for YHWH has done great things', which, as discussed above, completes a wordplay with the previous verse.[62] Joel 2:21 contrasts YHWH's agency in performing "great things" over and against the "great things" of the invading locust army that is doomed to destruction. Essentially, the land needs to fear no longer since YHWH promises to drive this seemingly great army into destruction outside its boundaries. Joel 2:21 shifts the emphasis for the implied audience's hope from YHWH's character to YHWH's actions; whereas the text's appeal to cry out to YHWH is rooted in the divine nature (Joel 2:13), the process of restoration shows YHWH's character in action. YHWH's "great deeds" cause the land to rejoice since they overcome and reverse the "great deeds" of the invading host.[63]

Joel 2:22 unfolds similarly to the previous verse. It begins with אַל־תִּירְאוּ, followed by an identification of the addressee in the vocative, and concludes by articulating the basis for assurance with clauses introduced

---

59. Conrad detects some resonance between Joel's use of the command not to fear and its use in Jer 46:27–28; Zeph 3:16–18a; and Isa 10:24–27. While the command not to fear could be addressed to warriors and kings, it also could be used to address a community for whom YHWH will fight as the divine warrior. Joel 2:21 and 2:22 both contain elements common to these other אַל־תִּירָא pericopes, including the command itself, a designation of the addressee and statements of the basis of assurance. Joel 2:21 and 2:22 differ from these other אַל־תִּירָא pericopes in that their addressees are non-human: the "earth" and "beasts of the field," respectively (E. Conrad, *Fear Not, Warrior: A Study of the 'al tira' Pericopes in the Hebrew Scriptures* [BJS 75; Chico, CA: Scholars Press, 1985] 122–23, 168–69). Joel 2:23, however, does address the "children of Zion," although with commands to "shout" and "be glad" instead. The parallels are not perfect, but the idea of YHWH acting powerfully on behalf of his covenant community may connect these verses with other אַל־תִּירָא pericopes.

60. All three of the imperatives in Joel 2:21 are in the feminine-singular form, taking their number and gender from אֲדָמָה 'land', which is the vocative addressee.

61. Deist, "Parallels," 64.

62. Simkins, *Yahweh's Activity*, 192.

63. Interestingly, this same declaration of YHWH's great deeds occurs in Ps 126:2–3, which is a psalm celebrating the return of the captives from exile thanks to YHWH's actions. Strazicich tries to draw the context of Ps 126 into this use of this phrase in Joel 2:21, arguing that the text is trying to relive the dream of restoration made explicit in Ps 126 (Strazicich, *Joel's Use of Scripture*, 180–81). This presumes, of course, that one can firmly date the composition of Joel after the composition of Ps 126, which may be likely but is not certain.

by כִּי.[64] The addressees on this occasion are the בַּהֲמוֹת שָׂדַי 'beasts of the field'. This resonantes with the way Joel 1:16–20 describes the deprivations suffered by the animals through its use of drought imagery, encapsulating their suffering with a description of their moans (מַה־נֶּאֶנְחָה בְהֵמָה). Joel 2:22, therefore, effectively reverses the picture of animal suffering by appealing to them not to be afraid before providing details of the agricultural renewal.

Joel 2:22 lacks an explicit statement attributing the restoration to YHWH, but one should infer it from the declaration of Joel 2:21 that YHWH has done "great things." Joel 2:22 details these "great things" and uses כִּי to introduce the first great deed; a vivid picture of a desert land producing lush vegetation. The verb is דָּשְׁאוּ 'they became green', whose only other appearance in the Old Testament is in Gen 1:11 in YHWH's command for the earth to fill with flora.[65] This calls to mind Joel 2:3, which describes the locust army as ravaging an Edenic landscape.[66] In employing a verb associated with the creation narrative, the text hints at the prospect of paradise restored because of YHWH's powerful acts. The object of דָּשְׁאוּ is נְאוֹת מִדְבָּר 'pastures of the wilderness', which the text is reusing from Joel 1:19, 20. In the earlier occurrence, fire consumed the נְאוֹת מִדְבָּר, putting an emphatic capstone on the image-world of drought that threatened the community's survival. In Joel 2:22, the text reverses the image completely since it declares that the fields will no longer burn. Instead, they will abound with vegetation.

The remaining phrases in Joel 2:22 echo and enhance the idea of renewed prosperity. The particle כִּי again introduces descriptions of renewed agricultural prosperity that give assurances that the addressee should heed the command to "fear not." These assurances include trees that bear their fruit (עֵץ נָשָׂא פִרְיוֹ), specifically mentioning fig trees and vines (תְּאֵנָה וָגֶפֶן) that yield rich produce. These same words appear in Joel 1:7 as part of the imagery depicting the totality of the locusts' ravaging. Now, they produce their fruit in remarkable abundance. The word חֵילָם 'their strength/ abundance' describes their output. The Old Testament uses it frequently to describe military strength, whether describing a great army or strong fighters in the army (cf. Judg 6:12; 11:1; 1 Sam 1:9; 16:18; 1 Kgs 11:28;

---

64. The command not to fear differs from Joel 2:21 in that this command is in the masculine-plural form as opposed to the feminine-singular. The vocative addressee of the verb in 2:21 is the land (אֲדָמָה), which agrees with the verb in number and gender. The vocative addressees of the verb in 2:22 are the beasts of the field (בַּהֲמוֹת שָׂדַי), a phrase that is a feminine-plural construct chain that does not agree with the gender of the verb. This lack of agreement probably reflects the convention that the masculine plural is the base form for verbs in the second person (cf. Ruth 1:4b; Amos 4:1). See Joüon, *Grammar*, 517; Dillard, "Joel," 298; Wolff, *Joel and Amos*, 55.

65. The presence of this verb and sequence of restoration that goes from land to animals to people seem to echo the creation order. See Strazicich, *Joel's Use of Scripture*, 181.

66. Crenshaw, *Joel*, 154.

2 Kgs 5:1; Jer 32:2; 34:1; Ezek 17:17; 27:10). Notably, the previous use of חַיִל in this text occurred in Joel 2:11, referring to the army that YHWH brings against Zion. In this instance, the text uses what was once a word indicating threat to announce blessing since it refers to the output of the vines and fig trees.

In the wake of the commands to the land and the animals, Joel 2:23 continues the progression of addressees by calling on the children of Zion to shout and rejoice in YHWH.[67] These commands echo Joel 2:21 by using similar imperatives that differ only in number and gender from those that the text directs toward the land (גִּילִי וְשִׂמְחִי 'rejoice and be glad!'). Joel 2:23 fronts the addressees, commencing with וּבְנֵי צִיּוֹן 'children of Zion', prior to the imperatives. This syntactic shift helps to mark this verse as the climax of the sequence of imperatives.[68] Joel 2:21–23 demonstrates the breadth of YHWH's restorative activity by moving from the land to the beasts to God's people: from inanimate to animate to human.[69] Each step draws closer to the implied audience who ought to respond to the text's dictates. Following the addresses to the land and the animals, the prophet now focuses specifically on YHWH's actions toward the children of Zion. The assurances that compel the "earth" and the "beasts of the field" to "fear not" also provide YHWH's community in Zion with reasons to rejoice.

Joel 2:23 announces the reasons for rejoicing by again employing the particle כִּי, which mirrors the syntax of the previous two verses. The first phrase articulating these reasons creates one of the more complicated interpretive issues in the entire book. The Masoretic Text states that YHWH will give to the community הַמּוֹרֶה לִצְדָקָה, the interpretation of which is the subject of significant debate. The LXX quite obviously has a different reading here since it translates it τὰ βρώματα 'food'. Suggestions for this reading include either המאכל לצדקה or הבריה לצדקה in the Hebrew text.[70] Within this specific rhetorical unit, the septuagintal reading seems to echo Joel 2:21–22 with the promise of food in the wake of commands to shout and rejoice.[71] It is difficult, however, to determine a text-critical error from either of these proposed original readings that would lead to the Masoretic form הַמּוֹרֶה. It

---

67. Dillard, "Joel," 289.

68. Prinsloo, *Theology*, 69.

69. Dempsey admirably expresses the scope of YHWH's restorative activity by noting that Joel 2:21–24 contains "hopeful words that speak of redemption and restoration, with humanity and the natural world in relationship with each other and God in relationship with both" (C. Dempsey, "Hope amidst Crisis: A Prophetic Vision of Cosmic Redemption," in *Creation Is Groaning: An Interdisciplinary Vision for Life in a Sacred Universe* [ed. C. Dempsey and R. Butkus; Collegeville, MN: Liturgical Press, 1999] 276). In these verses, YHWH inextricably intertwines restoration for the land and its inhabitants.

70. Simkins, *Yahweh's Activity*, 199; Wolff, *Joel and Amos*, 55; Dillard, "Joel," 289. Simkins notes that the root אָכַל 'to eat' occurs in Joel 1:16, which may strengthen the septuagintal reading since Joel 2:18–27 does explicitly reverse calamities found in Joel 1:15–20.

71. Simkins, *Yahweh's Activity*, 199.

is more likely that the LXX is trying to exegete a difficult passage by offering a reading that seems more contextually appropriate. In this case, the interpreter must wrestle with the complexities inherent in the Masoretic Text.

Attempting to determine the meaning of הַמּוֹרֶה לִצְדָקָה is challenging. The word הַמּוֹרֶה has multiple senses, two of which may be applicable in this context. First, it can refer to a teacher or instructor (Gen 12:6; Deut 11:30; Judg 7:1; Isa 30:20). This, along with the following לִצְדָקָה, leads to the translation 'teacher for righteousness', which the targum and Vulgate appear to have followed.[72] This has piqued scholarly interest in light of the discovery of the Dead Sea Scrolls and the Qumran community. Some seek to find parallels between this passage and the concept of a "teacher of righteousness" at Qumran. The absence of references to Joel 2:23 in the extant Qumran literature, however, argues against this explanation.[73]

A related possibility is that this phrase is a cryptic reference to a new Davidic figure as teacher and leader, derived from the political vacuum following the disappearance of Zerubbabel.[74] The degree of uncertainty surrounding the date of composition for this book, however, means that this proposal remains highly speculative. Further, the idea of a teaching figure appearing here in the middle of an extended description of YHWH's agricultural blessings is rather incongruous. If this is the sense that the text intends, one would expect further description of this figure and his import.[75] Instead, the text highlights YHWH's salvific deeds and offers no additional description of a promised leader who brings powerful teaching.

The other alternative is to understand הַמּוֹרֶה as a reference to rainfall, probably the autumn rains that prepare the ground for plowing and sowing.[76] This would be a rare use of the term, since Ps 84:7 is the only other passage that may contain מוֹרֶה with this meaning. The other term for this rain is יוֹרֶה, which occurs in Deut 11:14; Jer 5:24; and Hos 6:3. Despite its

---

72. Dillard, "Joel," 289. The targum reads מלפיכון בדכו 'teacher of merit', while the Vulgate reading is *doctorem iustitiae* 'teacher of justice'.

73. Roth suggests that the Qumran community interpreted this verse "out of its context" to appropriate the idea of a teacher of righteousness; there are, however, no references to this verse in any extant Qumran documents (C. Roth, "The Teacher of Righteousness in the Prophecy of Joel," *VT* 13 [1963] 93–95). See also Crenshaw, *Joel*, 155. Sellers suggests that לִצְדָקָה was a scribal addition brought on by the proximity of הַמּוֹרֶה. This scribe presumably would have belonged to a circle familiar with Qumran teachings (O. Sellers, "A Possible Old Testament Reference to the Teacher of Righteousness," *IEJ* 5 [1955] 93–95). This hypothesis, however, suffers from a lack of evidence to identify this scribe.

74. Ahlström, *Joel*, 107–10. Ahlström does not offer specifics of who this figure might represent other than to assert that he would be the leader of the Jerusalem cultus and perhaps also assert a certain degree of authority in the political sphere. The lack of specificity combined with the oddity of a reference to a teaching figure in the context of this passage render this proposal unlikely.

75. Crenshaw, *Joel*, 155.

76. Allen, *Joel*, 92–93.

rarity, there are strong reasons to consider 'rainfall' the most appropriate reading of this word in this context. The strongest evidence comes from the context of the remainder of the verse. Joel 2:23b declares that YHWH will cause precipitation using the unambiguous term גֶּשֶׁם 'rain' (cf. Gen 7:12; 8:2; Lev 26:4; 1 Kgs 17:7; 18:45; Isa 44:10; 55:10; Amos 4:7; Hos 6:3), followed by the appositional construction מוֹרֶה וּמַלְקוֹשׁ בָּרִאשׁוֹן. Again the disputed term מוֹרֶה appears, this time in conjunction with מַלְקוֹשׁ 'spring rain', which clearly refers to the rains that strengthen the crops before harvest (Deut 11:14; Prov 16:15; Job 29:23; Jer 5:24; Hos 6:3; Zech 10:1). The connection to מַלְקוֹשׁ, which follows גֶּשֶׁם, suggests that this phrase is a merism, by which מוֹרֶה וּמַלְקוֹשׁ explains that YHWH's sending of rain will extend over both expected rainfall seasons.[77] Looking back to the first half of the verse, it is reasonable to propose that, if מוֹרֶה refers to rain in Joel 2:23b, then it also refers to rain in 2:23a.[78]

Understanding מוֹרֶה as a synonym for rain still leaves the challenge of determining its relationship to the ensuing phrase לִצְדָקָה 'to/for righteousness'. At first glance it is difficult to see how the text intends to link rainfall to the concept of righteousness. One explanation is that לִצְדָקָה refers to order or a sense of what is right and appropriate.[79] In this case, the sense is that the rain will fall in its naturally allotted time and amount, which helps to guarantee the return of agricultural prosperity. This proposal is possible, but those who support it fail to provide further examples of לִצְדָקָה where it has the sense of 'appropriateness'. Another suggestion is that לִצְדָקָה should be understood in a collective sense, referring to "righteous ones," or those for whom YHWH will bring rain.[80] This proposal, however, also suffers from a dearth of evidence.

Arguably, the best trajectory to follow for determining the meaning of לִצְדָקָה is the proposal that the *lamed* simply denotes a relationship between

---

77. Allen, *Joel*, 93. See also Futato, who does excellent work categorizing the different words for rain in the Old Testament. He demonstrates that מָטָר and גֶּשֶׁם are the overarching terms for rainfall, while מַלְקוֹשׁ and יוֹרֶה/מוֹרֶה are restricted to describing rainfall in a specific season. He aptly characterizes the relationship between the two levels of words as that of "genus and species" (M. Futato, "Sense Relations in the 'Rain Domain' of the Old Testament," in *Imagery and Imagination in Biblical Literature: Essays in Honour of Aloysius Fitzgerald, F.S.C.* [ed. L. Boadt and M. Smith; Washington, DC: Catholic Biblical Association, 2001] 82–94).

78. In contrast to Ahlström, who asserts that it is unlikely for מוֹרֶה to have the same sense in both instances. Ahlström points to its articular use in Joel 2:23a versus its anarthrous use in 2:23b and attempts to make the argument that 2:23a is a title referring to a teacher (Ahlström, *Joel*, 108). This argument, however, does not carry enough weight to overturn the surrounding context, which focuses on rain and the gifts that it provides for the community.

79. Coggins, *Joel*, 48; Sweeney, *Twelve*, 172.

80. I. Rabinowitz, "The Guides of Righteousness," *VT* 8 (1958) 397. Rabinowitz find examples of צֶדֶק that he believes should be translated in a collective fashion (Isa 1:26; Jer 31:23; Qoh 3:16–17); however, he provides no other example for לִצְדָקָה.

the two words, and the concept expressed here is that YHWH will send rain in accordance with his righteousness and relationship with the community.[81] YHWH's actions bring righteousness in the sense that YHWH's saving act of bringing rainfall reveals this divine characteristic to the community (cf. Isa 46:12; 51:6; 56:1; 59:9; 60:17; 61:10). This suggestion gains further strength since it also resonates with other passages where the gift of rain represents covenant blessing (Lev 26:3–4; Deut 11:13–14), while the lack of rainfall represents covenant sanction (Lev 26:18–20; Deut 28:23–24; 1 Kgs 8:35–36).[82] This focus also corresponds with the concern of Joel 2:18–27 to reestablish the relationship between YHWH and the community that is experiencing YHWH's zeal and compassion.

The rhetorical strategy of Joel 2:23 takes shape in light of the discussion above. Essentially, Joel 2:23 continues to highlight the complete restoration of agricultural bounty through renewed rainfall as the result of YHWH's intervention. It begins by calling upon its implied audience to respond, commanding them to rejoice in light of YHWH's actions on their behalf. The descriptions of destruction in Joel 1:1–2:17 characterize a year of agricultural failure in all respects, while the celebration of restoration in Joel 2:18–27 describes a year of agricultural abundance in which every element necessary for prosperity, including abundant rainfall, comes to fruition.[83] The imagery extends below the surface of the earth since Joel 1:15–20 introduces the concept of drought on top of the locust plague and uses it to create other vivid pictures of famine and distress for both people and animals. In response, Joel 2:23 refers to abundant rains that raise the level of the water table to provide substantial water for both animals and crops.[84]

Following the description of the return of much-needed rain, the third-person prophetic speech concludes in Joel 2:24 with more pictures of agricultural prosperity. It introduces no new imperatives, instead offering further descriptions of YHWH's actions. This verse creates an inclusio with Joel 2:19 by again referring to grain, new wine, and oil as products that YHWH will supply. Joel 2:19 and 2:24 use the same words for new wine and oil (תִּירוֹשׁ וְיִצְהָר) but employ synonyms for grain (Joel 2:19 has הַדָּגָן; 2:24 has בָּר). The use of synonyms for grain may relate to a new element introduced in Joel 2:24 that associates the grain, new wine, and oil with their respective places of processing. The verse declares that the threshing floor (הַגֳּרָנוֹת)

---

81. Kapelrud, *Joel Studies*, 116; cf. Sweeney, *Twelve*, 172; Allen, *Joel*, 93. Kapelrud claims that "this solution, besides being the easiest, is also probably correct."
82. Dillard, "Joel," 289.
83. Nash, "Palestinian," 116.
84. Ibid., 122–24. It is not necessary to accept Nash's entire argument that this unit actually represents a physical year of good crops in order to make use of her observations concerning the totality of the restoration envisioned in this unit. The text positions the figure of the prophet as speaking during a time of bounty, and the imagery of turning every shortfall into abundance demonstrates the text's strategy to persuade the implied audience that following the instructed program would yield positive results.

will have the grain, while wine vats (הַיְקָבִים) overflow with new wine and oil. The term בָּר indicates clean grain after the completion of the winnowing process (Jer 23:28).[85] Mentioning the threshing floor and the wine vats places emphasis on the finished product that is ready for consumption; YHWH's restorative actions result in agricultural produce that meets the community's needs.

The repeated mention of agricultural produce stresses the reversal of Joel 1:10 and the cessation of sacrifices to YHWH because of the scarcity of these items. Abundance is again in view in light of the parallel verbs וּמָלְאוּ and וְהֵשִׁיקוּ, of which these crops are the subjects. While מָלֵא is a common verb referring to filling, שׁוּק is found only three times and indicates being filled to overflowing (Joel 4:13; Ps 65:10).[86] Thus, the end result of YHWH's "great things" is the guarantee of overwhelming prosperity and abundance that will completely satiate the community that suffered from want in the previous units.

Overall, Joel 2:21–24 details YHWH's restorative actions while adding commands to rejoice and celebrate. The scene transitions from devastation to restoration thanks to YHWH's actions, and the text tries to evoke a response from the implied audience based on the statement in Joel 2:21 that YHWH has done "great things." These "great things" are primarily the restoration of various crops from the conditions of drought and insect infestation. The addressees of the imperatives transition from the earth to the animals to culminate in the call to YHWH's covenant people in Zion to respond and rejoice. The totality of those whom the text calls to respond matches the totality of YHWH's restorative acts; both elements demonstrate that YHWH is now acting for the benefit of the implied audience.

Joel 2:25–27: YHWH's Promises

Joel 2:25 returns to first-person speech that the text places in the mouth of YHWH. This shift emphasizes again who it is that enacts these great promises of restoration. YHWH speaks, declaring וְשִׁלַּמְתִּי 'and I will make recompense' for the devastation that the locusts caused. The verb שָׁלֵם occurs elsewhere in legal contexts and designates payment for incurred losses (cf. Exod 21:34, 36–37; 22:1–5, 12–13).[87] The direct object of the verb is a matter of some dispute. The text appears to state that YHWH will repay הַשָּׁנִים 'the years' that the locusts have consumed. Some have suggested that

---

85. Dillard, "Joel," 290. For a detailed look at the process of threshing that results in the final grain product, see O. Borowski, *Agriculture in Iron Age Israel* (Winona Lake, IN: Eisenbrauns, 1987) 65–69.

86. Crenshaw, *Joel*, 156–57.

87. Ibid., 157. Given the semantic range of שׁלם in the Piel, it may be possible to consider it another piece indicating that the community was not necessarily guilty of a sin that drew the wrath of YHWH down on them. Crenshaw draws a parallel to Job, who was restored to prosperity after undeservedly losing what he owned. This parallel would be strong if שׁלם were found in Job 42.

it should instead be read as שְׁנַיִם 'double', indicating that the recompense will far exceed the damage.[88] This interpretation avoids the diachronic question whether the term 'years' is appropriate if both Joel 1:1–14 and 2:1–11 refer to the same locust infestation.[89] Dillard effectively defends the the 'years' interpretation, however, by noting that שְׁנַיִם is anarthrous and lacks the direct-object marker on the other rare occasions when it is used to indicate a double amount (cf. Exod 22:3, 6, 8; Deut 21:17; 2 Kgs 2:9).[90] His suggestion is that the impact of the locusts on one year's harvest would also affect that of the ensuing year; thus, the term הַשָּׁנִים is appropriate.[91] Ultimately, the significance of this issue fades when one considers the rhetorical strategy of the verse. Joel 2:25 attributes these words of restoration to Yʜᴡʜ, showing the continuing reversal of Yʜᴡʜ's intentions. The one who threatened punishment through the great locust army is now responding with blessing.

Joel 2:25 also makes important allusions to two earlier verses in its description of restoration. It refers to the locusts using a series of synonyms (הָאַרְבֶּה, וְהֶחָסִיל, וְהַגָּזָם, הַיֶּלֶק) that also occur in Joel 1:4.[92] In reusing all of the words for locust in this verse, the text emphasizes the totality of the restoration; just as the devastation came about in hammering waves, so the restoration will fully reverse each separate wave. The second allusion in this verse follows the words for locust and employs an appositional construction to identify them as Yʜᴡʜ's army (חֵילִי 'my army'). This refers back to Joel 2:11 and its description of Yʜᴡʜ thundering at the head of the invading army. The first-person pronominal suffix on חֵילִי stands out in a rhetorical unit where the text uses pronominal suffixes to emphasize the connection between Yʜᴡʜ and the implied audience. This suffix makes Yʜᴡʜ's leadership of the invading locusts explicit, but most importantly, the barrage of suffixes connecting Yʜᴡʜ to the covenant community reveals the new state of affairs. Thus, Joel 2:25 takes the previously prophesied disasters and claims that Yʜᴡʜ's restorative activity will overcome them.[93]

---

88. See, for example, Nash, "Palestinian," 126.

89. Barton, *Joel*, 89.

90. Dillard, "Joel," 292. The word that more frequently indicates double amounts is מִשְׁנֶה (cf. Gen 43:12, 15; Exod 16:22; Deut 15:18; Job 42:10; Isa 61:7; Jer 16:18; Zech 9:12).

91. See also Simkins (*Yahweh's Activity*, 193), who asserts that the locusts' activities occurred over the space of two years, positing two separate waves of locusts.

92. The order in which the text lists these words for locusts differs between these two texts. Joel 1:4 has הַגָּזָם, הָאַרְבֶּה, הַיֶּלֶק, הֶחָסִיל, while Joel 2:25 has הַגָּזָם, הֶחָסִיל, הַיֶּלֶק, הָאַרְבֶּה. This may provide further evidence that the differing words for locust are not referring to sequential stages in their development.

93. This verse may also help with the identification of the invading horde in Joel 2:1–11. In this verse, Joel appears to qualify the locusts as the "great army," which may strengthen the idea that 2:1–11 is a recapitulation of the locust invasion described in Joel 1.

Joel 2:26 continues to describe the reversal of what the locusts have done to the community. It commences with a rare grammatical construction in which two infinitives absolute אָכוֹל וְשָׂבוֹעַ 'to eat and to be satisfied' follow the initial conjugated verb וַאֲכַלְתֶּם 'you shall eat'. The first infinitive absolute also comes from the same root as the conjugated verb. This paranomastic construction typically strengthens the force of the conjugated verb, indicating that the community will eat in great abundance.[94]

The use of two postpositive infinitives absolute stresses the simultaneous or near-simultaneous nature of the two activities, which indicates the totality of the reversal from earlier images of starvation, since the eating leads swiftly to satiation (cf. Judg 14:9).[95] The choice of אָכַל 'to eat' in this verse is striking since the initial description of disaster in this book commences with a fourfold use of this verb to describe the activities of the locusts (Joel 1:4). The eating activities of the locusts effectively stripped the land bare and threatened the community with starvation; in response, Yhwh will make it so that the community itself can eat and satiate its hunger in repayment for what the locusts had eaten.

The act of eating in Joel 2:26 then guides the implied audience toward praise. This is an essential element of response that the text tries to evoke now that the situation has taken such a drastic turn. The text calls on the implied audience to acknowledge that Yhwh is the agent who causes these great reversals.[96] The text affirms Yhwh's reestablished relationship by stating to the community that it will praise "the name of Yhwh, your God." The second-person plural suffix on אֱלֹהֵיכֶם 'your God' emphasizes this connection. The concluding relative clause accentuates the power of Yhwh's actions, referring to Yhwh as the one who acts magnificently or wondrously (לְהַפְלִיא).[97] Again the text emphasizes that the implied audience is the recipient of this blessing, stating to them that it is 'among you' (עִמָּכֶם) that Yhwh performs these great deeds.

Joel 2:27 summarizes how Yhwh's restorative actions reaffirm his relationship with the community. This verse creates a "climactic affirmation of Yahweh's presence," emphasized in the opening clauses.[98] Joel 2:27 states in the first person, with Yhwh as the implied speaker, that the community will know that Yhwh is among them (וִידַעְתֶּם כִּי בְקֶרֶב יִשְׂרָאֵל אָנִי 'and you

---

94. GKC 342.

95. Joüon, *Grammar*, 395.

96. Prinsloo, *Theology*, 79.

97. For translating an infinitive construct preceded by a *lamed* adverbially, see GKC 351.

98. W. VanGemeren, "The Spirit of Restoration," *WTJ* 50 (1988) 83. Ogden correctly notes a threefold affirmation of Yhwh's character in this verse: (1) Yhwh is among the people; (2) Yhwh is their God; and (3) there are no other gods who can challenge Yhwh (G. Ogden and R. Deutsch, *Joel and Malachi: A Promise of Hope—A Call to Obedience* [ITC; Grand Rapids: Eerdmans, 1987] 26).

will know that I am in the midst of Israel').[99] The following clauses have
YHWH declaring divine uniqueness (וַאֲנִי יְהוָה אֱלֹהֵיכֶם וְאֵין עוֹד 'and I am YHWH
your God, and there is no other'). These statements reflect a modification
of the "divine recognition formula" that occurs in other parts of the Old
Testament, notably Ezekiel and Zechariah (cf. Exod 6:7; 10:2; 16:12; Ezek
6:7, 13–14; 7:4; 11:10, 15:7; 16:22; 29:6, 9, 16; Zech 2:9; 4:9; 6:15). This
recognition formula follows a declaration of YHWH's deeds, indicating that
YHWH's actions reveal the depth of the divine commitment to the implied
audience.[100]

The text's modification of the formula is notable in its insertion of the
declaration that YHWH is in the midst of Israel. This declaration has parallels in other prophetic books (Zeph 3:15; Hos 11:9b; Mic 3:11).[101] The
rhetorical strategy of explicitly stating YHWH's presence in the midst of the
community again reflects upon and reverses material from Joel 1:1–2:17.
Joel 1:15–20 concludes with an unanswered cry to YHWH, indicating divine
absence, while Joel 2:1–11 concludes by naming YHWH as the one leading
the assault. The first thing that Joel 2:27 emphasizes that the community
will now "know" is that the deity who was either absent or hostile is among
them, promising restoration.

After the declaration of YHWH's presence, Joel 2:27 continues with the
divine recognition formula. Interestingly, Joel 2:27 places extra emphasis
on the fact that it is the divine voice uttering these words through a double
use of אֲנִי. It is the last word of the first clause acting as the subject of the
phrase בְּקֶרֶב יִשְׂרָאֵל; it is also the first word of the next clause, in which
YHWH again identifies himself as אֱלֹהֵיכֶם 'your God' and asserts that there
are no rivals. The second-person plural suffix continues the trajectory introduced by the statement that YHWH is in the midst of Israel; YHWH's actions throughout this rhetorical unit restore the relationship between the
deity and the covenant community. This is in keeping with the typical use
of the divine recognition formula, which usually follows a statement or
prophetic declaration of YHWH's actions; through these acts, the implied
audience experiences the reality of YHWH's presence and power.[102]

Alongside its function in the divine recognition formula, the phrase "I
am YHWH your God" frequently asserts YHWH's claim to the implied audience. Significantly, it also commences both descriptions of the Decalogue

---

99. Ogden identifies texts in Isaiah (Isa 45:5–6, 22) that echo this theme, suggesting
that YHWH's self-revelation through divine actions on behalf of his people is a prevalent
theological theme (Ogden, *Promise of Hope*, 36).

100. Prinsloo, *Theology*, 74–75; Dillard, "Joel," 292.

101. The text uses "Israel" as a technical term to refer to all of YHWH's people, now
embodied in the implied audience whom the text constructs as those who dwell in Jerusalem and the surrounding land.

102. Dillard, "Joel," 292.

(Exod 20:2; Deut 5:6), which is relevant, seeing as how the following statement of Yhwh's incomparability mirrors the concerns of the first com-
mandment (Exod 20:3; Deut 5:7).[103] The declaration in Joel 2:27 of Yhwh's
uniqueness (וְאֵין עוֹד 'and there is no other') stresses the exclusive nature of
the relationship between Yhwh and the implied audience. It also evokes
images of Yhwh's restorative power as being put into action in connection
with the repeated use of this phrase in Isaiah (Isa 45:5, 6, 14, 18, 21, 22).
The magnitude of Yhwh's acts in Joel 2:18–27 highlights the authority that
Yhwh claims and the loyalty that Yhwh desires.

The text demonstrates the full range of Yhwh's commitment to the
implied audience in the final clauses of Joel 2:26 and 2:27, which both
employ the phrase וְלֹא־יֵבֹשׁוּ עַמִּי לְעוֹלָם 'and my people will be unashamed
for eternity'. These clauses are identical, leading some to view the second
occurrence of this particular line as dittography.[104] The rhetorical effect,
however, of placing these clauses in a passage that speaks so eloquently
about Yhwh's actions on behalf of the community argues against dittography. Instead, the use of repetition in Joel 2:26 and 2:27 recalls the repetition of the phrase וְאֵשׁ אָכְלָה נְאוֹת הַמִּדְבָּר 'and fire has devoured the pastures
of the wilderness' in Joel 1:19, 20. In both cases, these phrases demarcate
the conclusion of their respective rhetorical units, summarizing salient features of the prior discourse.[105]

In Joel 2:26 and 2:27, the divine assertion that Yhwh will not allow the
community to be shamed follows a liturgical expression of either Yhwh's
great deeds (Joel 2:26) or Yhwh's uniqueness and authority over his community (Joel 2:27).[106] The text strengthens this sense of authority in the
repeated clause by employing עַמִּי 'my people'. This marks the total transition from Joel 2:11, where Yhwh thunders at the head of "his army," which
he leads against those whom he now chooses to protect. In this rhetorical
unit, Yhwh is no longer the destroyer but the savior and protector of the
children of Zion. This final repeated summary statement in Joel 2:26 and
2:27 provides the powerful answer to the rhetorical question "where is
their God?" in Joel 2:17. Ultimately, the promises of divine activity and
restoration found in this unit reveal that Yhwh "their God" is among them
and will not let them fall into disrepute.

---

103. The phrase וְאֵין עוֹד also appears in Isa 45:5, 6, 18 in conjunction with other descriptions of Yhwh's great deeds that demonstrate his uniqueness and power.

104. Wolff, *Joel and Amos*, 56. Wolff asserts that the phrase is original in Joel 2:27
alone, while Barton hedges by declaring that this could be dittography, but that, if it is, it
produces a rhetorically pleasing effect (Barton, *Joel*, 90).

105. J. Thompson, "The Use of Repetition in the Prophecy of Joel," in *On Language,
Culture and Religion* (ed. M. Black and W. Smalley; The Hague: Mouton, 1974) 107. See also
Wendland, *Discourse Analysis*, 50.

106. Crenshaw, *Joel*, 159.

Summary

Joel 2:18–27 is an important turning point since it reverses the previous descriptions of insect infestation, drought, invasion, and terrifying cosmological phenomena. Prinsloo eloquently states, "[W]hat was a mere hope in the previous pericope is now realized, the 'perhaps' of 2:14 has been fulfilled; the prayer has been heard."[107] This rhetorical unit also demonstrates the validity of the character ascribed to Yʜwʜ in Joel 2:13. Yʜwʜ executes a "turn" back to the implied audience and definitively demonstrates gracious and compassionate qualities. Effectively, Joel 2:18–27 constructs Yʜwʜ's response to the prophet's proposal for the implied audience's response in Joel 2:12–17 and indicates that Yʜwʜ's actions move the situation from devastation to restoration.

The text indicates the transition toward restoration by interacting with previous rhetorical units. It ties many of the restorative promises to specific deprivations described in Joel 1:1–2:17, including agricultural ruin, interrupted worship, and fear of invasion. Joel 2:18–27 effectively "liquidates the lack" that dominates the imagery of the earlier rhetorical units.[108] Joel 2:18–27 also readdresses the concept of the community's honor and shame in Joel 1:11 and 2:17. The abundant offerings promised here will permit worship of Yʜwʜ to occur as prescribed while also demonstrating that Yʜwʜ acts mightily on behalf of the implied audience, which should free them from the implied mockery of foreign nations. Yʜwʜ expresses graciousness through mighty deeds that eliminate the invader and restore prosperity to and relationship with the implied audience. In return, the text calls the community to respond by praising Yʜwʜ again and acknowledging Yʜwʜ's status as the one true God, active among the people.[109]

Rhetorical Effectiveness

The consideration of the rhetorical effectiveness of Joel 2:18–27 is tied closely to that of the preceding rhetorical unit (Joel 2:12–17). On the level of the text itself, Joel 2:18–27 seemingly implies that the preceding unit was effective in provoking the desired response from the implied audience since it potentially answers the question "who knows? He may turn and have pity" (Joel 2:14) in the affirmative. Joel 2:18–27 goes to great length to detail the many elements of the "pity" that Yʜwʜ will show to the community through actions that both remove foreign threat and look forward to the return of prosperity and security. Unfortunately, Joel 2:18–27 lacks

---

107. Prinsloo, *Theology*, 76.

108. Deist, "Parallels," 74. The exacting specificity with which Joel 2:18–27 reverses the calamities of previous rhetorical units helps to inform Deist's perspective that this book constructs its images on a literary level only; there are no events in the "world behind the text" to which this text refers.

109. Prinsloo, *Theology*, 79.

an explicit description of the community responding to the prophetic call found in Joel 2:12–17. One expects an element of this sort to be present in order to justify the inauguration of the reversal of the catastrophes in the previous sections of the book.[110] As already noted, however, the text is also devoid of a description of the people's sin that would create a cause-and-effect relationship governing these catastrophes. This perhaps makes the ambiguity appropriate that was created by the absence of a definitive communal response.

Ultimately, we cannot know if the prophet is proclaiming this message of restoration in a textual world in which the community obeys the text's commands to turn back to Yнwн. The implication for the reading audience, however, is that the community responded to the prior prophetic commands as directed, clearing the way for this picture of complete restoration. The break between Joel 2:17 and 2:18 creates a "conceptual gap" that forces readers to enter the text and imagine what would prompt such a shift in tone.[111] The best way to bridge this gap is to accept the efficacy of the call to return in Joel 2:12–17 and to understand Yнwн's actions in Joel 2:18–27 as demonstrations of Yнwн's gracious and compassionate character.

Consideration of the rhetorical effectiveness of Joel 2:18–27 also involves noting the text's construction of Yнwн in the wake of its portrayal of the deity in previous rhetorical units. Yнwн has a major role in this rhetorical unit since Yнwн has the only agency that can ameliorate the situation. This stands in stark contrast to Joel 2:12–17, which turns on the text's ability to persuade its implied audience to act. Yнwн is briefly active in Joel 2:12, calling on the people to "return to me," but then Yнwн is essentially silent as the prophetic call to lament unfolds. Yнwн is active in Joel 2:1–11, but the text shockingly declares that Yнwн directs the activity against the covenant community, threatening them with the inbreaking of the day of Yнwн. In this milieu, the persuasive effect of Joel 2:18–27 is to restore Yнwн to the expected position as the deity who protects and intervenes on behalf of the covenant community. Joel 2:18–27 thus highlights Yнwн's capacity for unilateral action and Yнwн's freedom to bring both judgment and blessing. The text's effectiveness in reversing its previous portrayals of Yнwн is evident throughout the rhetorical unit. The initial *waw*-consecutive verbs in Joel 2:18 reorient the implied audience's perspective toward Yнwн, which is reinforced through the detailed descriptions of restorative actions that culminate in the divine recognition formula in Joel 2:27.

In order to consider further the rhetorical effectiveness of Joel 2:18–27, I find it helpful again to leverage Patrick and Scult's "hermeneutics of

---

110. Crenshaw, *Joel*, 147–48.
111. Strazicich, *Joel's Use of Scripture*, 163.

affirmation," in which the interpreter admits the ability to respond to the experience of the text.[112] From this perspective, Joel 2:18–27 is a necessary response that restores the interpreter's equilibrium after the text's shocking portrayal of Yhwh at the head of the terrifying invaders in Joel 2:10–11. There is a certain incongruity between the declaration of Yhwh thundering at the head of the invaders and the text's adaptation of the character credo in Joel 2:12; how could the gracious and compassionate figure of Yhwh come against the covenant community in such a frightening fashion? Joel 2:18–27, however, persuasively reaffirms the validity of the character credo from Exod 34:6–7. Yhwh does not abandon the people but, rather, acts powerfully to demonstrate a gracious and compassionate character. Joel 2:18–27 also effectively repatriates the use of the character credo in Jonah 4:2.[113] Whereas the text of Jonah universalizes Yhwh's compassionate character, the text of Joel demonstrates that Yhwh's character continues to work for the benefit of the covenant community. Thus, Joel 2:18–27 is effective in reestablishing an understanding of a gracious and compassionate deity who acts on behalf of the covenant community.

Overall, the rhetorical effectiveness of Joel 2:18–27 hinges on its ability to engage the interpreter in filling the narrative gap between Joel 2:17 and 2:18 and its efforts to reestablish Yhwh as the deity described in the character credo found in Joel 2:13. The description of Yhwh's actions is effective in persuading the interpreter to enter a textual world in which the community responds to the prophetic call of Joel 2:12–17 and where Yhwh returns to the expected position as the deity who restores the covenant community. Whereas Joel 2:1–11 reflects the nadir of the text with its portrayal of Yhwh as leader of the enemy, Joel 2:18–27 inaugurates Yhwh's program of restoration that begins with the promise of reversing the calamities of the locust invasion. Further rhetorical units build on this foundation.

Conclusion

Joel 2:18–27 is a pivotal rhetorical unit in the development of the text's persuasive argumentation. It builds on the climactic rhetorical question that concludes Joel 2:17 and goes to great lengths to assert that Yhwh will respond to this question positively. Joel 2:18–27 connects to previous rhetorical units when it portrays Yhwh as a deity who acts to restore all that the implied audience lost in the devastation described in Joel 1:1–14, 1:15–20, and 2:1–11. Joel 2:18–27 brings Yhwh's actions to the forefront, reversing Yhwh's silence or hostility from previous rhetorical units. Yhwh's explicit responses further help to fill in the conceptual gap between Joel 2:17 and

---

112. D. Patrick and A. Scult, "Rhetoric and Ideology: A Debate within Biblical Scholarship over the Import of Persuasion," in *The Rhetorical Interpretation of Scripture: Essays from the 1996 Malibu Conference* (ed. S. Porter and D. Stamps; JSNTSup 180; Sheffield: Sheffield Academic Press, 1999) 66–67.

113. Strazicich, *Joel's Use of Scripture*, 202.

2:18, suggesting that the implied audience heeded the prophetic call and responded appropriately, setting the stage for YHWH's magnificent actions. This description of YHWH as the one who reverses calamity and restores is a powerful rhetorical tool for persuading audiences to trust in the prophet's call to cry out to YHWH amidst desperate circumstances.

Chapter 7

*Pouring Out the Spirit of Y*HWH*: Rhetorical Analysis of Joel 3:1–5*

Introduction

Joel 3:1–5 is the second of the two locations in Joel where there is the greatest sense of disjunction.[1] From this point forward, images rooted in natural phenomena including the locust plague and the accompanying agrarian hardships fade into the background. The remainder of the book describes scenes of restoration through the outpouring of YHWH's Spirit, salvation for Judah, and judgment against foreign nations. There remains, however, significant continuity in imagery between Joel 3:1–5 and Joel 1:1– 2:27. Joel 3:1–5 echoes Joel 2:1–11 through its reuse of cosmological imagery and specific vocabulary that describes YHWH's appearance and reveals that YHWH leads the unstoppable invading force that assaults Jerusalem.[2] Now, beginning with 3:1–5, the text describes great acts of YHWH that again shake the cosmos and reveal YHWH's power over all creation. Joel 3:1–5 also relates to Joel 1:1–2:27 through its expansion of the promise of YHWH's presence in Joel 2:27. The outpouring of YHWH's Spirit makes manifest YHWH's presence among the people of the implied audience.[3]

Overall, the persuasive potential of Joel 3:1–5 is revealed through these echoes of earlier passages and through its emphasis on the power of YHWH's actions revealed throughout this rhetorical unit. Joel 3:1–5 employs the detailed description of the outpouring of YHWH's Spirit and the concomitant trembling of the cosmos to establish the necessity of calling upon the name of YHWH in the final verse. This response provides the potential rescue from the day of YHWH; now, security in Zion is promised rather than a divinely sanctioned assault, as in Joel 2:1–11.

---

1. J. Barton, *Joel and Obadiah* (OTL; Louisville: Westminster John Knox, 2001) 93; R. Simkins *Yahweh's Activity in History and Nature in the Book of Joel* (ANETS 10; Lewiston, NY: Edwin Mellen, 1991) 209. See also the above discussion of rhetorical units and the ways in which scholars divide the two proposed "halves" of Joel.

2. See the list of shared vocabulary in H. Wolff, *Joel and Amos* (Hermeneia; Philadelphia: Fortress, 1977) 8. It includes: בּוֹא יוֹם יְהוָה ('the coming of the day of YHWH'), חֹשֶׁךְ ('darkness'), and פְּלֵיטָה ('escaped group').

3. W. Prinsloo, *The Theology of the Book of Joel* (BZAW 163; Berlin: de Gruyter, 1985) 83.

Rhetorical Unit

The introductory formula וְהָיָה אַחֲרֵי־כֵן 'It will be after this' marks the aperture of Joel 3:1–5.[4] While its subject matter moves further away from Joel 1:1–2:27, this particular formula refers to the preceding unit in order to establish its foundation. It is "after" the events described in Joel 2:18–27 that the great cosmological shaking unfolds in Joel 3:1–5 (cf. Job 3:1; Isa 1:26; Jer 34:11).[5] Essentially, Joel 3:1–5 moves away from the promises of material restoration in Joel 2:18–27 and introduces a new horizon of YHWH's powerful presence into the discourse.[6] The closure of this unit occurs at Joel 3:5 and it is marked by the threefold repetition of the divine name in the final verse. The repetition of a key word or phrase like this may signal that a rhetorical unit is reaching its close (cf. Hos 1:9, 2:3, 25).[7] The presence of another introductory formula in Joel 4:1 (כִּי הִנֵּה בַּיָּמִים הָהֵמָּה וּבָעֵת הַהִיא) 'For behold in those days and in that time') also confirms that Joel 3:5 concludes this particular rhetorical unit.[8]

Within this short chapter, there are three subunits to consider. An inclusio using YHWH's declaration of his intent to pour out the divine Spirit identifies Joel 3:1–2 as the first subunit. Joel 3:3–4 continues the speech of YHWH and heightens the gravity of the situation by reflecting on the cosmological ramifications of the outpouring of the Spirit. Joel 3:3–4 also reintroduces the day of YHWH while reimagining its orientation toward Zion. Joel 3:5

---

4. Ibid., 80–81; A. Kapelrud, *Joel Studies* (UUÅ 4; Uppsala: Lundequist, 1948) 7. Contrary to the consensus position, Wolff argues that the divine recognition formula in Joel 2:27 וִידַעְתֶּם כִּי בְקֶרֶב יִשְׂרָאֵל אָנִי 'And you will know that I am in the midst of Israel') does not represent a conclusion; instead, it reflects a transition in a "two-stage self-disclosure formula" that continues through Joel 3:1–5 (Wolff, *Joel and Amos*, 65). Barton, however, successfully points out difficulties with Wolff's arguments. He notes that Wolff's construction of a "two-stage self-disclosure formula" involves viewing Joel 2:27 as only accomplishing a "temporary reversal," which runs contrary to the sense of finality inherent in the assertion that "my people will never again be put to shame." Further, the formula that begins Joel 3:1 suggests the aperture of a new rhetorical unit (Barton, *Joel*, 90–91). On the semantic function of phrases beginning with וְהָיָה, see C. van der Merwe, J. Naudé, and J. Kroeze, *A Biblical Hebrew Reference Grammar* (Sheffield: Sheffield Academic Press, 1999) 331.

5. See the discussion below under "Rhetorical Strategy" for an examination of the meaning of "after this" in the context of Joel 3:1–5.

6. Kapelrud, *Joel Studies*, 7. Kapelrud aptly suggests that Joel 3:1–5, "suits well in its place to mark the advance of the prophet's thought."

7. E. Wendland, *The Discourse Analysis of Hebrew Prophetic Literature* (MBPS 40; Lewiston, NY: Edwin Mellen, 1995) 50–51. Wendland illustrates the concept of repetition of key terms as signals of closure by appealing to the symbolic use of names in Hosea. He notes specifically the repetition of לֹא עַמִּי in Hos 1:9, the recurrence of עַמִּי and רֻחָמָה in Hos 2:3, and the repetition of לֹא רֻחָמָה and לֹא־עַמִּי in Hos 2:25. The use of symbolic names in Hos 1–2 may help to establish the validity of viewing the multiple repetitions in Joel 3:5 as a sign of closure for this rhetorical unit.

8. I consider the specific form and function of the introductory formula of Joel 4:1 in chap. 8, below.

concludes this chapter by reintroducing the prophet as the speaker and referring to YHWH in the third person. Joel 3:5 describes the manner in which
the implied audience ought to respond in order to survive the day of YHWH.

Rhetorical Situation

The shift away from the locust plague and its aftermath demonstrates
the continuing development in the rhetorical situation. Within the world
of the text, the original exigence of Joel 1:1–2:27 diminishes in Joel 3:1–
4:21. The locust plague and the ensuing agricultural disasters no longer
hover over the text; instead, Joel 3:1–5 employs richly textured images that
point to a coming day of YHWH and its impact on both YHWH's covenant
community and the other nations. This significant change in exigence
points to a development in the rhetorical situation. Joel 3:1–5 pushes forward the "life cycle" of the rhetorical situation since it focuses on different
issues in response to YHWH's promised salvation from the locust plague.[9]

The shift in exigence is rooted in the imminence of the prophetic predictions. Whereas Joel 1:1–2:27 reflects an imminent crisis and urgent need
for response to deal with the proximity of the fearful day of YHWH (Joel
1:15; 2:1), Joel 3:1–4:21 loses that sense of immediacy and appears to orient itself toward an unspecified time in the future.[10] The shift in exigence
is based on the prophesied resolution to the crisis found at the end of the
previous rhetorical unit. YHWH promised prosperity and protection as signs
of his presence among his people. Since Joel 2:26–27 assures YHWH's presence and protection, Joel 3:1–4:21 examines the ramifications of YHWH's
presence for the covenant community as well as for those who have stood
in opposition. The text constructs its implied audience in Joel 3:1–5 as having a renewed relationship with YHWH in the wake of the call to "turn" in
Joel 2:12–17. Now that YHWH has shown mercy in restoring prosperity and
security, the text strives to guide its implied audience to learn how YHWH's
presence among the people will affect their final fate.

Joel 3:1–5 constructs its implied audience somewhat differently from
preceding rhetorical units. The scope of the implied audience remains the
same since the text tries to frame itself so that it addresses the whole of the
Judahite community.[11] In this rhetorical unit, the totality of the implied
audience falls in the category of כָּל־בָּשָׂר 'all flesh', which it then subdi-
vides according to age, gender, and social standing.[12] The key feature that

___

9. G. Hauser, *Introduction to Rhetorical Theory* (2nd ed.; Long Grove, IL: Waveland,
2002) 60–62.

10. Barton, *Joel*, 29. I address the question of the temporal orientation of this passage
in detail in the section on "Rhetorical Strategy" below.

11. See the "elders" and "dwellers-in-the-land" merismus in Joel 1:2 and the appeal to
everyone, including priests, elders, children, and recently married people to gather to cry
out to YHWH in Joel 2:16–17.

12. See the discussion below in the rhetorical strategy section, which deals with the
intended scope of כָּל־בָּשָׂר in Joel 3:1. Despite the universalizing resonances of this phrase,

this construction of the implied audience emphasizes is that all of these different subgroups have the same access to the divine Spirit. Yнwн has the capacity to pour out the divine Spirit on both "your sons" and "your daughters," along with "your elders," "your young men," and even male and female servants. The range of Yнwн's gift of the divine Spirit helps to identify the contours of an implied audience whose subgroups have equal access to Yнwн's Spirit.

The text revisits the implied audience in Joel 3:5 when it offers the hope of survival to כֹּל אֲשֶׁר־יִקְרָא בְּשֵׁם יְהוָה 'all who will call on the name of Yнwн'. This restricts the implied audience to those who would make this call, suggesting that the outpouring of the Spirit in Joel 3:1–2 requires a declaration of exclusive loyalty to Yнwн in response.[13] Joel 3:5 further specifies as part of the audience פְּלֵיטָה 'an escaped group' and שְׂרִידִים 'survivors' whom Yнwн calls. These two terms occur in parallel in other places in the Old Testament, suggesting that שְׂרִידִים is probably a further explanation of פְּלֵיטָה (cf. Jer 42:17; 44:14; Obad 14).[14] The term פְּלֵיטָה is especially significant since it points to the idea of those who survive a time of ordeal.[15] The ordeal can reflect punishment for the audience's own sins (Isa 4:2–3; 10:20–23; Ezek 14:22) or other difficult circumstances such as foreign invasion (Isa 37:31–32). In Joel 3:1–5, the idea of survivors seems to define the implied audience as those who escape the threats mentioned in Joel 1:1–2:17 and find refuge in the wake of Yнwн's cosmos-rending actions. When the implied audience calls on the name of Yнwн, it activates the promise of escape from the day of Yнwн and guarantees the implied audience's continued existence.

Joel 3:5 also establishes the geographical location of the rhetorical situation. Yнwн offers the possibility of rescue on Mount Zion and Jerusalem. This is the first mention of Jerusalem in Joel, but the book does previously refer to Zion (Joel 2:1, 15, 23). This mention of Zion reflects the advancement of the rhetorical situation since the text portrays it as an abode of security, whereas previously the invading army encountered little difficulty in overrunning Zion (Joel 2:1–11). This use of Zion also offers further indication of the efficacy of the call to a Zion-based cultic response in Joel 2:15. The call to cry out to Yнwн for deliverance results in the provision of security in Zion.[16]

---

there are compelling arguments for restricting it to the Judahite community in this particular passage.

13. Simkins, *Yahweh's Activity*, 217; D. Hubbard, *Joel and Amos* (TOTC 25; Downers Grove, IL: InterVarsity, 2009) 76; J. Crenshaw, *Joel* (AB 24c; New York: Doubleday, 1995) 169.

14. Wolff, *Joel and Amos*, 68–69.

15. G. Hasel, "פָּלַט," *TDOT* 11:563.

16. L. Hoppe, *The Holy City: Jerusalem in the Theology of the Old Testament* (Collegeville, MN: Liturgical Press, 2000) 137.

Rhetorical Strategy

*Joel 3:1–2: Y*HWH *Pours Out the Divine Spirit*

Joel 3:1–2 consists of a first-person declaration of YHWH's intention to pour out the divine Spirit on a broad range of recipients. This coincides with the description of YHWH's actions to provide security and material restoration in Joel 2:18–27. The focus on YHWH's actions suggests that these verses adopt an epideictic approach, emphasizing YHWH's commitment to the implied audience.[17] These verses continue to build on YHWH's promise that the implied audience will never again be shamed (Joel 2:27) and describe further actions of YHWH on its behalf. YHWH's actions articulated in Joel 3:1–2 eventually invite the implied audience to consider an appropriate response, which the text provides in Joel 3:5.

As mentioned above, the formula וְהָיָה אַחֲרֵי־כֵן 'and it will be after this' in Joel 3:1 opens this rhetorical unit. Joel 3:1 is the only example in the Old Testament of the phrase אַחֲרֵי־כֵן occurring in conjunction with the verb הָיָה. There is some debate about the relationship that this phrase creates between Joel 3:1–5 and 2:18–27. One argument is that the phrase אַחֲרֵי־כֵן refers to a logical transition, functioning as a connective 'when' or 'and'.[18] VanGemeren sees examples of this logical connectivity in prophetic literature in Isa 1:26; Jer 21:7; 31:33 (cf. also Judg 16:4; 1 Sam 24:6; 2 Sam 2:1; 8:1; 2 Kgs 6:24; 2 Chr 24:4).[19] In these cases, the events that אַחֲרֵי־כֵן introduces may occur contemporaneously with those described in the preceding clauses. Following VanGemeren, Simkins argues that one should interpret the events of Joel 3:1–5 as happening at the same time as Joel 2:18–27.[20] The outpouring of the divine Spirit that informs the argument of this unit thus directly and immediately supplements the restoration of material blessing and renewed relationship with YHWH in Joel 2:18–27. In this way, the description of YHWH's restorative acts continues into this unit, with the

---

17. C. Perelman and L. Olbrechts-Tyteca, *The New Rhetoric: A Treatise on Argumentation* (Notre Dame, IN: Notre Dame University Press, 1969) 50. Perelman and Olbrechts-Tyteca assert that the function of epideictic rhetoric is to increase the audience's adherence to shared values, which should strengthen their disposition to act in the way that the rhetor desires. In Joel 3:1–5, focusing on YHWH's commitment to the implied audience may increase the probability that the people will act to become those who "call on the name of YHWH" in the final verse.

18. W. VanGemeren, "The Spirit of Restoration," *WTJ* 50 (1988) 85.

19. Ibid., 84–87. For example, in Isa 1:26 VanGemeren looks at the promised restoration of judges and counselors that will be followed 'after this' (אַחֲרֵי־כֵן) by a declaration of the people's righteousness. He suggests that the temporal sequence is secondary to the logical correlation between the people's restoration and their renewed character.

20. Simkins, *Yahweh's Activity*, 211. Simkins bases his argument, however, on his understanding of Joel 2:18–27 as an epexegetical interpretation of 2:12–17. See the discussion in the rhetorical strategy of 2:18–27 below for an analysis of why this is not the most appropriate understanding of the relationship between 2:12–17 and 2:18–27.

outpouring of the divine Spirit directly enhancing the material restoration described in Joel 2:18–27.

The arguments for logical connectivity are cogent, but there are also strong reasons to understand וְהָיָה אַחֲרֵי־כֵן as a sequential indicator. In this understanding, the events mentioned in Joel 3:1–5 follow the restoration of Joel 2:18–27 at a future time.[21] The phrase אַחֲרֵי־כֵן signifies temporal sequence on numerous occasions, which lends credence to this perspective (2 Chr 20:35; Jer 16:16; 34:11).[22] Another argument for temporal succession is the syntactic parallel between this phrase and the introduction found in Isa 2:2 (cf. Mic 4:1). That verse reads וְהָיָה בְּאַחֲרִית הַיָּמִים 'It will be after the days', which commentators typically take to indicate temporal progression.[23] This expression is introduced by וְהָיָה and contains a form of אַחֲרִי, which makes it markedly similar to the phrase that commences Joel 3:1. If וְהָיָה בְּאַחֲרִית הַיָּמִים indicates future time, it supports the temporal understanding of וְהָיָה אַחֲרֵי־כֵן in Joel 3:1–5.[24] The phrase וְהָיָה אַחֲרֵי in Jer 12:15 provides helpful evidence since it introduces a divine promise of further restoration following judgment. These parallels indicate the plausibility of a temporal understanding of וְהָיָה אַחֲרֵי־כֵן.

The best approach is to nuance the two understandings of וְהָיָה אַחֲרֵי־כֵן. In this first understanding, the outpouring of the Spirit and the heavenly

---

21. See, for example, Wolff, *Joel and Amos*, 58–59; G. Ahlström, *Joel and the Temple Cult of Jerusalem* (VTSup 21; Leiden: Brill, 1971) 133; T. Finley, *Joel, Amos, Obadiah* (WEC; Chicago: Moody Press, 1990) 77. Allen nicely summarizes the point of view of temporal succession, stating, "The bestowal of material blessing . . . is but the first stage. Further, deeper gifts of God's grace were in store, to be dispensed at a subsequent stage" (L. Allen, *The Books of Joel, Obadiah, Jonah and Micah* [NICOT; Grand Rapids: Eerdmans, 1976] 97–98).

22. VanGemeren, "Spirit," 84; R. Dillard, "Joel," in *The Minor Prophets: An Exegetical and Expository Commentary.* (ed. T. McComiskey; Grand Rapids: Baker, 1992) 294. Finley also locates numerous examples where וְהָיָה indicates "new predictions" in prophetic books (Isa 7:21; Jer 17:14; Ezek 38:10; Hos 1:5; Amos 8:9). He suggests that the blessings described in Joel 3:1–5 follow the restoration from the ravages of the locust plague (Finley, *Joel*, 71). This argument, however, cannot be held too strongly since there is a counterexample even within this rhetorical unit. Joel 3:5 also begins with וְהָיָה and, while it shifts focus from Yнwн to those whom Yнwн's actions impact, the temporal framework remains the same as the rest of the rhetorical unit since it introduces the appropriate response to the preceding description of the day of Yнwн.

23. Crenshaw, *Joel*, 164. Blenkinshopp understands the Isaianic temporal formula to indicate some time in the future; J. Blenkinsopp, *Isaiah 1–39* (AB 19; New York: Doubleday, 2000) 190. See also W. Brueggemann, *Isaiah 1–39* (Westminster Bible Companion; Louisville: Westminster John Knox, 1998) 23–34; O. Kaiser, *Isaiah 1–12* (OTL; Philadelphia: Westminster, 1972) 25–26. Shaw also preserves the futuristic outlook of Mic 4:1, translating the phrase, "In the days to come" (C. Shaw, *The Speeches of Micah: A Rhetorical-Historical Approach* [JSOTSup 145; Sheffield: JSOT Press, 1993] 98).

24. Concerning the issue of temporal succession in the history of reception, Dillard notes that temporal succession is clearly in view when Acts 2:17 cites Joel 3:1–5 since it introduces the prophecy with ἐν ταῖς ἐσχάταις ἡμεραις 'in the last days', which differs from the LXX's μετα ταυτα 'after this' (Dillard, "Joel," 294).

shaking that occurs in Joel 3:1–5 is "subsequent to, as well as consequent upon, the foregoing blessings."[25] Yhwh's guarantee of material restoration in Joel 2:18–27 thus lays the foundation for spiritual renewal. Although there remains some ambiguity, the arguments for maintaining that Joel 3:1–5 follows Joel 2:18–27 in some degree of temporal succession are more convincing than the attempts to argue for strictly logical succession or explicative commentary. Spiritual restoration is a logical counterpart to the material blessings found in Joel 2:18–27, but אַחֲרֵי־כֵן also suggests a second, different temporal framework.

Following the introductory phrases, Yhwh declares אֶשְׁפּוֹךְ אֶת־רוּחִי 'I will pour out my Spirit'. The fact Yhwh commences the action of this rhetorical unit is in keeping with the theme of divine agency that comes to the forefront in Joel 2:18–27. In this rhetorical unit, Yhwh is the principal actor, who sets the parameters for the responses attributed to the implied audience. This unit will make evident Yhwh's authority over both the created order and the people who dwell in it since Yhwh can give people the divine Spirit and secure deliverance for individuals who call on the name of Yhwh, while also dramatically affecting the activities of heavenly bodies.

The declaration that Yhwh will pour out the divine Spirit in Joel 3:1 also occurs in the final phrase of Joel 3:2. This creates an inclusio that distinguishes Joel 3:1–2 as a subunit within this chapter.[26] This repetition emphasizes the tremendous extent of Yhwh's promised gift of spiritual blessing.[27] Joel 3:1–2 indicates that those who receive Yhwh's Spirit engage in prophetic activities: וְנִבְּאוּ 'they will prophesy', חֲלֹמוֹת יַחֲלֹמוּן 'they will dream dreams', and חֶזְיֹנוֹת יִרְאוּ 'they will see visions'.[28] This is consistent with other passages that describe dreams and visions as legitimate expressions of di-

---

25. S. De Vries, *From Old Revelation to New: A Tradition-History and Redaction-Critical Study of Temporal Transitions in Prophetic Prediction* (Grand Rapids: Eerdmans, 1995) 87. De Vries asserts that וְהָיָה אַחֲרֵי־כֵן is a redactional expansion, set in poetic anacrusis with the rest of Joel 3:1–5. Unfortunately, he provides no evidence to support this redactional claim. Rhetorically, this phrase is valuable in this location for providing a connection to the previous rhetorical unit, indicating that the outpouring of the divine Spirit proceeds from the promise of divine presence in Zion (M. Sweeney, *The Twelve Prophets*, vol. 1 [Berit Olam; Collegeville, MN: Liturgical Press, 2000] 173).

26. Crenshaw, *Joel*, 164.

27. J. Thompson, "The Use of Repetition in the Prophecy of Joel," in *On Language, Culture and Religion* (ed. M. Black and W. Smalley; The Hague: Mouton, 1974) 103; D. Marcus, "Nonrecurring Doublets in the Book of Joel," *CBQ* 56 (1994) 61.

28. Crenshaw, *Joel*, 165. The classic study on the different types of interaction with the numinous in ancient Israel comes from Wilson, who looks at the nuances that Old Testament texts attach to prophesying, dreaming, seeing visions, fortune-telling, and divination. Interestingly, he notes a concern to preserve prophets as the only valid intermediaries. The outpouring of the divine Spirit in Joel, however, suggests that intermediation is a gift that Yhwh intends to spread throughout the community (R. Wilson, *Prophecy and Society in Ancient Israel* [Philadelphia: Fortress, 1980] 22–28, 241–51). Grabbe also comments on the terminology and characteristics of prophetic activity, emphasizing the lack of clear distinctions between various titles expressing divine intermediation (L. Grabbe,

vine intermediation (cf. Gen 28:12–17; 37:5–11; 40:8–23; 41:14–27; 1 Sam 28:6; Hos 12:11; Amos 7:1–8).[29] Notably, Num 12:6–8 establishes the validity of dreams and visions as forms through which Yhwh reveals himself to prophets, even as it elevates Moses' direct access to Yhwh.

While affirming the positive portrayal of all three prophetic activities, one can also make note of passages that negatively characterize claims of divinely inspired dreams (Jer 23:25–26; 27:9; 29:8; Zech 10:2).[30] This negative characterization, however, is directed at the content of the supposed prophetic communication rather than at the form of revelation itself.[31] Instead, this text synonymously employs three different verbs that denote different manifestations of Yhwh's Spirit.[32] Essentially, the range of recipients and the variety of intermediation highlight the magnitude of Yhwh's outpouring of the divine Spirit.

The concept of Yhwh pouring out his Spirit is an indicator of great divine favor. The unmistakable manifestations of Yhwh's presence in these verses are hopeful signs for the implied audience in the wake of the lengthy litany of difficult circumstances that dominates Joel 1:1–2:17. Ezekiel 39:29 provides the closest prophetic parallel, declaring that Yhwh will pour out the divine Spirit on the Israelites as a sign that Yhwh will defeat their enemies and guarantee their security.[33] Other references to Yhwh's pouring out the divine Spirit: look toward an idyllic future in Isa 32:15, promise blessings for Judah's descendants in Isa 44:3, and reaffirm the relationship between Yhwh and the covenant community in Zech 12:10 (cf. Prov 1:23; Isa 59:21).[34] The outpouring of Yhwh's Spirit manifests the divine presence

---

Priests, Prophets, Diviners, Sages: A Socio-Historical Study of Religious Specialists in Ancient Israel [Valley Forge, PA: Trinity, 1995] 107–18).

29. Barton, *Joel*, 95.

30. R. Coggins, *Joel and Amos* (NCBC; Sheffield: Sheffield Academic Press, 2000) 50–51. Coggins highlights the contrast that Jer 23 constructs between the dreamer and the one who actually possesses the word of Yhwh. However, the idea of divine communication through dreams is not always condemned. When Saul inquired of Yhwh, the text claims that Yhwh did not respond either through dreams or through prophets (1 Sam 28:6, 15). This expresses the validity of dreams as a form of divine communication.

31. Allen, *Joel*, 99; T. Overholt, *The Threat of Falsehood: A Study in the Theology of the Book of Jeremiah* (London: SCM, 1970) 66–68.

32. Crenshaw, *Joel*, 166.

33. J. Strazicich, *Joel's Use of Scripture and the Scripture's Use of Joel: Appropriation and Resignification in Second Temple Judaism and Early Christianity* (BIS 82; Leiden: Brill, 2007) 208. See the discussion below for analysis of the difference between Joel's claim that Yhwh will pour the divine Spirit on "all flesh" and Ezekiel's claim that the recipients of the divine Spirit constitute the "house of Israel."

34. The two passages in Isaiah employ different verbs for 'pouring out' from Ezek 39:29; Joel 3:1, 2; and Zech 12:10, which all use שָׁפַךְ. Isaiah 32:15 uses עָרָה, while Isa 44:3 employs יָצַק. These verbs appear to be synonymous, and their shared use of Yhwh's Spirit as the grammatical object makes it possible to suggest that these passages are discussing a similar phenomenon.

among its recipients.[35] This continues the trajectory of Joel 2:18–27, where
Yhwh acts on behalf of the implied audience.

Another way of demonstrating the magnitude of Yhwh's blessing is to
contrast this passage with others that view the lack of intermediation as a
sign of divine displeasure. First Samuel 3:1 claims that the word of Yhwh
was rare and that there were not many visions. This verse does not refer specifically to Yhwh's Spirit, but the association of the word of Yhwh
with visions suggests that it refers to a similar form of prophetic intermediation. The statement in 1 Sam 3:1 follows a prophecy against Eli's
house that decries the spiritual and moral bankruptcy of Israel's leadership
(1 Sam 2:27–36). The castigation for disobedience lays the groundwork for
the disappearance of prophetic intermediation. In the same vein, one of
the punishments for Israel's disobedience that Amos articulates is a famine of hearing the word of Yhwh (Amos 8:11–12; cf. Jer 18:18; Ezek 7:26;
Mic 3:6–7), which reflects a cessation of prophetic activity.[36] This creates
tremendous desperation among the community since their search will be
fruitless.[37] The abundant outpouring of Yhwh's Spirit in Joel 3:1–5 stands
in stark contrast to these signs of divine displeasure; whereas the propheti-
cally proclaimed punishment for disobedience is the removal of prophetic
intermediation, Joel declares that Yhwh will pour out the divine Spirit,
which manifests itself through intermediating activities.

Another important element of the rhetorical strategy of Joel 3:1–2 occurs in the interplay and reuse of previous rhetorical units. The description
of spiritual restoration here mirrors Joel 2:18–27's extended guarantees of
physical and material restoration from the ravages of the locust plague. In
Joel 2:18–27, Yhwh promises to restore prosperity as a sign of the divine
presence among the Judahite community (Joel 2:26–27). Joel 3:1–5 presents further proof of Yhwh's presence in the form of a powerful outpouring
of the divine Spirit. Further, the spiritual restoration found in Joel 3:1–5 reflects a distinct development in the situation articulated in Joel 1:1–2:17. In
those rhetorical units the text indicates that the relationship between Yhwh
and the people is in jeopardy since the sacrificial system is in shambles
(Joel 1:9, 13). Further, the prophet's cry to Yhwh (Joel 1:19–20) does not
lead to rescue but a divinely led assault on Zion (Joel 2:1–11). Essentially,
Joel 3:1–5 restores the broken spiritual relationship, which corresponds to
the restoration of physical security in Joel 2:18–27.[38] Not only will Yhwh

---

35. M. Boda, *Haggai, Zechariah* (NIV Application Commentary; Grand Rapids: Zondervan, 2004) 485.

36. S. Paul, *Amos* (Hermeneia; Minneapolis: Augsburg Fortress, 1991) 265.

37. Ibid., 266–67. Interestingly, there is similar imagery at work in both Israel's desperate search for the prophetic word in Amos 8:12 and the destruction of the invading locust
army in Joel 2:20. Both passages employ geographical merismus in order to stress the
totality of the absence of either the prophetic word (Amos) or the invading army (Joel).

38. F. Deist, "Parallels and Reinterpretation in the Book of Joel: A Theology of *Yom
Yahweh?*" in *Text and Context: Old Testament and Semitic Studies for F. C. Fensham* (ed.

satisfy the people's needs for sustenance and security, YHWH will provide continued prophetic intermediation through the presence of the divine Spirit.

The extent of the recipients of YHWH's Spirit in this passage is a matter of some dispute. Joel 3:1 states that YHWH will pour out his Spirit upon כָּל־ בָּשָׂר 'all flesh'. This is typically a universalizing term in the Old Testament, referring to all people, without ethnic or geographical restrictions (Deut 5:26; Job 12:10; Isa 49:26; 66:16). In some cases, the scope of this phrase even extends beyond humanity to reference all living beings (Gen 6:12, 13; 7:21; Num 18:15). Consequently, at first glance it appears that the text is declaring that YHWH will pour out the divine Spirit beyond the boundaries of Israel or Judah.[39]

The majority of interpreters, however, claim that the concept of "all flesh" here only refers to a democratization of YHWH's Spirit within the Judahite community.[40] This is an argument that must be made from the surrounding context since this would reflect a rare occasion on which כָּל־בָּשָׂר occurs in the Old Testament with a restrictive national sense (cf. Jer 12:12).[41] Evidence for this restrictive interpretation derives from the occurrence of the second-person pronominal suffixes on the groups who receive YHWH's Spirit in the rest of 3:1–2; for example, בְּנֵיכֶם 'your sons' and וּבְנוֹתֵיכֶם 'your daughters' receive this gift.[42] The referent of the second-person pronominal suffixes is then probably the prophet's implied audience, which comprises the members of YHWH's covenant community.[43]

When considering the parallel between this verse and the declaration of Ezek 39:29 that YHWH will pour out the divine Spirit on the "house of Israel," Strazicich helpfully suggests that the purpose of כָּל־בָּשָׂר is to

---

W. Claasen; JSOTSup 48; Sheffield: Sheffield Academic Press, 1988) 71. Deist helpfully points to Isa 55 as another passage where spiritual restoration occurs alongside physical restoration as a sign of YHWH's favor.

39. See especially W. Kaiser, "The Promise of God and the Outpouring of the Holy Spirit," in *The Living and Active Word of God: Studies in Honor of Samuel J. Schultz* (ed. M. Inch and R. Youngblood; Winona Lake, IN: Eisenbrauns, 1983) 119. It is interesting to note Peter's citation of Joel 3:1–5 in the Pentecost sermon of Acts 2:14–36. The outpouring of the Spirit that preceded that sermon appears to have taken place among the apostles and their Jewish audience at that time (cf. Acts 2:5–21), but it was not long afterward that Peter witnessed an unequivocal gifting of the Spirit to Gentiles (cf. Acts 10:44–48). For a nuanced study of the relationship between Joel 3:1–5 and its reuse in Acts 2, see D. Treier, "The Fulfillment of Joel 2:28–32: A Multiple-Lens Approach," *JETS* 40 (1997) 13–26.

40. Dillard, "Joel," 295; Crenshaw, *Joel*, 165; Allen, *Joel*, 98; Wolff, *Joel and Amos*, 67; Hubbard, *Joel*, 73.

41. Strazicich, *Joel's Use of Scripture*, 209. Jeremiah 12:12 occurs in the context of YHWH's pronouncing judgment on Judah. In this instance, "all flesh" seems to refer to the totality of the devastation that YHWH will bring on this community.

42. Dillard, "Joel," 295.

43. I return to the discussion of the scope of the implied audience in Joel 4, where the text directly addresses foreign nations and summons them to judgment.

emphasize that "really, truly, all members of the community" will receive the gift of the Spirit.[44] This includes the members who may not be ethnically Judahite.[45] Joel 3:5 also articulates a difference in fate between those who call on the name of Yʜᴡʜ and those who do not, which indicates that there are criteria that must be met in order to receive this outpouring of Yʜᴡʜ's Spirit.[46] This provides further evidence for a restriction of "all flesh." Thus, even though this verse extends the range of those who can receive Yʜᴡʜ's Spirit, the text appears to restrict it according to ethnic and religious boundaries.

Within these boundaries, the broad swath of social subgroups that receive Yʜᴡʜ's Spirit displays the immensity of this outpouring. Following the declaration that Yʜᴡʜ's Spirit will come upon "all flesh," Joel 3:1–2 details the particulars of that category. Joel 3:1 accomplishes this through a twofold usage of merismus. The first merismus indicates that the outpouring of Yʜᴡʜ's Spirit will cover both genders, since it will fall on both בְּנֵיכֶם 'your sons' and וּבְנוֹתֵיכֶם 'your daughters'. The second merismus is generational, and it indicates that Yʜᴡʜ's Spirit will affect people of all ages, from זִקְנֵיכֶם 'your elders' to בַּחוּרֵיכֶם 'your youths'.[47] This verse quite vividly demonstrates the freedom of Yʜᴡʜ's divine Spirit to come upon whomever Yʜᴡʜ chooses; there is no preference in gender or generation (cf. Mal 3:24).

Joel 3:2 then extends the outpouring of Yʜᴡʜ's Spirit further by stating that it will fall on עַל־הָעֲבָדִים וְעַל־הַשְּׁפָחוֹת 'the male and female servants', thus including the whole gamut of social strata, while continuing the theme of access for both genders. The emphatic adverb וְגַם introduces this clause, highlighting the significance of including this group among those who receive Yʜᴡʜ's Spirit.[48] Even though these servants could be foreigners, they are included as "marginal members" of the בֵּית אָב 'house of the father' kinship structure (Deut 5:12–15; 16:11, 14).[49] This identifies

---

44. Strazicich, *Joel's Use of Scripture*, 210.

45. See below for a further explication of the idea of including non-Judahite servants in the broader context of the covenant community.

46. Strazicich, *Joel's Use of Scripture*, 209. Strazicich asserts, "[I]f one is to assume a universalistic interpretation of כָּל־בָּשָׂר in 3:1, then one would also assume that the nations would appear in a salvific context in 3:5."

47. Prinsloo, *Theology*, 81. This is a similar generational merismus that the text employed in the summons to cry out to Yʜᴡʜ in Joel 2:16. Joel 2:16 calls everyone from 'elders' (זְקֵנִים) to 'children' (עוֹלְלִים), while Joel 3:2 uses a different term (בַּחוּרֵיכֶם) for young people. The term בַּחוּרֵיכֶם probably refers to young adults in their prime, so it still stands in contrast to the mention of elders in the previous clause (cf. Deut 32:25; Ps 148:12).

48. B. Waltke and M. O'Connor, *An Introduction to Biblical Hebrew Syntax* (Winona Lake, IN: Eisenbrauns, 1990) 663.

49. L. Perdue et al., *Families in Ancient Israel* (Louisville: Westminster John Knox, 1997) 175; S. Bendor, *The Social Structure of Ancient Israel: The Institution of the Family (beit ʾab) from the Settlement to the End of the Monarchy* (Jerusalem Biblical Studies 7; Jerusalem: Simor, 1996) 230–32.

them as part of the religious community, which allows them to receive the gift (Deut 5:14; 12:12; 16:11).[50] Ultimately, the purpose of Joel 3:1–2 is to explain the full scope of "all flesh" who can receive Yʜᴡʜ's gift. The text vividly demonstrates through the mention of these subgroups that everyone in the implied audience has equal access to the outpouring of Yʜᴡʜ's Spirit.

This reference to the outpouring of Yʜᴡʜ's Spirit alludes to another description of prophetic gifts in Israel's traditions. Joel 3:1–2 references Moses' desire for relief that prompts Yʜᴡʜ to endow 70 elders with the divine Spirit in Num 11:10–30.[51] These elders gather around the Tent of Meeting and begin to prophesy as a sign of the presence of Yʜᴡʜ's Spirit (Num 11:25). Significantly, two of the chosen elders, named Eldad and Medad, who were not present in the Tent of Meeting begin to prophesy elsewhere in the camp, which prompts Joshua to react with consternation at the potential threat to Moses' authority. Moses' response to Joshua expresses a desire that Yʜᴡʜ's Spirit would come upon all of Yʜᴡʜ's people so that they would prophesy since this would reflect a substantial outpouring of God's blessing (Num 11:29).

Therefore, one element of the rhetorical strategy of Joel 3:1–2 is to reflect on Num 11 and demonstrate that Yʜᴡʜ answered this prayer of Moses as part of Yʜᴡʜ's restorative actions.[52] Essentially, in the wake of the trials and torments experienced in the first half of the book, Joel 3:1–2 draws attention back to the religious traditions of the community and taps into the desire expressed by one of its seminal figures for a greater manifestation of Yʜᴡʜ's Spirit. A manifestation of this sort would be a clear sign of Yʜᴡʜ's care, concern, and presence.

In summary, the intention of Joel 3:1–2 is to inundate the audience with reminders that Yʜᴡʜ offers spiritual restoration that mirrors the material restoration of Joel 2:18–27, in the wake of the text's appeal to Yʜᴡʜ in Joel 2:12–17. The text achieves this goal by first issuing a generic statement about the outpouring of the Spirit, then following up with an exhaustive description of who receives this gift of Yʜᴡʜ. The list of subgroups emphasizes the range of Yʜᴡʜ's gift since it covers categories including gender, age, and social standing. This attention to detail is likely an effective strategy in persuading the implied audience that Yʜᴡʜ's gift pertains to them. It roots the promise of this gift in scriptural traditions that indicate the

---

50. Allen, *Joel*, 99. The inclusion of foreigners in the category of slaves may help to explain why the text drops the pronominal suffixes in this final clause. If the text referred to "your male servants," and "your female servants," its meaning could have been restricted to fellow Judahite slaves. Employing these terms without suffixes draws in the broadest possible range of people who could be said to be part of Yʜᴡʜ's community. See Strazicich, *Joel's Use of Scripture*, 211–12.

51. Dillard, "Joel," 294.

52. Ibid.

desirability of a powerful outpouring of the Spirit. The text does not offer
an opportunity for the implied audience to respond in these verses, but it
reveals the proper response in Joel 3:5.

Joel 3:3–4: Signs of the Day of Yʜᴡʜ

The remainder of Joel 3:1–5 considers the impact of the outpouring of
Yʜᴡʜ's Spirit. Joel 3:3 continues to present the words of Yʜᴡʜ in the first
person through the verb וְנָתַתִּי 'I will give', where Yʜᴡʜ declares what will
result from the outpouring of the Spirit. The speaker is harder to identify in
Joel 3:4 because the text refers to the day of Yʜᴡʜ using third person. It is
likely, however, that the Yʜᴡʜ is who continues to speak (first person) in
this verse, since Joel 3:4's cosmological phenomena seem to be a continuation of the list of responders to Yʜᴡʜ's actions in Joel 3:3. Further, the
reference to the day of Yʜᴡʜ does not necessitate a new speaker because it
is a fixed, technical expression (cf. Ezek 13:5; 30:3; Mal 3:23).[53]

Joel 3:3–4 continues the epideictic approach of describing the authority
that Yʜᴡʜ possesses over the cosmos. Joel 3:3–4 discusses powerful signs of
Yʜᴡʜ's actions and is especially notable for reinvoking the day of Yʜᴡʜ in
the final clause of 3:4. The location of this reference is significant considering the emphasis on Yʜᴡʜ's action created by the dual references to "my
Spirit" in 3:1–2. Yʜᴡʜ's actions in this unit, even though they affect the
entire cosmos, signify positive repercussions for the community, considering the promised outpouring of the divine Spirit that underlies Yʜᴡʜ's
commitment. The positive outlook that Joel 3:1–2 establishes is the preface
to this description of the day of Yʜᴡʜ.

This use of the day of Yʜᴡʜ in Joel 3:4 is striking because of the power
of the imagery that it invokes, as well as the way it echoes previous references to the day of Yʜᴡʜ. Joel 3:3 states that Yʜᴡʜ will display מוֹפְתִים
'signs' in heaven and on earth that include blood, fire, and columns of
cloud. The term מוֹפְתִים is significant, suggesting that the following phenomena point toward a powerful divine intervention.[54] Yʜᴡʜ is the agent
who causes these signs, a fact that gives this verse a theophanic flavor (cf.
Exod 19:18; Ps 18:9).[55] The description of these acts of Yʜᴡʜ also draws on
the traditions of the exodus plagues through which Yʜᴡʜ rescued Israel
from Egypt (cf. Exod 4:23; 7:3, 9; 11:9).[56] The plagues that Yʜᴡʜ unleashed

53. Crenshaw, *Joel*, 171.
54. Barton, *Joel*, 97; Allen, *Joel*, 100; Crenshaw, *Joel*, 167.
55. Allen, *Joel*, 101; K. Leung, *An Intertextual Study of the Motif-Complex Yom Yahweh in the Book of Joel* (Ph.D. diss., Fuller Theological Seminary, 1997) 179–81.
56. See, for example, Allen, *Joel*, 101; Strazicich, *Joel's Use of Scripture*, 213; J. Bourke, "Le jour de Yahvé dans Joël," *RB* 66 (1959) 33. Bergler connects the reference to מוֹפְתִים with the exodus plagues, reminders of which the plague of blood and the plague of darkness in Joel 3:3 seem to trigger (S. Bergler, *Joel als Schriftinterpret* [Frankfurt am Main: Peter Lang, 1988] 268–73).

against Egypt are examples of מוֹפְתִים par excellence.[57] Alluding to the exodus in Joel 3:1–5 further foreshadows the concerns of Joel 4:1–20, a passage that primarily describes the removal of foreign threat (including Egypt in Joel 4:19) and the preservation of Jerusalem.[58]

The sequence of the signs moves toward greater cosmological impact. The first three signs are blood, fire, and pillars of smoke, which may reflect various plagues of the exodus (Exod 7:14–24; 9:22–23).[59] Yhwh's actions in Joel 3:3 are also drawn from images of the day of Yhwh in Joel 2:1–2a, which uses the specter of a darkened cloud preceding the description of the locust army's overrunning the sanctuary of Zion. Further, in both Joel 3:3–4 and 2:1–11, the coming of this day dramatically affects the heavenly luminaries, a point that carries foreboding overtones. The description is slightly different in Joel 3, since 2:10 points to the darkening of both the sun and the moon, while 3:4 points to the sun's darkening and the moon's adopting a bloody hue.[60] This recalls the exodus plague of darkness, which was the final plague prior to the descent of the angel of Yhwh against the Egyptians (cf. Exod 10:21).[61] The images of darkening heavenly luminaries have a similar impact; they denote the final portent announcing the imminence of the day of Yhwh.

The parallel with the previous description of the day of Yhwh continues in the final line of Joel 3:4. It describes the day using the adjectives הַגָּדוֹל וְהַנּוֹרָא 'the great and terrible', which also link this reference to the day of Yhwh back to Joel 2:11, which employs the same vocabulary. Although the eventual targets of the day of Yhwh differ, this succinct phrase reveals the

---

57. See S. Wagner, "מוֹפֵת," *TDOT* 8:174–81. Wagner notes that over 19 of the 36 examples of this word in the Old Testament occur in contexts directly or indirectly related to the exodus event and the surrounding plagues. Consequently, when Joel employs this word to describe the harbingers of the day of Yhwh, it recalls the signs that Yhwh employed to liberate Israel from Egypt.

58. Strazicich (*Joel's Use of Scripture*, 213) argues that "the resignification of Yahweh's great power, exerted for the purpose of freeing the Israelites from the power of Egyptians, is now recontextualized into Yahweh freeing the Judeans from the oppression of foreign powers."

59. Bourke, "Jour," 26–27. Bourke argues that the strategy that Joel employs is to use evidence of Yhwh's deliverance from historical enemies to demonstrate Yhwh's ability to deliver the community from the peril described in Joel 1:1–2:17. Interestingly, Sweeney proposes that the triad of "blood, fire, and columns of cloud" also invoke images of sacrifice at the altar. The slain animal bleeds and then is set on fire, resulting in a thick column of smoke over the altar; Sweeney, *Twelve*, 175. It is difficult, however, to argue that sacrifice is in view in the manifestation of Yhwh's power in Joel 3:3–4.

60. Stephenson argues that solar and lunar eclipses were the impetus behind this reference, and he even identifies solar eclipses in 357 and 336 B.C.E. as potential incidents on which the prophet was drawing (F. Stephenson, "The Date of the Book of Joel," *VT* 19 [1969] 224–29). This assertion cannot be proved, however, and it is more useful to focus on the rhetorical function of drawing on images from the realm of cosmic activity.

61. Bergler, *Joel als Schriftinterpret*, 272; D. Stuart, *Hosea—Jonah* (WBC 31; Waco, TX: Word, 1987) 261.

immensity of the power and authority that YHWH exerts on this day.[62] The final description firmly establishes YHWH's control over the cosmos.

In summary, the rhetorical strategy of Joel 3:3–4 builds on the outpouring of the divine Spirit and heightens the significance of the situation. YHWH's actions invoke powerful signs of divine presence as the cosmos trembles alongside the gift of the divine Spirit.[63] The strategy of reinvoking the description of the day of YHWH found in Joel 2:10–11 effectively reminds the implied audience of the fearful nature of this day since these signs occur before the day of YHWH.[64] The dimming of the heavenly bodies and the signs of blood, fire, and smoke are only portents announcing the full manifestation of the day of YHWH. Consequently, the text establishes a progression from the outpouring of the Spirit to the shaking of the cosmos. The gift of the Spirit is a sign of great blessing while the portents of the day of YHWH remind the implied audience of the full scope of YHWH's power. The description of the portents of the day of YHWH should invoke a sense of urgency in the implied audience to find sanctuary. This strengthens the promise of rescue through calling on the name of YHWH in Joel 3:5.

Joel 3:5: Security in Zion

Following the description of cosmos-rending signs, Joel 3:5 articulates the essential distinction between the presentations of the day of YHWH in this rhetorical unit and Joel 2:1–11. Joel 3:5 claims that there is a way for the implied audience to escape its wrath. This verse is slightly distinct from Joel 3:3–4 since the focus shifts from YHWH to those who experience the day of YHWH. This shift occurs through the introductory phrase וְהָיָה כֹּל אֲשֶׁר־יִקְרָא 'and it will be [that] all who call'. Joel 3:5 thus offers commentary on the divine speech of Joel 3:1–4 and begins to discuss the response of those affected by the day of YHWH.[65] The nature of the response is implicit since the text remains in the indicative mood. However, the claim that those who call upon the name of YHWH will be saved provides the implied audience with a reason to cry out to YHWH in the wake of the portents announcing the day of YHWH.

The first statement of Joel 3:5 presents the possibility of refuge from the terrifying cosmological phenomena. This occurs in the statement that everyone who calls on the name of YHWH will find salvation. Similar to Joel 3:1, the interpretation of the "all" is debated. Since the reference to 'all

---

62. Crenshaw, *Joel*, 171.

63. Simkins, *Yahweh's Activity*, 217.

64. Coggins, *Joel*, 52.

65. Prinsloo, *Theology*, 83. Troxel examines the occurrences of the grammatical structure "וְהָיָה + fronted phrase + *yiqtol* verb" and notes that in 30 out of 35 cases it stands at the end of a rhetorical unit and implies or reveals consequences for the preceding discourse. This tightly links Joel 3:5 to what has unfolded in 3:1–4. See Ronald L. Troxel, "כֹּל אֲשֶׁר יִקְרָא: An Alleged Discontinuity between Joel 1–2 and 3" (paper presented at the annual meeting of the SBL, Chicago: Nov 18, 2012) 3.

flesh' (כָּל־בָּשָׂר) on whom Yhwh poured out his Spirit in Joel 3:1 probably
has ethnic restrictions, it is important to consider the extent of those who
could call on the name of Yhwh. Troxel convincingly shows that, in this
instance, the text employs כֹּל to mean "a maximal extension of a type,"
which refers to the community of Judahites receiving the gift of the Spirit
and witnessing the cosmological portents of the day of Yhwh.[66] Further,
the phrase כָּל־יִקְרָא בְּשֵׁם יְהוָה 'all who call on the name of Yhwh' helps to
define the meaning of כֹּל אֲשֶׁר.[67] The concept of "calling on the name of
Yhwh" typically denotes worship and thus identifies those who respond
in this way as adherents of Yhwh (cf. Gen 12:8; 13:4; 21:33; 26:25; Exod
33:19; 34:5; 1 Kgs 18:24; Isa 12:4; Zeph 3:9; Zech 13:9).[68] Only those who
call on the name Yhwh will escape the portents of the previous verses.[69]
This requirement coincides with the restrictive understanding of "all flesh"
in Joel 3:1 and continues the idea of salvation for the Judahite community
since it comprises the individuals who call on the name of Yhwh.

The next phrase continues to highlight the Judah-centric emphasis
of Joel 3:1–5. It extends the idea of those who escape the onslaught of
the day of Yhwh by providing them with a physical location in which
they find security. The text gives the location a dual reference, stating it
is Mount Zion or Jerusalem. There are parallels between Joel's reference to
sanctuary in Zion and Obad 17 (cf. Isa 4:2) on which Joel may rely.[70] The

---

66. Ibid., 13–14
67. Crenshaw, *Joel*, 169.
68. Genesis 4:26 is an exception since it declares that people began to call on the name
of Yhwh but does not provide an exclusive covenantal context. This verse, however, does
not necessarily universalize the concept of calling on the name of Yhwh. In the progression of the biblical narrative, Gen 4:26 precedes the flood and the dissolution of relationship between Yhwh and humanity. Yhwh then reestablishes a relationship with Abraham.
After that point, calling on the name of Yhwh typically reflects the relationship between
Yhwh and Israel/Judah. See J. Sailhamer, *The Pentateuch as Narrative* (Grand Rapids: Zondervan, 1992) 116.
69. Jeremias attempts to distinguish between those who receive the outpouring of the
divine Spirit in Joel 3:1 and those who call upon the name of Yhwh in Joel 3:5, suggesting
that the latter group is a subset of the former. For Jeremias, the gift of the divine Spirit in
Joel 3 does not guarantee salvation any more than the community's turn to Yhwh in Joel
2; he claims, "Ein Automatismus der Rettung ist in Joel 3 ebensowenig wie in Joel 2 im
Blick" (J. Jeremias, "'Denn auf dem Berg Zion und in Jerusalem wird Rettung sein' (Joel
3:5): Zur Heilserwartung des Joelbuches," in *Zion—Ort der Begegnung: Festschrift für Lauren-
tius Klein zur Vollendung des 65 Lebensjahres* [ed. F. Hahn et al.; Bodenheim: Hanstein, 1993]
41). Eventually, he differentiates between the escaped group (פְּלֵיטָה) and the survivors
(שְׂרִידִים) in Joel 3:5, suggesting that the latter group may include non-Judahites (pp. 35–
45). The distinction between the פְּלֵיטָה and the שְׂרִידִים seems syntactically questionable
since the two clauses are linked with a *waw*-copulative. Further, Joel 4 goes to great lengths
to intertwine the rescue of the Judahite community with the destruction of foreign nations, which would seem to render incongruous the idea that Joel 3 is looking beyond the
borders of the Judahite community.
70. Sweeney, *Twelve*, 175; Crenshaw, *Joel*, 169; R. Mason, *Zephaniah, Habbakuk, Joel*
(OTG; Sheffield: Sheffield Academic Press, 1994) 118. The text may employ a specific

first clause of Obad 17 reads וּבְהַר צִיּוֹן תִּהְיֶה פְלֵיטָה 'but on Mount Zion there will be an escaped group'. The only difference between this phrase and Joel 3:5 is its omission of Jerusalem as a phrase in parallel with Mount Zion. The day of YHWH informs both passages, with the Obadiah passage making more explicit the idea of judgment against foreign nations, represented by the house of Edom in Obad 18, while Joel 3:5 focuses more on Zion and Jerusalem and the existence of a group that can escape the day of YHWH.[71] The association with Obad 17 and its judgment of Edom also presages the judgment of the nations that occurs in Joel 4:1–20; the day of YHWH in Joel 3:5 offers salvation for those who call on the name of YHWH, while preparing the ground for the explicit judgment of foreign nations in the next chapter.

Joel 3:5 also displays a classical use of the Zion tradition, in which "Zion and Jerusalem are pre-eminently the abode of Yahweh, citadels of security and stability."[72] Zion is the only location where there is the guarantee of refuge from the cosmos-rending power of the day of YHWH. Again, this reveals a marked contrast with the portrayal of the day of YHWH in Joel 2:1–11. In that passage, YHWH leads the invading army against Zion, easily breaching its defenses and announcing destruction. In Joel 3:5, Zion/Jerusalem is now the one inviolable fortress into which YHWH is calling people to gather to escape the day of YHWH.

Continuing with the theme of those who "call on the name of YHWH," Joel 3:5 constructs an inclusio using the verb קָרָא 'to call' to emphasize the necessity of proper response; those who "call on the name of YHWH" at the beginning of this verse are probably also those "whom YHWH calls" (אֲשֶׁר יְהוָה קֹרֵא) at the end of the verse.[73] This implicit injunction to be among those who "call on the name of YHWH" most likely builds on the prophet's earlier explicit command to "return to YHWH" found in Joel 2:12–17.[74] For those who respond in obedience, the text now offers hope that the day of YHWH will not be a day of judgment since they will be among the survivors whom YHWH calls.[75] Instead, the terrors of the day of YHWH will fall on those who have not called on the name of YHWH.

---

quotation formula following the reference to the escaped group. The following clause confirms the existence of this escaped group, 'as YHWH has said' (כַּאֲשֶׁר אָמַר יְהוָה). Many understand this phrase as a citation formula, arguing that it directly cites Obad 17 (Strazicich, *Joel's Use of Scripture*, 218–19; Wolff, *Joel and Amos*, 68). This, of course, presumes the ability to identify correctly the date of composition for both books. Crenshaw suggests that it may also be possible that both passages rely on an unknown independent tradition (Crenshaw, *Joel*, 169–70).

71. Mason, *Zephaniah*, 118–19.
72. Prinsloo, *Theology*, 87.
73. Ibid., 81.
74. Simkins, *Yahweh's Activity*, 217.
75. J. Nogalski, "The Day(s) of YHWH in the Book of the Twelve," *SBL 1999: Seminar Papers* (SBLSP 38; Atlanta: Society of Biblical Literature, 1999) 629.

This verse also contains another link to the description of the day of YHWH in Joel 2:1–11. It states that in Jerusalem/Zion there will be a פְּלֵיטָה 'escaped group'—namely, those who call on the name of YHWH. The noun פְּלֵיטָה also occurred in Joel 2:3, describing the advance of the locust army. In that case, it stated that nothing could escape in the wake of that army, whereas in this case YHWH himself declares that he will allow some to escape. The promise of escapees should be powerful for the implied audience; whereas Joel 2:3 permits no escape, Joel 3:5 explicitly opens the door to survival. This opportunity should provide the implied audience with reason to heed the prophetic word.

The text gives the prospect of escape further weight in the following clause of Joel 3:5, which refers to this group as שְׂרִידִים 'survivors'. These two words (פְּלֵיטָה; שְׂרִידִים) occur in parallelism several times in the Old Testament in negated forms to emphasize complete defeat and destruction (Josh 8:22; Jer 42:17; 44:14).[76] The nominal form שָׂרִיד refers to survivors, typically of a military defeat (Num 21:35; Josh 8:22; Isa 1:9; Jer 42:17; 44:14).[77] The presence of survivors in this verse echoes the promise of an escaped group whom YHWH will protect. Again, whereas the description of the day of YHWH in 2:1–11 held out no hope of salvation, Joel 3:5 offers a way to avoid its onslaught for those discerning enough to cry out to YHWH.

In summary, Joel 3:5 simply states the guarantee of rescue from the day of YHWH, but one can effectively argue that the illocutionary intent of this verse is to persuade the implied audience that it ought to call on the name of YHWH and trust that YHWH would honor the promises of protection rooted in Zion.[78] The shift in voice in Joel 3:5 thus contains another clue to the unit's rhetorical strategy. In the wake of the potentially devastating consequences of the day of YHWH, the prophet proclaims that those who call on the name of YHWH find sanctuary. The implied audience is expected to conclude that it is incumbent on them to be among those who "call on the name of YHWH" so that they will avoid the portended destruction.[79]

---

76. Joshua 8:22 describes the total defeat of Ai, while the two passages in Jeremiah claim that those who flee to Egypt will find only destruction.

77. This stands in contrast to the Greek tradition, which describes those who escape the destruction of the day of YHWH as εὐαγγελιζόμενοι, that is, 'the ones receiving good news'. In Hebrew, this would be derived most likely from ומבשרים. This is probably an erroneous reading, as Prinsloo points out by citing the Aquila and Theodotion recensions, which read καὶ ἐν τοῖς καταλελειμμένοις, a reading that follows the Masoretic Text (Prinsloo, *Theology*, 81). Interestingly, Crenshaw notes that Peter's citation of this passage in his Acts 2 sermon does not reflect the Greek tradition, even though it would seem to have fit his context quite well (Crenshaw, *Joel*, 172).

78. On the illocutionary potential of prophetic oracles, see K. Möller, "Words of (In-)evitable Certitude? Reflections on the Interpretation of Prophetic Oracles of Judgment," in *After Pentecost: Language and Biblical Interpretation* (ed. C. Bartholomew, C. Greene, and K. Möller; SHS 2; Grand Rapids: Zondervan, 2001) 370–71.

79. Some have used this as evidence for a certain sectarian division in the historical audience that Joel was addressing. For example, Ahlström and Plöger argue that "calling on

Yʜᴡʜ's appearance shakes the cosmos in Joel 3:1–5, but there is an explicit guarantee of sanctuary for those who appeal to Yʜᴡʜ. Therefore, the rhetorical strategy of Joel 3:5 is rooted in the shift from first- to third-person speech and the opportunity for response grounded in the promise of rescue and sanctuary in Zion for those who call on the name of Yʜᴡʜ.

Summary

Joel 3:1–5 moves the audience away from the concerns of the locust plague and drought that dominated the image-world of the preceding units. Joel 3:1–5 continues the description of restoration begun in 2:18–27 by offering an abundant spiritual renewal to go along with Yʜᴡʜ's promise of a return to agricultural prosperity. The abundance of the outpouring of Yʜᴡʜ's Spirit reveals the rich nature of the blessing that Yʜᴡʜ brings in the divine response to the appeals of Joel 2:12–17. Further, this unit articulates a significant development in the concept of the day of Yʜᴡʜ from its previous uses in Joel 1:15 and 2:1–11. Most notably, Joel 3:1–5 shifts the primary target of the wrath inherent in the day of Yʜᴡʜ. In Joel 1:15 and 2:1–11, the warnings of the day of Yʜᴡʜ indicate a time when Yʜᴡʜ acts and threatens to bring destruction on Judah and Jerusalem, a fate from which the prophet directs them to cry out in hope of deliverance.

Joel 3:1–5 offers refuge in Zion to those who call upon the name of Yʜᴡʜ, identifying themselves as adherents of Yʜᴡʜ. This creates an implicit understanding that the proper response to the outpouring of the divine Spirit is to call on the name of Yʜᴡʜ. The text juxtaposes the immensity of Yʜᴡʜ's blessing with Yʜᴡʜ's authority over all creation. The portents of the day of Yʜᴡʜ persuade the implied audience to receive the gift of Yʜᴡʜ's Spirit and respond so that they can find sanctuary in Zion.[80] The identification of refuge from the day of Yʜᴡʜ effectively introduces the rest of the

---

the name of Yʜᴡʜ" implies that there must be a correct way to do so, a way that perhaps stood in contrast to the established cult of the time (Ahlström, *Joel*, 54–55; O. Plöger, *Theocracy and Eschatology* [trans. S. Rudman; Richmond: John Knox, 1968] 125). Redditt suggests that the democratization of Yʜᴡʜ's Spirit in this section reflects the book's growing disillusionment with the priestly leadership and suggests a longing for more immediate evidence of Yʜᴡʜ's presence (P. Redditt, "The Book of Joel and Peripheral Prophecy," *CBQ* 48 [1986] 240–41). In contrast, Wolff understands this passage to reflect a warning against cultic restoration and the supremacy of Torah that would diminish the authority of the prophetic spirit that declared that Yʜᴡʜ would act (Wolff, *Joel and Amos*, 67). No explicit support for these interpretations exists, however, in the rest of the text. Consequently, a more specific identification of those who "call on the name of Yʜᴡʜ" requires an appeal to extratextual evidence to determine a time and place for the composition of Joel, which is a task that has yet to lead to conclusive results.

80. Prinsloo, *Theology*, 84–85. Prinsloo refers to the occurrence of the day of Yʜᴡʜ in Joel 3 as "ambivalent," since the dual prongs of destruction and salvation are evident. The promise of restoration for the implied audience, however, emphasizes the positive potential of the day of Yʜᴡʜ. The day of Yʜᴡʜ plays a similar role in Joel 4, where it announces judgment against the nations while guaranteeing security for Yʜᴡʜ's covenant community.

book since Joel 4:1–21 focuses on the fate of other nations while promising protection for those who worship YHWH in Jerusalem.

Rhetorical Effectiveness

The consideration of the rhetorical effectiveness of this particular unit involves again reflecting on its relationship to the appeals found in Joel 2:12–17. That particular passage takes the announcement of the impending day of YHWH as a signal to urge the people to cry out for deliverance. Joel 3:1–5 continues the trajectory begun in Joel 2:18–27 and operates under the presumption that the implied audience responded to the prophetic appeal to cry out to YHWH. As a result, YHWH's zeal and compassion govern YHWH's actions in both Joel 2:18–27 and 3:1–5. YHWH's actions on their behalf should persuade the implied audience to heed the implicit appeal to call out to him so that they can receive the status of "those who call on the name of YHWH." The guarantee of material restoration in Joel 2:18–27 effectively provides the foundation for the promises of spiritual restoration, which should persuade the implied audience that it should respond to the deity, who offers deliverance.

Joel 3:1–5 further persuades the implied audience to heed the text's message by reinterpreting the day of YHWH. Following the progression of the book, Joel moves the implied audience to see the devastation created by the locusts as a sign of YHWH's approaching day, calls them to turn to YHWH so that "perhaps" he will turn and have compassion, and now gives evidence that "perhaps" their plea will be answered in the affirmative. Joel essentially employs the day of YHWH first to persuade the implied audience of the impossibility of resisting YHWH when he chooses to act. Joel does not intend for this powerlessness to lead to paralysis, however, since the text commands the implied audience to cry out to YHWH. Now that YHWH is acting from zeal and compassion, the text again employs the day of YHWH. On this occasion, however, the text demonstrates the efficacy of responding as it directs by placing the promise of deliverance alongside the announcement of the day of YHWH.

Overall, Joel 3:1–5 maintains the terror of the day of YHWH through the harrowing description of cosmological portents. The effects of these portents are different, however, since they occur in a context where the implied audience now has promises of the outpouring of the Spirit and sanctuary rooted in Zion. By activating these positive outcomes, the text effectively communicates to the implied audience that, although the day of YHWH is coming, the people no longer need to fear its ramifications if they respond appropriately.

Another way to consider the rhetorical effectiveness of Joel 3:1–5 is to look beyond the immediate implied audience of the text. Specifically, the way in which Joel 3:1–5 delves into the theme of the outpouring of the divine Spirit is worthy of consideration. Joel 3:1–5 takes the trajectory at which Num 11:10–30 hints and expands it so that the fervent wish of

Moses for all Y_HWH's people to receive the divine Spirit becomes a prophetic promise of divine blessing in the wake of the desperate circumstances articulated in Joel 1:1–2:17. For a universal audience, this passage is powerful in proclaiming the desire of Y_HWH to pour out the divine Spirit across many different boundaries; neither age, nor gender, nor social category is a barrier to accessing the divine Spirit.[81] Although the discussion above notes that the scope of those included in the category of "all flesh" is probably restricted to the Judahite community in the immediate context, Joel 3:1–5 invites the universal audience to consider Y_HWH's intention to pour out the divine Spirit on a wide range of people, permitting a universal audience to consider themselves people to whom Y_HWH gives the divine Spirit. This elevates the persuasive potential of Joel 3:1–5 and permits it to influence audiences that continue to read this text.

Conclusion

Joel 3:1–5 continues the trajectory of restoration that commences in Joel 2:18–27. The rhetorical situation advances beyond the specter of the locust plague and orients itself toward a future time of Y_HWH's powerful intervention. The image of the overwhelming outpouring of the divine Spirit portrays the lavish extent of Y_HWH's guarantee of spiritual restoration; this, in turn, mirrors the description of material restoration in Joel 2:18–27. Joel 3:1–5 effectively bridges distinctions of age, gender, and social standing to reveal that Y_HWH's gift of the divine Spirit is available to every member of the implied audience. The gift of the divine Spirit precedes portents of the day of Y_HWH, which it reconfigures by reusing similar images of darkness and fearfulness while promising hope for rescue. The promise of refuge and the gift of the Spirit should persuade the implied audience to respond by calling on the name of Y_HWH, since the text now proclaims that Y_HWH is acting on their behalf.

Further, the lavish outpouring of the divine Spirit invites all audiences to consider themselves among those upon whom Y_HWH can call. It explores a scriptural tradition that eagerly desires an outpouring of Y_HWH's Spirit and provides a prophetic promise that it will occur. Finally, Joel 3:1–5 prepares the way for further divine activity in Joel 4:1–21, which expands on the pouring out of the divine Spirit and the rending of the cosmos to issue judgments against foreign nations and guarantees of security for those who call on the name of Y_HWH. There is deliverance in Zion for those who call upon the name of Y_HWH, but Joel 4:1–21 explores the fate of the nations who do not find this sanctuary.

---

81. Garrett effectively captures the power of the range of groups included in this gifting of the divine Spirit, stating that "in an era in which men (not women), the old (not the young), and the landowners (not slaves) ruled society, Joel explicitly rejected all such distinctions as criteria for receiving the Holy Spirit" (D. Garrett, *Hosea, Joel* [NAC 19A; Nashville: Broadman & Holman, 1997] 367).

Chapter 8

The Promise of Yhwh's Presence: Rhetorical Analysis of Joel 4:1–21

Introduction

The final chapter of Joel builds on the outpouring of the divine Spirit and the cosmological imagery of Joel 3:1–5. Yhwh's actions are again the focus of Joel 4:1–21, and they set up a contrast between Yhwh acting salvifically toward the Judahite community and Yhwh bringing judgment against foreign nations. The text alternates between portraying these nations as a collective entity and highlighting the offenses of specific nations. Again, various rhetorical techniques combine to portray the fate of the Judahite community and its enemies. These strategies reveal Yhwh's commitment to the Judahite community, to whom it promises paradisiacal prosperity, while removing the threat of outside nations. This reminds the Judahite community of the need to remain committed to Yhwh while Yhwh acts on its behalf.

Rhetorical Unit

Joel 4:1–21 follows the "great and dreadful" day of Yhwh and the lavish outpouring of the divine Spirit in Joel 3:1–5. It details the response to Yhwh's promise of intervention. After an introductory כִּי הִנֵּה, the phrase בַּיָּמִים הָהֵמָּה וּבָעֵת הַהִיא 'in those days and at that time' marks its aperture. This exact phrase occurs elsewhere only in Jer 33:15; 50:4, 20.[1] It also resonates with Joel 3:1 and its reference to a portentuous day when Yhwh appears (cf. Zeph 3:20).[2] The addition of כִּי הִנֵּה reinforces the thematic shift that

---

1. The passages in Jeremiah in which this phrase is found point toward future salvation for Judah and Israel through either Yhwh's raising up a Davidic scion (Jer 33:15) or authorizing the destruction of Babylon (Jer 50:4–20).

2. R. Dillard, "Joel," in *The Minor Prophets: An Exegetical and Expository Commentary* (ed. T. McComiskey; Grand Rapids: Baker, 1992) 300; S. De Vries, "Futurism in the Minor Prophets," in *Thematic Threads in the Book of the Twelve* (ed. P. Redditt and A. Schart; BZAW 325; Berlin: de Gruyter, 2003) 261; W. Prinsloo, *The Theology of the Book of Joel* (BZAW 163; Berlin: de Gruyter, 1985) 92. De Vries argues that the introductory formula in Joel 4:1 points toward "the world's penultimate day," with powerful portents that presage the final great and terrible day of Yhwh that reaches its pinnacle in Joel 3:4. De Vries points to the presence of כִּי as introducing Joel 4:1 to suggest that Joel 4 is an exposition of the announced day of Yhwh (S. De Vries, *From Old Revelation to New: A Tradition-History and Redaction-Critical Study of Temporal Transitions in Prophetic Prediction* [Grand Rapids: Eerdmans, 1995] 70).

renders this a new rhetorical unit. It marks a change of subject from the divine assurance of safety in Zion to the fate of YHWH's antagonists.[3] The fate of YHWH's people is mentioned again in Joel 4:18–21, where the text uses it to provide the mirror-image for its final statement concerning the fate of the foreign nations.

Within this final rhetorical unit, there are four subunits to consider. Joel 4:1–3 introduces the final unit and promises that YHWH will summon הַגּוֹיִם 'the nations' to attend a judgment of YHWH. It declares both judgment on these nations and restoration for the Judahite community. Essentially, Joel 4:1–3 foreshadows the major concerns of the subsequent verses. This demonstrates the appropriateness of considering Joel 4:1–21 as a single rhetorical unit since what follows reflects either YHWH's commitment to "restore the fortunes of Judah and Jerusalem" (Joel 4:1) or YHWH's intention to judge the nations (Joel 4:2–3).

Joel 4:4–8 begins to add further detail by identifying some of these nations and issuing specific judgments for their crimes against Judah and Jerusalem. Joel 4:9–17 directly summons the nations as a collective entity to gather and face divine judgment. Joel 4:9–17 also projects the result of the nations' doomed challenge to YHWH's authority. Finally, Joel 4:18–21 looks beyond the confrontation between YHWH and the nations and interweaves promises of paradisiacal blessing for Judah and Jerusalem with continued assertions of the fate of YHWH's enemies.[4] These verses cohere around repeated images drawn from the semantic domain of liquid, which starkly contrasts with the images of drought and desiccation found in Joel 1.[5] Joel 4:18–21 brings closure to this final rhetorical unit by describing in vivid detail the full nature of what it means for YHWH to "restore the fortunes" of Judah and Jerusalem.

Rhetorical Situation

The rhetorical situation of Joel 4 expands the range of those whom the text addresses, drawing foreign nations into the implied audience. Whereas Joel 1–3 mostly focuses internally on the situation of YHWH's covenant people, Joel 4 develops a distinct situation in which YHWH issues directives to antagonistic nations.[6] Joel 4:1–3 commences the process by announc-

---

3. J. Crenshaw, *Joel* (AB 24c; New York: Doubleday, 1995) 173.

4. M. Sweeney, *The Twelve Prophets*, vol. 1 (Berit Olam; Collegeville, MN: Liturgical Press, 2000) 181.

5. E. Wendland, *The Discourse Analysis of Hebrew Prophetic Literature* (MBPS 40; Lewiston, NY: Edwin Mellen, 1995) 301. There is some debate regarding whether Joel 4:17 concludes the subunit that begins at Joel 4:9 or whether it introduces the final subunit. Wendland's identification of imagery deriving from miraculous fruitfulness and liquidity provides a persuasive reason for beginning a new subunit at Joel 4:18.

6. Crenshaw, *Joel*, 173. Crenshaw suggests that כִּי הִנֵּה at the outset of Joel 4:1 has a disjunctive function that emphasizes the shift in the text's perspective.

ing YHWH's intention to bring the nations into judgment for their crimes against "my people and my inheritance Israel." Joel 4:4–8 then directly addresses Tyre, Sidon, and Philistia, while Joel 4:9–17 issues a sequence of commands to unnamed nations, summoning them to face YHWH's judgment. Again, while there is no evidence that this prophetic proclamation was ever spoken to these foreign nations, on the level of the "world of the text" there is an indentifiable shift in the identity of the addressees.[7] The nations, named and unnamed, are rhetorical foils against which the text can juxtapose its vision of ultimate destiny for Judah and Jerusalem.

The inclusion of other nations as addressees of divine imperatives represents an interesting development in the shape of the text's implied audience. The purpose of addressing these nations is made evident in the final promises of restoration and blessing for the Judahite community. Joel 4:17 presents an address from YHWH to the Judahite community that includes the phrase יְהוָה אֱלֹהֵיכֶם 'YHWH your God', while Joel 4:18–21 details the aftermath of YHWH's declaration to dwell in Zion. Consequently, even though on the surface the text addresses foreign nations, underneath there is an implied Judahite audience in view who hears YHWH's commitment to it expressed through the interactions with the nations.

Essentially, the purpose of Joel 4:1–21 is to explore the ways in which YHWH will "restore the fortunes of Judah and Jerusalem." The implied audience whom the text calls to mourn and cry out to YHWH in previous rhetorical units now awaits the final resolution of its exigences through YHWH's engagement with foreign nations.[8] Just as the use of the unvoiced opinion of "the nations" in Joel 2:17 functions rhetorically as a prophetic strategy for urging divine action, so here the inclusion of foreign nations as the addressees of divine commands has a rhetorical function aimed at

---

7. Interestingly, Raabe considers the possibility of prophetic oracles against foreign nations traveling outside the boundaries of Israel or Judah. He notes specifically Jer 27, which may include envoys from foreign powers, and Isa 21:11–12, which may reflect an inquiry from Seir. Further, Raabe suggests the possibility of prophetic osmosis, by which word of Israelite prophetic speech informally spread and reached non-Israelite ears, citing 2 Kgs 6:8–14 as a possible example (P. Raabe, "Why Prophetic Oracles against the Nations?" in *Fortunate the Eyes That See: Essays in Honour of David Noel Freedman in Celebration of His Seventieth Birthday* [ed. A. Beck et al.; Grand Rapids: Eerdmans, 1995] 252). There is no evidence, however, that the prophetic judgments in Joel 4 were announced beyond the borders of the Judahite community. This leaves the interpreter to consider the rhetorical strategy behind intertwining judgment of foreign nations with promises of salvation in Joel 4.

8. J. Hester, "Speaker, Audience and Situations: A Modified Interactional Model," *Neotestamentica* 32 (1998) 79. Hester notes that, when the interests of the speaker and the audience intersect in this manner, it becomes possible for the audience to modify the exigence because of the speaker's communication. Joel 4:1–21 presents a slightly different case since the text does not open up any doors for the implied audience to respond; YHWH's actions dominate the entire chapter.

presenting YHWH's commitment to the Judahite community and YHWH's unmistakable sovereignty over all nations.

The discussion over the nature of the implied audience in Joel 4:1–21 resonates with the progression of the exigences that drives the text's rhetorical strategies. Previous rhetorical units within Joel deal with threats directed against the Judahite community through a combination of imagery relating to locust infestations, droughts, and military invasion, culminating with the revelation that the day of YHWH is going to be unleashed against YHWH's own community (Joel 1:1–2:11). After calling for a return to YHWH (Joel 2:12–17), the exigences of the following rhetorical units reveal the ways in which YHWH chooses to act on behalf of the Judahite community through both physical and spiritual restoration (Joel 2:18–27; 3:1–5). Joel 4 focuses on the prospect of external threat to YHWH's claim over the community, articulating in significant detail that YHWH will triumph over all nations.

The text establishes the situation of the implied audience in a manner that activates the need for YHWH's intervention. In spite of the preceding promises of YHWH's presence, Joel 4:2–3 and 5–6 suggest that the nations have sold the Judahites into slavery and looted the land. Consequently, the text portrays the implied audience as weak and unable to resist the outside nations. In this state of affairs, YHWH's claim of ownership over the land and its inhabitants offers hope for the amelioration of the rhetorical situation. Joel 4:1–21 dramatically reverses the situation of the foreign nations, who go from ravaging Judah to being unable to stand against the unleashed authority of YHWH. Joel 4:1–21 thus resolves the external exigence that threatens the implied Judahite audience. This is the necessary counterpart to the concerns of previous rhetorical units. Now that the relationship between YHWH and the implied audience is restored in Joel 1–3, the text can focus on other threats.

Shifting toward external exigence and divine agency also helps shift the nature of the constraints that govern its rhetorical situation. In previous passages, constraints on the rhetorical situation include the necessity for the text to gain a hearing among the various facets of the implied audience identified in Joel 1:1–14, as well as the necessity for the audience to respond appropriately in Joel 2:12–17 in order to allow the text to transition from threat to deliverance. In Joel 4:1–21, the fact that YHWH is the primary agent means that the text can declare what is going to happen while minimizing the role of any other actors, especially those whom the text constructs as hostile to YHWH.[9] The text can declare that what YHWH commands will occur because of the authority attributed to YHWH.

---

9. Taking a broader diachronic perspective, LaRocca-Pitts argues for a progression toward divine agency in the prophetic construction of the day of YHWH. YHWH's acts become the focus, and the responses of other actors fade into insignificance (M. LaRocca-Pitts, *The Day of Yahweh as Rhetorical Strategy among the Hebrew Prophets* [Ph.D. diss., Har-

Rhetorical Strategy

The primary feature of Joel 4:1–21 is the way it extends the scope of Yhwh's sovereignty, speaking powerfully about Yhwh's coming judgment against foreign nations as a means of bringing restoration to Judah and Jerusalem. This shows a marked transition from preceding rhetorical units where the voice of the nations speak only briefly, in Joel 2:6 and 2:17.[10] Joel 4:1–21 is oriented toward the judicial genre, declaring the offenses of the nations (Joel 4:2–3, 5–6) and promising to enact judgment (Joel 4:7–8, 9–16, 19). This judicial speech, however, needs to be considered in light of the declaration of Yhwh's intentions to "restore the fortunes of Judah and Jerusalem" in Joel 4:1. The detailed discussion of the rhetorical strategies below reveals that this judicial language also provides persuasive reasons for the implied audience to have confidence in God since Yhwh removes external threats while promising restorative action.

Joel 4:1–3: Introduction of Restoration through Judgment of Foreign Nations

Joel 4:1–3 builds from the hinge of 2:18, where Yhwh transitions from destroyer to protector and provider for the Judahite community. The text establishes this shift clearly in Joel 4:1b by having Yhwh declare אָשׁוּב אֶת־שְׁבוּת 'I will restore the fortunes' of Judah and Jerusalem at this time. Variations of the phrase שׁוּב שְׁבוּת occur 27 times in the Old Testament, and although its precise origins are disputed, in its literary contexts it usually points toward a reversal of Yhwh's judgment and restoration for the Judahite community (Jer 30:3, 18; 31:23; 32:44; 33:7, 11).[11] The occurrence

vard University, 2000] 333). This trajectory certainly appears to describe aptly what occurs within the framework of Joel 1–4 since the announcements of the day of Yhwh in Joel 1:15; 2:1, and 11 lead to a call to response in Joel 2:12–17.

10. See the description of the nations trembling in Joel 2:6 as the invading horde passes by and the assertion that the Judahite community will be a laughingstock among the nations if Yhwh does not intervene in Joel 2:17.

11. Preuschen and Baumann attribute the noun שְׁבוּת to the root שָׁבָה 'to make captive', while Dietrich argues that it is derived from שׁוּב 'to turn/return'. See E. Preuschen, "Die Bedeutung von שׁוּב שְׁבוּת im Alten Testamente," *ZAW* 15 (1895) 1–74; E. Baumann, "שׁוּב שְׁבוּת: Eine exegetische Untersuchung," *ZAW* 47 (1929) 17–44; E. Dietrich, "שׁוּב שְׁבוּת: Die Endzeitliche Wiederherstellung bei den Propheten [BZAW 40; Berlin: de Gruyter, 1925] 27–28). Borger highlights the difficulty of determining the etymology of שְׁבוּת by noting the presence of *Kethiv/Qere* issues that render it almost impossible to differentiate between the two proposed roots (R. Borger, "שׁוב שבו/ית," *ZAW* 66 [1954] 315–16). In the case of Joel 4:1, if שְׁבוּת makes reference specifically to exile, then it may be possible to argue that the text has in mind the Babylonian captivity, which would lend credence to arguments for understanding the book as postexilic. Simkins, however, makes a convincing argument that the phrase in question has in view the events described in Joel 4:4–8, where Yhwh reverses the depredations of the nations against Judah. In this view, when Yhwh "restores the fortunes" of Judah and Jerusalem, these depredations cease. Further, the imagery surrounding שׁוּב שְׁבוּת may indicate that the prophet is describing a larger reversal of fortune,

of this phrase in Joel 4:1 is congruent with the understanding of reversal since this chapter eliminates the threat of invasion from enemies in the preceding chapters (Joel 1:6–7; 2:1–11) and promises inescapable divine judgment on those who plunder Judah.[12]

Joel 4:2 then states that, as an integral part of the restoration process, YHWH will claim sovereignty over the rest of humanity. YHWH acts and exercises divine agency in order to gather the nations and bring them into judgment.[13] The phrase כָּל־הַגּוֹיִם 'all nations' in this verse emphasizes the universality of this judgment, while the nations' anonymity permits the activation of this text in the context of any threat against Jerusalem.[14] The location of judgment in this passage demonstrates a rhetorical flourish. YHWH declares that he will bring the nations to the Valley of Jehoshaphat (עֵמֶק יְהוֹשָׁפָט), and there he will judge them (וְנִשְׁפַּטְתִּי). The name of the valley and the action that YHWH promises to perform both derive from the root שָׁפַט 'to judge'. Thus, the name of this valley is a pun on the activity of judging that YHWH promises to perform.

While many have searched for a physical location for this valley—typically either the Valley of Berechah where Jehoshaphat defeated a coalition of Moab, Ammon, and Edom (2 Chr 20:26) or the Kidron Valley—no conclusion has been reached. It is more fruitful to consider that the significance of the valley is symbolic rather than topographical.[15] The connection

rather than a more limited promise of return from exile (R. Simkins, *Yahweh's Activity in History and Nature in the Book of Joel* [ANETS 10; Lewiston, NY: Edwin Mellen, 1991] 225). Price aptly suggests that "the image has stretched the idiom far beyond the exile and return framework" (R. Price, *A Lexicographical Study of* glh, šbh *and* šwb *in Reference to Exile in the Tanach* (Ph.D. diss., Duke University, 1977) 122. See also Dillard, "Joel," 300.

12. J. Bracke, "*šûb šebût*: A Reappraisal," *ZAW* 97 (1985) 241.

13. De Vries, "Futurism," 262. De Vries finds contradictions between the declaration in Joel 4:1–2 that YHWH will judge the nations and the "incipient universalism" of Joel 3:1. As argued above, however, the case for universalism in Joel 3:1 is weakened by the apparent restriction of the phrase "all flesh" to the Judahite community in this instance. Consequently, there is no necessary contradiction between the promises of restoration through the outpouring of YHWH's Spirit and the divine judgment of foreign nations.

14. M. Sweeney, "The Place and Function of Joel in the Book of the Twelve," *SBL 1999: Seminar Papers* (SBLSP 38; Atlanta: Society of Biblical Literature, 1999) 586.

15. Ibid., 177. Second Chronicles 20:20–26 describes King Jehoshaphat telling the Judahites to believe in YHWH and YHWH's prophets and leading them in songs of praise as they engaged their enemies. It is interesting to note that Jehoshaphat defeats a coalition of Judah's foes when the promise of the Valley of Jehoshaphat is that all foreign nations will face divine judgment and destruction. Sweeney also correctly notes that the mention of the Valley of Jehoshaphat is not definitive in determining the historical setting of Joel (Sweeney, "Sequence and Interpretation," 53). For the identification of the Valley of Jehoshaphat with the Kidron Valley, see A. Merx, *Der Prophetie des Joel und ihrer Ausleger von den ältesten Zeiten bis zu den Reformatoren: Eine exegetisch-kritische und hermeneutisch-dogmengeschichtliche Studie* (Halle: Waisenhaus, 1879) 197–99. For the emphasis on the symbolic value of this valley, see Crenshaw, *Joel*, 175; Simkins, *Yahweh's Activity*, 226; L. Allen, *The Books of Joel, Obadiah, Jonah and Micah* (NICOT; Grand Rapids: Eerdmans, 1976) 108–9. Since the concern of my project is with the rhetorical function of the book of Joel,

to the Valley of Berechah in particular is probably allusive for Joel rather than historical. Second Chronicles 20:15 provides a prophetic message to King Jehoshaphat and the rest of Judah, telling them not to fear a forthcoming battle against numerically superior opposition because it is YHWH's battle, not theirs (לֹא לָכֶם הַמִּלְחָמָה כִּי לֵאלֹהִים 'not for you [is] the battle, but for God'). In the same way, the restoration in Joel 4:1–3 rests on YHWH; divine actions alone will restore Judah's fortunes.[16]

Further, this mention of the Valley of Jehoshaphat resonates with broader prophetic traditions of divine judgment. These traditions are evident in passages such as Isa 22:1–5; Ezek 38–39; and Zech 14, which all place YHWH's judgment in valley settings that have a great deal of symbolic significance.[17] Specifically, there may be a parallel between the Valley of Jehoshaphat and the judgment on Gog that culminates in the Valley of Hamon-Gog in Ezek 38–39.[18] Both passages use the same verb for divine judgment (וְנִשְׁפַּטְתִּי in Ezek 38:22; Joel 4:2), and the description of Gog's destruction in Ezek 38:22 includes references to blood and fire that recall the unfolding of the day of YHWH in Joel 3:3–4.[19] Ezekiel identifies Gog with the northern foe (Ezek 38:15; cf. Joel 2:20), which is a prophetic metaphor with multivalent referents.[20] Consequently, Joel is most likely appropriating the symbolic significance rather than the geographical location of the valley where YHWH enacts judgment.

Also supporting the symbolic interpretation of the Valley of Jehoshaphat is the connection between YHWH's judgment in the valley and the day of YHWH. All four valley judgment texts (Isa 22:1–5; Ezek 38–39; Joel 4; Zech 14) make at least oblique reference to the day of YHWH through various phrases associated with that day.[21] The introduction of the Valley of Jehoshaphat and the parallel "valley of decision" in Joel 4:12 effectively

---

it is more appropriate to follow this line of reasoning and concentrate on the symbolic resonances of calling for divine judgment in this particular valley.

16. J. Strazicich, *Joel's Use of Scripture and the Scripture's Use of Joel: Appropriation and Resignification in Second Temple Judaism and Early Christianity* (BIS 82; Leiden: Brill, 2007) 225.

17. A. Kapelrud, *Joel Studies* (UUÅ 4; Uppsala: Lundequist, 1948) 144–48. Kapelrud examines these passages and draws attention to what he describes as their mythological nature. He notes, however, that in all of these cases, this valley would seem to stand in proximity to Jerusalem.

18. Simkins, *Yahweh's Activity*, 226. See also the "valley of vision" in Isa 22:1 and the valley in Zech 14:4 that forms when YHWH splits the Mount of Olives when the deity fights for Jerusalem.

19. Strazicich, *Joel's Use of Scripture*, 226.

20. See the above discussion of the northern foe in the rhetorical strategy section of Joel 2:18–27.

21. Simkins, *Yahweh's Activity*, 226–27. Isaiah 22:5 refers to a 'day of panic, confusion and subjugation for YHWH God of Hosts' (יוֹם מְהוּמָה וּמְבוּסָה וּמְבוּכָה לַאדֹנָי יְהוָה צְבָאוֹת), while Ezek 39:11 looks to the destruction of God 'on that day' (בַּיּוֹם הַהוּא), and Zech 14:1 speaks of a 'day coming to YHWH' (יוֹם־בָּא לַיהוָה).

links Joel 4:1–3 with the day-of-Yнwн tradition, which is mentioned in 4:14.[22] On this occasion, the judgment that occurs on the day of Yнwн falls on the nations summoned to judgment in the appropriately named valley, which marks a significant transition from the first half of this book, where the day of Yнwн is a day of woe for the implied audience.

The latter half of Joel 4:2 and the entirety of Joel 4:3 articulate the nations' offenses, providing the judicial tone of this chapter. Joel 3:1–5 and 4:1–2a indicate that Yнwн's powerful arrival has a devastating effect on those not fortunate enough to be among the survivors (שְׂרִידִים) whom he calls. Until this point, however, the text has offered no rationale for the terrifying manifestation of Yнwн's power. Now, the latter half of Joel 4:2 continues with a wordplay on שָׁפַט, employing a verb from that root to reveal that Yнwн is stepping in to render judgment (וְנִשְׁפַּטְתִּי).

The text gives this judgment a personal flavor, employing three first-person suffixes that connect Yнwн with the Judahite community. Yнwн justifies judgment and acts on behalf of עַמִּי וְנַחֲלָתִי 'my people and my inheritance', whom these nations scattered.[23] As a further offense, they also divided אַרְצִי 'my [Yнwн's] land'. These suffixes are significant because they show Yнwн's identification with the Judahite community, which has been an important issue throughout the book. Notably, the two impassioned pleas in Joel 2:17 employ עַמֶּךָ 'your people' and נַחֲלָתְךָ 'your inheritance', respectively, to motivate Yнwн to act, while 2:18 attributes the programmatic restoration to Yнwн's zeal and pity לְעַמּוֹ 'for his people' and לְאַרְצוֹ 'for his land'.[24] Joel 4:2b builds and strengthens Yнwн's claim of ownership over the covenant community and the land. These suffixes also have the effect of continuing to answer the doubts raised in the pleas of Joel 2:17; at this point, Yнwн is clearly on the side of the Judahite community.

After establishing Yнwн's claim over the land and its people, Joel 4:2b employs an אֲשֶׁר clause to commence the actual process of judgment. The text states that these nations have scattered Yнwн's people, claimed Yнwн's land for themselves, and engaged in slave trading. The text treats the first two offenses succinctly, but it gives maximum impact to the final charge of enslavement, making three separate statements in Joel 4:3. The first statement claims that these invaders cast lots, using a verb (יַדּוּ) that occurs only on two other occasions in the Old Testament (Obad 11; Nah 3:10). This verb conjures up imagery of dividing plunder after a military

---

22. Ibid., 227.

23. G. Ogden and R. Deutsch, *Joel and Malachi: A Promise of Hope—A Call to Obedience* (ITC; Grand Rapids: Eerdmans, 1987) 41. Ogden comments on the use of וְנַחֲלָתִי, suggesting that it refers to the land that Yнwн has given to Judah, and by extension, those living in it. He notes the use of this concept in lament psalms as part of the pleas for Yнwн to intervene salvifically (Pss 28:9; 74:2; 79:1).

24. Further examples of "my/his people" occur in Joel 2:19; 2:26–27; 4:3; and 4:16, while 1:6 also refers to Yнwн's ownership of the land (אַרְצִי).

victory, a degrading fate to befall human beings.[25] The context of Obad 11 is especially appropriate since it references the actions of Edom in the wake of the fall of Jerusalem. Joel 4:3 refers to the same crime as Obad 11, but it does so in a more general context, accusing unnamed nations of engaging in this practice.[26] The text then heightens the offense in the final two statements of Joel 4:3 by revealing that these foreigners use Judahite children as a means of barter by means of a merismus in which the captors exchange the boys for the services of prostitutes and the girls for wine.[27] These offenses root Yʜᴡʜ's judgment in the guilt of the nations who have oppressed his people.

Overall, this brief subunit introduces the theme of divine judgment on the enemies of Yʜᴡʜ's covenant people that dominates the remainder of the book. Essentially, Joel 4:1–3 is a "short *résumé* of the contents of the whole oracle."[28] It refers back to preceding units by mentioning Yʜᴡʜ's restorative acts for Judah and Jerusalem, and it reasserts Yʜᴡʜ's claim to the community by calling them "my inheritance" and "my people Israel." For the most part, however, this unit looks toward a time of judgment for foreign nations. This particular unit begins to detail the offenses of the foreign nations that will lead to their punishment.

Joel 4:4–8: Judgment against Specific Nations

This subunit breaks away from Yʜᴡʜ's statement of intent to bring the nations as a whole into judgment. The emphatic adverb וְגַם introduces instead a special instance of divine judgment on three specific enemy nations—namely, Tyre, Sidon, and Philistia.[29] The genre reflected in this subunit is judicial, focusing on the crimes of these specific nations while also detailing their punishment.[30] The effect of using judicial speech in this subunit is interesting when one considers the nature of the text's audiences. Joel 4:4–8 is constructed as divine speech directed at Tyre, Sidon, and Philistia, detailing Yʜᴡʜ's grievances against them. While Yʜᴡʜ

---

25. Crenshaw, *Joel*, 176. Amos notably employs this theme in his oracle against Israel, condemning it for selling the innocent for silver and the poor in exchange for shoes (Amos 2:6).

26. Strazicich, *Joel's Use of Scripture*, 227; Sweeney, *Twelve*, 179; S. Bergler, *Joel als Schrift-interpret* (Frankfurt am Main: Peter Lang, 1988) 305–6.

27. Dillard, "Joel," 301. Dillard argues that the preposition in בַּזּוֹנָה is properly understood as a *bêt* of price or a *bêt* that introduces the object acquired. Other examples include Ps 44:13 and Amos 2:6. See also H. Wolff, *Joel and Amos* (Hermeneia; Philadelphia: Fortress, 1977) 71; B. Waltke and M. O'Connor, *An Introduction to Biblical Hebrew Syntax* (Winona Lake, IN: Eisenbrauns, 1990) 197. This is in contrast to the LXX reading ἔδωκαν τὰ παιδάρια πόρναις, which suggests that the boys were sold into prostitution.

28. Kapelrud, *Joel Studies*, 7.

29. Crenshaw, *Joel*, 178.

30. G. Kennedy, *New Testament Interpretation through Rhetorical Criticism* (Chapel Hill: University of North Carolina Press, 1984) 20. Kennedy lists defense and prosecution as the positive and negative forms of judicial rhetoric. Joel 4:4–8 appears to fit into the prosecution category rather neatly.

announces judgment, it is also helpful to consider the implied Judahite audience who hears Yʜᴡʜ's declarations. For this audience, Yʜᴡʜ's dialogue with the nations reinforces Yʜᴡʜ's commitment to act on their behalf that has been active since Joel 2:18. Thus, the judicial rhetoric of Joel 4:4–8 also strengthens the case for the implied audience to have confidence in Yʜᴡʜ.

Many have argued that Joel 4:4–8 reflects a later, redactional insertion since it appears to be more prosaic in style than other subunits in Joel 4 and because it narrows the scope from a universal condemnation of nations to focus on three of Israel and Judah's "minor" foes.[31] Wolff detects a shift in vocabulary in Joel 4:6 and 4:8, which refer to the בְּנֵי יְהוּדָה 'children of Judah' and the בְּנֵי יְרוּשָׁלִַם 'children of Jerusalem'.[32] He sets these phrases in contrast to Joel 4:2–3, in which Yʜᴡʜ expresses an explicit claim through first-person suffixes, such as עַמִּי 'my people' and נַחֲלָתִי 'my inheritance'. Further, Wolff suggests that the chain of rhetorical questions in Joel 4:4 and the increase in subordinate clauses in these verses indicate that this is a secondary piece, since these are foreign to the rest of the book.[33] This has significant ramifications for interpreting the rhetorical progression of this chapter. On the basis of arguments of this sort, some scholars even omit this passage when developing the argument of the book, opining that it is "clearly intrusive and secondary."[34]

The identification of Joel 4:4–8 as secondary, however, is disputable. Even if one accepts that Joel 4:4–8 is written in a more prosaic style, this does not necessarily indicate its secondary stature. Further, in the case of a rhetorical reading of the text for the implied audience that it constructs, it is difficult to justify omitting a passage from consideration. Ahlström shows continuity between Joel 4:4–8 and the surrounding subunits by suggesting that the mention of slave trading in Joel 4:2–3 provides a reason for Joel 4:4–8 to engage this motif.[35] This leads to a reversal in which Yʜᴡʜ decrees that the Judahites will sell the slave traders themselves into captivity. After reaching this conclusion, the text is then ready to resume a more oracular form for the remainder of the chapter.

Other unifying features include the occurrence of the key word מָכַר 'to sell' across the entirety of Joel 4:1–8 (Joel 4:3, 6, 8).[36] Further, there may be elements of a prophetic lawsuit in Joel 4:1–8 that resonate through this

---

31. Wolff, *Joel and Amos*, 74, 77–8; Crenshaw, *Joel*, 185; J. Barton, *Joel and Obadiah: A Commentary* (OTL; Louisville: Westminster John Knox, 2001).

32. Wolff, *Joel and Amos*, 74–75.

33. Ibid., 75. Of course, rhetorical questions do appear elsewhere in Joel, although they concern the character and action of Yʜᴡʜ; cf. Joel 2:11, 14, 17.

34. K. Nash, *The Palestinian Agricultural Year and the Book of Joel* (Ph.D. diss., Catholic University of America, 1989) 226.

35. G. Ahlström, *Joel and the Temple Cult of Jerusalem* (VTSup 21; Leiden: Brill, 1971) 134–35.

36. Dillard, "Joel," 303. Conversely, Wolff does note the repetition of מכר but suggests instead that it appears in order to link this redactional piece with 4:1–3 (Wolff, *Joel and Amos*, 74–75).

entire passage (cf. Isa 3:13–15; Ps 50:2–23; Hos 2:4–17; 4:1–3; Mic 6:1–5).[37] These elements include summoning the "accused" in Joel 4:1–2a, reading the accusations in 4:2b–3, asking rhetorical questions typical of lawsuit interrogations in 4:4, specifying the charges in 4:5–6, and announcing the verdict in 4:7–8.[38] Ultimately, the issue of Joel 4:4–8's "originality" will probably never be resolved, but at the very least there is warrant to conclude that this subunit adds a significant dimension to the description of YHWH's judgment. Effectively, it aims at "concretizing and specifying the vague, general assertions of the previous pericope section [*sic*]."[39]

The rhetorical purpose of this subunit is to provide a logical exposition of the claims put forward in Joel 4:1–3. Joel 4:1–3 begins from a very broad perspective, surveying the situation in order to describe in general terms the fate of those "nations" who defy YHWH and face divine judgment. Now, in Joel 4:4–8, the text adopts a more focused perspective and highlights the errors of specific nations and the punishment that YHWH will bring to bear. Interestingly, a similar juxtaposition of broad and narrow points of view occurs later on in this chapter, when Joel 4:18–21 responds to YHWH's defeat of the nations as a whole by highlighting the specific effects on Egypt and Edom. For Joel 4:4–8, the primary focus is on taking the general charges of raiding and slave trading in 4:2–3 and identifying the people responsible for these despicable activities.[40]

The nations accused in this section are Tyre, Sidon, and all the regions of Philistia. Philistia achieved notoriety in the Old Testament as the great enemy of Israel during the periods of the latter judges and early monarchy (cf. Judg 13–16; 1 Sam 4). Tyre and Sidon are portrayed as allies of David and Solomon (cf. 2 Sam 5; 1 Kgs 5), but then prophets such as Amos and Ezekiel announce doom oracles against them for their sins against YHWH (cf. Ezek 26–29; Amos 1:9–10). Interestingly, in Amos's oracles against nations, the

---

37. On the form and function of prophetic lawsuits, see K. Nielsen, *Yahweh as Prosecutor and Judge* (trans. F. Cryer; JSOTSup 9; Sheffield: JSOT Press, 1978) 74–83; J. Limburg, *The Lawsuit of God in the Eighth Century Prophets* (Ph.D. diss., Union Theological Seminary, 1969) 296–99; H. Huffmon, "The Covenant Lawsuit in the Prophets," *JBL* 78 (1959) 285–95. Laney identifies two modes of prophetic lawsuits. The first details a complaint brought by an offended party against the offender, while in the second, a third party brings the accusation on behalf of the aggrieved party (J. Laney, "The Role of the Prophet in God's Case against Israel," *BSac* 138 [1981] 313–25). This latter form may resonate with what is occurring in Joel 4, where YHWH brings an accusation against the guilty nations as part of the process of restoring Judah and Jerusalem. More recently, the validity of prophetic lawsuit as a prophetic form has been called into question. See M. De Roche, "Yahweh's *Rîb* against Israel: A Reassessment of the So-Called 'Prophetic Lawsuit' in the Pre-Exilic Prophets," *JBL* 102 (1983) 563–74; D. Daniels, "Is There a 'Prophetic Lawsuit' Genre?" *ZAW* 99 (1999) 339–60. While resolving questions of oracle form is beyond the purview of this book, the presence of unifying literary features demonstrates coherence in reading Joel 4:4–8 as an integral part of the text's rhetorical strategy.

38. Dillard, "Joel," 300–301.

39. Prinsloo, *Theology*, 110.

40. Dillard, "Joel," 303.

oracles against Philistia and the Phoenician cities of Tyre and Sidon are placed next to one another. Amos also condemns both regions for slave trading, accusing them of selling Israelite captives to Edom (Amos 1:6–10). The resonance between the Joelian and Amosian references may reveal a shared tradition of grievances against this particular coalition of enemy nations.[41]

Naming these nations is rhetorically powerful since it provides a specific way in which Yhwh is acting restoratively for the Judahite community. Joel 4:4–8 demonstrates Yhwh's authority and intention to remove enemies and guarantee security, which are welcome statements in the wake of the portended destruction in Joel 1:1–2:17. One of the suggested functions of oracles against foreign nations is to offer hope to a despairing audience that Yhwh will rescue them.[42] This function is active in Joel 4:4–8 since Yhwh promises to move against Judah's enemies to eliminate their threat. Although Tyre, Sidon, and Philistia are not mentioned in Joel 1:1–2:17, they still serve the rhetorical purpose of demonstrating Yhwh's intention to rescue the Judahite community.

The precise manner in which Joel 4:4 presents these accusations is worthy of further consideration. Joel 4:4 makes Tyre, Sidon, and the regions of Philistia the targets of two successive rhetorical questions that Yhwh asks.[43] The first question is general in nature and asks rather obscurely, "What are you to me?" The implied answer to this question is that they are of little or no account in the eyes of Yhwh. The second question brings the meaning into closer view. It asks הַגְּמוּל אַתֶּם מְשַׁלְּמִים עָלָי 'are you recompensing me?' The idea behind this question is to inquire whether Tyre, Sidon, and Philistia believe that they have a legitimate case against Yhwh and are attacking Judah out of a sense of aggrieved justice.

The first word of the second rhetorical question is גְּמוּל 'recompense', which is key to understanding the rhetorical purpose of Joel 4:4. It occurs three times within this verse, first in this rhetorical question and then twice more in Yhwh's answer. This repetition suggests that Yhwh's judgment against these nations reflects their guilt.[44] Yhwh's use of הַגְּמוּל subverts the argument of the nations since it is Yhwh who can legitamely repay them for their actions against Yhwh's people. Yhwh's response makes it evident that these nations will reap their just rewards from him, not the other way around.

---

41. Another perspective comes from Sweeney, who argues that Joel's propensity to re-work material from Obadiah (which condemns Edom) led him to Amos's condemnations of nations who sold captives to Edom. See Sweeney, *Twelve*, 178.

42. Raabe, "Why Prophetic Oracles?" 249. Other functions of these oracles that Raabe lists are: (1) warnings against foreign alliances, (2) warnings against desiring the nations' gods, (3) necessary background for indictments directed against Israel and Judah.

43. Allen, *Joel*, 111. Allen uses these rhetorical questions to suggest that Yhwh is adopting the role of plaintiff in a lawsuit before acting as judge and executing the divinely ordained punishment.

44. Crenshaw, *Joel*, 179.

The crimes that these nations commit extend beyond their forays into the slave trade. The first half of Joel 4:5 indicates that they have aggrieved Yhwh by taking treasure to adorn their palaces or temples.[45] The repeated use of the first-person pronominal suffix in this verse (כַּסְפִּי וּזְהָבִי 'my silver and my gold') emphasizes Yhwh's claim of ownership over these items.[46] The second half of Joel 4:5 is a parallel that uses the relatively rare word מַחְמַד as a synonym for כֶּסֶף and זָהָב (cf. 1 Kgs 20:6; 2 Chr 36:19; Isa 64:10; Ezek 24:21). This is a more general term that refers to precious or valued items. Again, this word possesses the first-person singular suffix, emphasizing Yhwh's ownership of these items.

Joel 4:6 brings the slave trade fully into view and accuses the guilty nations of taking the children of Judah and Jerusalem into captivity and selling them to a group called the בְּנֵי הַיְּוָנִים 'children of Javan', whom most commentators identify as Ionians or Greeks.[47] Interestingly, Ezek 27:13 also mentions this people-group in an oracle against Tyre and describes them as exchanging slaves for Tyre's merchandise, which echoes the concerns of Joel 4:6 (cf. Zech 9:1–13).[48] Joel 4:6 fronts the grammatical objects (וּבְנֵי יְהוּדָה וּבְנֵי יְרוּשָׁלַ͏ִם 'children of Judah and children of Jerusalem'), emphasizing the captured peoples' identity. A subordinate clause introduced by לְמַעַן follows, stating that these nations purport to send their captives away from their land. This verse also contains two third-person plural suffixes, on הַרְחִיקָם 'sending them afar' and גְּבוּלָם 'their borders'—'them' and 'their' referring to the Judahite community.[49] The statement that the captors will send the "children of Judah" outside their land sets up the response of Yhwh that follows. Yhwh's restoration is first to return them home, then to mete out judgment on their former captors.

Joel 4:7–8 announces the verdict on these nations for their crimes. Just as Joel 4:4–6 identifies the offenses of the nations as crimes against Yhwh,

---

45. The noun הֵיכָל can refer to both temples (1 Sam 1:9; 2 Kgs 18:16) and palaces (1 Kgs 21:1; 2 Kgs 20:18; Ps 45:9; Dan 1:4). This passage does not provide any explicit context for specifying one location over another. Crenshaw suggests that 'palaces' makes more sense because one would probably expect a reference to foreign gods if a religious meaning were in view (ibid., 181). In any event, the basic idea that these nations are guilty of plundering what is Yhwh's for their own display is evident.

46. Ibid. The claim in this verse extends beyond the treasures found in the temple, which the Babylonians captured. In this case, the silver and gold probably refer to the plunder and spoil of raiding, since there is no suggestion that a Philistine-Phoenician alliance ever looted the Jerusalem temple. See Barton, *Joel*, 102.

47. Crenshaw, *Joel*, 182; Barton, *Joel*, 101. References to Greeks are infrequent in the Old Testament, but they do appear in several other prophetic passages (cf. Isa 66:19; Dan 8:21; 10:20; 11:2; Zech 9:13).

48. Zechariah 9:1–13 also shows a progression from Tyre and Sidon to the Philistine cities in its portrayal of the march of the divine warrior. This passage also mentions בְּנֵי הַיְּוָנִים, with the indication that Yhwh is going to stir up the Judahites to fight against them.

49. Crenshaw, *Joel*, 182. Demoting the Judahite community to the status of grammatical objects may evidence their change in status from owning property to becoming property.

so these final two verses declare that YHWH will enact punishment.[50] YHWH first promises to restore the Judahite community to their homeland before describing divine retribution against the guilty nations. The key word גְּמוּל occurs for the fourth and final time in Joel 4:7, this time with the second-person masculine-plural pronoun suffixed to it (גְּמֻלְכֶם). This again emphasizes that it is YHWH's גְּמוּל against these nations that carries the day, not the גְּמוּל that these nations claim to have against YHWH. Joel 4:4–8 thus dramatically employs the concept of *lex talionis*: the punishment for selling YHWH's people into slavery is for YHWH to sell the offending nations into slavery. These nations receive a judgment identical to their offense against YHWH and the Judahite community, which is "one of the clearest examples of poetic justice in the prophets."[51]

The use of geographical locations in Joel 4:7–8 deepens the picture of poetic justice. The response to the raiding and enslaving activities of the "seaboard coalition" of Philistia, Tyre, and Sidon, who sell the Judahites into slavery across the sea to the northwest is the promise that the Judahites will sell them into slavery to the Sabeans, who control the trade routes to the southeast. Consequently, those who sell the Judahites into slavery will themselves go into slavery in a region that is as alien as conceivable (Gen 10:7; 1 Chr 1:9; Ps 72:10; Isa 43:3).[52] The Sabeans also probably represent a region that is the farthest imaginable distance from the text's implied audience, thus indicating the complete devastation and dislocation that YHWH

---

50. Ogden, *Promise of Hope*, 43–44. Ogden rightly notes that YHWH is the primary actor in this dialogue with the nations; YHWH alone is the one who will correct injustice. The Judahite community whom these nations have wronged are called implicitly to subordinate their own potential desires for retribution to the divine promise of retribution.

51. P. Miller, *Sin and Judgment in the Prophets: A Stylistic and Theological Analysis* (SBLMS 27; Chico, CA: Scholars Press, 1982) 76, 122–32. Miller places Joel 4:4–8 in context with other passages that emphasize the correspondence between the offense and the divinely prescribed punishment (cf. Isa 3:9b–11; Jer 50:16; Hos 8:7; Obad 15–16). Lichtenstein details examples of poetic justice principally in wisdom literature and psalms (Pss 7:16; 35:8; 57:7; Prov 28:10; Qoh 10:8) but also considers biblical narrative, notably, Haman's hanging on his own gallows (Esth 7:10). Lichtenstein uses the same terminology as Miller, stating that "divine retribution often exhibits a measure for measure correspondence between a crime and its punishment" (M. Lichtenstein, "The Poetry of Poetic Justice: A Comparative Study in Biblical Imagery," *JANESCU* 5 (1973) 255–65. This accurately reflects the intention of Joel 4:4–8. Bovati stresses the potential for positive outcome for the innocent party when divinely ordained retribution occurs, as in Joel 4:4–8 (P. Bovati, *Re-establishing Justice: Legal Terms, Concepts and Procedures in the Hebrew Bible* [trans. M. Smith; JSOTSup 105; Sheffield: Sheffield Academic Press, 1994] 376–80).

52. J. Nogalski, *Redactional Processes in the Book of the Twelve* (BZAW 218; Berlin: de Gruyter, 1993) 29; W. Müller, "Seba," *ABD* 5:1064. There is also a text-critical issue here where the LXX reads εἰς αἰχμαλωσίαν 'into captivity'. Dillard suggests that the retroversion for this reading would be לַשְּׁבִי or לַשְּׁבוּת. Context probably favors the Masoretic reading since naming a specific nation at this point would complete the parallel with Joel 4:6, which mentions the nation to whom the Judahites were sold (Dillard, "Joel," 304).

promises to bring on Judah's enemies.[53] The text describes the Sabeans as a גּוֹי רָחוֹק 'far-off nation', which supports idea that the text imagines the greatest possible dislocation for YHWH's enemies.

This subunit concludes with the declaration כִּי יְהוָה דִּבֵּר 'for YHWH has spoken'. This is the second of only two oracular formulas that Joel employs (cf. Joel 2:12). This formula authenticates divine address and typically concludes a speech from YHWH (cf. 1 Kgs 14:11; Isa 1:2; 22:25; 24:3; 25:8; Jer 13:16; Obad 18).[54] The presence of this formula adds more weight to the judgments pronounced against these "guilty" nations by stating incontrovertibly that YHWH has declared their fate. This formula differs from the remainder of Joel 4:4–8 by shifting from a first-person to third-person depiction of YHWH. At the climax of the subunit, the text provides a prophetic declaration that YHWH has spoken. This shift effectively emphasizes the finality of YHWH's judgment.

Overall, Joel 4:4–8 provides an exposition of the declarations expressed in 4:1–3. These verses highlight the offenses of three specific nations and indicate what YHWH will do in response. YHWH's claim to be able to judge these nations and the artful fashion in which the text constructs the punishment provides the implied audience with reason for hope. As the implied audience hears the dialogue between YHWH and the nations, it receives assurance that YHWH is acting on its behalf.

Joel 4:9–17: Judgment against the Nations in General

Joel 4:9–17 continues to describe YHWH's actions and their repercussions for the nations who set themselves in opposition. Joel 4:9–17 looks back to 4:1–3 and widens the perspective from the focus that is on Tyre, Sidon, and Philistia in 4:4–8. Joel 4:9–17 resumes the process of judging the "nations" in general. This subunit commences with a lengthy series of imperatives directed at the nations, commanding them to come up against YHWH and test their strength. In this way, Joel 4:9–17 is the direct counterpart to the indirect summons offered in 4:1–3. Joel 4:1–3 details YHWH's intention to judge but does not specifically begin the process. Joel 4:9–17 actualizes the declarations of 4:1–3 by explicitly summoning the nations and unleashing the day of YHWH.

The process of bringing judgment on the nations commences in Joel 4:9 with a string of four imperative phrases. The identity of the one issuing these imperatives is not readily apparent. Joel 4:4–8 concludes with the declaration that YHWH has spoken, perhaps laying the foundation for a

---

53. Sweeney, *Twelve*, 180.

54. Crenshaw, *Joel*, 184. Interestingly, this formula is used both to introduce and to conclude prophetic oracles, even within the same prophetic book. It occurs in Isa 1:2 to bolster the prophet's initial attempt to gain an audience, while also occurring in Isa 22:25 to bring an oracle of judgment to an emphatic conclusion.

change of implied speaker in the following verse.[55] Sweeney argues that the prophet is the implied speaker, but he intersperses first-person statements from YHWH to add further weight to the claims of the text (cf. 4:12, 17, 21a).[56] The appeal for YHWH to bring down the heavenly host in Joel 4:11 may support this position. On the other hand, Prinsloo suggests that YHWH resumes the role as speaker, based on the first-person verb in 4:12 (אָשֵׁב 'I will return').[57] This confusion renders it difficult to distinguish the implied speaker in all cases. The text, however, portrays the prophet as a divine herald who is issuing imperatives that will be carried out. Consequently, the specific identity of the implied speaker in this section is not critical to understanding the text's persuasive strategies.

The first three imperative phrases consist of only two or three words, creating a sharp, staccato rhythm that emphasizes the urgency to respond to these commands.[58] This fits well with the intensity of the subject matter and the gravity of the conflict that the words presage. The first command is קִרְאוּ 'proclaim' what follows among the nations. The direct object of the command to proclaim is זֹאת 'this', which in this case anticipates what follows, rather than looking back to previous statements.[59] This first command also identifies the recipients of the following commands; they target the collection of unnamed "nations." In Joel 4:2, the text portrays YHWH as declaring the divine intention to gather the nations in order to judge them. The first imperative of Joel 4:9 begins to actualize the process of judgment.

On the way to issuing final judgment, however, the text takes an interesting rhetorical twist. While it preserves the judicial sense of this chapter by declaring YHWH's intention to judge the nations and announcing the day of YHWH, it presents an intermediate step that calls the nations to a last-ditch attempt to resist their inevitable fate. The imperatives that follow the initial command for prophetic proclamation in Joel 4:9 command the nations to prepare for war, ostensibly offering these nations the opportunity to resist YHWH. In a prophetic "call to war," there are typically three aspects: (1) statements about the call to arms and the army's advance; (2) statements about the preparation of weapons; and (3) statements about the war itself (cf. Jer 6:4–6; 46:3–4; 50:14–15, 16, 21, 26–27, 29; Hos 5:8; Mic 4:13; Obad 1).[60] As the following analysis demonstrates, Joel 4:9–12

---

55. E. Wendland, *Prophetic Rhetoric: Case Studies in Text Analysis and Translation* (Longwood, FL: Xulon, 2009) 26.

56. Sweeney, *Twelve*, 181. Sweeney considers Joel 4:9–21 to be one discrete unit of which the prophet is the implied speaker. His division of the text requires reading over what appears to be an apparent introductory formula in Joel 4:18 (וְהָיָה בַיּוֹם הַהוּא).

57. Prinsloo, *Theology*, 97.

58. Dillard, "Joel," 306.

59. Crenshaw, *Joel*, 187.

60. Simkins, *Yahweh's Activity*, 231. See also R. Bach, *Die Aufforderungen zur Flucht und zum Kampf im Alttestamentlichen Prophetenspruch* (Neukirchen-Vluyn: Neukirchener Berlag, 1962) 62–72.

contains phrases that admirably fit the first two categories, but the third is notably absent.

The reason for the absence of statements concerning the conflict itself resides in the text's understanding of the futility of opposing YHWH. The futility of the nations' assembly and march against YHWH is inevitable. It does not warrant further description that might suggest that they could successfully resist their fate. Despite YHWH's assured victory, however, the imperative phrases commanding the nations to assemble against YHWH create a rhetoric of delay reminiscent of Joel 1:2–3. The delay that Joel 4:9–12 creates before the text unleashes divine judgment in 4:13 heightens the nations' implied sense of hubris since they respond to YHWH's summons by preparing to take part in a battle where the result is foreordained.

The second imperative phrase in Joel 4:9 commences the "call to arms" and draws upon the prophetic summons to battle which is one part of the imagery derived from the realm of holy war.[61] The nations are commanded

---

61. There is a great deal of literature on the concept of holy war in the Old Testament. Von Rad is credited with the seminal study on the motif, in which he delineates the elements of holy war as: (1) mustering by trumpet blast, (2) gathering the camp to be consecrated as the people of YHWH, (3) offering sacrifices and receiving a divine oracle of victory, (4) YHWH leading the way and engaging the enemy, (5) Israel remembering not to fear but to trust YHWH, (6) war cry and divine terror overtaking the enemy, (7) devoting the spoils to YHWH, and (8) the warriors returning home to their tents. Consequently, von Rad conceives "holy war as an eminently cultic undertaking—that is, prescribed and sanctioned by fixed, traditional, sacred rites and observances" (G. von Rad, *Holy War in Ancient Israel* [trans. B. Ollenburger; Grand Rapids: Eerdmans, 1991] 41–51). Another contributor to the discussion is Patrick Miller, who argues for resonance between the mythic elements of YHWH's battles found in poetic literature (Exod 15; Judg 5) and the historically oriented accounts of YHWH's defeating Israel's enemies. Miller also helpfully describes three theological dimensions that holy war literature engages: (1) salvation, which is where YHWH delivers Israel from its enemies; (2) judgment, which is where YHWH fights against Israel as the price for disobedience; (3) kingship, which is where YHWH supports claims of wideranging divine dominion through defeating Israel's foes (P. Miller, *The Divine Warrior in Early Israel* [HSM 5; Cambridge: Harvard University Press, 1973] 161–62, 173–75). See also F. Cross, "The Divine Warrior in Israel's Early Cult," in *Biblical Motifs: Origins and Transformations* (ed. A. Altmann; Cambridge: Harvard University Press, 1966) 11–30; T. Longman III and D. Reid, *God Is a Warrior* (SOTBT; Grand Rapids: Zondervan, 1995) 31–88. Sherlock traces the theme of holy war through both testaments and considers its appearance in Joel as evidence of tension juxtaposed between ideas of universal salvation and universal cataclysm (C. Sherlock, *The God Who Fights: The War Tradition in Holy Scripture* [Rutherford Studies in Contemporary Theology 6; Lewiston, NY: Edwin Mellen, 1993] 201–21). Kang engages in a comparative analysis with other ancient Near Eastern cultures that finds parallels between the exaltation of YHWH as the divine warrior over other deities and suggests that divine warrior literature seems to appear at the time of a nation's ascendancy (S. Kang, *Divine War in the Old Testament and in the Ancient Near East* [BZAW 177; Berlin: de Gruyter, 1989] 223–24). Lind roots the idea of holy war in the ancient poem of Exod 15, where YHWH alone saves Israel. Israel's role was to believe and await deliverance. He argues that this perspective belongs to the earliest strata of the Old Testament and is not a later theological interpolation. Lind also finds the same process at work in Judg 5, where the Israelite militia does not adopt a cooperative role until after YHWH delivers the decisive

קַדְּשׁוּ מִלְחָמָה 'sanctify a battle'. This same imperative occurs in Joel 1:14 and 2:15–16, which commands the covenant community to sanctify a fast. The connection between Joel 4:9 and 2:15–16 is especially notable since both passages contain the dual imperatives קִרְאוּ 'call' and קַדְּשׁוּ 'sanctify'. The two imperatives appear in opposite order in Joel 4:9, which may reflect the opposing viewpoints that the two passages take concerning YHWH.[62] The purpose of sanctifying a fast for YHWH's community in Joel 2:15–16 is to entreat YHWH to respond redemptively in the midst of desperate circumstances. In contrast, the nations are called to sanctify a battle in Joel 4:9, demonstrating their opposition to YHWH. This command presupposes a holy war setting in which YHWH fights, and a priest sanctifies an army (not necessarily Israelite) to act as YHWH's agents (cf. Deut 20:1–20; Isa 13:2–3; Jer 6:4; 22:7; 51:27–28; Hos 5:8; Mic 4:13; Obad 1).[63] In this context, however, YHWH issues the command to the opposing forces to sanctify this battle; they are to come and meet YHWH in a conflict in which they will be defeated.

The remaining two imperative phrases of Joel 4:9 continue to describe the call to arms. The first imperative phrase is the two-word command הָעִירוּ הַגִּבּוֹרִים 'rouse the warriors'. The imperative הָעִירוּ indicates that the warriors will work themselves into a state of excitement and battle lust in preparation for the conflict.[64] The final imperative phrase is longer and begins with the two jussives יִגְּשׁוּ יַעֲלוּ 'let them draw near, let them go up' directed at the warriors. The stark nature of these jussive commands without even an interlinking *waw* suggests a rapidly issued series of commands as the time for battle looms.[65] The subject of these jussives suggests a picture of hurried and harried mobilization. The subject is כֹּל אַנְשֵׁי הַמִּלְחָמָה 'all men of battle', which parallels the הַגִּבּוֹרִים in the previous phrase. It further stresses the commitment required since everyone capable of wielding a weapon is called to advance against YHWH.

Joel 4:10 continues to describe this subunit's call to total war while also providing a fascinating example of the prophet's rhetorical technique. It

---

blow (M. Lind, *Monotheism, Power, Justice: Collected Old Testament Essays* [Text-Reader Series 3; Elkhart, IN: Institute of Mennonite Studies, 1990] 189–90; idem, *Yahweh Is a Warrior* [Scottdale, PA: Herald, 1980] 46–54, 169–74). This resonates with the events of Joel 4 where the prophet summons the nations to battle against YHWH, then summons YHWH's host in response (see the discussion of 4:11b). In Joel 4, the Judahite community does not participate in the "battle" that achieves restoration; YHWH alone summons the nations to the Valley of Jehoshaphat, where they will face their inescapable fate.

62. Wendland, *Prophetic Rhetoric*, 26; Strazicich, *Joel's Use of Scripture*, 232. Wendland correctly identifies a strong sense of irony in the imagery of nations' being consecrated for a futile fight against YHWH.

63. Sweeney, *Twelve*, 181.

64. Crenshaw, *Joel*, 187. This is one of the few occasions on which the verb רוע is used transitively (cf. Jer 51:11; Hag 1:14), calling on YHWH's heralds to stir the nations to warlike activity.

65. Ibid., 188.

continues the series of imperatives calling the nations fully to assume a warlike posture. In the first line of this verse, the prophet commands the nations to "beat your plowshares into swords, your pruning hooks into spears," which effectively commands YHWH's enemies to mobilize completely and to turn even agricultural implements into weapons of war.[66] The following phrase, "Let the weak say, 'I am strong,'" conjures up images of non-warriors' being drafted into military service, so that the nations coming to YHWH will confront the highest possible complement of soldiers and weaponry.[67] This final phrase contains one of only four appearances of the first-person-singular pronoun אֲנִי in Joel. Interestingly, YHWH is the pronoun's antecedent in the other three cases (twice in Joel 2:27 and once in 4:17). The weakling's use of a pronoun otherwise reserved for YHWH in the book of Joel intensifies the irony of the nations' challenge to YHWH in Joel 4:9–17.[68]

One of the most significant features of Joel 4:10 is that it explicitly invokes and reverses a prophecy found in both Isaiah and Micah. Isaiah 2:2–4 and Mic 4:1–4 both envision an idyllic time when weapons of war will become agricultural implements. The occurrence of this idea in two different prophetic books suggests that it was a well-known prophecy, and there is potential to achieve a significant rhetorical impact by inverting it.[69] A preponderance of shared vocabulary words makes apparent the connection between these three passages. The same verb כָּתַת 'beat' governs the actions of all three passages, and all of the passages employ the same words for the agricultural implements (אֵת for 'plowshares', מַזְמֵרָה for 'pruning hooks') and for swords (חֶרֶב).[70] The words for the other weapon differ (רְמָחִים in Joel and חֲנִית in Isaiah/Micah), but these words are synonymous, both indicating spears.[71] This degree of lexical and syntactic recursion certainly

---

66. C. Mariottini, "Joel 3:10 [H 4:10] 'Beat Your Plowshares into Swords,'" *Perspectives in Religious Studies* 14 (1987) 127–29.

67. Ibid., 129–30. The idea of turning farm implements into weaponry suggests a context of climactic battle, when there is no longer any need for agricultural tools. All that matters is to assemble as powerful a military force as humanly possible.

68. Crenshaw, *Joel*, 189.

69. Sweeney, *Twelve*, 182. Commentators are nearly universal in claiming that Joel is reworking the Isaianic material. Allen views it as an example of the way Joel echoes older Scripture, sometimes to reverse it (Allen, *Joel*, 115). Wendland cites this among other examples of Joel's use of Scripture to argue for a postexilic date for Joel's prophecy (Wendland, *Discourse Analysis*, 247).

70. Crenshaw, *Joel*, 188.

71. R. Coggins, "Interbiblical Quotations in Joel," in *After the Exile: Essays in Honour of Rex Mason* (ed. J. Barton and D. Reimer; Macon, GA: Mercer University Press, 1996) 78. Coggins also suggests that perhaps this change of vocabulary is intended to be a conscious marker of the reversal of meaning in Joel 4:10 (R. Coggins, *Joel and Amos* [NCBC; Sheffield: Sheffield Academic Press, 2000] 56–57). While this cannot be proved conclusively, the shift in vocabulary does at least call attention to the differences between these passages.

shows that Joel is deliberately invoking and inverting the prophecy found in Isaiah and Micah.

The rhetorical effect of this sort of inversion is a question worthy of consideration. Wendland refers to Joel 4:10 as an example of *defamiliarization*, which he defines as an intertextual recursion that reverses the connotation or expectation of the original passage.[72] It is an ironic parody of the expected prophetic word presented with the same form but invoking the opposite meaning. Whereas Isaiah and Micah envision an idyllic future in which the nations submit to Yhwh's authority and have no need of weaponry, Joel's inversion indicates that Yhwh will need to break the power of the nations militarily. Joel 4:10 also inverts the idea of a pilgrimage in which foreign nations come to Zion in order to submit to Yhwh: whereas the Isaianic promise of peace takes place as foreign nations come to "the mountain of Yhwh" in order to be instructed (Isa 2:3), Joel's summons to the nations calls them to the Valley of Jehoshaphat to receive final judgment (cf. Zech 8:21–23).[73]

The rhetorical effect of these calls to full-fledged armed resistance in Joel 4:10 is to make a mockery of the nations that trust in their military strength to withstand Yhwh.[74] The repetition of the commands to the nations to gather their military strength is ironic given its ultimate futility. Joel 4:10 thus asserts the supremacy of Yhwh to the utmost degree since Joel inverts a prophecy of future peace and uses this inversion to command the nations to "do their worst," even though it will have no impact on their eventual fate. The summons to total war contained in this verse is in effect a summons to final judgment since the nations will not be able to stand against Yhwh's unleashed power.[75]

Joel 4:11 continues the string of imperative clauses, but the interpretation of this verse is the subject of significant debate. Joel 4:11a clearly is congruent with Joel 4:9–10 since this half-verse continues to issue commands to the nations who challenge Yhwh. There are two imperatives at the beginning of Joel 4:11. While the second (וּבֹ֔אוּ 'and come') is straightforward, the first (עֻ֣שׁוּ) is difficult since it is a hapax legomenon. Scholars have put forward multiple proposals to resolve the issue of its meaning, including different emendations and attempts to follow readings from vari-

---

72. Wendland, *Discourse Analysis*, 251.

73. Strazicich, *Joel's Use of Scripture*, 233; B. Zapff, "The Perspective on the Nations in the Book of Micah as a 'Systematization' of the Nations' Role in Joel, Jonah and Nahum? Reflections on a Context-Oriented Exegesis in the Book of the Twelve," in *Thematic Threads in the Book of the Twelve* (ed. P. Redditt and A. Schart; BZAW 325; Berlin: de Gruyter, 2003) 308–10.

74. H. Wolff, "Swords into Plowshares: Misuse of a Word of Prophecy," *Currents in Theology and Mission* 12 (1985) 134. "The phrase 'plowshares into swords' makes a blunt mockery of the world powers, who think that by completely arming themselves with much effort they will have power and superiority over the people of God."

75. Prinsloo, *Theology*, 112.

ous versions, but none has gained significant traction.[76] Its proximity to וּבֹאוּ suggests that it is a parallel command, but even this is conjecture.

The addressee of the imperatives in Joel 4:11 is the collection of nations whom Joel 4:9–17 calls to war against YHWH. The text here emphasizes the broad scope of this collection since the recipients of the commands in this half-verse are כָל־הַגּוֹיִם מִסָּבִיב 'all nations from around'. The scope of the appeal resonates and reinterprets the call for the Judahite community to come before YHWH in Joel 2:15–17. In that case, the text commands the entire community to gather before YHWH by using the merismus of the very young and the very old and the image of the bride and bridegroom leaving their chamber as statements of the commitment required. Joel 4:9–11 now appropriates the command for a full gathering through its call for the nations fully to mobilize by reinterpreting Isaianic prophecy and appealing to the "weaklings" to arm themselves to march against YHWH.[77] Whereas the call for the entire Judahite community to gather before YHWH ultimately leads to its salvation, this call for the nations to mobilize themselves fully only sets the stage for their imminent destruction.

The remaining clause in Joel 4:11a (וְנִקְבְּצוּ שָׁמָּה) is also the subject of some confusion. First, identifying וְנִקְבְּצוּ שָׁמָּה 'and gather there' as a clause requires the interpreter to ignore the Masoretic accentuation, in which an *athnach* has been placed under the verb וְנִקְבְּצוּ. This would indicate that שָׁמָּה is the first word of Joel 4:11b.[78] In contrast, the LXX reads συνάχθητε ἐκεῖ, suggesting that וְנִקְבְּצוּ שָׁמָּה is a distinct clause.[79] This issue defies conclusive resolution, but reading וְנִקְבְּצוּ שָׁמָּה is preferable since it provides an object for the verb and sets apart the plea to YHWH (הַנְחַת יְהוָה גִּבּוֹרֶיךָ) 'bring down,

---

76. BHS proposes either עוֹרוּ 'rouse yourselves' or חוּשׁוּ 'hurry', although there is no versional support. Crenshaw tentatively supports the latter proposal "on the basis of context and the remote possibility of an aural mistake by a scribe" (ח for ע), while Simkins considers it irresolvable and leaves it untranslated (Crenshaw, *Joel*, 189; Simkins, *Yahweh's Activity*, 229). The versions do not offer any greater clarity. The LXX instead reads συνάχθητε, which means 'to gather', from which Wolff conjectures a Vorlage of נרעו (Wolff, *Joel and Amos*, 72). However, this would be a rare retroversion for συνάθροιζειν, which typically translates the Niphal of קבץ. The Syr ('tknšw) and Tg. J. (יתכנשון) follow the lead of the LXX. The Vulgate reads *erumpite* 'to break forth', which may either mean that it is reading from a different Vorlage or that it is trying to make sense of the MT as it stands.

77. F. Deist, "Parallels and Reinterpretation in the Book of Joel: A Theology of *Yom Yahweh*?" in *Text and Context: Old Testament and Semitic Studies for F. C. Fensham* (ed. W. Claasen; JSOTSup 48; Sheffield: Sheffield Academic Press, 1988) 72. Deist draws a broader connection between Joel 2:1–17 and 4:9–17, arguing that the framework of total war informs both passages. This is not entirely accurate since the thrust of the military imagery in Joel 2:1–11 is that the approaching invader is unstoppable. The point of the "mobilization" of the entire Judahite community in Joel 2:15–17 is to call on YHWH to intercede on their behalf; they do not mobilize to engage in military activities; instead, the text calls for them to commit fully to imploring YHWH to fight their battle.

78. See Sweeney, *Twelve*, 182, for an example of an interpreter who follows the Masoretic punctuation.

79. Dillard, "Joel," 306.

O Yʜᴡʜ, your warriors') that Joel 4:11b comprises. Since Joel 4:11a commenced with imperative forms, it is seems reasonable to suggest that Joel 4:11b mirrors that structure.

Second, the verb וְנִקְבָּצוּ is in the affix form, where context suggests an imperative to fit with the imperatives that began Joel 4:11.[80] Wolff and Simkins follow the lead of the LXX (συνάχθητε) and replace וְנִקְבָּצוּ with the imperative וְהִקָּבְצוּ in order to preserve syntactical continuity, while Allen claims that it could be an obscure form of the imperative.[81] Crenshaw refers to this verb as a Niphal jussive without explaining how this form could represent a jussive. He does capture the essential purpose of this clause, however, noting that it "indicates the goal and result of the previous two imperatives."[82] Consequently, it may be preferable to read this as a result clause, indicating that the nations will heed the commands to assemble that are indicated by the first two imperatives. They will gather after assembling their full force, as indicated in Joel 4:10, and meet their fate. Ultimately, the purpose of Joel 4:11a is to move the scene toward the time and place of Yʜᴡʜ's final judgment. Yʜᴡʜ instructs the nations to move toward the place of judgment.

Joel 4:11b is also difficult to interpret since it breaks away from the string of imperatives commanding the nations to assemble and prepare for battle. Instead, 4:11b offers up what is most likely a vocative plea הַנְחַת יְהוָה גִּבּוֹרֶיךָ. This apparent lack of continuity with the surrounding text puzzles many interpreters, who seek alternative explanations. The LXX reading of ὁ πραΰς ἔστω μαχητής 'let the meek become a warrior' echoes the sentiments expressed in the preceding verse.[83] This possibility, however, is unlikely since πραΰς translates עָנִי in its other occurrences in the LXX, meaning that in this instance it was probably guessing at how to handle a difficult text.[84] Wolff and Simkins prefer a reading based on the Syriac and targum, which would reflect a Vorlage of ויחת יהוה גבורין, where the verb ויחת is a Hiphil jussive form of חתת 'to shatter'.[85] As a result, this final phrase expresses the prophet's desire for Yʜᴡʜ to defeat the nations' warriors.

One defense of the Masoretic Text is to suggest that, amidst this flurry of summons to the nations, the prophet (not unreasonably) calls for Yʜᴡʜ's own army to assemble in opposition, because the text is constructing a

---

80. Coggins, *Joel*, 59; Crenshaw, *Joel*, 189.

81. Wolff, *Joel and Amos*, 72; Simkins, *Yahweh's Activity*, 229; Allen, *Joel*, 107. Allen bases this proposal on a tentative suggestion in Gesenius's grammar, which cites this verb as a possible example of stress-shifting in the Niphal conjugation (GKC 139). It claims that this would result in the "rejection" of the initial ה that would signal the imperative tense.

82. Crenshaw, *Joel*, 189.

83. D. Stuart, *Hosea–Jonah* (WBC 31; Waco, TX: Word, 1987) 265.

84. E. Hatch and H. Redpath, *A Concordance to the Septuagint and the Other Greek Versions of the Old Testament (Including the Apocryphal books)* (Oxford: Clarendon, 1897) 1201.

85. Wolff, *Joel*, 73; Simkins, *Yahweh's Activity*, 229.

judgment scene (cf. Isa 13:1–5; Jer 50:14–16, 21).[86] Dillard helpfully cites Zech 3:5 as an example of a brief prayer from the prophet interrupting a prophetic discourse. Thus, although the Syriac/targumic reading may seem to fit better in the context, the Masoretic reading is still comprehensible.

Rhetorically, this prophetic interjection offers a poignant counterpoint to the preceding imperatives of Joel 4:9–11a. The text places in the mouth of the prophet an "emotive, exclamatory plea to God for immediate judicial and punitive action."[87] While Joel 4:9–11a commands the nations to assemble and gird for battle, the interjection in Joel 4:11b offers a sharp reminder that this mobilization will meet powerful resistance.[88] The interplay of addressees is fascinating. The nations, to whom the text directs the summons in Joel 4:9–11a, now hear a prophetic plea for YHWH to intervene that seals their fate. The implied Judahite audience hears this as an oracle of salvation since they know that the summons to the nations will encounter a response from YHWH. Thus, even when the text is in the midst of summoning the nations, it indicates to the implied audience that the people ought to trust in YHWH.

The appeal in Joel 4:11b also expresses symmetry with the following verse in its calls for the divine warriors to descend to meet the nations. Subsequently, Joel 4:12 calls the nations to ascend (וְיַעֲלוּ) to face YHWH and the heavenly host.[89] The nations go up only to encounter YHWH and the heavenly host coming down to meet them. Essentially, Joel 4:11b heightens the tension by inverting the text's point of view and giving the reader a view of the other side of the story; the nations assemble in full force, but this verse also anticipates the divine response.

---

86. Dillard, "Joel," 306–7. In a diachronic study of what he terms the "war oracle," Christensen views the prophetic use of a metaphorical summons to battle as the development of an ancient form in which a charismatic figure would summon the nation to engage in warfare to preserve its existence (cf. Exod 17:9; Num 21:34, 31:3–4; Josh 3:5; 1 Sam 11:7). Essentially, "the war oracle as tactical element in military strategy was transformed into the literary mode of a prophetic judgment speech against both military foes and the nations of Israel" (D. Christensen, *Transformations of the War Oracle in Old Testament Prophecy: Studies in Oracles against the Nations* [HDR 3; Missoula, MT: Scholars Press, 1975] 47, 282–83). Christensen's study does not include Joel 4, although he mentions this passage as worth considering for its development of this prophetic form. It is sufficient, however, to note here that the interjection of Joel 4:11b that summons the divine host bears some correspondence to the prophetic use of the idea of a battle summons.

87. Wendland, *Prophetic Rhetoric*, 26.

88. The word used for the divine army is גִּבּוֹרֶיךָ 'your warriors', which is frequently used to describe human warriors (cf. Josh 10:2; 1 Kgs 1:8, 10; Job 16:14; Ps 33:16; Hos 10:13; Nah 2:4; Zeph 1:14). However, Miller notes that this term is also applicable to heavenly warriors in Ps 103:20 and Judg 5:23 (Miller, *Divine Warrior*, 138). Miller also posits that the idea of YHWH's heavenly warriors is conflated with the concept of the divine council for whom prophets served as heralds or messengers (P. Miller, "The Divine Council and the Prophetic Call to War," *VT* 18 [1968] 100–107). The identification of this force as גִּבּוֹרֶיךָ may also separate it from identification of the locusts as YHWH's army in Joel 2:10 (חֵילוֹ).

89. Miller, *Divine Warrior*, 138.

Joel 4:12 concludes the divine summons to judgment by summarizing the different features of Joel 4:9–11. Joel 4:12 again encourages action by foregrounding the two jussive verbs יֵעוֹרוּ וְיַעֲלוּ 'let them gather and go up'. The location to which this verse summons the nations is the same as Joel 4:2, employing the same pun on the name of the valley and the activity that occurs there. The Valley of Jehoshaphat (יְהוֹשָׁפָט) is the place where YHWH will sit in order to judge (לִשְׁפֹּט) these nations. The occurrence of this title here clarifies any issues in identifying the referent of שָׁמָּה from the preceding verse.[90] Joel 4:12 also connects to the preceding summons by reusing and reinterpreting the phrase describing the scope of the summoned nations from the previous verse (כָל־הַגּוֹיִם מִסָּבִיב).

Beyond summarizing preceding features, Joel 4:12 actualizes the nations' judgment by YHWH. The invitation for the nations to gather and go up in the first half of Joel 4:12 is a dare; it encourages these unnamed nations to ascend to the place of inescapable judgment detailed in the second half of the verse.[91] There is also an ironic element to Joel 4:12 since the nations realize that, although they are summoned to battle in Joel 4:9, they are instead going to experience divine judgment when YHWH adopts the victor's role and declares the fate of the vanquished.[92] Finally, Joel 4:12 concludes the summons found in Joel 4:9–12. These verses together command the nations to gather in an aptly named valley with their full might so that YHWH might confront them and announce the divine decision.

Joel 4:13 introduces the results of the summons to the nations.[93] Again, the nations have little agency in this verse; they respond to the summons only to be subjected to inescapable divine judgment. The nations' lack of agency is evident in the preponderance of imperatives from YHWH that govern this verse, directed at the heavenly host whom the prophet summons to answer the nations' mobilization in Joel 4:11 (cf. Zech 14:5).[94] The imperatives that commence Joel 4:13 build from YHWH's declaration in the previous verse and make it evident that YHWH is the driving force behind the nations' fate. Keller aptly states, "Cette grandiose scène du jugement est réalisée par un seul acteur, YHWH. Tous les autres personnages—les foules

---

90. Prinsloo, *Theology*, 99.

91. Crenshaw, *Joel*, 190.

92. Wendland, *Discourse Analysis*, 300. In contrast, Good draws together the realms of warfare and judgment in prophetic imagery and considers the summons to the nations as a medium through which YHWH acts as judge (R. Good, "The Just War in Ancient Israel," *JBL* 104 [1985] 385–400). Consequently, for him there is less irony at work since YHWH's authority to judge derives from the divine ability to defeat the nations. Good is correct to draw attention to the close linkage between YHWH's role as warrior and YHWH's role of judge over the nations, but the lack of mention of an actual battle in Joel 4:9–12 is still surprising in the wake of the detail given for the process of mobilization.

93. Sweeney, *Twelve*, 181.

94. Nogalski, *Redactional Processes*, 31; Crenshaw, *Joel*, 191.

des nations, les serviteurs de YHWH—ne sont que des comparses."[95] Joel
4:13 reveals that the nations' assembly is an act of futility; there is no place
allotted for them to strive against YHWH's judgment since this verse moves
from summons to the declaration of final judgment.

The imagery of this verse comes from the agricultural realm, and it presents two vivid pictures of YHWH's judgment. The first is that of a field ready
for harvesting, with YHWH issuing the command שִׁלְחוּ מַגָּל 'send in the
sickle'. The second image is a command to trample grapes since the winepress is full. Again, imperatives govern Joel 4:13: the command to begin
the harvest is matched with the dual imperatives בֹּאוּ רְדוּ 'come! trample!'
to begin the process of crushing grapes. The use of imperatives again reinforces YHWH's authority since these divine commands commence the
process of judgment.

The common link between the two agricultural images is that the appropriate time has arrived, because fields are harvested and grapes are trampled
when crops have reached maturity.[96] The text makes this apparent through
its threefold use of כִּי in Joel 4:13, which introduces three declarations that
the time is appropriate for the actions that YHWH commands.[97] Further,
both the image of the grain field and the image of grapes resonate with
other passages that employ metaphors of ripeness to indicate judgment
(cf. Isa 17:5; Jer 24:2; 48:32; Hos 2:9; Amos 8:1–2). In particular, Isa 63:1–6
vividly depicts YHWH as the Divine Warrior stained with the blood of the
enemies whom he tramples like grapes in a winepress. In the case of Joel
4:13, YHWH declares that the time has arrived to judge the nations; it is
time to reap the divine harvest.

Joel 4:13 also details the magnitude of the harvest. The final clause of
this verse begins with the phrase הֵשִׁיקוּ הַיְקָבִים 'the vats overflow', which
conjures up an image of such abundance that the process of trampling
overflows the allotted containers. Interestingly, this same phrase also occurs in Joel 2:24, where it helps to describe the enormity of YHWH's restorative actions for the Judahite community. The image of overflowing vats
takes on a different metaphorical sense in Joel 4:13, with the fullness of
the vats reflecting the ripeness of the time for judgment.[98] In Joel 4:13 the
image also adopts negative connotations, where the filling of vats reflects
the imminence of the outpouring of YHWH's wrath because of the nations'

---

95. E. Jacob, C. Keller, and S. Amsler, *Ósee* (Genève: Labor et Fides, 1965) 151.

96. Sweeney, *Twelve*, 182. Sweeney states that the first image "presupposes the imagery
of standing grain that is cut down at harvest time to portray the fall of enemy soldiers,"
while the second image "presupposes the imagery of grapes being tread at harvest time,
which symbolizes the blood shed by the fallen enemy warriors."

97. Wendland, *Prophetic Rhetoric*, 27. The first כִּי introduces the declaration that the
harvest is ripe, the second כִּי introduces the declaration that the winepress is full, while
the final כִּי introduces the declaration that the nations' wickedness is of a quantity that
requires divine judgment.

98. D. Marcus, "Nonrecurring Doublets in the Book of Joel," *CBQ* 56 (1994) 63.

immense guilt. While Joel 2:18–27 declares Yʜᴡʜ's intention for full and overflowing divine restoration, Joel 4:13 declares that the time is ripe for divine judgment.

Joel 4:14 continues to describe the results of the summons. Two separate instances of repetition characterize this short verse beginning with its first two words, הֲמוֹנִים הֲמוֹנִים 'multitudes, multitudes'. This word is employed often in martial contexts, suggesting that the "multitudes" are preparing for battle (cf. Judg 4:7; 1 Kgs 20:13; Dan 11:10). Repeating this noun indicates a superlative quality, suggesting in this case that the nations who answer Yʜᴡʜ's summons are beyond count (cf. Isa 13:4; 17:12; Ezek 39:11).[99] The statement that there are innumerable foes may allude to earlier references to the locust hordes that the text describes as uncountable (Joel 1:6).[100] The difference, however, is that Yʜᴡʜ's power and authority are now active on behalf of the Judahite community, which renders irrelevant the vast quantity of foes.

The singular form of the noun הָמוֹן is found at Isa 13:4, another "day-of-Yʜᴡʜ" passage that describes Yʜᴡʜ's power over the nations to which Joel has previously made reference (cf. Joel 1:15 and Isa 13:6).[101] The Isaianic reference draws from a different part of the semantic range of הָמוֹן, referring to the noise that an assembly of peoples would create.[102] The passages, however, share a common orientation concerning the certainty of Yʜᴡʜ's triumph over the gathered nations. Both texts demonstrate that no collection of nations can challenge Yʜᴡʜ's authority. Further, the conflation of the senses of grouping and noise may also indicate that the repetition of הֲמוֹנִים הֲמוֹנִים has an onomatopoetic effect. The sound of the repeated word essentially echoes the chaos and confusion found in the babbling voices of a large crowd.[103]

The second example of repetition in Joel 4:14 provides the location to which Yʜᴡʜ summons this collection of foes. The aforementioned multitudes assemble בְּעֵמֶק הֶחָרוּץ 'in the Valley of Decision' to await their fate.[104]

---

99. Kautsch, *Gesenius'*, 396.

100. Wendland, *Prophetic Rhetoric*, 27.

101. Coggins, *Joel*, 60.

102. Isaiah 13:4a reads קוֹל הָמוֹן בֶּהָרִים דְּמוּת עַם־רָב 'a sound of tumult upon the mountains, a likeness of many people'.

103. Crenshaw, *Joel*, 192; Wendland, *Prophetic Rhetoric*, 27. Wendland acknowledges, however, the difficulty of gauging onomatopoeia without knowing the sound-sense correspondences present in the original language; Wendland, *Discourse Analysis*, 229. Schart notes that Joel 4:14 is the only occasion where הָמוֹן occurs in a plural form and suggests that the reduplication of the otherwise unattested הֲמוֹנִים has a superlative function. The sound of the nations gathered together is extraordinary, but ultimately it has no bearing on their fate since Yʜᴡʜ controls the events in this valley (A. Schart, "Deathly Silence and Apocalyptic Noise: Observations on the Soundscape of the Book of the Twelve," *Verbum et Ecclesia* 31 [2010] §§30–34).

104. This is the only place in the Old Testament that uses חָרוּץ as a noun. See Coggins, *Joel*, 60. Coggins suggests that it draws from the same semantic range as the verb

Joel 4:14b then declares that the day of Y<small>HWH</small> is near in the "Valley of Decision." This repetition expresses the certainty of Y<small>HWH</small>'s final verdict, with its full unveiling set for the approaching day of Y<small>HWH</small>.[105] The name assigned to the valley in Joel 4:14 changes from 4:2 and 4:12, which refer to it as the "Valley of Jehoshaphat." The two titles are synonymous, however, with the text stressing the idea of judging in Joel 4:2 and 12 and providing the final verdict here in 4:14. Further, the text may be engaging in double entendre through the change of name. There is a suggestion that this verse plays off a double meaning of חָרוּץ, which is also glossed as an instrument of cutting or a 'threshing sledge' (cf. Job 41:22; Isa 28:27; Amos 1:3).[106] Thus, in concert withDeuteronomy the imagery of Joel 4:13 that concerns harvesting agricultural produce, the עֵמֶק הֶחָרוּץ may evoke another image of threshing to describe Y<small>HWH</small>'s judgment.

Joel 4:14 is also significant for reintroducing the day of Y<small>HWH</small> into the rhetoric of the text. Interestingly, this is the third occasion on which the text describes the day of Y<small>HWH</small> as קָרוֹב 'near' (see Joel 1:15; 2:1). In the first two instances, the text warned the Judahite community about the coming of Y<small>HWH</small>'s day, probably as a rhetorical strategy to push people to adopt the prophetic program of response (see Joel 2:12–17). On this occasion, the nearness of Y<small>HWH</small>'s day signals divine deliverance since the "multitudes" who have gathered are the ones against whom Y<small>HWH</small> acts. The repeated description of the nearness of the day of Y<small>HWH</small> is a deliberate echo of the previous passages.[107] This echo demonstrates how radically the situation changes throughout this prophetic book. In Joel 1:15 and 2:1, the announcement of the proximity of the day of Y<small>HWH</small> is a cause for great alarm among the Judahite community, whereas in Joel 4:14, the proximity of the day of Y<small>HWH</small> signals salvation for those who call on the name of Y<small>HWH</small>

חָרַץ, which helps to suggest an understanding of 'decision' in this verse (cf. 1 Kgs 20:40; Isa 10:22–23).

105. Marcus, "Doublets," 61; J. Thompson, "The Use of Repetition in the Prophecy of Joel," in *On Language, Culture and Religion* (ed. M. and W. Smalley; The Hague: Mouton, 1974) 103.

106. Ahlström, *Joel*, 81; Merx, *Die Prophetie*, 74. Strazicich points to the text's potential use of other multivalent terms, including the "Valley of Jehoshaphat" in Joel 4:2 and 12, to suggest that the ambiguity of meaning is probably intentional in this case (Strazicich, *Joel's Use of Scripture*, 237). Another less plausible suggestion is that the name is derived from חָרִיץ, which is a type of cheese. This has led to this valley's being associated with Josephus's Valley of Tyropoeon (derived from a Greek word meaning 'cheese makers, cheesemongers'), which runs through Jerusalem. See Dillard, "Joel," 300, 309.

107. Schwesig argues for an even more detailed connection between the day-of-Y<small>HWH</small> passages, identifying elements of reversal from Joel 2:1–11 in 4:1–3 and 9–17 as the day of Y<small>HWH</small> transitions from destruction to salvation for the Judahite audience (P. Schwesig, *Die Rolle der Tag-J<small>HWHS</small>-Dichtungen im Dodekapropheten* [BZAW 366; Berlin: de Gruyter, 2006] 174–79). These include the sanctity of Zion, the advance of armies, and the voice of Y<small>HWH</small>. His identification of a parallel construction requires excising Joel 4:4–8 which, as discussed above, does play an important role in constructing the meaning of this chapter.

(Joel 3:5) while promising final judgment on the foreign nations when
Y<small>HWH</small> renders the verdict in the "Valley of Decision."[108]

Following the reintroduction of the day of Y<small>HWH</small> in Joel 4:14, Joel
4:15–16 begins to describe its effects.[109] Again, divine agency drives these
verses since the trembling of the heavenly bodies and Y<small>HWH</small>'s establishment of divine authority in Zion is reminiscent of themes derived from
the march of the Divine Warrior (cf. Isa 13:10; Judg 5:20; Hab 3:11).[110] In
the process of invoking these cosmological themes, Joel 4:15–16 is also
notable for its interaction with Joel 1–2. Joel 4:15 quotes 2:10b with its
description of the darkening of the heavenly luminaries. Joel 4:15 and
2:10b also share close proximity to a reference to the day of Y<small>HWH</small> (cf. Joel
2:11, 4:14). The parallels continue into Joel 4:16 which begins with a roar
from Y<small>HWH</small>, echoing how Y<small>HWH</small> shouts in front of his army in 2:11.[111]
Further, Joel 4:16 and 2:10 both describe a convulsing that encompasses
both heaven and earth, pointing to the immense power of the one who
causes the shaking.[112]

Interestingly, the text changes the order of activities in the two passages.
In Joel 2:10–11, the progression is: (1) trembling of earth and heavens,
(2) darkening of heavenly luminaries, and (3) Y<small>HWH</small>'s loud shout. In Joel
4:15–16, the order is: (1) darkening of the luminaries, (2) Y<small>HWH</small>'s roar, and
(3) shaking of the heavens and the earth.[113] The reuse and reconfiguration
of this imagery helps to highlight Joel's progression in depicting the day
of Y<small>HWH</small>. In Joel 2:10–11, the focus is internal; the image of frightening
cosmological events is the capstone to a description of the terror that the
day of Y<small>HWH</small> would bring upon Zion. It moves from the earth to the heavens, culminating in Y<small>HWH</small>'s voice's breaking in to announce the day of
Y<small>HWH</small>. In Joel 4:15–16, the focus is external, following a description of

---

108. J. Bourke, "Le jour de Yahvé dans Joël," *RB* 66 (1959) 22.

109. Ibid. The transition from the proximity of the day of Y<small>HWH</small> to descriptions of its
impact is consistent with Bourke's assertion that the two most striking characteristics of
the day of Y<small>HWH</small> in Joel are its "proximité et grandeur."

110. Miller, *Divine Warrior*, 118. Simkins claims that "[t]hese are the convulsions of nature which are typically associated with the divine warrior's cosmogonic battle" (Simkins,
Yahweh's Activity, 235). When the heavenly luminaries shake, Y<small>HWH</small> asserts supremacy
over the nations who challenge Y<small>HWH</small> and over the created order, which can only convulse in response.

111. The two phrases differ in the verb tense that they employ. Joel 2:11 employs
the suffix conjugation (נָתַן קוֹלוֹ) while Joel 4:16 employs the prefix conjugation (יִתֵּן קוֹלוֹ).
However, this distinction does not outweigh the similarity of the imagery.

112. In both Joel 2:10 and 4:16, the verb describing the convulsions of the heavens
and the earth is רעשׁ. Kessler suggests that, when this verb occurs with an impersonal
subject/object, such as the heavens and the earth, it takes on a hyperbolic meaning. The
intention is to stress the awesome power of the one who causes what should be fixed objects to shake in this fashion (J. Kessler, "The Shaking of the Nations: An Eschatological
View," *JETS* 30 [1987] 161).

113. Crenshaw, *Joel*, 194.

Y_{HWH}'s enacting his day against unspecified "multitudes."[114] Accordingly, the divine roar in Joel 4:16 originates from within Jerusalem as a signal of protection since Y_{HWH} dwells there as defender instead of coming against Zion, leading the locust horde.

The latter half of Joel 4:16 solidifies the fact that this day of Y_{HWH} is actually a signal of Y_{HWH}'s desire to protect the Judahite community. It states that Y_{HWH} will be מַחֲסֶה לְעַמּוֹ וּמָעוֹז לִבְנֵי יִשְׂרָאֵל 'a refuge for his people and a stronghold for the children of Israel'. This fits with the progression of Divine Warrior imagery in which, after victory, the deity returns to a sacral location in order to establish kingship.[115] Y_{HWH}'s presence in Zion after the darkening of the heavenly luminaries indicates divine triumph over the nations' challenge and the promise of future presence and protection for those who dwell under divine protection. This half-verse consists of two parallel verbless clauses that both have Y_{HWH} as their subject, which emphasizes that Y_{HWH} is the one who acts to bring salvation and security. This half-verse may also invoke liturgical language to describe the sufficiency of Y_{HWH}'s protection (cf. Pss 14:6; 46:2; 61:4; 71:7. cf. Isa 17:10; 25:4; Jer 16:19).[116] Thus, even as the heavenly bodies darken and convulse, Y_{HWH}'s people find safety and security rooted in the divine presence.[117]

Joel 4:16 also shifts the scene from the "Valley of Decision" described in 4:15 to Zion, which is the setting for the remainder of the chapter.[118] Essentially, the preceding verses in this chapter fulfill the promise to "restore the fortunes" of Judah and Jerusalem in Joel 4:1 by concentrating on the fate of those who oppose Y_{HWH}. Now the focus shifts as the text details what the restoration of fortunes might entail for those fortunate enough to be in Zion under the aegis of Y_{HWH}. Joel 4:16 effectively reaffirms that

---

114. Prinsloo, *Theology*, 100. Matthews emphasizes the sense of reversal between Joel 2:10–11 and 4:14–16, where the change in terms describing cosmological events presages the change in target against which Y_{HWH} directs the heavenly army (S. Matthews, "The Power to Endure and Be Transformed: Sun and Moon Imagery in Joel and Revelation," in *Imagery and Imagination in Biblical Literature: Essays in Honour of Aloysius Fitzgerald, F.S.C.* [ed. L. Boadt and M. Smith; Washington, DC: Catholic Biblical Association, 2001] 39).

115. L. Greenspoon, "The Origin of the Idea of Resurrection," in *Traditions in Transformation: Turning Points in Biblical Faith* (ed. B. Halpern and J. Levenson; Winona Lake, IN: Eisenbrauns, 1981) 272. Greenspoon examines Divine Warrior texts in both the Old Testament and other ancient Near Eastern cultures and proposes the following rubric for the march of the Divine Warrior: the Divine Warrior marches to battle, which results in the natural world's convulsing and languishing. After the Divine Warrior's triumph, the deity returns to take up kingship (usually among other deities on a holy mountain), and nature responds with fertility and joy.

116. Crenshaw, *Joel*, 194.

117. Coggins, *Joel*, 60.

118. Barton sees this geographical distinction as evidence that this is a separate oracle, unconnected with the preceding verses; Barton, *Joel*, 106. However, this devalues the text's poetic imagination; instead, these are complementary visual images explaining Y_{HWH}'s actions at this time. See Crenshaw, *Joel*, 192–93.

Zion regains its expected status of inviolability since Yhwh's presence is firmly rooted within it (Pss 46:2–4; 48:5–9; 76:4–10).[119] Whereas Joel 2:10–11 threatens the existence of Zion because of the presence of Yhwh among the attackers, Yhwh's divine roar reasserts Zion's status as place of protection thanks to the presence of the deity.

One additional rhetorical feature of Joel 4:16 is its connection to other prophetic literature. The first clause of Joel 4:16 is וַיהוָה מִצִּיּוֹן יִשְׁאָג וּמִירוּשָׁלַם יִתֵּן קוֹלוֹ 'Yhwh roars from Zion, and from Jerusalem he utters his voice', which notably appears in exactly the same form in Amos 1:2.[120] This raises the question of the relationship between the passages (cf. Jer 25:30). Nogalski suggests that the divine roar is a redactional piece in Joel that anchors Joel 4 to the judgment material of 2:1–11 and anticipates the oracles against nations that begin the book of Amos.[121] At the very least, the citation from Amos provides another example of Joel's willingness to reshape prophetic material to serve its purposes. There is some similarity between the two passages since Amos uses this utterance to introduce a collection of oracles against nations, oracles that resonate with Yhwh's actions of judging the foreign nations in the Valley of Jehoshaphat.[122] Both passages picture Yhwh as the one who roars, an image that appeals to the authority of Yhwh as a judge as well as a lion announcing its powerful presence.[123]

Joel and Amos, however, use the image of Yhwh's roar for different purposes. Amos creates a geographical merismus (shepherds' pastures/top of Carmel) to state that Yhwh's roar powerfully affects the whole land, whereas Joel employs a merismus involving the heavens and the earth. The effect of the divine roar is also different in Joel and Amos. Amos springs a rhetorical trap that eventually announces judgment against both Judah and Israel, while Joel uses Yhwh's roar to promise deliverance for Judah from its oppressors. The declaration that Yhwh is a refuge and a stronghold in Joel 4:16b emphasizes the protective nature of the divine roar in Joel. The juxtaposition of images is visible since Amos's focus is on divine punishment for specific crimes that culminate with Israel's and Judah's of-

---

119. Renz asserts that "the assumption that Zion is an especially protected place is the inevitable conclusion from the premise that God is present in the city" (T. Renz, "The Use of the Zion Tradition in the Book of Ezekiel," in *Zion, City of Our God* [ed. R. Hess and G. Wenham; Grand Rapids: Eerdmans, 1999] 84).

120. Wendland, *Prophetic Rhetoric*, 28. Wendland takes note of the first clause in Joel 4:16 (וַיהוָה מִצִּיּוֹן יִשְׁאָג), noting how it positions Zion before the verb describing Yhwh's action. He calls this "locative constituent focus," and it helps to shift the geographical locale of this subunit from the climactic valley to Yhwh's dwelling in Zion.

121. Nogalski, *Redactional Processes*, 37.

122. Prinsloo, *Theology*, 103. Prinsloo notes that Yhwh's coming in judgment after he "roars from Zion" is the common link between Jer 25:30; Amos 1:2; and Joel 4:16.

123. Ogden, *Promise of Hope*, 46. Ogden looks to psalms of lament to find other juxtapositions of both aspects, in which the fear-inducing judge is also the protector of the weak and vulnerable (Pss 31:2, 4; 43:2; 61:3).

fenses against Y<small>HWH</small>, while the association of Y<small>HWH</small>'s roar with the day of
Y<small>HWH</small> as a day of judgment on the attacking nations in Joel points toward
restoration.[124] This fits well with the overarching purpose of Joel 4, which
describes Y<small>HWH</small> as acting restoratively by announcing judgment against
foreign nations.[125]

Joel 4:17 responds to these pronouncements of Y<small>HWH</small>'s activity with a
divine self-identification formula that reads וִידַעְתֶּם כִּי אֲנִי יְהוָה אֱלֹהֵיכֶם 'then
you will know that I am Y<small>HWH</small> your God'. This verse returns to first-person
speech, which provides a powerful assurance of Y<small>HWH</small>'s presence. Previous
verses state that Y<small>HWH</small> shakes the heavens and roars, while Joel 4:17 details
Y<small>HWH</small>'s promise. This exact phrase occurs in Exod 6:7 and 16:12, where
Y<small>HWH</small> declares that Israel will know that Y<small>HWH</small> is their God because Y<small>HWH</small>
will rescue them from Egypt and care for them in the wilderness. A simi-
lar phrase is found in Joel 2:27, where the text states that Y<small>HWH</small>'s restorative acts in the wake of the locust infestation will cause the community
to know that Y<small>HWH</small> is in their midst.[126] Taken together, "the formulas of
knowing God serve to resolve with glorious certainty the cautious question
'Who knows?' concerning God in 2:14."[127] The hope expressed in Joel 2:14
is rooted in the acknowledgment of Y<small>HWH</small>'s gracious and compassionate
character. The divine self-identification formulas in Joel 2:27 and 4:17 are
powerful confirmations of this portrayal.

The succeeding statements in Joel 4:17 are also significant in light of
what has previously transpired. The next clause of Joel 4:17 builds on the
divine self-identification formula and declares that Y<small>HWH</small> is שֹׁכֵן בְּצִיּוֹן הַר־
קָדְשִׁי 'dwelling in Zion, my holy mountain'. This declaration resonates with
Joel 4:16, which establishes Zion as the location from which Y<small>HWH</small> roars.
Further, it continues to reverse the threat articulated in Joel 2:1, which mentions Zion and Y<small>HWH</small>'s holy mountain but commands the people to sound
an alarm before describing a divinely sanctioned assault that breaches the
walls. Joel 2:10–11 ultimately reveals that the cause for this alarm is Y<small>HWH</small>,
who is coming as conqueror against what should have been the sanctuary
guaranteed by the divine presence.

Joel 4:17, however, articulates that Y<small>HWH</small>'s renewed presence provides
protection from further calamity since "where Yahweh resides, one need

---

124. Strazicich, *Joel's Use of Scripture*, 239.

125. J. Nogalski, "Intertextuality and the Twelve," in *Forming Prophetic Literature: Essays on Isaiah and the Twelve in Honour of John D. W. Watts* (ed. J. Watts and P. House;
JSOTSup 235; Sheffield: Sheffield Academic Press, 1996) 107. Nogalski claims that the Joelian version of the divine roar broadens it into "a universal portrayal of judgement, the
purpose of which is to encourage Yahweh's people."

126. Wendland, *Prophetic Rhetoric*, 28. The reuse of the divine recognition formula
"forges an important thematic link between the deliverance (2:27) and vindication of
God's people vis-à-vis their erstwhile enemies."

127. L. Allen, "Some Prophetic Antecedents of Apocalyptic Eschatology and Their Hermeneutical Value," *Ex Auditu* 6 (1990) 21.

not fear locust plagues, drought, fire, or armies."[128] The text replaces the locust army in Joel 2:1–11 that climbed over the walls and even invaded the homes with the declaration that זָרִים 'strangers' will not pass through Jerusalem any longer.[129] Whereas Joel 2:1 commences a rhetorical unit with the holiness of Zion before detailing its violation, Joel 4:17 concludes a rhetorical subunit that guarantees Zion's continued holiness thanks to the presence of Yhwh in its midst. This use of recursion is rhetorically powerful in directing the implied audience to recall the prophet's previous words while promising a complete change in fate.

Joel 4:17 continues to use recursion when it echoes Joel 3:5. Joel 3:5 finishes its unit by promising that those who call on the name of Yhwh will find salvation on Mount Zion and in Jerusalem in the wake of the earth-rending signs that presage the day of Yhwh. Essentially, the promise of security for Jerusalem in Joel 4:17 at the end of the subunit that summons the nations to judgment makes explicit the event from which Yhwh will save those whom Yhwh calls in 3:5.[130] This further detail should persuade the implied audience that calling out to Yhwh is the necessary response since Yhwh promises security through his presence in Jerusalem.

Finally, Joel 4:17 concludes this subunit that describes Yhwh's defeat of the nations and ultimate residence in Zion. Again, recursion signals the conclusion of this subunit with the repetition of the key words *Zion* and *Jerusalem* in both 4:16 and 4:17. Zion is the "synecdochic equivalent of 'Jerusalem' which in turn acts as a metonymic designation for . . . the faithful and holy people of God."[131] In this case, the presence of references to Zion and Jerusalem seems to mark the end of this particular thought unit, which climaxes with the promise of divine protection guaranteed by Yhwh's presence in Zion.

Essentially, the rhetorical strategy of Joel 4:9–17 is to portray a summons to the nations, calling them to battle against Yhwh in a symbolically named valley, where Yhwh unleashes judgment, shakes the foundations of the cosmos, and guarantees the security of the Judahite community by

---

128. J. Crenshaw, "Freeing the Imagination: The Conclusion of the Book of Joel," in *Prophecy and Prophets: The Diversity of Contemporary Issues in Scholarship* (ed. Y. Gitay; Atlanta: Scholars Press, 1997) 143–44. Crenshaw looks at this verse and the equivalent final declaration of Yhwh's presence in Zion in Joel 4:21 as the keys to understanding the conclusion of this prophetic book. All of the calamities and soul-searching in the book are resolved by the prophetic promise that Yhwh resides within the community, in Zion.

129. L. Snijders, "The Meaning of זָר in the Old Testament," in *Oudtestamentische Studiën* (ed. P. A. H. de Boer; OtSt 10; Leiden: Brill, 1954) 39–40. Snijders understands the term זָרִים to refer to "strangers who do harm to the people and destroy them," while pointing "to the distance between *zarīm* and the holy." Snijders also understands the promised sanctity of the divine presence as a reversal of the slave-trading activities referenced previously, in Joel 4:4–8.

130. Strazicich, "Joel's Use of Scripture," 207.

131. Wendland, *Discourse Analysis*, 282.

establishing divine reign in Zion. Throughout the summons and its aftermath, these verses make it clear to the implied audience that YHWH's judgment will prevail. Joel 4:9–17 reverses the scenario of 4:1–3, where the nations scatter YHWH's people and take possession of their land. These assurances of YHWH's victory should persuade the implied audience that maintaining their faith and trust in YHWH is the correct course.

Joel 4:18–21: Restoration Resulting from Judgment

The final subunit of Joel builds off the established description of the nations' fate and shifts the focus back to the Judahite community. The judicial genre remains in evidence especially in the pronouncements against Egypt and Edom. The positive repercussions for Judah and Jerusalem flow out of YHWH's judgment made manifest in the day of YHWH.[132] Joel 4:18 begins with the temporal formula וְהָיָה בַיּוֹם הַהוּא 'and it will be on that day', which recalls similar formulas in Joel 3:1 and 4:1 that introduce occasions for decisive divine action.[133] The use of this formula in Joel 4:18 resembles the pattern of Zech 14, which commences with a temporal formula invoking the day of YHWH (יוֹם־בָּא לַיהוָה 'a day comes for YHWH'), while using בַיּוֹם הַהוּא 'on that day' (Zech 14:4, 6, 8, 13, 20) to mark various events that it foretells. Essentially, the temporal formula in Joel 4:18 recalls the formula of Joel 4:1 and reorients the implied audience's perspective back to the time when YHWH will intervene restoratively.[134]

---

132. Keller, *Ósee*, 152; Prinsloo, *Theology*, 116. Keller and Prinsloo argue that these verses follow an "ABA" pattern in which "A" represents salvation for Judah (cf. 4:18, 20–21), and "B" reflects doom for the nations, identified in this particular verse as Egypt and Edom (cf. 4:19). This scheme, however, involves splitting hairs too finely because the text ties these concepts closely together. The text clearly connects the doom of Egypt and Edom to Judah's previous unfortunate state, which YHWH's mighty acts will restore. Further, discussion of Joel 4:21 will reveal that this verse tightly interweaves the judgment of enemies and the blessing of YHWH's people.

133. Dillard, "Joel," 312. See De Vries's full study on this phrase, in which he understands it to mark a significant moment in the language of divine-human interaction (S. De Vries, *Yesterday, Today and Tomorrow* [Grand Rapids: Eerdmans, 1975] 279–323). De Vries's study is unapologetically diachronic and derives a significant portion of its understanding of textual composition from redactional schemes that are not fully convincing. He claims that "surely it was a late editor" who added the וְהָיָה בַיּוֹם הַהוּא phrase to Joel 4:18, on the grounds that it differs from "original" Joelian temporal phrases in Joel 3:1 and 4:1. This raises the question of whether or not it would be possible for a prophet creatively to employ different temporal phrases for certain rhetorical purposes. Regardless of the conflict between diachronic and synchronic sensibilities, De Vries's claim that בַיּוֹם הַהוּא references intend to present opportunities for divine or human decisive action provides a useful perspective on the rhetorical purpose of this temporal phrase.

134. The similar opening phrases of Joel 3:1, 4:1, and 4:18 interlink with explicit references to the day of YHWH in 3:4 and 4:16. The phrases in Joel 3:1, 4:1, and 4:18 focus on promises of restoration for the Judahite community, while the overt references to the day of YHWH evoke images of judgment and terror for the nations (Wendland, *Discourse Analysis*, 275–76). The connection to Joel 4:1 is especially notable since 4:18–21 essentially fulfills the promise of 4:1 to "restore the fortunes" of Judah and Jerusalem. Whereas Joel

The remainder of Joel 4:18 presents various images of Yʜᴡʜ's promised restoration. The details are hyperbolic, moving far beyond the reversal of what was lacking in Joel 2:18–27. These verses offer pictures of almost miraculous fruitfulness (cf. Isa 65:17–25; Zech 14:6–11). Several images related to liquid combine to build this picture, which stands in stark contrast to the scenes of arid desolation that mark Yʜᴡʜ's absence in Joel 1. The images of restoration begin with the claim יִטְּפוּ הֶהָרִים עָסִיס 'the mountains will drip sweet wine', which echoes the sentiments expressed in Amos 9:13.[135] This promise reverses one of the reasons for lament: Joel 1:5 called on the wine-drinkers to mourn the loss of wine. The next phrase parallels the promise of renewed wine, declaring that milk will flow from the hills, which recalls the ancient promise of Canaan with its references to the "land of milk and honey" (Exod 3:8; Lev 20:24).[136] This image indicates that the cattle will have an unceasing supply of grass so that they will be able to produce milk constantly—a reversal of Joel 1:18, which lamented the destruction of fodder for the animals.[137]

The idea of these liquids flowing and dripping from the mountains is hyperbolic, pointing to tremendous bounty and blessing.[138] These images of abundant liquid continue in the next clause with the declaration that all the אֲפִיקֵי יְהוּדָה 'stream-channels of Judah' will flow with water. The use of watercourses alongside the previous images focusing on the mountains and the hills creates a geographical merismus in which the high and low points of the land work together to demonstrate Yʜᴡʜ's blessing.[139] The use of אָפִיק also points to a reversal of Joel 1:20, in which the stream-channels dry up because of the drought that followed the locust infestation. The overflowing presence of water and other liquids in Joel 4:18 is a vivid promise of prosperity and blessing in the context of a land in which the supply of water is always tenuous.

The final image of Joel 4:18 continues to use the idea of liquid but takes it even further into the realm of hyperbole. It leaps from the natural world to depicting a מַעְיָן 'stream' flowing out of the house of Yʜᴡʜ. The idea of

---

4:1–17 focuses on removing the threat of the foreign nations, while also guaranteeing Yʜᴡʜ's presence in Zion, 4:18–21 elaborately details the outpouring of blessing for Judah and Jerusalem.

135. J. Nogalski, "The Day(s) of Yʜᴡʜ in the Book of the Twelve," in *SBL 1999: Seminar Papers* [SBLSP 38; Atlanta: Society of Biblical Literature, 1999] 630. This phrase in Joel 4:18 is not an exact citation since the form of the verb is different. Joel 4:18 employs a Qal prefix form (יִטְּפוּ), while Amos 9:13 uses a Hiphil suffix + *waw* relative form (וְהִטִּיפוּ). It is noteworthy that, in verses that are close together (Joel 4:16, 18), the text draws in both the beginning and the end of the book of Amos. See E. Ben Zvi and J. Nogalski, *Two Sides of a Coin: Juxtaposing Views on Interpreting the Book of the Twelve / the Twelve Prophetic Books* (Analecta Gorgiana 201; Piscataway, NJ: Gorgias, 2009) 12.

136. Strazicich, *Joel's Use of Scripture*, 243.

137. Crenshaw, *Joel*, 199; Nash, "Palestinian," 200.

138. Prinsloo, *Theology*, 118.

139. A. Schökel, *A Manual of Hebrew Poetics* (Rome: Pontifical Biblical Institute, 1988) 84.

water springing forth from either Jerusalem or the temple itself also appears in Ps 46:5; Ezek 47:1–12; and Zech 14:8.[140] Ezekiel 47 is probably the most similar to Joel 4:17 since both primarily point toward restored fecundity for the land, with Ezek 47:12 even pointing to the growth of trees alongside this river's banks.[141] The totality of the restoration further "strikes paradisi- acal chords" by employing the same verbs (יָצָא; שָׁקָה) as Gen 2:10, which de- scribes the river flowing out of Eden.[142] Joel 4:18, along with its Ezekielian counterpart, thus conflates Edenic imagery with the imagery of the temple. This combination reflects hope for future harmony and blessing since the location of Yhwh's dwelling is also the life-giving center of all creation.[143] This provides a stark contrast to the beginning of Joel with its images of a locust-ravaged landscape and the cessation of sacrifices in the temple. Whereas the devastation of Joel 1:1–14 and 1:15–20 reflects Yhwh's silence and absence, the fructifying streams of Joel 4:18 reflect Yhwh's promise of divine presence in Zion and the restoration of the temple.

Joel 4:18 concludes by stating that the temple-sourced stream will water the נַחַל הַשִּׁטִּים 'Wadi Shittim'. This location is otherwise unattested, leading to various speculations about its geographical location.[144] The most

---

140. N. Ho Fai Tai, "The End of the Book of Twelve: Reading Zechariah 12–14 with Joel," in *Schriftprophetie: Festschrift für Jorg Jeremias zum 65. Geburtstag* (ed. F. Hartenstein, J. Krispenz, and A. Schart; Neukirchen-Vluyn: Neukirchener Verlag, 2004) 344–45. Ho Fai Tai focuses on the relationship between Joel 4:18 and Zech 14:8, noting the presence of shared vocabulary (מַיִם, יָצָא) and suggesting that Ezek 47:1–12 influences both passages. He also draws attention to differences including the claims in Zech 14:8 that water will flow both to the east and to the west (contra Joel 4:18, where it flows to the east) and that the water flows out of Jerusalem itself, rather than out of the house of Yhwh. He suggests that Zech 14:8 is a conscious modification of the Joelian text, conflating the idea of Jerusalem with the sanctity of the temple.

141. Crenshaw, *Joel*, 200. Zechariah 14 also differs in that it envisions two rivers, one flowing eastward while the other flows westward.

142. Ahlström, *Joel*, 41. See also Strazicich, *Joel's Use of Scripture*, 243. Hoppe draws further attention to the image of life-giving water originating in Jerusalem by noting the presence of the Gihon spring in the list of the four rivers sourcing the Garden of Eden in Gen 2:13 (L. Hoppe, *The Holy City: Jerusalem in the Theology of the Old Testament* [Collegeville, MN: Liturgical Press, 2000] 27–29). The Gihon was the actual source of water for Jerusalem but clearly reaches superlative stature in the Genesis narrative. Leppäkari provides a useful synopsis of the concept of the paradisiacal nature of Zion (M. Leppäkari, *Apocalyptic Representations of Jerusalem* [NBS; Studies in the History of Religions 3; Leiden: Brill, 2006] 83–86).

143. M. Fishbane, *Biblical Interpretation in Ancient Israel* (Oxford: Clarendon, 1985) 370–71; Hoppe, *Holy City*, 27–29.

144. Crenshaw, Dillard, and Allen argue that the most likely location is some exten- sion of the Kidron Valley between Jerusalem and the Dead Sea (Crenshaw, *Joel*, 200; Dil- lard, "Joel," 312; Allen, *Joel*, 124). In contrast, Milik identifies it as the Wadi Qaddûm between the Mount of Olives and Jerusalem (J. T. Milik, "Notes d'épigraphie et de topog- raphie palestinienne," *RB* 66 [1959] 553–55). However, none of these identifications has definitive proof. There are other references to "Shittim" in Num 25:1; 33:49; Josh 2:1; and 3:1; however, none of them refers to it as a wadi. Further, this Shittim is on the plains of

plausible suggestion is that the Wadi Shittim is a symbolic name, similar to the Valley of Jehoshaphat mentioned previously in this chapter.[145] In this way, even without identifying an actual location, it is possible to point to the rhetorical impact of using this name. The noun שִׁטִּים refers to acacia trees, which grow in arid environments; thus, the idea that the stream flowing from Yhwh's house could reach even this region probably symbolizes the rejuvenating power of this water.[146] In conjunction with the rest of Joel 4:18, the mention of the Wadi Shittim points toward an idealized future, where Yhwh's provenance will eliminate any wants from the land; Yhwh's promised presence in Zion leads to a guarantee of matchless prosperity, emphasized by the presence of continually flowing water.

The text then transitions in Joel 4:19–20 by juxtaposing themes of judgment and blessing. In Joel 4:19, the prophet promises judgment against Egypt and Edom because of their offenses against Judah and Jerusalem.[147] Multiple instances of constituent fronting mark the description of the fate of these nations, with Egypt and Edom appearing as the first word in their respective clauses, followed by nouns describing their status. The judgment on Edom echoes and enhances the judgment on Egypt: the text first declares that Egypt will become לִשְׁמָמָה 'for a desolation', and Edom then becomes לְמִדְבַּר שְׁמָמָה 'for a desert of desolation'.[148] This is again reassuring for the implied Judahite audience since the text vividly contrasts the fate of the nations with the promised future for Yhwh's own people, who see

---

Moab, across the Jordan River, rendering it highly unlikely that a stream flowing out of Jerusalem could reach this location. Ahlström, however, notes that Shittim in Josh 3:1 is the place from which Israel crosses the Jordan to enter the Promise Land and inaugurate a new era of divine blessing, suggesting that the text is invoking this memory to inaugurate salvific activity of Yhwh in Joel 4:18 (Ahlström, *Joel*, 92–93). Sweeney suggests that Joel could be pointing to a complete transformation of the region surrounding the Dead Sea and the Jordan Valley, thus rendering plausible the Moabite location of Shittim (Sweeney, *Twelve*, 184). This again, however, is speculative.

145. Simkins, *Yahweh's Activity*, 239. Luria comments further, "In vain have Bible scholars sought to identify this valley of Shittim; this is not an actual but only a symbolic valley" (B. Luria, "And a Fountain Shall Spring Forth from the House of the Lord," *Dor le Dor* 10 [1981] 49).

146. Crenshaw, *Joel*, 200. Some of the cultic items for the tabernacle were made from acacia wood (cf. Exod 25:10; 25:23–24; 26:15; 27:1; 30:1); however, Joel does not appear to be importing this nuance.

147. The reasons for the selection of Egypt and Edom as the enemies to mention in this verse are unclear. This chapter has primarily made general references to unnamed nations against whom Yhwh will act (cf. Joel 4:2, 11, 12), although Joel 4:4–8 did break in to mention Tyre, Sidon, and Philistia specifically. There is a certain geographical symmetry created with the inclusion of Egypt and Edom; enemies from the south (Egypt) and east (Edom) balance out those from the north (Tyre and Sidon) and west (Philistia).

148. Crenshaw attributes the additional marker of desolation on Edom to the two countries' respective access to consistent water sources, claiming that "Edom, never so fortunate as Egypt with regard to water, will find itself even harder pressed to discover enough of it for survival" (Crenshaw, *Joel*, 200).

even their arid regions become bountiful and productive. Meanwhile, the enemies of Yhwh suffer a fate similar to that described in Joel 2:3, with their own prosperous regions becoming like deserts in the wake of Yhwh's punishment.[149]

The second half of Joel 4:19 provides the rationale for this harsh punishment on Egypt and Edom, claiming that this is the result of their cruel treatment of the Judahites. The condemnation of Edom in Obad 10 may be alluded to by the use of חָמָס 'violence' in Joel 4:19.[150] Obadiah condemns Edom for doing this to "your brother Jacob," making the crime especially heinous since it is committed against close kin. Joel further describes the violence, claiming that שָׁפְכוּ דָם־נָקִיא 'they poured out innocent blood'. The reference to pouring out is interesting since the text's previous reference to pouring out referred to the gifting of Yhwh's Spirit in Joel 3:1–2.[151] Instead of mentioning unmitigated blessing, however, the text charges these enemy nations with shedding the blood of innocents, thus justifying their imminent destruction. This verse adopts a persuasive strategy found throughout Joel 4:1–21, which is to assure the implied audience that Yhwh will eliminate external threats to their prosperity and security.

Joel 4:20 commences with an adversative *waw* that sets up Zion and Jerusalem as the counterparts to Egypt and Edom. Whereas Yhwh's wrath against these hostile nations leads to their becoming uninhabitable, Yhwh's blessing guarantees eternal dwelling in the city. The two clauses are set up as parallel to the verse fronting Judah and Jerusalem in their respective clauses, which is equivalent to Joel 4:19's treatment of Egypt and Edom. The text thus emphasizes the different locations before moving into a description of their respective fates. In both clauses in Joel 4:20, the next element is a temporal description pointing toward eternal duration.

---

149. This measure-for-measure devastation of the landscape again reflects the symmetry of the book of Joel. The devastation of Judah in the wake of the locust army's advance is mirrored by the promise that Yhwh will mete out devastation against enemy nations (Marcus, "Nonrecurring," 63–64).

150. The potential allusion to Obadiah in Joel 4:19–21 is an oddity when compared with Joel's use of Scripture throughout the rest of the book. Sweeney correctly notes that Joel has a tendency to eliminate the specific referents of the alluded texts, so that they can be constructed typologically to deal with any enemy that might arise (M. Sweeney, "The Priesthood and the Proto-Apocalyptic Reading of Prophetic and Pentateuchal Texts," in *Knowing the End from the Beginning: The Prophetic, the Apocalyptic and Their Relationships* [ed. L. Grabbe and R. Haak; JSPSup 46; London: T. & T. Clark, 2003] 169–70). This is notable in Joel 4 with the reference to a Valley of Jehoshaphat without mention of the foes that Jehoshaphat defeated there (cf. 2 Chr 20). Joel 3:5 further removes the context of judgment against Edom in its connection to Obad 17.

151. Dillard, "Joel," 312–13. Simkins highlights the mention of דָם־נָקִיא as something that builds into his interpretation of Joel 2:12–17; perhaps offering further evidence that there is no underlying sin behind the devastation of the locust plague (Simkins, *Yahweh's Activity*, 240). See the extended discussion of the issue of Judah's potential guilt in the analysis of rhetorical strategy in Joel 2:12–17, above.

The final element in the first clause is the verb תֵּשֵׁב 'she [Judah] will dwell', which the second clause elides.[152] Both clauses of Joel 4:20 reinforce the fact that, because of Yhwh's continued presence, Jerusalem will be inhabited continually.

Joel 4:20 also alludes to Isa 13:20 and its description of the aftermath of the day of Yhwh directed against Babylon. The two passages share the verb יָשַׁב, and the temporal construction לְדוֹר וָדוֹר 'from generation to generation'. The shared vocabulary stands in contrast to the opposing consequences of Yhwh's actions; whereas in Joel 4:20, Yhwh guarantees eternal dwelling in Jerusalem, in Isa 13:20, Yhwh guarantees that Babylon will not be inhabited in the wake of its destruction.[153] The inhabitation of Judah and Jerusalem in Joel 4:20 thus contrasts with the desolation of Egypt and Edom in Joel 4:19 and the prophesied fate of Babylon in the wake of the day of Yhwh in Isa 13:20. Joel 4:20 powerfully guarantees Yhwh's restorative power by contrasting the fate of Jerusalem with the fate of the nations who defy Yhwh.

The book then concludes in Joel 4:21 with a verse that has provoked serious debate. Joel 4:21a is notoriously difficult to interpret, a fact that has occasioned several different proposals. The Masoretic Text reads וְנִקֵּיתִי דָּמָם לֹא־נִקֵּיתִי 'I will hold innocent their blood I have not held innocent'.[154] At first glance, these clauses seem self-contradictory and also rather terse since there is no conjunction or preposition between them.[155] The declaration of innocence in the first verb makes it evident that the antecedent of the pronominal suffix on דָּמָם 'their blood' is Judah/Jerusalem, but the second clause in the Masoretic Text seems to contradict Joel 4:19, which chastised Edom and Egypt for pouring our Judah's innocent blood. It is difficult to see how the people with דָם־נָקִיא 'innocent blood' in Joel 4:19 could also be deemed by Yhwh as people whom לֹא־נִקֵּיתִי 'I will not hold innocent' in 4:21.

One suggestion is that the first clause, וְנִקֵּיתִי דָּמָם, is an unmarked rhetorical question; this is possible when the phrase follows a conjunction (cf. Job 2:10; 10:9; 10:11; 11:11; 17:4b; 23:17; 30:24; 38:8; 40:24, 25; Jer

---

152. This verb is in the feminine-singular form, which Crenshaw finds unusual, claiming that Judah typically takes the masculine form of verbs. He speculates that the nearby presence of Jerusalem, which always takes a feminine verb, influenced the selection here (Crenshaw, *Joel*, 202).

153. Sweeney, *Twelve*, 185; Strazicich, *Joel's Use of Scripture*, 246. Strazicich asserts that the shared vocabulary "makes this allusion understandable."

154. Barton, *Joel*, 109. According to this reading, Yhwh will now overlook the sins of Judah that he used to punish. Ahlström suggests that, in this instance, the root נָקָה could be related to the Akkadian *neqū* 'to pour out'. See Ahlström, *Joel*, 95. According to this reading, the suffix on דָּמָם 'their blood' would refer to Egypt and Edom and point to their ultimate punishment. However, this would be the sole case in the OT where נָקָה had this meaning, rendering this interpretation suppositional at best.

155. Dillard, "Joel," 313.

25:29).[156] Jeremiah 25:29 in particular resonates with Joel 4:21 since it also is governed by the root נָקָה, although it is a Niphal rather than a Piel (וְאַתֶּם הִנָּקֵה תִנָּקוּ לֹא תִנָּקוּ). This solution is possible, but it would be rather surprising for a rhetorical question concerning the fate of foreign nations to intrude here after the explicit statement of judgment rendered in Joel 4:19.[157]

An appeal to other textual witnesses may shed some light on the issue. The LXX reading of the first clause is potentially either ἐκδικήσω on the basis of the Alexandrinus uncial or ἐκζητήσω according to Vaticanus and Sinaiticus.[158] It is likely, however, that both Greek verbs have ונקמתי 'I will avenge' as their underlying Hebrew text, which means that the choice of Greek verbs is between synonyms and not due to a difference in Hebrew source-texts.[159] Many commentators prefer the LXX reading since it seems to make clear the meaning of Joel 4:21a, declaring that YHWH will avenge the blood of the Judahite community.[160] From a text-critical perspective, it is plausible that the מ in ונקמתי dropped out of the Masoretic Text due to confusion with the dual מs in the following word. This strengthens the plausibility of the LXX.

The LXX's rendering of the second verb (לֹא־נָקֵיתִי) is οὐ μὴ ἀθῳώσω 'I will not leave unavenged'. This suggests that the LXX is reading the affix form of the Masoretic Text as a prefix form (לֹא־אֲנַקֶּה).[161] The LXX reading is more plausible because it fits better syntactically after the *waw* relative + affix conjugation verb that appears in the first part of the verse. Following this reading means that, instead of contradiction, Joel 4:21a contains two statements that reinforce each other. YHWH will mete out punishment to those who have harmed YHWH's people. This appears to be the best solution to the textual issues of this half-verse. Essentially, Joel 4:21a conveys unalloyed blessing for Judah, a reading that fits seamlessly with the declaration

---

156. GKC 473. This grammar proposes that ו is the conjunction that introduces unmarked questions most frequently. Allen and Stuart also adopt this line of reasoning (Allen, *Joel*, 117; Stuart, *Hosea–Jonah*, 265). On the characteristics of unmarked rhetorical questions, see L. de Regt, "Discourse Implications of Rhetorical Questions in Job, Deuteronomy and the Minor Prophets," in *Literary Structure and Rhetorical Strategies in the Hebrew Bible* (ed. L. de Regt, J. de Waard, and J. Fokkleman; Assen: Van Gorcum, 1996) 53–54.

157. Simkins, *Yahweh's Activity*, 237.

158. J. Ziegler, *Duodecim Prophetae Septuaginta* (3rd ed.; Göttingen: Vandenhoeck & Ruprecht) 198, 239.

159. Crenshaw, *Joel*, 202–3.

160. See, for example, Crenshaw, *Joel*, 203; Barton, *Joel*, 109; D. Garrett, *Hosea, Joel* (NAC 19A; Nashville: Broadman & Holman, 1997) 397.

161. In this view, the א prefix beginning the second verb disappeared in the Masoretic Text through haplography with the preceding לֹא. As a result of this, the Masoretic scribes confused the ה of the prefix form with the ת of the affix form and also inserted two *yods* into the word. However, it could also be a case of dittography, whereby the LXX Vorlage copied in the second א and then omitted the two *yods* and confused the ת with a ה. Since it is possible to make the argument for textual corruption in both directions, the broader context of the verse helps to provide criteria for distinguishing between these readings.

of Yʜᴡʜ's presence that follows.[162] Its rhetorical purpose is to conclude the stream of thought related to the punishment of the nations and the final fate of the Judahite community; the nations' attack on Yʜᴡʜ's people results in their final and complete overthrow, guaranteeing the security of Judah and Jerusalem.

The final phrase of Joel 4:21 is an emphatic capstone to the message of the book—namely, וַיהוָה שֹׁכֵן בְּצִיּוֹן 'Yʜᴡʜ is dwelling in Zion'. This coincides with the promise in the previous verses for rich blessing and the eternal inhabitation of Zion and Jerusalem. Essentially, Yʜᴡʜ's presence guarantees the security of the city (cf. Ezek 48:35). Joel 4:21 also marks the final reversal of the questions surrounding Yʜᴡʜ's presence and attitude toward the implied audience posed throughout the remainder of the book. Specifically, this climactic statement engages Joel 2:1–11, which calls for the sounding of an alarm because Yʜᴡʜ leads an army against Zion. It also provides the final, resounding answer to the rhetorical question "where is their God?" in Joel 2:17.[163] This final clause declares that "their God" dwells in their midst, guaranteeing their security and prosperity in the aftermath of defeating those who have the temerity to challenge Yʜᴡʜ's fidelity and commitment to the Judahite community.

Summary

Joel 4:1–21 broadens the scope of the book and looks beyond the borders of Judah and Jerusalem. Joel 1–3 concentrates primarily on the relationship between Yʜᴡʜ and the Judahite community, describing difficult circumstances, directing the people to cry out to Yʜᴡʜ, and promising a divine response. Joel 4:1–21 now brings outside nations into view in the prophet's discussion of Yʜᴡʜ's restorative activities. The statement in Joel 4:1 that Yʜᴡʜ is going to "restore the fortunes of Judah and Jerusalem" provides the context for the discussion of the nations; their downfall is part of Yʜᴡʜ's restorative plan. The text's perspective oscillates between the nations in general and specific nations who are condemned for particular offenses, all the while demonstrating Yʜᴡʜ's authority over them.

Ultimately, the text uses these nations as a foil to set apart the greatness of Yʜᴡʜ and his care and concern for his people. This is evident throughout the chapter as Yʜᴡʜ enters into judgment on the nations with regard to their relationship with the Judahite community in Joel 4:1–3; promises *lex talionis* justice against Tyre, Sidon, and Philistia in 4:4–8; summons the nations to their ultimate defeat in 4:9–17; and promises final destruction for Egypt and Edom in 4:18–21. The text portrays the nations as unable to resist the unleashed might of Yʜᴡʜ, picturing an attempt by the nations to assemble their strongest possible force, only to go down to certain defeat (Joel 4:14). The rhetoric of delay in Joel 4:9–17 heightens the tension

---

162. Barton, *Joel*, 110.
163. Wendland, *Discourse Analysis*, 320.

before the declaration of the day of Y<small>HWH</small>, which is now a day of salvation for Judah against its enemies. Joel 4:1–21 concludes with a description of the ultimate restoration that follows the day of Y<small>HWH</small>. The abundance of water and the restoration of prosperity approach the miraculous, but the presence of Y<small>HWH</small> in the temple in Zion guarantees final deliverance for the Judahite community. The promises of prosperity intermix with the declarations of judgment, offering a dual-pronged approach that indicates the scope of Y<small>HWH</small>'s commitment to the implied audience. This provides further support to the prophet's program of response in Joel 2:12–17. Joel 4:1–21 indicates that crying out to Y<small>HWH</small> can bring restoration from all manner of devastation.

Rhetorical Effectiveness

Categorizing rhetorical effectiveness is challenging in Joel 4:1–21 since the prophet does not command the Judahite community that is the implied audience to undertake any concrete actions to alleviate its situation. As has been the case since the narrative snippet in Joel 2:18–19a, the primary actor in Joel 4:1–21 is Y<small>HWH</small>, who commands these disparate nations to gather to face divine judgment. Y<small>HWH</small> acts restoratively throughout this chapter without requiring any further action from the Judahite community. These acts should help the implied audience to know that Y<small>HWH</small> is their God, but the text does not acknowledge whether they do (cf. Joel 2:27). Even the imperatives that the prophet places in the mouth of Y<small>HWH</small> do not lend any real agency to other actors. These imperatives are directed either to Y<small>HWH</small>'s servants, who wordlessly obey, or to the collection of nations whose activities against Y<small>HWH</small> are ultimately futile.

With the aforementioned challenges in mind, we may consider the rhetorical effectiveness of Joel 4 by examining how it completes the idea of full restoration for the Judahite community. The significant amount of attention that Joel 4:1–21 devotes to foreign nations, both named and unnamed, presents Y<small>HWH</small> as a deity who removes external threats, whereas the previous chapters focus more on the situation internal to the Judahite community. Joel 1:1–2:17 articulates the gravity of the situation facing the community, and Joel 2:18–3:5 provides promises of material and spiritual deliverance, but there are still external threats to consider. The "nations" make a brief appearance in Joel 2:17 as an imaginative construct: the text portrays them as mocking Judah's distress. Y<small>HWH</small>, however, does not explicitly deal with their threat until this chapter.[164] This chapter thus balances the prophet's promises to the people; not only will Y<small>HWH</small> turn and

---

164. Joel 2:20 details Y<small>HWH</small>'s destruction of the locust army that previous rhetorical units characterized as an instrument of Y<small>HWH</small>'s judgment, referring to it as "the northerner," which suggests a foreign foe. The discussion is abrupt, however, because it quickly returns to Y<small>HWH</small>'s promises of agricultural renewal in 2:21–27. The text holds the details of deliverance from foreign foes in abeyance until Joel 4.

bring back material blessing and the promise of his presence, YHWH will also act powerfully and guarantee this community's security from its enemies. This effectively completes the movement of this book from the cataclysmic dystopia of the locust invasion to a near utopia marked by YHWH's presence, peace, and prosperity.

The predominance of divine activity in Joel 4:1–21 also has rhetorical effects worth considering. This chapter roots YHWH's salvific activity in divine dwelling in Zion, where the deity provides refuge for the implied audience. One significant element of the Zion tradition is the idea that rescue comes to those who depend on YHWH alone and not human strength (cf. Pss 9:10–13; 20:2–3; Isa 30:1–4; 31:1–3).[165] Joel 4:1–21 requires the implied audience to rely solely on YHWH since this rhetorical unit opens up no opportunity for the implied audience to act to ameliorate the situation on its own. The other actors in this chapter are the nations whose agency only sets them in opposition to YHWH and assures their destruction. Thus, this prophetic message effectively directs the implied audience toward full dependence on YHWH since the optimal response is to trust that YHWH will accomplish what this chapter promises.

We move beyond the effectiveness of this unit to the unit's immediate entextualized rhetorical situation: Joel 4:1–21 speaks powerfully concerning the authority that YHWH claims over all human powers, regardless of their allegiance. Essentially, in this chapter, YHWH claims authority over the entirety of the "universal audience," since the text does not grant the members of the audience any autonomy to avoid responding to YHWH's summons to judgment.[166] The claim of authority over the nations is a common prophetic trope, visible in passages such as oracles against nations (Isa 13–23; Jer 46–51; Ezek 25–32; Amos 1:3–2:3; Obad 1–21; Nah 1:1–3:19; Zeph 2:4–15; Zech 9:1–8)[167] and other declarations of YHWH's supremacy (Amos 9:7; Jonah 3:4–5). It effectively asserts YHWH's authority since, according to Joel 4:1–21, YHWH can summon and pronounce judgment on all nations, including those who would serve other deities.

The final element of rhetorical effectiveness found in this passage is in its presentation of positive hope for those who follow YHWH. The utopian imagery augurs a future in which those who claim allegiance to YHWH find their toil reaping great rewards. Adopting Patrick and Scult's model of a hermeneutics of affirmation—the hope provided in Joel 4:1–21 is an

---

165. B. Ollenburger, *Zion the City of the Great King: A Theological Symbol of the Jerusalem Cult* (JSOTSup 41; Sheffield: JSOT Press, 1987) 69–70. Ollenburger helpfully claims that "the security to be found in Zion calls forth a particular response, designated as trust."

166. Perelman and Olbrechts-Tyteca, *New Rhetoric*, 30–36.

167. Raabe, "Why Prophetic Oracles?" 236–57. Raabe calculates that 13.6% of the corpus of the Latter Prophets contains oracles against nations. Raabe also mentions Joel 4 as a passage that does not fit the specific genre of "oracles against nations" but still proclaims doom for foreign nations.

impetus calling the audience to greater commitment and fidelity to Y<small>HWH</small>. Taking this approach helps to "integrate the interpreter into the mainstream of the text's readership, which also most likely read the text as discourse which genuinely aspired to speak the truth."[168] In reading the rhetoric of Joel and allowing him/herself to be persuaded by it, the interpreter can further identify with the implied audience of the text, understanding the trials and turmoil that the text portrays as part of the divine call to faithfulness and commitment. Joel 4:1–21 offers encouragement that this faithfulness bears ultimate fruit: that Y<small>HWH</small> promises to "restore the fortunes" of those whom Y<small>HWH</small> calls.

Conclusion

Joel 4:1–21 concludes this prophetic book by bringing closure to the exigence of an external threat against the Judahite community. This chapter creatively constructs foreign nations as the recipients of divine commands that reveal their subordination to Y<small>HWH</small>. Y<small>HWH</small>'s promise to "restore the fortunes" of Judah and Jerusalem governs the flow of this chapter, with the text detailing how Y<small>HWH</small>'s defeat of foreign foes will guarantee Judah's and Jerusalem's restoration. Joel 4:1–21 again depicts the acts of Y<small>HWH</small> in both specific and general terms, discussing how Y<small>HWH</small> will pay back those who attacked the Judahite community and summon the nations as a whole to judgment. This judgment is rooted in Y<small>HWH</small>'s authority, which the text expresses by means of Y<small>HWH</small>'s roar and rending of the cosmos on the day of Y<small>HWH</small>. This leads to a paradisiacal restoration that reverses all the calamities of Joel 1:1–2:11. Further, the promised presence of Y<small>HWH</small> in Zion secures this restoration. Joel 4:1–21 effectively calls on the implied audience to trust in the actions of Y<small>HWH</small>, while demonstrating Y<small>HWH</small>'s sovereignty over all nations. The promise of ultimate restoration also calls all audiences to trust in Y<small>HWH</small>, whose prophesied actions reveal the divine presence among the people.

---

168. D. Patrick and A. Scult, "Rhetoric and Ideology: A Debate within Biblical Scholarship over the Import of Persuasion," in *The Rhetorical Interpretation of Scripture: Essays from the 1996 Malibu Conference* (ed. S. Porter and D. Stamps; JSNTSup 180; Sheffield: Sheffield Academic Press, 1999) 66.

Conclusion

Summary of Results

My goal in this book is to demonstrate the usefulness of rhetorical-critical methods for the study of prophetic books. By investigating the rhetorical strategies with which the text constructs its arguments, I have considered the persuasive nature of Joel. I have demonstrated that Joel is a unified work of prophetic literature that moves from scenes of devastation to promises of restoration in persuading people to call and rely on Yhwh in all circumstances and persuading Yhwh to respond to their call. This study is rooted in the broader context of Joel studies, reflecting on the longstanding debate over Joel's date of composition and literary unity. It lends support to theories of the textual cohesion of Joel's literary composition. It also emphasizes the usefulness of reading Joel as a discrete literary unit in the context of the Book of the Twelve. While Joel interacts with the rest of the Book of the Twelve and contributes significantly to the shape of that corpus, it is a literary unit of its own. It also interacts with texts outside the Book of the Twelve—a fact that permits us to develop intertextual approaches. This study leverages some of the results of those approaches in order to articulate the persuasive effects of this prophetic book.

The refinement and development of Kennedy and Möller's rhetorical-critical methodology is also important to this study. The practitioners of this model—notably Kennedy, Möller, and Shaw—use similar approaches to delineate rhetorical units and consider the rhetorical strategies revealed through the text's literary devices and structural arrangements. The ways in which one ought to approach the rhetorical situation and rhetorical effectiveness, however, are much more inconclusive in their approaches. In this book, I break with Bitzer's seminal definition of the rhetorical situation and propose that it is appropriate to locate it within the world that the text constructs. This text-immanent move is a response to the challenges of "getting behind the text" of Joel, due to the fact that there is little consensus about its time of composition. I have attempted to push rhetorical effectiveness in the direction of the implied audience constructed within the text itself and other reading and hearing audiences. This is necessary since one cannot state conclusively how the actual audience of Joel's prophecies reacted, beyond the fact that this text was preserved and included in a collection of sacred Scripture.[1] This study grounds the discussion of rhetorical

---

1. M. Fox, "The Rhetoric of Ezekiel's Vision of the Valley of the Bones," *HUCA* 51 (1980) 4. Fox notes that prophets were effective rhetoricians on some level since they gained followers who preserved and retransmitted their words.

effectiveness in Patrick and Scult's hermeneutics of affirmation, reading the text in such a way that the interpreter can experience the text's persuasive authority.

Elements of Persuasion in Joel

In most of this study, I have considered the book of Joel by using the model of rhetorical criticism detailed above. I commenced with an analysis of Joel 1:1–14 that locates the rhetorical situation of the text as being a response to the exigence of a locust infestation and drought. The prophet constructs the implied audience by first using a merismus of "elders" and "dwellers of the land," then employing a sequence of imperatives that summon subgroups in the broader community to assemble under cultic leadership and cry out to Yhwh. These cries invoke the day of Yhwh before detailing the suffering of the land and its human and animal inhabitants. The effectiveness of Joel 1:1–14 lies in its fusion of the catastrophes with the agency of Yhwh, calling on the implied audience to see the hand of Yhwh in what it experiences.

In chap. 2, I consider the prophetic appeal to Yhwh to act in the midst of desperate circumstances in Joel 1:15–20. This passage offers the first layer of response to the command to cry out to Yhwh that concludes Joel 1:14. Joel 1:15–20 is also significant in the broader rhetorical flow of the book since it introduces the day of Yhwh and directs it against the implied audience created in Joel 1:1–14. This is the point of departure for Joel's use of the day-of-Yhwh motif, which shifts from announcing devastation to promising protection and restoration. Joel 1:15–20 also effectively identifies the prophet with the implied audience. The prophet then offers a personal appeal to Yhwh alongside the laments that he undertakes with the community (cf. Joel 1:16). When it connects the prophet to the implied audience, Joel 1:15–20 also assures the validity of crying out to Yhwh in the midst of desperate circumstances, offering it as part of the process of prophetic intermediation.

Joel 2:1–11 continues the description of the catastrophes facing the community. An inclusio involving the day of Yhwh demarcates the boundaries of this rhetorical unit. This reuse of the day of Yhwh adds more detail to the succinct mention that it is "near" in 1:15. Joel 2:1–11 again indicates its imminence while adding imagery that emphasizes its cosmological significance, visible through the trembling and darkening of the heavenly bodies. Joel 2:1–11 develops the portrayal of the implied audience, directing the scene toward Zion. The exigence shifts slightly since the text takes the locusts from 1:1–14 and provides them with the characteristics of a well-disciplined, awe-inspiring army.[2] The rhetorical strategies of this unit

---

2. On the blend of image-worlds, see E. Wendland, *Prophetic Rhetoric: Case Studies in Text Analysis and Translation* (Longwood, FL: Xulon, 2009) 34.

effectively emphasize the invulnerability of the invader, detailing how it despoils the land in its march and overcomes all obstacles in its approach to Zion. Joel 2:6 demonstrates a powerful use of perspective when the text provides a glimpse of the victims, who can only writhe in anguish. This creates the context for the description of the assault against Zion in which the invading horde easily overruns the city.

The rhetorical strategy of Joel 2:1–11 culminates in the final two verses which reveal that Yʜᴡʜ, the one who should dwell in Zion, is actually at the head of the army that overruns Zion. This is undoubtedly the nadir of the book. It is also a shocking response to the previous rhetorical units since it reveals that neither the call for the implied audience to cry out to Yʜᴡʜ (Joel 1:14) nor the prophet's personal appeal offered on behalf of the community have alleviated the threat (Joel 1:19–20). The shock that it creates is undeniably effective in capturing the attention of the implied audience. Identifying Yʜᴡʜ as the invaders' leader effectively guides the progression of the prophetic passage; the implied audience would want to learn if there is any hope of turning aside the power of Yʜᴡʜ. Joel 2:1–11 creates a disquieting picture of Yʜᴡʜ that requires further resolution in the portrayal of the divine character and actions in the following rhetorical units.

Joel 2:12–17 is an essential rhetorical unit in the progression of the persuasive argumentation of this book. It commences with a call to return to Yʜᴡʜ and concludes with a detailed description of what form this return should take, culminating in a powerful rhetorical question that challenges Yʜᴡʜ's commitment to the implied audience. The exigences described in previous rhetorical units set the stage for the prophetic program of response, since the fate of the implied audience hangs in the balance. The strategy of response is rooted in the call for the people to return to Yʜᴡʜ both through external actions and through heartfelt commitment. The prophet constructs the ways in which the implied audience ought to return, including providing the location where they should assemble and the words of their cry.

Attention to detail reveals that Joel 2:12–17 moves beyond the calls to cry out to Yʜᴡʜ in 1:1–14 and 1:15–20. Instead of general commands to assemble, fast, and cry out (1:13–14) or appeals that reflect on the grave situation (1:19–20), Joel 2:12–17 provides a detailed description of the implied audience's ideal response and adopts a strategy of calling on Yʜᴡʜ to act in order to preserve Yʜᴡʜ's divine reputation in the wake of the community's return. This detailed program of response is ideally situated following the nadir of 2:11, which heightens its persuasive potential. The interplay of responses that the text tries to evoke in Joel 2:12–17 is visible in the creative word play on the verb בוש that shifts the onus for action from the implied audience to Yʜᴡʜ.

The urgency of the call to return to Yʜᴡʜ raises the question of the community's implied guilt and sin. The lack of an explicit statement about errors is rare in prophetic literature, and attempts to identify a specific offense through accusations of idolatry or lack of regard for the prophetic word are highly speculative. The language of shame and disgrace informs the prophet's proposed cry to Yhwh in Joel 2:17 since it calls for Yhwh to act so that the nations will not view the community as an object of scorn because Yhwh did not rescue the people. However, the intertextual interaction of Joel 2:12–17 with Solomon's prayer in 1 Kgs 8:35–48 and the divine character credo of Exod 34:6–7, including its reuse in Jonah 4:2, implies that there is sin from which the community needs to turn.[3]

The most fascinating element in the discussion of rhetorical effectiveness is the conceptual gap between Joel 2:17 and 2:18, where the text transitions from the prophet's articulation of how the community should cry out to Yhwh to declarations of Yhwh's intention to restore. Use of a conceptual gap can be an effective rhetorical technique since it requires its audiences to engage the world of the text and provide the necessary transition to the following rhetorical unit. Each rhetorical unit helps to prepare the way for what follows, but there is usually some level of indeterminacy in the transition. If the gap between units is more pronounced, then audiences must be more active to bridge it in order to preserve the text's coherence.[4]

A gap is evident between Joel 2:17, where the text is still commanding the implied audience to gather and cry out to Yhwh, and Joel 2:18, where Yhwh's zeal and pity are piqued, and Yhwh promises a restorative response. In the space between these two verses, it appears that the text requires its reading and hearing audiences to enter into the fray and posit that the implied audience heeded the prophetic call to return to Yhwh. Joel 2:12–14 calls for the Judahite community to return to Yhwh because of who Yhwh is, indicating that this return may lead Yhwh to turn back to the community. Joel 2:18 then abruptly begins to describe Yhwh's restorative actions; these actions are most plausible in a context in which the community first returned to Yhwh as directed.

On the other side of the conceptual gap, Joel 2:18–27 begins the process of linking Yhwh's restorative actions to the catastrophes enumerated throughout Joel 1:1–2:17. Its connection to previous rhetorical units helps to demonstrate the essential unity of Joel's rhetoric. Joel 2:18–27 commences with a narrative introduction that details Yhwh's commitment to act and concludes with the epiphoric claim that Yhwh will no longer permit the implied audience to fall into disgrace and shame. Joel 2:18–27 advances the life cycle of the rhetorical situation to emphasize divine response, and it also shifts from the call for the implied audience to respond in Joel 2:12–17

---

3. M. Boda, *A Severe Mercy: Sin and Its Remedy in the Old Testament* (Siphrut 1; Winona Lake, IN: Eisenbrauns, 2009) 306–7. See Boda's list of the various reuses of Exod 34:6–7, which all seem to appear in contexts of sin.

4. W. Iser, "Indeterminacy and the Reader's Response in Prose Fiction," in *Aspects of Narrative: Selected Papers from the English Institute* (ed. J. Miller; New York: Columbia University Press, 1971) 39.

to a detailed listing of Yʜwʜ's actions. The rhetorical strategy of this unit is rooted in the reversal of the calamities described in previous passages. Yʜwʜ destroys the locusts that ravage the landscape in Joel 1:1–14 and returns agricultural bounty to the land and its inhabitants, which were threatened with starvation in Joel 1:1–14 and 1:15–20. It also promises protection and security in Zion, reversing the image of Zion's fall in Joel 2:1–11.

Joel 2:18–27 also dramatically shifts the responses of the implied audience. Whereas in the previous rhetorical unit the text calls on the people to assemble and cry out to Yʜwʜ, in this passage the text calls them to rejoice while Yʜwʜ acts on their behalf. This also reestablishes the nature of Yʜwʜ as portrayed in the character credo in Joel 2:13; Yʜwʜ's graciousness and compassion are on full display. Joel 2:18–27 also sets the tone for the remainder of the book, which delves into the full nature of Yʜwʜ's commitment to the covenant community and the way that Yʜwʜ intends to act on its behalf.

Joel 3:1–5 continues the process of restoration through the agency of Yʜwʜ's action. It commences with a phrase that casts this unit into a different temporal orientation and considers what Yʜwʜ will do following the actions detailed in Joel 2:18–27. It concludes with a word play on the concept of calling: those who call on the name of Yʜwʜ inform those whom Yʜwʜ calls. Joel 3:1–5 unifies the implied audience through its declaration that the gift of Yʜwʜ's Spirit bridges all ages, genders, and social situations. This is reflective of the creation of the implied audience in Joel 1:2 and 14, which use the merismus of "elders" and "dweller of the land" to emphasize the inclusiveness of this audience. It also commences the process of reversing the imagery related to the day of Yʜwʜ found in Joel 1:15 and 2:1–11. Joel 3:1–5 connects to previous mentions of the day of Yʜwʜ since it still promises the rending of the cosmos and the darkening of heavenly luminaries (cf. Joel 2:10). However, Joel 3:1–5 also provides the potential for escape for those whom Yʜwʜ chooses to protect. This effectively recalls the prophetic appeal to the implied audience to turn in Joel 2:12–17, suggesting that this response could rescue them from the day of Yʜwʜ.

In chap. 8 of this book, Joel 4:1–21 concludes the process of announcing restoration by focusing on the removal of external threats to the implied audience's future existence. This chapter commences with the declared intention of Yʜwʜ to restore the fortunes of Judah and Jerusalem and concludes with the announcement that Yʜwʜ dwells in Zion, a guarantee of Yʜwʜ's restorative presence. The promise of the divine presence answers the rhetorical question in Joel 2:17, where the text constructs the nations as mocking the implied audience because of Yʜwʜ's silence. Joel 4 also advances the life cycle of the rhetorical situation by dealing with the exigence of external nations. This is a natural progression from the previous units, which address the need to reverse material and spiritual threats to the Judahite community itself.

The rhetorical strategies of Joel 4:1–21 are rooted in Yʜᴡʜ's authority over all nations. The text announces judgment for the crimes that these nations commit in Joel 4:1–3 and provides specific examples through the display of *lex talionis* justice in Joel 4:4–8 that artfully constructs a punishment worthy of the crime. Joel 4:1–21 employs symbolic geographical locations to tie into the tradition of divine judgment in a valley. In this case, the names attributed to the valley manifest the inevitability of divine judgment. This chapter then dramatically highlights the nations' hubris by providing a call to battle that is ultimately futile. This unit explicitly engages and reverses other prophetic declarations by commanding the nations to gather the greatest fighting force they can muster. This challenge ends in defeat when Yʜᴡʜ unleashes the day of Yʜᴡʜ. This use of the day of Yʜᴡʜ also completes its reversal since it uses similar imagery from Joel 2:10–11 about the darkening of heavenly luminaries, the shaking of the cosmos, and Yʜᴡʜ's roar. The same images that announce doom and destruction for the implied audience in Joel 2:10–11 now portray salvation and security in Zion.

Joel 4:1–21 concludes with promises of paradisiacal bounty and final judgment on specific foreign nations. Yʜᴡʜ's presence in Zion places the capstone on the promises of restoration; from Zion Yʜᴡʜ will enact blessing for the implied audience and judgment for their enemies. This completes the journey of the prophetic book from dystopia to utopia for the implied audience thanks to Yʜᴡʜ's restorative actions. The progression of this chapter provides the implied audience with reasons to continue to rely on Yʜᴡʜ, who is now visibly acting on their behalf. Joel 4:1–21 also effectively emphasizes Yʜᴡʜ's authority over all nations. Their challenge is futile, and this chapter reveals that the deity who dwells in Zion claims sovereignty over the nations of the earth.

The Persuasive Potential of Joel

After looking at the rhetorical situations and strategies of the individual subunits, we will also find it helpful to draw back and consider the persuasive potential of Joel as a whole literary unit. In tracing its flow, we can see how Joel juxtaposes divine and human responses in order to emphasize the authority of Yʜᴡʜ and the necessity for the human audience to acknowledge and submit to it. Joel first moves its readers through multiple exigences (locusts, drought, invasion, mockery of the nations) that threaten the destruction of the implied audience that it constructs. Throughout its portrayal of the exigences, the text repeatedly focuses on the response of the implied audience, commanding it to cry out to Yʜᴡʜ and maintain communion with Yʜᴡʜ by gathering under priestly leadership to lament. This culminates in the prophet's program of response presented in Joel 2:12–17. There is no indication that the implied audience can deal with any of the exigences without the intervention of Yʜᴡʜ, but the calls to assemble and appeal to Yhwh (Joel 1:13–14, 19–20; 2:12–13, 15–17) engage the implied audience in the fray.

Beginning in Joel 2:18, the text focuses on Yhwh as the active agent who answers the question "who knows?" from Joel 2:14. Yhwh responds to the prophet's presentation of the implied audience's cry by becoming jealous and compassionate. The text never specifically links Yhwh's response to the implied audience's cry, thus preserving Yhwh's freedom to act as Yhwh chooses, but it is likely that the text is indicating that turning to Yhwh "with all your heart" is the appropriate strategy to adopt amidst all of the exigences it portrays. Yhwh's responses then explicitly resolve the crises described in Joel 1:1–2:17, including a reversal of the day of Yhwh. Although the unit maintains the imagery of the day of Yhwh's proximity and power, it shifts focus so that the day of Yhwh promises salvation rather than desolation. In Joel 2:18–4:21, Yhwh also removes the invading locust army, restores the landscape, provides the gift of the divine Spirit, and asserts authority over all nations while promising divine dwelling in Zion.

While Yhwh acts in this manner, the text mutes the responses of the implied audience in Joel 2:18–4:21. It does, however, call on the audience to rejoice in the wake of Yhwh's actions (Joel 2:23). Otherwise, the appropriate responses to Yhwh's actions seem to be implicit, with the text guiding the implied audience to conclude that its members should call on the name of Yhwh to be saved (Joel 3:5) and acknowledge that Yhwh is their God when Yhwh removes the threat of the foreign nations (Joel 4:16–17). Yhwh's restorative responses persuade the audience that crying out to Yhwh and acknowledging that Yhwh is God are the correct reactions.

The rhetorical power of Joel lies in the interweaving of the divine and human responses to the exigences it presents. The text deftly captures the reader's attention with the scope of its crises, plunging downward into despair when it appears that the day of Yhwh is inescapably imminent against the implied audience. Joel, however, then presents a window of hope through its appeal for the implied audience to respond by crying out to Yhwh and its description of Yhwh's character. It then effectively supports its characterization of Yhwh through Yhwh's salvific response. The implied audience cannot enact its own restoration, but returning to Yhwh fully and crying out to the God who is "gracious and compassionate, slow to anger, abounding in love, and relents from sending calamity" may activate Yhwh's zeal and pity. Joel does not presume to know the mind of Yhwh and does not indicate that this sort of appeal is certain to be effective. Joel does persuade us, however, that, if Yhwh chooses to respond, Yhwh has the authority and the ability to turn dystopia into utopia. As a result, when crises arise, the proper response is to acknowledge the gravity of the situation and cry out to Yhwh so that Yhwh can provide hope of restoration through the promise of Yhwh's presence.

Index of Authors

Index of Scripture

Lamentations (cont.)
  2:21   175
  2:22   97
  3:40   146
  4:8   122
  4:21   182

Esther
  4:3   152
  4:14   156
  7:10   232

Daniel
  1:4   231
  7–12   114
  8:21   231
  9:3   153
  9:4   133
  9:7   180
  10:20   231
  11:2   231

Daniel (cont.)
  11:10   244

Ezra
  3:13   153
  8:17   71
  8:21   153
  8:25   71
  8:30   71
  8:33   71

Nehemiah
  1:5   133
  4:8   133
  7:2   113
  8:18   89
  9:1   153
  9:17   154
  9:31   154
  9:32   133
  10:33–40   71
  13:12   176

1 Chronicles
  1:9   232
  12:33   126
  12:35   126
  15:28   158
  15:29   125

2 Chronicles
  6:38   150
  11:1–4   110
  15:14   118, 158
  20   255
  20:3   153
  20:15   225
  20:20–26   224
  20:26   224
  20:35   203
  24:4   202
  30:6   152
  36:19   4, 231

Apocrypha

Sirach
  49:10   13

New Testament

Matthew
  7:28–29   56

Luke
  6   56
  12:1–13:9   48

John
  15–17   51

Acts
  2   207, 215
  2:5–21   207
  2:14–36   207
  2:17   203

Acts (cont.)
  10:44–48   207

Revelation
  9:2–11   114, 115
  9:3–4   115
  9:7   124
  9:10   115

www.ingramcontent.com/pod-product-compliance
Lightning Source LLC
Chambersburg PA
CBHW021958090426
42811CB00001B/73